ANGELIC ECHOES:
HERVÉ GUIBERT AND COMPANY

Angelic Echoes

Hervé Guibert and Company

Ralph Sarkonak

UNIVERSITY OF TORONTO PRESS
Toronto Buffalo London

© University of Toronto Press Incorporated 2000
Toronto Buffalo London
Printed in Canada

ISBN 0-8020-4794-7

Printed on acid-free paper

University of Toronto Romance Series

Canadian Cataloguing in Publication Data

Sarkonak, Ralph, 1949–
  Angelic echoes : Hervé Guibert and company

  (University of Toronto romance series)
  Includes bibliographical references and index.
  ISBN 0-8020-4794-7

  1. Guibert, Hervé – Criticism and interpretation.   2. Guibert,
  Hervé – Friends and associates.   I. Title.   II. Series.

  PQ2667.U4612Z92 2000   843'.914   C00-930074-0

University of Toronto Press acknowledges the financial assistance to its publishing program of the Canada Council for the Arts and the Ontario Arts Council.

This book has been published with the help of a grant from the Humanities and Social Sciences Federation of Canada, using funds provided by the Social Sciences and Humanities Research Council of Canada.

University of Toronto Press acknowledges the financial support for its publishing activities of the Government of Canada through the Book Publishing Industry Development Program (BPIDP).

*In memory of
my friend and colleague Gordon McGregor
who died of AIDS-related illness in 1986*

Contents

Acknowledgments ix

Illustration Credits xi

Abbreviations xiii

Introduction 3

1 Traces and Shadows 9

2 The Deaths of Desire 28

3 The Pursuit of Pleasure 66

4 Memories of the Blind 86

5 Searching for Vincent 115

6 For an AIDS Aesthetics 149

7 Writing on Writing on ... 193

8 Partners in Writing 218

9 Ghost Writing 256

Afterword 284

Bibliography 291

Index 305

Illustrations follow page 146

Acknowledgments

First, I should like to thank Les Éditions Gallimard, Les Éditions de Minuit, Les Éditions du Seuil, and *Gai Pied* for allowing me to consult their archives. I sincerely thank Albert Dichy and Hélène Favard, who facilitated my always time-pressed research of the Hervé Guibert archives housed at the Institut Mémoires de l'Édition Contemporaine. My research in France was funded by a grant from the Social Sciences and Humanities Research Council of Canada, for which I am most thankful. I gratefully acknowledge the financial support of the Dean of Arts Office and the Dorothy Dallas Fund of the Department of French, Hispanic and Italian Studies of the University of British Columbia. A special debt of gratitude is owed the always helpful people at the interlibrary loan service of the Koerner Library for obtaining books and articles that I had despaired of ever finding. I have been aided by many individuals – among whom are numerous students and colleagues, both here in Vancouver and elsewhere – whose questions and comments have helped me clarify my ideas. I was extremely privileged to meet several people who knew Hervé Guibert: Agathe Gaillard, Christine Guibert, Jérôme Lindon, Mathieu Lindon, and one other person whose name I shall not divulge. I am most grateful to Christine Guibert for allowing me to consult the manuscripts of several of Guibert's novels, to include the extracts quoted, and to reproduce the photographs that are part and parcel of Hervé Guibert's oeuvre. I should like to thank the following individuals for their help and encouragement, none of whom of course is responsible for any of my interpretations: Jan Baetens, Larry Bongie, Françoise Gaillard, Alec Globe, Richard Hodgson, Alistair MacKay, Gloria Onyeoziri, Charles Porter, Pierre Saint-Amand, Anne Scott, Anne Simpson, Tom Tomlinson, and Michael Worton.

Illustration Credits

Photographs by Herve Guibert (Figures 1–11, 13, 14, and 18–21) are courtesy of Christine Guibert.

Ship of Fools, painting by Hieronymus Bosch (Figure 12), is courtesy of the Musée du Louvre, Paris. Reprinted from Sandra Orienti and René de Solier, *Hieronymus Bosch.*

Saint Sebastian, painting by Sodoma (Figure 15), from Palazzo Pitti, Florence, is courtesy of the Ministero per i Beni e le Attività Culturali. Reprinted from Charles F. Clark, *AIDS and the Arrows of Pestilence.*

Self-portrait (Figure 16) is courtesy of the The Estate of Robert Mapplethorpe. Copyright 1988.

After the Duel, painting by Antonio Mancini (Figure 17), is courtesy of Museo Civico, Turin.

Abbreviations

Ami	À l'ami qui ne m'a pas sauvé la vie
AS	Les Aventures singulières
Av.	Des aveugles
Bl.	Blindsight
CMV	Cytomegalovirus: A Hospitalization Diary
CP	The Compassion Protocol
Cyto.	Cytomégalovirus: journal d'hospitalisation
Friend	To the Friend Who Did Not Save My Life
FV	Fou de Vincent
G	Les Gangsters
Gang.	The Gangsters
GI	Ghost Image
HB	L'Homme blessé
HCR	L'Homme au chapeau rouge
I	L'Incognito
IF	L'Image fantôme
LA	Les Lubies d'Arthur
Let. É.	Lettres d'Égypte: du Caire à Assouan, 19..
Mes	Mes parents
MP	La Mort propagande et autres textes de jeunesse
MRH	The Man in the Red Hat
MV	Mauve le vierge
My	My parents
P	Le Paradis
PA	La Piqûre d'amour et autres textes suivi de La Chair fraîche
PC	Le Protocole compassionnel
Photo.	Photographies

SV	*Le Seul Visage*
V	*Vice*
VD	*Vole mon dragon*
Vous	*Vous m'avez fait former des fantômes*
Voy.	*Voyage avec deux enfants*

ANGELIC ECHOES:
HERVÉ GUIBERT AND COMPANY

Introduction

> J'ai eu l'impression, par la force des choses, d'être mon propre personnage, mais d'être aussi un corps mis en jeu dans des narrations, dans des situations, dans des rapports, j'ai aussi l'impression que c'est l'histoire d'un corps, effectivement d'un corps qui vieillit, d'un corps qui est malade, d'un corps qui est abîmé, d'un corps ceci, d'un corps cela, d'un corps qui renaît un peu, tu vois, mais d'un corps monstrueux aussi, d'un corps difforme, et j'ai l'impression que c'est l'histoire de ce corps.
> Interview with Christophe Donner, 145

> I had the impression, by force of circumstances, of being my own character, but also of being a body brought into play in narratives, situations, relationships. I also have the impression that my work is the story of that body, in fact a body that is growing old, a sick body, a body in ruins, a body like this or like that, a body that is coming back to life somewhat, you understand, but also the impression of a monstrous body, a deformed body, and I have the impression it's all about this body.[1]

On 27 December 1991 Hervé Guibert died as a result of complications arising from an unsuccessful suicide attempt two weeks earlier. The author of some thirty creative works, including a film scenario, a video, and numerous books – eight of which have been translated into English

---

1 Translations of works not published in English are my own. When I have changed a quotation from a published translation in the interest of greater textual accuracy or more idiomatic expression in North American English, this is indicated by "trans. alt." (translation altered) after the page reference.

to date[2] – Guibert gained wide recognition and notoriety with the publication in 1990 of *À l'ami qui ne m'a pas sauvé la vie* (*To the Friend Who Did Not Save My Life*). This novel, one of the most famous AIDS fictions in French or any language, recounts the battle of the first-person narrator not only with AIDS but also and especially with the medical establishment on both sides of the Atlantic, including the friend who "did not save his life." Guibert had been the photography critic for the newspaper *Le Monde* from 1977 to 1985. Earlier on he worked for several magazines, including one entitled *Vingt ans* in which he, an eighteen-year-old gay man, passed himself off as a straight in an advice column for teenage girls. Guibert was born in Paris in 1955; in 1970 his family moved to La Rochelle, where he finished high school. It was there that he discovered what were to become the three main loves of his life: men, photographs, and words. He returned to Paris in the early 1970s, where he published his first book *La Mort propagande* (1977), which was reissued the year he died in an expanded edition that included important juvenilia.

Guibert was no stranger to scandal. Without anyone's permission, he published a personal letter that Roland Barthes had written to him a few years before his death. Guibert's autobiographical text, *Mes parents* (1986), seems to leave no stone unturned in the family's past, no skeleton uncovered, as one critic remarked: "what shamelessness! What exhibitionism! What a display! ... To read *Mes parents* is like secretly reading the diary of a neighbor, a friend, a brother. What would be quite intolerable in a novel ... becomes almost totally unbearable because readers get trapped in their own voyeurism" (Gaudemar, "Livret d'infamille," 35). And in *À l'ami qui ne m'a pas sauvé la vie*, the work that provoked the greatest scandal of all, he wrote of a philosopher named Muzil whose battle with AIDS precedes and foreshadows the narrator's own. The novel was read, at least at first, largely as a *roman à clés*, with the emphasis on the clues, as the title itself seemed to invite. (I discuss this in chapter 7.) It would probably be safe to say that most of France had heard about Guibert after his two appearances on French television: *Apostrophes* (16 March 1990) and *Ex libris* (7 March 1991). When he announced on the first program that he had given up on books, he received thousands of letters encouraging him to go on writing. The result was his second –

---

2 In the order of their original publication in French, these are *Ghost Image, Blindsight, The Gangsters, My Parents, To the Friend Who Did Not Save My Life, The Compassion Protocol, The Man in the Red Hat*, and *Cytomegalovirus: A Hospitalization Diary*. See the bibliography for publication details.

and some would say his best – book about AIDS, *Le Protocole compassionnel* (1991), and an invitation from a television producer challenging him to continue his story by making a video. The home video that he made of himself over a period of several months consisted of some twenty-five forty-five-minute cassettes; eventually, it was edited down to a fifty-eight-minute movie, *La Pudeur ou l'Impudeur*, showing him doing his exercises, sitting on the toilet, playing Russian roulette with the poison that he had written about in his AIDS novels, and also visiting his beloved island – Elba. It was finally shown on TV on 30 January 1992, but only after a huge debate in the French media. Even in death, or rather after death, Guibert still could provoke scandal.[3]

For many years Guibert's books were not widely known beyond a select circle of faithful readers and book reviewers. But during the years 1990 to 1992 he became a great media success. Today, however, there is little if any mention of Guibert in the French press, but where the journalists have dropped the baton, academic critics have picked it up. In May 1994 an international conference devoted entirely to his work was held at the University of London, and the proceedings were published the next year.[4] In 1997 I edited a collection of essays published under the title *Le Corps textuel d'Hervé Guibert*. Today Guibert's works are studied in universities in the United States, Canada, Australia, and the United Kingdom. No doubt it will take somewhat longer for his books to become part of the sacrosanct university canon in France, given the conservative notions that country's academics hold to concerning what is worthy to be considered literature. As for Guibert's literary antecedents, they are impeccable if not always traditional, since his writing was influenced, among others, by Jean Genet, Georges Bataille, and Thomas Bernhard, not to mention Sade. Edmund White has pointed out the Proustian element in some of Guibert's books ("Love Stories," 5).

Guibert was, before his death, the subject of numerous interviews, book reviews, articles, and two early books, photographic albums by his friend Hans Georg Berger who made Guibert his sole subject in *L'Image de soi, ou l'injonction de son beau moment?* (1988) and *Dialogue d'images* (1992). Hervé Guibert was handsome, and almost every book review published in France mentions his good looks or includes a photograph

---

[3] Further biographical information may be found in François Buot's *Hervé Guibert: Le jeune homme et la mort*, including reproductions of photographs of Guibert when he was a child.

[4] The papers were published in *Nottingham French Studies* in the spring of 1995. This special issue edited by Jean-Pierre Boulé contains a bibliography of Guibert's fiction and non-fiction, including most of the articles published in *Le Monde* from 1977 to 1985.

of the "hyacinthian, ringleted," "earnest wide-eyed" young man.[5] Guibert, so often accused of narcissism, seemed bemused by this fetishization of his own body by the press, and toward the end of his life he said that so many people were thinking about him that he almost didn't need to exist ("Le Coeur fatigué," 23).

That Guibert himself was ever obsessed by bodies, both live and dead, is demonstrated in his fiction from the very outset, including *La Mort propagande*, which contains a description of an autopsy performed on the body of the narrator! This obsession is also exemplified by a little-known text entitled *Vice* (1991) that describes spaces as varied as the storage rooms of condemned museums full of preserved bodies and body parts, and the steam baths and dungeons of an unnamed city where the bodies of men are transformed into mummified immobility (chapter 3). The body is always there in his writings, and in much – though not all – of his photography. As in Balzac, Guibert's characters can be traced from one book to another even though they sometimes appear in various guises and under different names or initials, before appearing in a photograph since so many were based on his real friends!

Guibert the photographer and Guibert the writer have become better known to us since the posthumous publication of several works. *L'Homme au chapeau rouge*, the last of the so-called AIDS novels; *Cytomégalovirus*, a hospital diary; and *Le Paradis*, a novel about a supposedly straight love story, were all published in 1992. To follow were *Photographies*, an album of photographs (1993); *La Piqûre d'amour et autres textes* suivi par *La Chair fraîche*, a collection of short stories and a novella (1994); *Vole mon dragon*, a play (1994); and a collection of letters to his friends, *Lettres d'Égypte: du Caire à Assouan, 19..* (1995). Perforce, Guibert the journalist, given the transitory nature of the medium, is less well known at least at this stage, although this may change with the publication of a selection of his articles written for *Le Monde*.[6]

One of the most blatant characteristics of Guibert's fiction is that he never wrote in a vacuum: we have only to think of his activities as a photography critic and a photographer in his own right to realize how much his writing was linked to visual images. But no doubt the real backbone – the tree trunk – of his fiction is his personal diary, most of which to date remains unpublished. It is in his diary that many works, including

---

5 The words quoted are taken from Edmund White's article "Love Stories" (3).
6 A number of Guibert's book manuscripts and copies of his journalism are housed at the IMEC (Institut Mémoires de l'Édition Contemporaine) at 9 rue Bleue, 75009 Paris.

À l'ami qui ne m'a pas sauvé la vie, germinated. In an interview he explained that when a theme or a character began to take on consistency and depth, he would perfom a textual transplant, moving to a new manuscript the diary extracts that were beginning to take on a life of their own: "Every book is an outgrowth, a branch. Every time when something in the diary becomes obsessive, carries the whole thing off course, it leads to the birth of book" (interview with Gaudemar, "Les aveux permanents"). Clearly, in reading Guibert we are dealing with a fictive universe with many branches and ramifications.[7]

Throughout Guibert's books, autobiography and fiction are woven together in what appears to be a seamless fabric so that one is never sure of just how referential his writing is. For example, the only early work of his to gain wide acclaim, *Des aveugles* (1985), was based on his volunteer work at the Institute for Blind Youth in Paris (chapter 4). In *Adultes!*, a thinly disguised autobiographical novel that Guibert never completed, he wrote that the problem "Gaspar" had with his work was its relationship to the truth: "He is bored by telling a story when it is false, entirely false, and he is equally bored when it is entirely true ... [Gaspar] has the knack of getting himself in situations that are unbelievable but true" (f. 57; quoted with the permission of Christine Guibert). Speaking about the influence of AIDS on his writing, Guibert articulated the troubling relation between truth and fiction that underpins so much of his fiction: "AIDS has allowed me to make even more radical certain techniques of narration, the relation to truth, the staging of myself beyond what I had ever thought possible" (Interview with Gaudemar, "La vie sida," 21). In the end, Guibert and his writing became so identified with AIDS in France that many people forgot that most of his work is not about the syndrome, although his AIDS fictions are no doubt the culmination of his career and the ultimate litmus test of his desire to reveal all (chapter 6).

Guibert's is a smaller universe than Proust's but it presents its own unique complexity, intertextual references, and thematic clusters, all of which evolve and revolve around the principal narrator's preoccupations, obsessions, and relationships including his relationship with himself and his self-image (chapters 2 and 5). In this monograph I will not attempt a detailed description of all of Guibert's works, since that has already been done by Jean-Pierre Boulé in *Hervé Guibert: Voices of the Self* (1999). Rather I will concentrate on important works, themes, and writ-

---

[7] The French critic who has written the most extensively about Guibert, Raymond Bellour, compared his oeuvre to a rhizome ("Hervé Guibert, l'inéluctable," 68).

ing practices, ranging from a comparison of his photography and his writing (chapter 1) to identifying some of the ties that link his works with the writing of several of his contemporaries (chapters 8 and 9).

Guibert's first artistic interests were theater and cinema; later he would become fascinated with painting. Largely through his work at *Le Monde* – though not always – Guibert met, photographed, and wrote about many famous people, including artists, actresses, film directors, and photographers. Perhaps this is why two of my readers detected a gossipy feel to this study. To which I reply by quoting a sentence from Edmund White's *Farewell Symphony*, complete with its Foucauldian undertones: "I didn't want to be a historian but rather an archaeologist of gossip" (355). It is true that to speak of Guibert is not an easy task. Nor is it an innocent gesture, not only because his texts reveal supposed secrets, or blend fiction and nonfiction, or institute a troubling relationship between the textual and the visual, but also because his writing brings us into such intimate contact with the fragile materiality of his own body. By writing about himself in almost every imaginable state, whether thinly disguised, masked, or unveiled, his main character is his own body. It is not by chance that he was impressed, as he told an interviewer a few months before he died, by what Montaigne wrote in the introduction to his *Essais*: "I would have portrayed myself ... naked."[8] The effect was so profound that it gave him a flash of inspiration ("ça a fait tilt"). As Guibert said, the words of Montaigne could be the epigraph for everything he wrote (Interview with Donner, 145).

I never met Hervé Guibert. But readers of this study will become aware that I have a personal investment, involvement, and identification with his writing. Such significant disclosure, as it might be termed, does not need justifying. I offer it here for what it is worth – a statement about my desire to share the "pleasure of the text" that the works of Hervé Guibert have afforded me. If even a small portion of that pleasure is shared by my readers, then I will have succeeded in this sometimes perilous enterprise.[9]

---

8 "Que si j'eusse esté entre ces nations qu'on dict vivre encore sous la douce liberté des premières loix de nature, je t'asseure que je m'y fusse très-volontiers peint tout entier, et tout nud" (Montaigne, *Essais*, vol. 1, 1) [If I were in (one of those) nations that are said to be living still in the gentle liberty of the first laws of nature, I assure you that, very willingly, I would have portrayed myself completely, totally naked].

9 Three of the chapters of this study are revised versions of articles that appeared previously: chapter 1 in *Yale French Studies*, chapter 3 (in French) in *Nottingham French Studies*, and chapter 7 (also in French) in *TEXTE*.

Chapter One

Traces and Shadows

> J'ai l'impression d'avoir fait une oeuvre barbare et délicate.
> *Le Protocole compassionnel*, 113

> I have the feeling I've created a work both barbarous and delicate.
> *The Compassion Protocol*, 96

On the wall above and to the left of my computer hangs a photograph. It represents the head of a man in his early thirties with shortish hair and well-defined features: the forehead is high, the chin strong, and the nose long and straight, the lips full. But what strikes, or as Roland Barthes would have said, punctuates my gaze are the piercing eyes, the extraordinary light and shadow of the composition – more than three-quarters of the photo is made up of black and various shades of gray – the back of the subject's head seen in a mirror image, and, in the border beneath the photo, towards the right-hand margin, the traces of twelve lower-case letters written in a legible hand: *hervé guibert* (figure 1).

In the summer of 1994, after returning to Paris from Berlin, I visited the Galerie Agathe Gaillard to look once again at the photographs, including the self-portraits, of Hervé Guibert.[1] I wanted to buy all of them, preferably one bearing the signature of the writer whose work I had been researching at the Bibliothèque Nationale, the Centre Georges-Pompidou, and the Institut Mémoires de l'Édition Contemporaine. This or that one, I couldn't make up my mind. Agathe was about

---

1 Guibert's photographs can be seen at the Galerie Agathe Gaillard, 3 rue du Pont Louis-Philippe, 75004 Paris.

to leave for the provinces; I had to hurry; but none seemed quite right. At that point someone arrived with a large brown paper parcel that contained the photographs of an exhibition recently held outside of Paris. We opened the package; I fell upon the one I liked, paid for it, had it wrapped, and left in a rush. Then, the tiring pre-Eurostar train-boat-train journey to England, a one-night stay in a hotel near the University of London where the Guibert conference had been held a few weeks earlier, the train trip to Gatwick airport, and the long-haul voyage from Europe to Vancouver – all of this happened to me in a panic-driven daze. I was "stealing" Guibert, his image, his referential imprint, his trace, his portrait, and what is more his signed *self-portrait*, like some modern equivalent of a Montaigne manuscript. Did I have any right to this photo? Was it going to be damaged? (The package was cumbersome and hard to manage.) As the jet flew on and on – over Scotland, the Atlantic, Greenland, northern Canada, the Prairie provinces, the Rockies, and then beyond – I wondered if he would have approved. Eventually I did arrive home, had the photograph framed with a wide white mat and a charcoal black border, and put it on the wall. I should have been content, shouldn't I? The icon of the writer and photographer whose work had fascinated me since I first read his 1990 bestseller *À l'ami qui ne m'a pas sauvé la vie* was not really in my possession – for one can never possess the "air" of a photographic subject[2] – but rather in my potential line of vision. But the photograph continued to trouble me, and I would only attempt to steal a glance at Hervé at night after the computer was turned off as though I were a thief in my own apartment.

Another trip, to the Foucault conference organized by Paul Bouissac in Toronto, fall 1994. This time I ended up buying the poster, a drawing by Juno Youn, a young artist from the Ontario College of Art who managed to capture visually the intensity of Foucault's face and to transpose the transgressive side of his work in typographical terms by playing with the bilingual title of the conference: "MICHEL.F'S & LA;LITTERATURE AND: LITERATURE PROGRAMME?PROGRAMEE=." F'S recalls *Fuchs*, "fox," Foucault's nickname when he was a student at the École Normale Supérieure (Macey, *The Lives of Michel Foucault*, 30). Framed, the Foucault conference poster also found its way into my study, where it hangs on the wall opposite the photo of Guibert. It was only then that I began to be able to look at the self-portrait of Guibert without doubt or

---

2 "[T]he air is that exorbitant thing which induces from body to soul – *animula*, little individual soul ..." (Barthes, *Camera Lucida*, 109).

guilt, imagining his happiness at being lodged in afterlife opposite his old friend – as he is in the text that best describes the times when he and Foucault were neighbors in the XVe arrondissement in Paris, that is, *À l'ami qui ne m'a pas sauvé la vie*. And as the likenesses of Hervé and Michel – two writers who enjoyed an intense intergenerational friendship and who both died because of AIDS – look upon me, they have constructed a space of tranquillity in which I too can write my piece, including these fragments about an oeuvre made up of texts and photos, watched over by Saints Foucault and Guibert.[3]

AN ANGEL IN FRANCE

In the beginning, in the artistic beginning, there was not Hervé and his parents but rather Hervé and his two great aunts (figure 2). In Guibert's first photo text, *Suzanne et Louise* (1980), he tells the unusual story of these two old ladies, the one a haughty widow of a pharmacist and owner of an *hôtel particulier* – Suzanne, the woman seated – and the other a former Carmelite nun – Louise, the woman in black who seems to disappear into the background and the shadows, making her appear remote, almost out of the picture despite her central position – whom Suzanne literally bought back from the religious order only to make her sister into her personal factotum. Suzanne and Louise are characters in one of Guibert's early texts, "Histoire d'une sainte" (*La Mort propagande*), but they also appear in his autobiography, *Mes Parents*, and *Les Gangsters* (1988), as well as other texts that make passing reference to these eccentric women. In fact, they were to populate Guibert's life, imagination, and work up to and including the video *La Pudeur ou l'Impudeur*, in which he talks to his aunts about AIDS, old age, and the will to live. This early self-portrait of Guibert in the company of his aunts also reminds us that his angelic looks were an object of intense fascination to journalists. Even when he began to look his age after his curls were cut off, magazines continued to publish out-of-date photos contemporaneous with the one shown here of Hervé and his aunts.

---

3 On the idea of Foucault as a gay saint, see David Halperin, *Saint Foucault: Towards a Gay Hagiography*. One also thinks of Sartre's *Saint-Genet*, a work devoted to a writer who had a considerable influence on Guibert. The relationship of Foucault and Guibert was based on an intense friendship, which is why I believe they can be seen as a modern version of Saints Serge and Bacchus, that couple of athletic, martyred warriors whose names are invoked in so many of the offices described by the late John Boswell in his magnificent book *Same-Sex Unions in Premodern Europe*.

12 Angelic Echoes

This photo of the "sacred family," in which Louise appears as the stronger, almost god-like figure presiding over the "marriage" of the more vulnerable Hervé and Suzanne, can be considered emblematic of the troubling relationship between photographic *Spectra* and texts that characterizes Guibert's oeuvre. The fragments in *Suzanne et Louise*, which reproduce Guibert's regular handwriting, accompany the photographs, but rarely if ever refer to them. As Daniel Arsand says, "The text seems independent of the photos: Or rather, the text shows that the photographic subjects have a story and that this story is unphotographable. The story precedes the photos, continues them, neglects them, forgets them" (69). In many of Guibert's other works the link between text and image is even more problematical.[4] For example, *L'Image fantôme* (1981) describes photos, real and imaginary ones, actual photos and memories of photos that might have been, photographic fantasies and photographic *actes manqués*. But this book contains no photographs. In *Vice* there is an obvious relationship between some of the texts and the photographs grouped together in the middle of the book, but there are also texts that have no relationship to any photo. *Le Seul Visage* (1984), Guibert's only true album, contains an introduction, but the photos are unaccompanied by any text save for the captions, a model that was followed in the posthumous *Photographies* album. Clearly, the photograph in Guibert's books is askew in relation to the text that might "explain" it; conversely, only by searching through all the texts is one able to find the hidden clues in the form of initials, real names, and pseudonyms that nonetheless entwine the visual and the textual. The original caption of figure 2 is perhaps the most traditional, as well as a direct link between the written word and the image: "À la fin ils reviennent pour saluer ..." But do the "characters" of *Suzanne et Louise*, the only book in which words and text are juxtaposed, however problematically, come back like actors to take a bow or like ghosts to haunt the pages of a book that remains out of print, as well as an entire oeuvre?

In the 1970s Guibert's fascination with bodies was to lead him to photograph and write about the Musée Grévin, France's equivalent of Madame Tussaud's Wax Works. In figure 3 we see the androgynous head of a model being ravished by an equally androgynous Guibert. Here "Au

---

4 Jean-Pierre Boulé has pointed out that the series entitled "Photo + Texte" published in *L'Autre Journal* in 1985 and 1986 "represents perhaps the only point in the whole of Guibert's work where photo and text meet in harmony ..." (*Hervé Guibert: Voices of the Self*, 116).

musée Grévin" in *La Mort propagande* (265–78) and "La Tête de Jeanne d'Arc" in *Mauve le vierge* (83–100) make up the missing intertext, not to mention an autographically inspired character who lives with just such a wax head in *Des aveugles* (117 [*Bl.*, 97]). It turns out that the head that seduced Guibert – so much so that he claimed to have stolen it from the storeroom where it languished – had been used for the wax models of *both* Joan of Arc and Louis XVII, the boy king who never reigned but to whom historians pay the courtesy of attributing a Roman numeral in honor of his lost heritage. But is the angelic Hervé symbolically making love to these two national icons, embracing the idea of androgyny, or acting out his enthrallment with the representation of a dead body whatever its gender? Or perhaps the title gives us the key, *Self-portrait*.

There are many self-portraits of Guibert, the ultimate attempt at portrayal of the self being reached in the poignant AIDS video, *La Pudeur ou l'Impudeur*, in which he filmed himself going about his daily life while the sound track is made up mostly of excerpts of his diary read by him. At one moment this baring of the soul and the body seems, as Derek Duncan has pointed out (110), to have reached the limits of what is bearable or sayable: Suffering from diarrhea, Guibert covers his face in a gesture born less of defeat or a desire for privacy, as I read it, than of an open acknowledgment of a final, visceral fatigue. But to come back to the early photograph of Guibert and Joan or Guibert and Louis, what I see is a doubling of the self-portrait as the wax model mimics the young writer's still unblemished face. Like Narcissus looking in the river, H.G. the ephebe looks upon his own desire in this mirror image. But H.G.'s desire is not just for himself but for the most perfect representation of a body. Guibert's on-going fascination with bodies is incarnated here by a wax body part of the right size and shape. The detached head is thus a kind of three-dimensional photograph, one that has been blown up, almost but not quite "embodied," thereby allowing Guibert to reach beyond the grave and the lens towards a doubly absent referent.

FRIENDS

Michel Foucault was Hervé Guibert's best and most famous friend. The photo of Michel (figure 4) is also very famous, having been used for the cover of James E. Miller's controversial biography of the great thinker, *The Passion of Michel Foucault*. In the photo a very gentle Foucault is surrounded on either side by reflections of himself. As he so often does, Guibert has made extensive use of shadow contrasted with bright light against which Foucault, wearing a kimono, appears like a Zen master caught between "reality" and its many representations. Such a likeness is, I believe, not by chance. Guibert knew Foucault, saw or spoke with him almost every day, and was part of his coterie from 1977 until his death in 1984. That Foucault must have talked about his work in progress would seem inevitable. It is my belief that some of Guibert's writing, for example, *Des aveugles*, can be read as a fictionalization of Foucault's theories, as we shall see in chapter 4.

The scandal caused when *L'Ami* was published was subsequently rekindled by the way in which Miller used Guibert's earlier short story about the illness and death of a famous philosopher, "Les secrets d'un homme" (*MV*, 101–12). What provoked the scandal is Miller's interpretation of the three secrets that, shortly before his death, Foucault is supposed to have told Guibert (*The Passion of Michel Foucault*, 354–74). Given the apparent lack of documentary evidence about Foucault's death and the poignancy of Guibert's description of the death of Muzil – the name is based on one of the novelist's other favorite writers, Robert Musil – it is perhaps not suprising that *all* of Foucault's biographers have made use of *L'Ami*.[5] However, Didier Eribon, who was the first biographer to write about Foucault's homosexuality and his friendship with Guibert, was shocked by the way Miller uses Guibert's short story in order to arrive at a hypothesis about the "truth" concerning Foucault's life and works, as though three short confessions could ever explain a long and complex career of teaching, writing, and political involvement that saw several radical shifts in focus, tactics, and method (*Michel Foucault et ses contemporains*, 28–30). (I shall return to "Les secrets d'un homme" in more detail in chapter 7.) Admittedly, Eribon himself could have made his second book about Foucault more convincing if he had not limited his study of Foucault's contemporaries to philosophers. Despite their age difference and the different styles of writing they practiced, Foucault and Guibert were every bit as much contemporaries as Foucault and Georges Dumézil, another intellectual friendship marked by an age difference.[6]

---

5 See Didier Eribon, *Michel Foucault (1926–1984)* and David Macey, *The Lives of Michel Foucault*. Guibert's biographers seemed to have missed a number of passing references to Foucault ("M.," "Michel," "Muzil," or 'l'ami") in some of Guibert's other works: *Voy.*, 14–15, 103; *Mes*, 169 (*My*, 155); *G*, 55–6 (*Gang.*, 55); *MV*, 101–11; *I*, 81, 128; *FV*, 70–1; *PC*, 72, 165 (*CP*, 141); *P*, 121–2; *Cyto.*, 17, 40–1, 47, 64 (*CMV*, 10, 31, 38, 54); *Let. É.*, 53.
6 See also Halperin's dialogue with Eribon and his own very detailed criticism of Miller's approach in the second chapter of *Saint Foucault: Towards a Gay Hagiography*, "The Describable Life of Michel Foucault."

15   Traces and Shadows

That Guibert loved to work in the tricky zone where life and fiction meet, that he excelled at turning the banal into the extraordinary, and that his works provide us with a kind of fictional *veritas* that in the end may well turn out to be more true than supposedly nonfictional truth – all of this seems self-evident to me. It is also equally clear that Guibert's texts, unlike most of his photography, which appears tame in comparison, have shocked some readers. In fact, he had more apprehension about taking photographs of friends and loved ones than he did about writing no-holds-barred scenes about his (semi-)fictitious characters. Guibert said that secrets are meant to be told, to be passed on, to be "betrayed," by which he meant written down.[7] While his fiction is definitely more adventuresome than his photography, both genres – in their own unique way – bear witness to his love for his friends and his desire to give testimony to this love:

> When I write there are no limits, no scruples because there is really only me involved; the others become merely abstract beings hidden by initials. But when I take photos of the bodies of others, family members, friends are there, and I am always somewhat apprehensive: Am I not betraying them by transforming them into objects to be seen? Fortunately, this question is soon replaced by an idea, the notion that by revealing these familiar bodies, these beloved bodies to others, to the bodies of indifferent strangers and passersby (I can also imagine them as accomplices), I am doing only one thing, something enormously important I believe, something, in any case, that is the goal of all my creative efforts: bearing witness to my love. (*SV,* [5])

What moves me in *L'Ami* are not only the passages describing Muzil's illness, but also Guibert's homage to his character's research. It takes the form of a description of the evolution of Muzil's *Histoire des comportements,* which stands in for Foucault's *History of Sexuality.* That the philosopher had the honesty to change his mind is characteristically described by Guibert in concrete terms, as though Foucault were the master planner, builder, and engineer of some vast city. Such is the lesson of Guibert: it is the truth of metaphor grounded in the depth of feeling and under-

---

7 "Every book carries with it a crime. Each one always contains a knife-thrust sentence [*une phrase coup de couteau*]. I am very upset when the time comes to dedicate my books: each time they betray secrets, and these secrets are not only mine. To write is to betray, to commit a crime" (Interview with Gaudemar, "Les aveux permanents").

standing that the younger man had for the older man. I believe that this truth has much to do with a gay aesthetic: the mutual attraction these two men felt for each other's company, conversations at once casual and serious, narcissistic betrayals, and the telling of secrets typical of the life of gay bars, as well as the braiding together of life's daily trials – including illness, depression, and fear – with the outrageous *jouissances* of sex and the creative act. It is the truth of a friendship of two kindred spirits, each caught up in his own manner in a web of words, yet still full of admiration for his friend's unique form of literary praxis.[8] It is also what the photograph, so lovingly affectionate and so full of mutual confidence between the photographer and his subject, shows us without words.

Another dear friend of Guibert was T., a.k.a. "Bibi" and "Jules," who is portrayed in a 1976 photo (figure 5). The play of light and shadow forms a series of arabesques against which we see the passive, pensive body of a beautiful man with downcast eyes. The photo is definitely homoerotic and not pornographic, to use Guibert's own criteria (*IF*, 100–4 [*GI*, 92–5]), which is no doubt why *T.* reminds me of the early self-portraits of Peter Berlin. More than the photographic *studium* I experience while looking at this image, I am hit with a personal *punctum* because for me Guibert's portrait of the beloved carries with it the weight and impact of time past. T.'s body is a very 1970s body: they just don't seem to make men like that any more, for nowadays men come complete with muscles but hardly any hair! Looking at T., I am transported back to the Toronto of the seventies and all the long-haired, thin boys who used to amble along Yonge Street on their colorful, high-heeled shoes, wearing tight little leather jackets. In the photo of T. – unlike the bodies displayed in today's skin magazines and many of Robert Mapplethorpe's photos – the sensuality is not lodged in the rock-hard flesh beneath the skin. Rather, the sensuality is located in the touch and feel of the body's outer envelope. Fittingly enough for the period, it is a structuralist sensuality based on the notion of a tactile, even textual difference, as in the Barthesian body.[9] Hence the importance of the play of light and shadow, of black and white, of light skin and dark hair.

In *À l'ami qui ne m'a pas sauvé la vie* Hervé and Jules live their lives, their

---

8 In his preface to a 1982 catalogue of the photography of Duane Michals, Foucault wrote as follows: "I love forms of works that do not develop like an oeuvre, but rather open themselves up because they are drawn from experiences: Magritte, Bob Wilson, *Under the Volcano, The Death of Maria Malibran,* and, of course, H.G." (quoted in English by Miller, *The Passion of Michel Foucault*, 461n6).

9 See Pierre Saint-Amand, "The Secretive Body: Roland Barthes's Gay Erotics," 162–3.

diagnoses as HIV-positive, and their descent into hell as mirror images of each other. To juxtapose a text with the photo of the "model" for one of an author's characters might appear to be a critical "obscenity." But given the nature of Guibert's fiction, his dual praxis of photography and writing, and the links that both unite and separate them, I feel justified in doing so. In fact, not to do so would be a cop-out, as well as a form of censorship, for T. is an integral part of Guibert's entire oeuvre. As one of Guibert's friends has written, "He wrote as he photographed: just as a photographer collects instants of reality and, on his contact sheets, makes the necessary choices that correspond to his intentions; giving up what is now no longer useful, Hervé Guibert took from life, without pity but not without love, instants of reality that were necessary to the writing of his fiction. His friends accepted the blind risk of becoming his characters, of course, never as they expected" (Gaillard, n.p.). What is important is not to attempt to identify T., as would have been done in the days of biographical criticism, but to recognize that T. is at once a photographic subject, the dedicatee of several of Guibert's books,[10] a character who reappears in a great many of his books, and his (soul) mate. Let us not forget either that, as the opening of *Le Protocole compassionnel* recounts, the AIDS triology only exists thanks to Jules's giving his friend the ddI medication that made such a difference in his friend's ability to cope with the disease and its treatment, and to continue writing, in short, to go on living. Thus, in the context of such a complex series of interrelationships between life and writing, *T.* is not just a photograph of one of Hervé Guibert's models. It is, in a very real sense, a photo of the oeuvre itself. Just as the photograph adds an uncanny dimension of reality to the books, the fictions provide the text, intertext, and subtext of one of the most poignant of Guibert's photographic subjects.

The following passage, which I quote despite its length, is one of the most vivid, the most painful, and the most magnificent in *À l'ami qui ne m'a pas sauvé la vie*. It describes Hervé and Jules making out not just in spite but in the face of the terrible disease that at once unites and separates them:

> Je réattaquai ses tétons, et lui rapidement, mécaniquement, s'agenouilla devant moi, les mains imaginairement liées derrière le dos, pour frotter

---

10 *Les Chiens* ("À T. et C."); *L'Image fantôme* ("À T., échappé du roman général. Et à mes parents."); *Vous m'avez fait former des fantômes* ("À T."); et *L'Homme au chapeau rouge* ("À mes modèles").

ses lèvres contre ma braguette, me suppliant par ses gémissements et ses grognements de lui redonner ma chair, en délivrance de la meurtrissure que je lui imposais. Écrire cela aujourd'hui si loin de lui refait bander mon sexe, désactivé et inerte depuis des semaines. Cette ébauche de baise me semblait sur l'heure d'une tristesse intolérable, j'avais l'impression que Jules et moi nous étions égarés entre nos vies et notre mort, et que le point qui nous situait ensemble dans cet intervalle, d'ordinaire et par nécessité assez flou, était devenu atrocement net, que nous faisions le point, par cet enchaînement physique, sur le tableau macabre de deux squelettes sodomites. Planté au fond de mon cul dans la chair qui enrobait l'os du bassin, Jules me fit jouir en me regardant dans les yeux. C'était un regard insoutenable, trop sublime, trop déchirant, à la fois éternel et menacé par l'éternité. Je bloquai mon sanglot dans ma gorge en le faisant passer pour un soupir de détente. (*Ami*, 156)

I went after his nipples again, and his hands tied by an imaginary cord behind his back, he quickly, automatically knelt down in front of me, rubbing his lips against my crotch, begging me with his grunts and his groans to give him my body once again, as deliverance from the pain I was inflicting on him. Writing this today, at such a distance from him, gives me a hard-on again after weeks of inaction and lifelessness. At the time this attempt at fucking struck me as unspeakably sad: I felt as though Jules and I had become lost somewhere between our lives and our deaths, that our location in this no-man's-land, ordinarily and necessarily rather nebulous, had suddenly become atrociously precise, that we were taking our places, through this physical coupling, in a macabre tableau of two sodomitical skeletons. Jammed all the way up my ass, deep in the flesh around my pelvic arch, Jules made me come as he gazed into my eyes. It was an unbearable look, too sublime, too wrenching, both eternal and threatened by eternity. I intercepted the sob in my throat, making it sound like a sigh of relief. (*Friend*, 141; trans. alt.)

It is a sob that we continue to hear. According to the chronology published at the end of *Photographies*, T. died on 14 July 1992, less than seven months after his friend.

WRITING AND READING

Figure 6, *Writing*, is no doubt one of the most sensuous of Guibert's photographs. The warmth of the bed, which the writer's and the photographer's bodies seem to have just left, seems almost palpable. The naked subject who has been captured in the act of writing is caught between the shadows and the light that caresses his sensuous body, especially the shoulder, arm, and back. It is an intimate, even *intimiste* scene that reminds us of the autobiographical character of so much of Guibert's writing.

Guibert's first drafts were done by hand, including the many interviews he did when working for *Le Monde*; the rewriting was done on an old manual typewriter inherited from one of his father's uncles.[11] The artisan-like nature of writing is emphasized here by the rough plaster of the walls, the coarse weave of the carpet upon which the writer's feet rest, the small wooden table, not to mention the four different types of cloth present – the sheets, the towel upon which the writer sits, the translucent curtains, and the sheet suspended from the ceiling to frame the subject. A drawing of a phallic figure recalls the shape of the candle, the love-making that has gone on before or will continue after the taking of the photo, and which, in fact, is continuing as the photographer aims his camera at the back of the attractive male posing as a writer. Taking photos and writing amidst decors made up entirely of various shades of white, gray, and black – for me it is impossible to conceive of what any of the "real" colors might have been – lead to the traces and shadows that he has left us of past moments of sensuality.

The next two photos continue to display the scene of writing, except that now there is no writer present. Taken in 1980, figure 7, whose intertextuality is particularly rich, shows the view from Guibert's sixth-floor apartment at 293 rue de Vaugirard to which he moved in the mid-1970s. (Foucault was a nearby neighbor, since he lived on the same street.) A translucent curtain both masks and highlights a neighboring apartment building with modern balconies. In contrast, the old manual typewriter set up on a table in front of the window forms a solid mass of metallic black that "recalls" and interacts with a curious object above and to the

---

11 At some point – perhaps when he had grown too weak to use the manual typewriter – he began to use an electronic typewriter with a small memory, as seen in some of the last images of the video *La Pudeur ou l'Impudeur*. At the end of the video, Guibert gets up from his desk and leaves the room, as the typewriter prints out what he has just entered. This final scene can be read as a companion piece to the photograph entitled *Rue du Vaugirard*, except that this time the author is nowhere to be seen; there is not even an X-ray of him. But the printing goes on in his absence, which one could interpret as an allusion to the works that were to be published posthumously, i.e., to the fact that even after his death Guibert would go on "writing."

left that has been taped to the window looking out onto Guibert's own balcony.[12] The object in question is an X-ray, taken at age seventeen, of Hervé's upper body clearly showing his left arm, his chin, the lead apron worn to protect his genitals, and – the most problematic part of all – his upper torso.[13] The reason for the X-ray was that Guibert suffered – and the word is not too strong – from a concave chest. Whether this deformity was caused by a lack of calcium during his formative years or his mother's difficult pregnancy, there can be no doubt as to Hervé's complex about his hollow torso. In *Mes parents* he writes that his life could be cut in two, dating before and after the day when as a child he was told by another boy that "I am not like him" (*Mes*, 50 [*My*, 41]). This revelation turns up again in *À l'ami qui ne m'a pas sauvé la vie*, albeit indirectly, when an incompetent doctor diagnoses the source of Hervé's ills to be his "dysmorphophobia." And in *L'Image fantôme* he wrote:

> en affichant là, et à la vue de tous (des voisins comme des visiteurs), cette radiographie, je placarde l'image la plus intime de moi-même, bien plus qu'un nu, celle qui renferme l'énigme, et qu'un étudiant en médecine pourrait facilement déchiffrer. (*IF*, 68)

> by placing this x-ray where anyone could see it (neighbors as well as visitors), I was displaying the most intimate image of myself – much more intimate than any nude, one that contained an enigma, and that a medical student could easily decipher. (*GI*, 65)

This time the writer is represented not by a self-portrait but by the photograph of a negative, so to speak, that is, the X-ray that clearly shows certain body parts in white against a black background; only the intertext allows us to make the connection with Guibert himself. The writer as a person is absent from the scene, anonymous. All that remains are the place of work and the instrument of writing, the black typewriter. I interpret this photo as a visual rendering of the "death of the author" about which both Foucault and Barthes wrote. I do not know if

---

12 In a letter written to Guibert on 23 July 1983, Foucault described looking at a young man who appeared each morning on a similar balcony, wearing only a small blue towel or blue underpants. The text of Foucault's playful letter is reproduced in "L'autre journal d'Hervé Guibert" (69).
13 For the intertext, see the following: *MP*, 110, 211, 224, 290–2; *IF*, 68 (*GI*, 65); *Voy.*, 85, 93, 97; *LA*, 116; *Mes*, 50–2, 100–1, 124–5 (*My*, 41–2, 90, 113–14); *MV*, 40–2; *FV*, 58; *PC*, 47 (*CP*, 37); *PA*, 108–9.

Guibert was familiar with Barthes's text; clearly, he knew about Foucault's ideas because, in "Les secrets d'un homme," he wrote:

> Pourtant les livres n'étaient pas lui-même, cela il l'avait un jour écrit, et il s'en souvenait encore: que le livre n'était pas l'homme, qu'entre le livre et l'homme il y avait le travail qui les désidentifiait, et qui parfois les repoussait comme deux ennemis. (*MV*, 107)

> But the books weren't him, he had once written that, and he still remembered it: that the book was not the man, that between the book and the man there came the work which separated them, and which sometimes drove them apart like two enemies.

Barthes died in 1980, Foucault in 1984. The photo dates from 1980 and the text from 1984 although it was only published in 1988.

The third scene of writing (figure 8) is even more devoid of any human presence than the last photo. In this one, we see Guibert's desk at the Villa Médicis where he held a fellowship from 1987 to 1989. Unlike *L'Incognito* – the novel in which Guibert, as in some farcical black comedy, describes the time spent by a certain Hector Lenoir at a fictitious Académie espagnole in Rome – the photo shows all the Baudelairian "luxe, calme et volupté" ("L'Invitation au voyage") that appear to have surrounded Hervé Guibert in real life. However, what fascinates me is not the apparent discrepancy between the photo and the novel, but rather the *punctum* of this deliberate staging, in particular, one element: the light bulb that Guibert has managed to capture hanging from the high ceiling, set off against the rise and fall of the tall drapes that hang behind the desk. This odd icon makes the desk look like an altar on which Guibert, the putative chief priest of some pagan cult, will sacrifice his victims' bodies as they are incorporated into the pages of the manuscript that appears to the right of the typewriter. What is more, the incandescent rays of the carbon filament seem to spell out the letters of the word *club*, making one think of the gay night club that is the focus of so many of the suspicious activities that go on in the novel *L'Incognito*, named after it. *L'Ami* is usually considered to be the first AIDS novel by Guibert, but this is not entirely true, for the syndrome made its appearance simultaneously in two works published in 1989: *Fou de Vincent* and *L'Incognito*. I believe that the light bulb symbolizes the threat that hangs over the absent Guibert/Lenoir, and serves to highlight the manuscript upon which lies a watch, as though it were a time bomb. Despite numerous references to AIDS in *L'Incognito*, the novel can hardly be considered very shocking: it "outs" neither Muzil nor Guibert as Persons Living with AIDS (PLAs), something for which *L'Ami* was so severely – and so unreasonably – attacked in the French press. I would argue that the manuscript beside the typewriter in the photo is *not* the 1989 novel but rather *L'Ami* itself, which was written in Rome and which can be considered a true time bomb, at least given the tenor of the times. In any case, Guibert described it as such in an interview (Jonquet, 111). Viewed thus, this photo takes on a multitude of symbolic meanings, all of which revolve around the secrets that the novelist was about to divulge, "secrets" that the photographer could visually capture in a very special *mise en scène*.

Figure 9, *Reading*, takes the progression of absence one step farther: now not only is the writer absent, so too is the reader who has left the book he or she is reading lying on the floor of earthenware tiles on which Guibert's camera – like that of some "spy," perhaps a child or an animal – focuses. A table cloth acts like a canopy that, together with the legs of the table and chairs, gives this photograph a feeling of perfect immobility, almost like a domestic scene from Pompeii, frozen in time. This is, for me, a photo of immense sadness, as one senses the "presence" of the absent reader who has left the imprint of his or her body in the canvas deck chair behind the table. As Alain Buisine has said about Guibert's photographs, "it is the traces of an absence that are photographed: someone is missing since so many 'remains' of his/her presence are visible" ("Le photographique plutôt que la photographie," 40). This is no doubt an example of all that is best in Guibert's photography: he succeeds in capturing a moment, a scene of seemingly perfect banality, only to turn it into something else. Here we wonder about the title of the book, the identity of the absent reader, why and where he or she has gone, what the reader is doing now, and when the book will be picked up and read again, if ever. And if so, by whom? In other words, just as the absence of a photograph in *L'Image fantôme* leads to the writing of a *récit photographique*, so too an actual photo asks us to "write" the untold story behind the photo. What is more, it is our story, for it is the story of a reader: owing to the absence of any body in the photo, we are literally in the picture.

To recapitulate: the photo of absence generates a fiction in the same way that the absence of a photograph can – and often does – lead to the writing of a Guibert text. This helps explain the problematic relationship between photos and texts, for to provide the story of a photo directly, immediately – in the same space, as in a photo text – would have the effect of canceling the absence, filling the void, and curtailing our imagination. It is no doubt for this reason that when there is an intertext to a particular photo, it is usually fragmented, dispersed, and disseminated among the written works, rather than directly juxtaposed to the image that it "explains." The figures of past, present, and future absences that haunt Guibert's writing are thus reified in a photo such as this one by the play of light and shadow that emphasizes the link between photography and an absent referent. Perhaps never has a photographer/writer managed so well to write and to photograph what is the essence of all photography – the eerie concomitance of presence and absence.

LE CLUB DES CINQ

Figure 10 shows five figurines whose purchase Guibert describes in *L'Ami*:

> Dans le passage couvert d'une cour d'immeuble qui jouxtait la vitrine d'une épicerie, dans le quartier de Graça à Lisbonne, j'avais perçu en contre-jour un étalage de figurines translucides qui paraissaient soufflées dans le sucre, j'y retournai pour les acheter, c'étaient des têtes en cire de garçonnets que des parents, autrefois, allaient déposer comme ex-voto à l'église quand leur enfant avait une méningite. (*Ami*, 208–9)

> In the Graça quarter in Lisbon, in the covered passageway of a courtyard adjoining a grocery store, I noticed a display of translucent figurines in the store window, lit up from behind so that they seemed made of spun sugar; I went back to buy them, and they turned out to be wax figures, the heads of little boys, which parents at one time used to place in churches as ex-votos when their children had meningitis. (*Friend*, 190; trans. alt.)

The author of some four hundred books, Enid Blyton (1897–1968), one of the most translated of English-speaking authors at the time of her death – after Agatha Christie and Shakespeare – wrote a series of children's novels that involve the same set of five characters (Julian, Dick, George, Anne, and Timmy – a dog), for example, *Five Go off to Camp*, *Five Go Down to the Sea*, *Five on a Secret Trail*, and *Five Get into Trouble*. The first volume of the Famous Five Club, as the series was called, appeared in the Collection Verte in France in 1955, the year of Guibert's birth. The link between the purchase of the figurines and Blyton's novels is provided earlier on in *L'Ami* when Jules uses the expression "Le Club des cinq" to describe the little family made up of Hervé, Jules, Berthe – Jules's companion and the mother of their children – Loulou and Titi.

Placed at different angles and different distances from each other, the five figurines are lit from behind, as they were when Hervé first saw them. As such, they represent this nontraditional family made up of two gay lovers; the two children of one of those men; and the woman who is their mother, the lover of one of the men, and later the wife of the "other man," Hervé, whom she would eventually marry. Do the two figurines that face each other at the left of the photograph represent Hervé and Jules? or Jules and Berthe? or Hervé and Berthe? or perhaps Loulou and Titi? What is certain is that this representation of a family threatened by AIDS can be compared with the more traditional portrait of Guibert and his two great-aunts. As in the photo of the head of Joan of Arc or Louis XVII, the human figure has been displaced by a group of three-dimensional representations of a part of the human body. And like the photos of desks and empty rooms, absence has found its usual place in a Guibert photo. Finally, light and shadow serve once again, sharply – even violently – to underscore the anonymity but also the individuality of the discrete bodies represented by the figurines.

The photo of Suzanne, Louise, and Hervé taken in 1979 or 1980 is a portrait of a group of people related by blood. On the other hand, one might initially interpret the photo of *Le Club des cinq* as having nothing to do with a family portrait. In fact, this would be wrong, because the significance of the 1988 photo and of the 1990 and 1991 novels that describe this group lies precisely in the family links that form the intense bond between the five individuals "portrayed" here, even – especially – when Guibert can only hope that there is no blood link:

> J'aimais ces enfants, plus que ma chair, comme la chair de ma chair bien qu'elle ne le soit pas, et sans doute plus que si elle l'avait été vraiment, peut-être sinistrement parce que le virus HIV m'avait permis de prendre une place dans leur sang, de partager avec eux cette destinée commune du sang, bien que je priasse chaque jour qu'elle ne le soit à aucun prix, bien que mes conjurations s'exerçassent continuellement à séparer mon sang du leur pour qu'il n'y ait jamais eu par aucun intermédiaire aucun point de contact entre eux, mon amour pour eux était pourtant un bain de sang virtuel dans lequel je les plongeais avec effroi. (*Ami*, 212)

> I loved those children, more than my own flesh, as though they'd been flesh of my flesh even though they weren't, and probably more than if they really had been, and perhaps ominously so, because the HIV virus had allowed me to become part of their blood, to share with them this common fate of our blood, even though I prayed every day that this would never be, no matter the cost, that my blood would have always been separate from theirs so that there could never have been any contact whatsoever between them, but still my love for them was a potential bloodbath, into which, terrified, I plunged them. (*Friend*, 194; trans. alt.)

The blood link and all that goes with it, so essential to the bourgeois family tree – one thinks of the archetypal tales of hidden treasure and lost inheritances that crop up from time to time in Guibert's works from *Mes parents* and *Les Gangsters* to *La Pudeur ou l'Impudeur* – have become the terrible tale of whose body's fluids have been directly exposed to whose other body fluids. The extended family of the nineteenth century, already made so much larger in recent times by remarriage and bisexuality, gains new meaning as the all-important lineage becomes that of the HIV virus itself.

So-called family values have been turned upside down by extremist right-wing politicians and homophobic fundamentalists, so that the family can be constructed as an artificial, antiseptic entity that has nothing to do with sex, and certainly not gay or lesbian sex. Nonetheless, as has often been pointed out, gays and lesbians are not the products of miraculous births. And yet at the same time that scientific discourse seems to indicate more and more that homosexuality, like left-handedness, is a genetic trait, and as such should be no more subject to value judgments, moralistic condemnations, or in the final analysis all that much discussion as regards its etiology, some people still seek to make those whom they regard as genetically warped feel guilty about their sexual orientation. The "logic" cries out for a Barthesian paradox or a queer critique, such as David Halperin's eloquent study *Saint Foucault: Towards a Gay Hagiography*. Gays and lesbians are "guilty," not because of what they have or have not done, but because of the gender of the desired one. In these sad times, much of the world is still intent on reliving the errors, the hate, and the terror of the 1930s and the 1940s. The positive – but still fragile – side of all of this is the fascinating ways lesbians and gay men have engaged in various cultural practices to live with and ward off the essentialist homophobia that still characterizes so much of the ambient society we live in.

Guibert was never a gay liberation activist. Even his attitude toward homosexuality was somewhat ambivalent. In *L'Image fantôme*, he does explain why homoerotic desire forms an integral part of his writing about photography, to which I shall return in the next chapter. Later on, he would speak of his own problematic relationship with homosexuality: "it's like the word *homosexuality*, for me it's a word that has never really related to me, strangely enough, since it clearly does relate to me, but I don't see things like that, it's not the way I live, it's not the way I feel, I have the impression that I am elsewhere than in those ..." (Interview with Donner, 157; original ellipsis). The issue came up at the end of a long interview, which is a pity because despite Guibert's evident malaise with the subject, he might have had more to say if the interviewer had broached the issue earlier on. Derek Duncan sees homosexuality in Guibert's work as an indication of artistic marginality and not as a gay identity as such. "A homosexual without obvious relations within the gay community, Guibert realized his sexual identity through his faithfulness to a handful of members of the Parisian artistic and intellectual elite who were hostile to all aspects of bourgeois provincialism associated – although not exclusively – with homophobia and heterosexism. Guibert's homosexuality is an indication of the marginality of an artist and not of a gay identity; consequently, AIDS threatens Guibert's identity as a writer as much as it threatens a subjectivity based on sexual preference ..." ("Gestes autobiographiques," 101). For Guibert what is most important is his primary desire to bare his soul and body, his "project of self-revelation" (*Ami*, 247; *Friend*, 228), whether through writing fiction, taking photographs, or making a video of himself. More than homosexuality as such, AIDS was the true catalyst that enabled Guibert to get closer to his goal (Pratt, "De la désidentification à l'incognito," 72).

Nonetheless, *À l'ami qui ne m'a pas sauvé la vie* and the subsequent media publicity probably did more for the consciousness raising of thousands if not millions of people in France and elsewhere about gay life and love than many more "politically correct" works. Furthermore, I believe that, in its own way, the photograph *Le Club des cinq*, like the 1990 novel and its sequel, *Le Protocole compassionnel*, is not only a document, but a kind of political statement in and of itself. It makes us realize how far the notion of the family can be and has been extended in the shadow of AIDS, a time of lost talents, immense fatigue, and suffering, not to mention the burden of hate – and sometimes, as in the case of Guibert, of spurious adoration – that is borne by PLAs. This is the price this new family must pay for the conversion to HIV-positive status of one or more of its members. But there is another side, and it is that other positive side that Guibert also reminds us of in this last, very special photo. Despite the terrible uncertainty, the panic, and the fear that permeate every page of Guibert's first AIDS novel, what unites this little "sacred band" is love. It is a love that speaks to and of a new kind of family.[14] As the old family recedes into the background – Suzanne, like Michel, was to die before Hervé – the members of Hervé's last queer family represented by the five figurines face their destiny at once alone and united, in the dark about their future even in the blinding light of day in which they face each other and the world about them.

In his writing about photography, Guibert emphasizes the photos that were taken but didn't turn out, the photos that should or could have been taken. Similarly, many of his actual photographs portray lifeless models, statues, or decors in which someone seems to have just left. On the other hand, there are family portraits, portraits of friends, and self-portraits. *Le Club des cinq* is all of these, for it is a self-portrait, a photo of figures that represent absent bodies, and – most of all – a symbolic portrait of a real family, not a *memento mori* but a memento of love, valor, and compassion with which surely we all can identify.

---

14 "[B]y a kind of grace, with vigilance on part of all, through a certain sense of discretion, of delicacy, of acceptance, it happened finally that I loved a couple, a family. I have a relationship with this man, I have a relationship with this woman, with this couple. This family. And each of these relationships is different and makes me happy" (Interview with Françoise Tournier, "Chronique d'une mort annoncée," 183).

Chapter Two

The Deaths of Desire

> J'eus peur que cette lettre reste entre nous, à jamais, comme une tache noire, un regret, un faux pas.
>
> *L'Image fantôme*, 150

> I was afraid this letter would remain between us forever like a dark stain, a regret, a blunder.
>
> *Ghost Image*, 138

Among the photographs taken by Hervé Guibert there is none of Roland Barthes, which at first might seem surprising. Though his relations with Roland Barthes are less well known than his friendship with Michel Foucault, Guibert knew Barthes, whose work he admired. Guibert claimed that his passion for Barthes's books went back a long time, whereas he admitted to not having read those of Foucault until after the philosopher's death in 1984 (Interviews with Donner and Eribon). Guibert's most detailed chronicle of his friendship with Foucault a.k.a. Muzil can be found in *À l'ami qui ne m'a pas sauvé la vie*. But just as there is no photograph of Barthes, there is no novel about him. This doesn't mean, however, that there are no textual traces of their onagain, off-again relations, for in fact there are many. The major difference is that in Barthes's case, all the traces are fragmentary, dispersed in many different works. Given the complexity of the personal and intertextual relationship, I shall attempt a fragmentary narrative, following a chronology that covers the years 1977 to 1991.

Just eleven days after Roland Barthes's inaugural lecture at the Collège de France on 7 January 1977, Hervé Guibert's first book *La*

Mort propagande was published. He sent copies of this slim volume – one hundred and thirty-seven pages – to three older gay men whose work he admired: Francis Bacon, Roland Barthes, and Michel Foucault. While we do not know what their reactions were, one can well imagine the interest that the book must have provoked just by its title, as well as the front and back covers. The front cover reproduces part of a large painting, *Le Christ au tombeau* (1839) by the Belgian painter Antoine Wiertz (1806–65), whose grandiose works have been compared to Rubens. The illustration represents a half-naked androgynous-looking male with pouting lips wearing a white loincloth and partly wrapped in a great piece of red silk, the folds of which are entwined around his arms and head. Grasping one end of the fabric is a right hand, whose index finger is pushed deep into his naked left nipple. On the back cover, superimposed over a black and white photograph of Hervé Guibert – with his curly hair, wide-open eyes, and drooping head, he looks rather like Diana the late Princess of Wales – is a publicity blurb signed "H.G." in which he speaks of his ambition to "Entretenir un rapport sadomasochiste à l'écriture: par elle, disséquer son corps, et la disséquer elle-même" (Foster a sadomasochistic relationship with writing: to use writing to dissect his body and writing itself). Guibert describes his body as homosexual, his writing as "anal-phallic."[1]

We know that Guibert had read more than one of Barthes's books, since although he claimed to have a passion for *Roland Barthes by Roland Barthes*, he admitted that Barthes's most autobiographical work was perhaps not his best (Interview with Eribon, 88). In general, for Guibert, reading an author and writing about him tend to go hand in hand, and in this Barthes was no exception: "I believe it is by being a reader that one becomes a writer. The writer whom I was reading – his shadow or his ghost – almost became a character in the fiction I was writing. He was both a character and a model. I have never had the fantasy of modernity, of literary invention. I never wanted to do something brand new, different. I have felt love for various writers and I tried to let myself be supported by them" (ibid.). As this quotation indicates, Guibert was at heart a postmodernist, refusing the myth of originality. But one would be hard put to find anything Barthesian in the pages of *La Mort*

---

1 For readers more familiar with the second edition of *La Mort propagande et d'autres textes de jeunesse*, it should be pointed out that the first edition corresponds only to pages 186–211; the last sentence on page 211 included in the first edition is "Il s'agit donc d'un crime sexuel, ou crime de moeurs."

propagande and its tales of dissection and sex; clearly, at this point in his career, Guibert was more influenced by Genet and Bataille. In Guibert's later work, *Mes parents*, however, there are definite echos of Barthes's own autobiography in Guibert's narrative about growing up in Paris and the provinces.

But let us return to early 1977. One day a film critic told Guibert he should attend Barthes's lectures and that the great man himself would let them in "par une petite porte," thereby avoiding the unpleasantness of both the crowd and a long wait. Guibert turned up at the Collège de France one Saturday morning, and Barthes did indeed let him into the amphitheater by a little door. Like Cunégonde at Candide's autodafé, he was well placed, but unfortunately he found what Barthes had to say "mortally boring" (ibid., 89).[2] He left in full view of both Barthes and the audience, presumably by the front door, and returned home, only to find a letter from Barthes in his mailbox! In his letter, Barthes claimed to have read Guibert's book and expressed a wish to dialogue with the young writer about the relationship between fantasy and writing. The only condition that Barthes placed on this dialogue was that it must occur without his actually meeting Hervé: it was to take the form of letters. Though the two men did exchange correspondence, for some reason they couldn't resist meeting in the flesh, and they would have dinner together. Guibert himself said that as far as his friendship with Barthes went, he was in a secondary zone, whereas he "entered the primordial zone of friendship with Foucault" (ibid.).

Guibert was looking for a mentor cum master;[3] and since he admired Barthes's work, what better choice could he make? But things didn't work out that way. Refusing to play his intended role, Barthes said to Guibert: "'I'm not worried the least about you (*toi*), I believe in the charm of your writing'" (ibid.) As Guibert goes on to say, in some ways Foucault was more of a master for him, although not in terms of writing.

2 In *Adultes!* Guibert describes a "fictional" character called Gaspar who attended a lecture given by a certain Thess: "À peine Thess égrène-t-il le subtil fil de son discours que Gaspar étouffe, il a envie de hurler, il se sent humilié, il veut être le seul à écouter ça, ou ne jamais l'écouter" (f. 59, quoted with the permission of Christine Guibert) (Thess had scarcely begun to weave the subtle thread of his talk when Gaspar suffocated, felt like screaming, he felt humiliated, wanted to be the only one to hear it, or never hear it at all).

3 Also in the manuscript of *Adultes!* is to be found the following sentence: "Il [Gaspar] voulait être le disciple unique d'un maître adoré" (f. 7; quoted with the permission of Christine Guibert) (Gaspar wanted to be the only disciple of a beloved master.) Guibert explains that this is why Gaspar did not continue with his university education.

The Deaths of Desire

(Apparently, Foucault thought so little of Guibert's short pornographic text *Les Chiens*, supposedly written for him, that he never mentioned it to his younger friend.) As for Barthes, Guibert claimed to have truly liked him, even if he found him boring: "He never stopped complaining. He was always overwhelmed by celebrity, by requests for prefaces that he couldn't write" (ibid.).

As a result of this friendship between the newest gay writer to be discovered by Parisian literati and one of the best-known literary theorists of the time, Guibert was encouraged to write a text entitled "La mort propagande n⁰ 1" (*MP*, 229–40). Guibert told Barthes about one of his childhood fantasies about naked men in an underground room of pleasure, as he called it. Without speaking and without touching, men take their places in stall-like compartments where flames that are at once gaseous and liquid bathe their nether regions. In the dream-fantasy, Guibert, the only child among this company of adults, waits his turn before taking his place for a firey douche. One can easily imagine Barthes encouraging Guibert to write down such a savory fantasy! In any case, Guibert was to return to the same fantasy in his autobiographical work *Mes parents* where we learn that the precocious Hervé was only four or five years old when he first dreamed of the sauna-like establishment (*Mes*, 23, 40; *My*, 14, 31). Whatever its primary origin, the text was supposed to be published with a preface by Barthes, on one condition: Guibert would agree to sleep with him (Interview with Eribon, 89). But the younger man felt that he could not have sex with someone as old as Barthes: at the time, Barthes was sixty-one, Hervé twenty-two.

We now lose track of the two of them together, but one can still get some idea of their activities that spring and summer of 1977. For example, in May Barthes's best-selling *Fragments d'un discours amoureux* (translated as *A Lover's Discourse: Fragments*) was published. The next month, the Cerisy-la-Salle conference "Prétexte: Roland Barthes" brought together some of Barthes's most ardent admirers from France and abroad. The newly elected holder of the Chair of Semiology at the prestigious Collège de France was at the apogee of his career; but according to his biographer Louis-Jean Calvet this was the most painful summer of his life (270). The reason was that his beloved mother was dying. As Barthes wrote on 13 July 1977, "*Sombres pensées, peurs, angoisses: je vois la mort de l'être cher, m'en affole*" (*Le Bruissement de la langue*, 402) (Dark thoughts, fears, anxieties: I can see the death of the beloved one, I am panicked by it).

Guibert also had an eventful summer. After spending some time with his parents at their home in Porquerolles, where he felt suffocated by their excessive attentions for his person, he read his play "Suzanne et Louise" at the Gueuloir of the Festival d'Avignon. The Gueuloir was a locale in which new plays were read out loud by young playwrights. Hervé wrote an amusing text about his experiences in Avignon, and sent it to his favorite newspaper, *Le Monde*, which published it in August. This was to lead to his being hired as photography critic for France's premier newspaper, a post he was to hold until 1985 when his friend and mentor Yvonne Baby left the paper.

We next pick up the trail of Guibert's relations with Barthes in the fall of 1977. Had the two men written to each other over the course of the summer? It is possible, for we do know that there was correspondence in either direction, much of it "stormy," according to Guibert (Interview with Eribon, 89). There were also attempts to arrange dinners together, but in the fall Barthes refused all of Guibert's invitations, because of his mother's illness. Guibert never met Henriette Barthes, but he spoke with her on the telephone. In a section entitled "La mort au plus près," in *L'Image fantôme*,[4] a series of meditations on photography, he describes how he imagined Barthes at this time:

> Sa voix à lui est de plus en plus faible, et triste au bout du fil, d'une politesse un peu lasse. Je l'imagine, dans cet appartement sombre, renfermé, de la place Saint-Sulpice, jouer du piano, très doucement, pour cette vieille dame très pâle, très fatiguée, reposant entre ses draps blancs, mais continuant toujours à se lever, je l'imagine, pour faire la cuisine à son fils. Et lui en retour lui faire la lecture, la divertir paisiblement, chantonner pour elle, apposer ses lèvres sur ses paupières lourdes de fièvre. (*IF*, 148)

> His own voice on the phone has become weaker and weaker, and sad, marked by a weary politeness. I picture him in that dark, stuffy apartment on the Place Saint-Sulpice, playing the piano very softly for the pale, tired old woman resting between her white sheets, but always managing to get up – I can see her now – to cook dinner for her son. And in return, he would read to her, amuse her quietly, sing softly to her, place his lips on her eyelids heavy with fever. (*GI*, 137; trans. alt.)

Guibert's fascination with the bodies of old women, the chief among whom were his great-aunts Suzanne and Louise, got the better of him,

---

4 Guibert's title reprises *L'Afrique fantôme* of Michel Leiris and, of course, Wagner's *Der fliegende Holländer*, known in French as *Le Vaisseau fantôme*.

and he contacted Barthes by letter, asking if he could take a photograph of him with his mother. As Guibert was to write later,

> La photo pouvait être simple et banale en soi (j'imaginais d'ailleurs une photo un peu plate: sa mère allongée, ou assise sur une chaise, et lui debout près d'elle, lui tenant peut-être la main), elle pouvait même être ratée techniquement, elle était de toute façon forte. Elle était "la" photo, la seule photo pour moi, en ce moment, de R.B. (*IF*, 149)

> The photograph could have been simple and ordinary in itself (moreover, I imagined a rather trite picture: his mother lying down or seated in a chair, he standing near her, perhaps holding her hand), it could even have been technically faulty, it would still have been strong. At that moment, it was "the" photograph of R.B., the only one possible for me. (*GI*, 137–38; trans. alt.)

We would do well to remember that Guibert wrote this after reading *La Chambre claire*, echoes of which are clearly evident here, especially the "platitude" of the anticipated photograph. In any case, there was no response.

Ten days later, worried by the thought that he might not have taken sufficient rhetorical precautions in his letter, Guibert telephoned Barthes, only to learn that Henriette Barthes had died on 25 October 1977:

> Je me confondis en excuse, mais il éluda mon excuse, et reporta encore le moment de me voir, sous le prétexte de ce temps de suspension provoquée par la mort, le déplacement du corps, les papiers de succession, mais aussi la retombée de la peine, l'habitude de l'absence, l'entrée très lente et très pénible dans un monde nouveau, le monde sans elle, le monde sans maman ... (*IF*, 149–50; original ellipsis)

> I apologized profusely, but he ignored my excuses and again delayed seeing me, using as a pretext the interruption of events caused by death, the removal of the body, the inheritance papers, but also the renewal of pain, the growing accustomed to absence, the very slow and difficult entrance into a new world, the world without her, the world without *maman* ... (*GI*, 138; trans. alt.)

In *L'Image fantôme*, Guibert then switches from this painful *faux pas* to the general principle that he deduces, that is, the link between photography and death, or rather the morbid desire harbored by so many people to see photographs taken as near to the actual moment of death as possible. Here one thinks of *Suzanne et Louise*, in which he staged deathlike tableaus of his great-aunts. The *démarche* in this fragment – but not the ideas – is pure Barthes: after a personal experience (Barthes himself would not have been so specific, so long about it, but …), comes the general principle as it applies to Guibert, followed in turn by a universal semiotic rule: The photo that represents death "sera reproduite, et multipliée à l'infini; elle restera dans les imaginations, innombrable et suspendue, toujours vibrante, comme une petite menace, ou la délectation d'être soi hors du cadre, et de voir encore" (*IF*, 151) ("will be reproduced and multiplied an infinite number of times, it will remain in our imagination in innumerable copies, suspended, filled with emotion, like some tiny threat, or like our delight at being outside the frame and yet able to see" [*GI*, 139; trans. alt.]).

In November 1977, writes Barthes at the beginning of the second half of *Camera Lucida*, he found himself looking at photographs of his mother, searching for the image that best represented her essential goodness, her *air*, as Barthes will say later. Eventually, after putting aside many photos including recent ones, he was to find the truest one. Although the photograph of the Winter Garden showed Henriette as a little girl, it is the one that "spoke" the most directly to her son: in fact, it is the only one in which he recognized her *air*, thereby re-establishing contact with her through a kind of referential radiation that Barthes sees as the essence of all photography: "Ainsi, la Photographie du Jardin d'Hiver, si pâle soit-elle, est pour moi le trésor des rayons qui émanaient de ma mère enfant, de ses cheveux, de sa peau, de sa robe, de son regard, *ce jour-là*" (*Oeuvres complètes* (henceforth *OC*), 3:1166) ("Hence the Winter Garden Photograph, however faded, is for me the treasure trove of rays emanating from my mother as a child, from her hair, her skin, her dress, her gaze, *on that day*" [*Camera Lucida*, 82; trans. alt.]).[5]

In following the story of the on-again off-again relations between Barthes and Guibert, let us now turn to the latter's contribution to his column "Notes-Photo" published 10 November 1977. In it he reviewed two works, one of which was the fourth issue of the review *Créatis*, devoted to the photographs of Daniel Boudinet with a text by Barthes.[6] Guibert has

---

5 Henceforth *Camera Lucida* be will abbreviated as *CL*.
6 Boudinet's photographs and Barthes's originally untitled text are reproduced in the *Oeuvres complètes* (3:705–18). The title of Guibert's article was "Une matière de feuillage."

little to say about the photographs, and it is clear that Barthes thought more highly of them than did the photography critic of *Le Monde*. What does impress Guibert, however, is the beauty of the older man's style in these thirteen fragments:

> Barthes pourrait écrire n'importe quoi sur n'importe qui, ce serait toujours aussi séduisant, somptueux, inutile et musical, sans jamais être complaisant. Le texte qui commente les photos de Boudinet est si beau qu'on serait tenté ici de le recopier, de le resavourer.

> Barthes could write anything about anyone, it would still be as seductive, sumptuous, useless and musical, without ever being complacent. The text that comments Boudinet's photos is so beautiful that one is tempted to reproduce it here in order to savor it again.

At this point in his review Guibert does quote one sentence from the text,[7] which, by the way, anticipates the *studium/punctum* opposition Barthes will explore in more detail in *La Chambre claire*. Was Guibert disinterested here? Perhaps not entirely – he wanted a mentor and Barthes was sure to read the review – but I do not think that he was being hypocritical. I believe that he was a genuine admirer of Barthes's writing and appreciated its sensuousness, its concreteness, its corporeity – traits he will incorporate into his own writing, albeit in texts that are quite different from those of his wished-for "writing master."

In early December, Guibert's relations with Barthes reached a crisis point. After having dinner together one evening, Barthes invited Hervé to his apartment. At some point, the older man asked if he could kiss the younger man's hand. Hervé refused, Barthes was deeply hurt, and an exchange of letters ensued. We do not have access to those of Guibert, but since he later published one of Barthes's, we know his

---

7 "[C]e qui me saisit, ce n'est pas un spectacle, une scène, une 'vue', c'est une matière de feuillage, un tissu délicat: la substance est à la fois touffue et légère, désordonnée et centrée; ces frondaisons verticales sans air, sans ciel, inexplicablement, me donnent à respirer, elles m'élèvent l'"âme' (aurait-on dit il y a cent ans: mais l'âme, c'est toujours le corps), et pourtant, je veux aussi m'enfoncer dans l'obscur de la terre: bref, une moire d'intensités" (*OC*, 3:707) (What captivates me is not a spectacle, a scene, a "view," it's the living matter of the leaves, like a delicate fabric: their substance is at once dense and light, untidy but centered; inexplicably, this vertical foliage without air or sky allows me to breathe, uplifts my "soul" [as one would have said a hundred years ago, but a soul is always a body], and yet I also want to plunge into the darkness of the earth: in short, a moiré effect of shimmering intensities).

thoughts about the incident. Barthes's letter takes the form of fragments, which could rightly be considered as a kind of coda to the book published earlier that same year, *Fragments d'un discours amoureux*. The title of Barthes's letter to Hervé, "Fragments pour H.," says it all in a way, when one recalls what Barthes wrote about the letter "H" in *Roland Barthes by Roland Barthes*. In the fragment entitled "The goddess H." he refers to the "blissful potential of a perversion" as inscribed by the initial letter of the words *homosexualité* and *haschisch* (*OC*, 3:143; 63). Now Hervé has become another type of perversion! As a result of Guibert's refusal to allow himself to be kissed, Barthes finds himself marginalized in relation to his already marginal position as he perceived it. The actions and words of the younger gay man send him back to the hated *doxa* and a role he finds abhorrent – he is the "horny old man" who made an unsuccessful pass and was rebuffed for his unwelcome advances.

In the first part of "Fragments pour H." Barthes writes that Guibert's second letter was the meanest, since "elle *dit* à l'autre que son corps est indésirable" (*OC*, 3:1297) (it *tells* the other person his body is undesirable). Throughout the fragments, Barthes never mentions Guibert by name and refers to him only in the third person, reducing him to an anonymous and distant *he*. Barthes objects to what he perceives to be Hervé's desire to parcel out parts of him that are desirable – his ideas about writing, for example – while refusing the other parts – his untouchable body. Such an idea is not new to Barthes, for he had adressed the identical schema, only in reverse, in his 1977 bestseller about love: "qui m'aime 'pour moi-même', ne m'aime pas pour mon écriture" (*OC*, 3:532) ["if you love me 'for myself,' you do not love me for my writing" (*A Lover's Discourse*, 79)].[8] Barthes would have liked to be found desirable for his body *and* for his writing. In "Fragments pour H." he takes care to emphasize that he did not desire Hervé sexually but sensuously: "Aucun désir de 'génitalité,' mais l'envie d'une 'sensualité' commune. Sensualité: champ du rapport défini (limité) par cela qu'un corps *ne m'est pas interdit*. Distinguer: 'ne pas être interdit'/'être accessible.' Vivre selon, sur des nuances" (*OC*, 3:1297) (No desire for "genital" involvement, but a longing for a common "sensuality." Sensuality: the sphere of a relationship defined (limited) by the fact that a body *is not forbidden to me*. Differentiate: "not to be forbidden"/"to be accessible." To live accordingly, according to nuance).

---

8 Henceforth, *A Lover's Discourse: Fragments* will be abbreviated as *LD*.

Barthes then goes on to describe the scene from the point of view and the memory of one for whom Hervé had constructed the role of "dirty old man":

> Le sens de la scène est le suivant: en éloignant spectaculairement son corps du mien, en se reculant au fond de la pièce, en la quittant hâtivement, il me *constituait* en sauteur: j'allais sauter sur lui et, à l'avance, il se garait. Constitution si forte, si bien réussie qu'après son départ, je me suis retrouvé seul dans l'appartement, collant à l'image d'un salaud qui a échoué dans son entreprise. (ibid.)
>
> The meaning of the scene is the following: by spectacularly withdrawing his body from my own, by stepping back to the far end of the room, by leaving so hurriedly, he *constructed* me as a seducer: I was going to jump on him, and he was going to stay clear. The construction was so strong, so successful that after he left, I found myself alone in the apartment, stuck with the image of a bastard who failed in his undertaking.

The word *scene* is encoded with strong negative connotations in Barthes. According to his book about amourous discourse a scene happens when "deux sujets se disputent selon un échange réglé de répliques et en vue d'avoir le 'dernier mot'" (*OC*, 3:649) ("two subjects argue according to a set exchange of remarks with a view to having the 'last word'" [*LD*, 204]). In point of fact, it conjures up what must have been one of the most repugnant images for Barthes, namely, that of the couple legally joined in mariage until death do them part, for he goes on in the following terms: "ces deux sujets sont *déjà* mariés: la scène est pour eux l'exercice d'un droit, la pratique d'un langage dont ils sont copropriétaires; *chacun son tour*, dit la scène, ce qui veut dire: *jamais toi sans moi*, et réciproquement" (*OC*, 3:649) ("these two subjects are *already* married: for them the scene is the exercise of a right, the practice of a language of which they are co-owners; *each one in turn*, says the scene, which means: *never you without me*, and vice versa" [*LD*, 204; trans. alt.]).[9] But Hervé and Roland were *not* married, and thus the scene was not just ridiculous, like the scenes portrayed in plays about bourgeois marriage; it was simply inappropriate. In spite of himself, Barthes found himself playing the role of the villain,

---

9 No doubt the highest praise that Barthes can pay his mother in *La Chambre claire* is when he tells us that during a lifetime of living together, she never reproached him with anything, never made a "single observation" (*O.C.*, 3:1158; *CL*, 69).

given the dramatic reaction of the "victim," who – need I add here – resembled an angel at the time. So strong was Hervé's acting out that even after he left, Barthes found himself alone in the apartment – all of this takes place only weeks after his mother's death, so that to be there alone must have been traumatic in itself – like some actor on stage waiting to deliver a soliloquy. He identifies with the dramatist and novelist Jean Genet, reminding Guibert of Sartre's analysis of the great homosexual writer: "Ainsi le Genet de Sartre se fait (est fait) voleur et pédé parce qu'enfant, il reçoit un jour dans le dos l'appellation 'Voleur'" (*OC*, 3:1297) (Thus Sartre's Genet becomes (is made into) a thief and a fag because one day as a child he heard someone call him "thief" behind his back). Like the Autodidacte in *Nausea*, Barthes has been labelled a pervert – he deliberately uses the Sartrean term *salaud*, "bastard" – in the most essentialist manner possible not only by what the other said but also by his actions. Perhaps he considered himself lucky that Hervé did not strike him like the librarian in Sartre's novel who beats up the Autodidacte upon discovering his timid advances towards a high school student!

Barthes goes on to clarify his initial request. Clearly, Guibert had written that Barthes wanted to put his tongue on his skin, for the fragment begins as follows: "Je ne voulais nullement 'ma langue sur sa peau', mais seulement, ou autrement 'mes lèvres sur sa main'" (*OC*, 3:1297) (I didn't at all want to put "my tongue on his skin" but only, or otherwise, "my lips on his hand"). The nuance between tongue on skin and lips on hand is a literary one, as Barthes emphasizes: "La nuance est littéraire (puisqu'elle tient au langage)? Mais je vis selon la littérature, j'essaie de vivre selon les nuances que *m'apprend* la littérature" (*OC*, 3:1297–8) (The nuance is literary [since it derives from language]? But I live according to literature, I try to live according to the nuances that literature *teaches me*). No doubt Guibert had intimated in one of his letters that he had no time for such a "purely" literary distinction; whatever the case, the message here is that if Hervé wants to become a writer, then at least he should try to understand literature! It is his ignorance of nuance that is the source of the whole malentendu! Barthes is only being consistent with himself and with his "philosophy": "Né de la littérature, ne pouvant parler qu'à l'aide de ses codes usés, je suis pourtant seul avec ma force, voué *à ma propre philosophie*" (*OC*, 3:480) ("Born of literature, able to speak only with the help of its well-worn codes, yet I am alone with my strength, devoted *to my own philosophy*" (*LD*, 23; trans. alt.]). Like Proust and Guibert himself, no doubt Barthes could only live life with the story of living that life in mind.

"Fragments pour H." must be situated in the context of not only the published fragments about the discourse of love, but also the intertext which underpins that work. I believe that Barthes was thinking of *The Sorrows of Young Werther* (1774), the key text in the literary and psychoanalytical corpus on which *A Lover's Discourse* is based, when he made his unfortunate request to Guibert. I have found three possible quotations that Barthes may have had in mind: "I bent down and kissed her hand, and now there were tears in my eyes too as I looked into hers again" (*The Sorrows of Young Werther*, 42); "I ran to meet them, and I shivered as I took her hand and kissed it" (ibid., 68); "Today I walked into her room, she came to meet me, and I kissed her hand, my heart overflowing with joy" (ibid., 90). Casting himself in the role of the Romantic hero and Guibert as heroine, Barthes wanted to kiss Lotte alias Hervé. In other words, he wanted the young man to participate in a kind of intertextual reenactment in order to realize the all-important kiss in Goethe, a "figure," as Barthes called it, about which he must have lectured in the seminars leading up to the publication of *Fragments d'un discours amoureux*.[10] According to Barthes, Werther is not a fetishist interested only in hands: he is a lover. Hence in the best Proustian tradition of the lover qua semiotician, he creates meaning everywhere: "et c'est le sens qui le fait frissonner: il est dans le brasier du sens" (*OC*, 3:521) ("it is meaning which thrills him: he is in the crucible of meaning" (*LD*, 67]). In fact, Barthes gives an example from Proust, that is, the episode when Charlus takes Marcel's chin in his hand and "slides his magnetized fingers up to the ears 'like a barber's fingers'" (ibid., 68).[11] Perhaps we should even think of casting Hervé in the role of the narrator of *À la recherche du temps perdu*, ostensibly a naïve heterosexual who, though fascinated by everything queer, misunderstands the gestures, body language, and voice of Charlus, whom he supposes to be a lunatic, a thief, or a spy rather than a homosexual attracted by

---

10 Alternately, Barthes may have been thinking of the intertwined hands portrayed on the cover of *Fragments d'un discours amoureux*, which reproduces a painting of *Tobias and the Angel*. We can imagine that Barthes was casting himself not just as Werther but also as Tobias led by an angelic-looking Guibert!

11 "'Comment! vous ne savez pas vous raser, même un soir où vous dînez en ville vous gardez quelques poils', me dit-il en me prenant le menton entre deux doigts pour ainsi dire magnétisés, qui, après avoir résisté un instant, remontèrent jusqu'à mes oreilles comme les doigts d'un coiffeur" (Proust, *À la recherche du temps perdu*, 2:851) ("'What, you don't know how to shave! – even on a night when you've been dining out, you have still a few hairs here,' he said, taking my chin between two fingers which seemed magnetized, and after a moment's resistance ran up to my ears like the fingers of a barber" [*Remembrance of Things Past* 2:584, trans. alt.]).

Marcel! Interestingly, in his best-selling book, Barthes underscores how an insignificant gesture can lead to a "demand for love": "Ce geste insignifiant, que je commence, est continué par une autre partie de moi; sans que rien, physiquement, l'interrompe, il bifurque, passe de la simple fonction au sens éblouissant, celui de la demande d'amour" (*OC*, 3:521–2) ("This trivial gesture, which I begin, is continued by another part of myself; without anything interrupting it physically, it branches off, shifts from a simple function to a dazzling meaning, that of the demand for love" [*LD*, 68]).

While Guibert thought that Barthes's request referred to something sensual, Barthes based his own need on a "kind of festival not of the senses but of meaning," to (re)coin the binary opposition found in *A Lover's Discourse* (*OC*, 3:521; *LD*, 67). But in his fragments written for H. he is more concrete, more direct, more full of self-pity:

> Un *effet de littérature* se produit lorsque la littérature (la langue bien faite) modifie quelque chose dans le réel. Renvoyé par les mots au dégoût de "ma langue sur sa peau," c'est peu dire que je renonce à lui: je renonce à moi-même; je vais oublier mon corps. (*OC*, 3:1298)
>
> A *literary effect* is produced when literature (language well-wrought) modifies something in reality. Put off by the words of disgust "my tongue on his skin," it would be an understatement to say I give up on him: I give up on myself; I'm going to forget my body.

Playing on the double sens of *langue*, "tongue" and "language," he tells Guibert how disgusted he is with the image that is being thrown in his face. We note how he continues to play with the pronouns, refusing to use the second-person pronoun, which allows him to avoid the choice of the *vous* over the *tu* that he had hitherto used when speaking with or writing to Hervé. As Barthes wrote in the public fragments, "Le troisième pronom est un pronom méchant: c'est le pronom de la non-personne, il absente, il annule" (*OC*, 3:630) ("The third-person pronoun is a wicked pronoun: it is the pronoun of the non-person, it eclipses, it annuls" [*LD*, 185; trans. alt.]).

The problem with a so-called literary effect is that, like irony, it risks being misunderstood by the other person. Significantly, there is nothing in the nine fragments reproduced first in *L'Autre Journal* and then in complete works of Barthes that would let the reader – Guibert, us – know exactly to what he is referring. It is possible that the reenactment that Guibert refused to play in – preferring to "write" his own scene, the hysterical performance ending in his melodramatic exit, and the follow-up explanatory letters – was not text- or image-specific. Perhaps Barthes was thinking not just of Werther and Lotte (as portrayed by Goethe), or Charlus and Marcel (as described by Proust), or Tobias and the Angel (as represented by the anonymous painter of the school of Verrocchio), but of *all three*. Such an interpretation would have the added semiotic pleasure of combining a woman, a young man, and a decidedly boyish-looking angel, presumably sexless. It would also combine heterosexual, homosexual, and divine love. Or perhaps Barthes was thinking of all the scenes in literature in which a lover steals a kiss, a furtive squeeze of the hand, a brushing of knees beneath the table. Rejected, like Charlus, by someone who misreads his complicated encoding of messages, his literary allusions, who remains blind to the all-important festival of meaning based on a literary effect, all Barthes can do is register his defeat the morning after:

> Catharsis: un nouveau jour se lève sur un paysage un peu désolé, image d'un contrat réduit – mais désormais sûr. De moi à lui, plus aucune consistance charnelle; substantiellement, je verrai son corps à peu près comme je vois celui de Marchais à la TV! Et de lui à moi: il acceptera désormais, sans essayer de la critiquer ou de s'en plaindre ou de la forcer, "cette politesse un peu lasse" qui est un deuil: le deuil insistant, irréparable, du corps de l'autre.
> A bientôt (dis-je, quant à moi). (*OC*, 3:1298)

> Catharsis: a new day rises on a somewhat desolate landscape, the image of a reduced – but henceforth certain – contract. Between me and him, no more carnal consistency; I will look upon his body substantially in the same way I look at that of Marchais on TV! And between him and me: he will accept from now on, without trying to criticize, complain or force his way through "that rather weary politeness" that is a mourning: the insistent, irreparable mourning for the other's body.
> (As for me, I say) Bye for now.

Here Barthes refers to the original contract that Guibert described in the Eribon interview – a night of love for a preface – the terms of which recreate the contract proposed in Balzac's novella *Sarrasine* – a night of love for a story – that Barthes analyzed in such detail in *S/Z*. Now the terms of contract between Barthes and Guibert have changed. On the one hand, Barthes's thoughts about Hervé will no longer have any "carnal consistency," by which he means that he will look upon the young man's body with the same indifference as he would on seeing a televised image of the leader of the French Communist party, Georges Marchais, which is about as great an insult as any gay Frenchman of the time could imagine! Guibert, for his part, must accept, without criticizing or complaining, Barthes's "rather weary politeness," an expression presumably quoted from one of Guibert's letters that he was to use again, as we have already seen (p. 32). Indeed, Barthes tired politeness has a meaning heretofore undetected by Guibert, for it signifies a mourning "for the other's body." Clearly, Barthes was deeply hurt, and his mourning for his beloved mother becomes a weapon to be used in the face of Guibert's hostile gestures.

Originally written on ten sheets of paper, the fragments are unnumbered and untitled. One fragment – I presume the first, introductory one – is missing from both of the published versions of the letter. The ending raises another mystery, for there is no evidence that Barthes and Guibert ever saw each other again, just as there is no evidence that they did not. All we can learn by the date is how close this drama was to the death of Barthes's mother, enacted in the very *sanctum sanctorum* of the apartment in which she had lived and died. As Barthes wrote in *A Lover's Discourse*, mimicking Mallarmé's "Jamais un coup de dés n'abolira le hasard," to have the last word is to dominate: "it is the last throw of the dice which counts" (*OC*, 3:652; *LD*, 208). Considering that Guibert published Barthes's letter without the permission of his literary executors and that it was prefaced by this introductory sentence, it might well seem that it was Hervé who had the last word:

> *Fragments d'un discours amoureux*, "ce livre 'chaste'" – comme il l'écrira dans une dédicace – est sorti en mai 1977. Le 10 décembre, en réponse à une lettre qui l'a blessé, Roland Barthes envoie et offre à une connaissance – étrange cadeau pour apaiser chez l'autre la blessure qu'il vient de commettre – ce texte bouleversant, qu'il intitule "Fragments pour H." (*OC*, 3:1298)

> *Fragments d'un discours amoureux*, "that 'chaste' book," as he described it in a dedication, was published in May 1977. On 10 December, in answer to a letter that hurt him, Roland Barthes sent and gave to an acquaintance – a strange gift to soothe the wound inflicted by the other – this deeply moving text entitled "Fragments for H."

In the Complete Works this sentence is reproduced after the letter, whereas in the original publication in the magazine *L'Autre Journal*, it preceded the letter. Whether or not Guibert understood all the allusions in Barthes's letter, either in 1977 or nine years later when he published it, is unclear, but it seems likely, given the adjective he chose to describe it: *bouleversant*, "deeply moving" or "overwhelming." By recognizing the wound he had inflicted, Guibert also seems to be indicating that it is the older man who has had the last word, but to read this letter in the Complete Works of Roland Barthes, in which it was included presumably because of its earlier publication by Guibert, is a strangely disturbing experience as one comprehends the superimposed levels of the hurt involved.

Let us now consider very briefly the events of the last years of Barthes's life. Between 15 April and 3 June 1979 he wrote the forty-eight chapters of *La Chambre claire* (*Camera Lucida*), an inverted numerical cipher corresponding to the eighty-four years his mother lived, a type of homage that Guibert himself would make use of later in his own works. On 17 September 1979 in "Soirées de Paris," Barthes wrote about a young man named Olivier G. who came for lunch (and no doubt more if Barthes had had his way), concluding in the following terms: "Puis je l'ai renvoyé, disant que j'avais à travailler, sachant que c'était fini, et qu'au-delà de lui quelque chose était fini: l'amour d'*un* garçon" (*OC*, 3:1286) ("Then I sent him away, saying I had work to do, knowing it was over, and that more than Olivier was over: the love of *one* boy" [*Incidents*, 73]). Unlike the "Fragments pour H.," the fragment about Olivier's prophetic visit is softly melancholic, and the leave-taking is at the request of Barthes himself. This time there is no *scene*, no hysteria, just the calm realization of the death of desire.[12]

On 25 January 1980 *La Chambre claire* was published and exactly one month later on 25 February, after having lunch along with several other intellectuals and the first secretary of the Socialist party, François Mitterrand, who was to be elected president of the Republic in 1981, Barthes was hit by a truck in front of the Collège de France. Three days later, *Le Monde* published a review of Barthes's book under the title "La sincérité du sujet." The author? Hervé Guibert, the photography critic, of course. One wonders if Barthes was told about the review while he was in hospital. Guibert begins by praising Barthes's voice, presumably his textual or

---

12 Barthes's biographer Louis-Jean Calvet attributes great importance to the episode with Olivier: perhaps it even explains why Barthes, as some said, "let himself die" (298–9).

writerly voice, although one can hear a description of RB's actual voice, so unmistakedly seductive and melodious:

> C'est une voix menue, douce, prudente, obligée, un peu nonchalante, qui ne piétine pas, non, mais qui avance par petits bonds, par petits scintillements, par petits chipotages d'écriture. S'il y a une vérité ici, c'est celle de la sincérité du sujet. ("La sincérité du sujet")

> It's a voice that is thin, soft, prudent, grateful, slightly nonchalant, it doesn't mark time, no, but advances by short leaps, brief glitterings, and quick nibblings of writing. If there is a truth here, it is that of the subjet's sincerity.

After rehearsing the Barthesian opposition *studium* versus *punctum*, Guibert goes on to describe the second part of the book, where Barthes speaks about the death of his mother: "C'est la deuxième partie du livre la plus limpide, la plus authentique, la plus nécessaire, et donc la plus belle" (ibid.) (The second part of the book is the most limpid, the most authentic, the most necessary, and hence the most beautiful). Guibert even adresses Barthes's tendency to use the word *mourning* instead of *death*: "Barthes dit plus volontiers 'deuil,' comme s'il prêtait aux mots une vertu émolliente" (ibid.) (Barthes prefers to say "mourning," as though he ascribed a healing power to words). We recall that Barthes also used the word *deuil* in his "Fragments pour H." Overall, the review is positive. Guibert compliments Barthes for mixing erudite vocabulary with popular images, for example, *faire tilt*.[13] Guibert concludes that *Camera Lucida* will undoubtedly sell fewer copies than Barthes's previous work, *A Lover's Discourse*, and that Barthes's notes on photography will not be of much use to photographers. Rather, he situates the book's appeal in the musicality of its style. Guibert was right in all three cases. One wonders how many readers of *Le Monde* who read this article were aware of Guibert's troubled relationship with the author of the book he was reviewing!

Almost one month later, on 26 March 1980, Roland Barthes died in hospital. But Guibert's dialogue with Barthes was far from over. For

---

13 *Faire tilt* is a popular expression often heard in French cafés where young people play electronic pinball machines. Figuratively, it means "to capture one's attention" or "to have a flash of inspiration." Guibert would use it himself in his interview with Christophe Donner when he described the effect that Montaigne's preface had on him (see Introduction).

example, on 8 April he published an article entitled "Beau à tout prix." The interest of this article, which was later included in *L'Image fantôme* in a slightly rewritten version (*IF*, 137–9; *GI*, 126–8), is that it is a direct response to the most important tenet of *Camera Lucida*: the self-authenticating character of photography.[14] Basing his theory – or perhaps it would be more accurate to say his ardent desire – about referential emanation, Barthes is able to convince himself that there is a direct, almost corporeal link between the photograph of his mother taken in the Winter Garden and himself: "Une sorte de lien ombilical relie le corps de la chose photographiée à mon regard: la lumière, quoique impalpable, est bien ici un milieu charnel, une peau que je partage avec celui ou celle qui a été photographié" (*OC*, 3:1166) ("A sort of umbilical cord links the body of the photographed object to my gaze: light, though impalpable, is here a carnal medium, a skin I share with the one who has been photographed" [*CL*, 81; trans. alt.]). To be sure, he does acknowledge that trick photography exists, but he is unwilling to admit just how common it is: "les artifices, rares, qu'elle permet, ne sont pas probatoires; ce sont, au contraire, des truquages: la photographie n'est laborieuse que lorsqu'elle triche" (*OC*, 3:1169) ("the [rare] artifices it permits are not probative; they are, on the contrary, trick pictures: the photograph is laborious only when it fakes" [*CL*, 87]). What then was the subject of Guibert's article published in *Le Monde* on 8 April? The secrets of a retoucher:

> Entre les agences de publicité, les médias et les consommateurs, les retoucheurs font figure d'agents secrets, d'exécuteurs obscurs et innombrables, de grands exterminateurs de l'imperfection. La retoucheuse déblaye et embellit la réalité. Mais elle est aussi une magicienne: elle peut faire voler les avions au repos, mettre des cheveux sur les crânes

---

14 "La Photographie ne dit pas (forcément) *ce qui n'est plus*, mais seulement et à coup sûr, *ce qui a été* ... Cette certitude, aucun écrit ne peut me la donner. C'est le malheur (mais aussi peut-être la volupté) du langage, de ne pouvoir s'authentifier lui-même. Le noème du langage est peut-être cette impuissance, ou, pour parler positivement: le langage est, par nature, fictionnel ... mais la Photographie, elle, est indifférente à tout relais: elle n'invente pas; elle est l'authentification même ..." (*O.C.*, 3:1169) ("The Photograph does not necessarily say *what is no longer*, but only and for certain *what has been* ... No writing can give me this certainty. It is the misfortune (but also perhaps the voluptuous pleasure) of language not to be able to authenticate itself. The *noeme* of language is perhaps this impotence, or, to put it positively: language is, by nature, fictional ... but the Photograph is indifferent to all intermediaries: it does not invent; it is authentication itself ..." [*CL*, 85–7]).

> chauves pour les publicités de lotions contre la calvitie. Elle peut fermer des yeux ouverts et rouvrir des yeux fermés, elle peut faire marcher les morts. (*IF*, 139)

> Among the advertising agencies, the media, and consumers, retouchers play the part of secret agents, obscure and unnameable executioners, great exterminators of imperfection. The retouching artist cleans up and embellishes reality. But she is also something of a magician: she can make a grounded airplane fly, can put hair on a bald head for an advertisement of a lotion that prevents baldness. She can close eyes that are wide open and open eyes that are closed. She can make the dead walk. (*GI*, 128)

Although Guibert does not mention Barthes in his article, it would have been difficult for readers of the time who were familiar with *La Chambre claire* to ignore the "coincidence." Guibert was deconstructing Barthes's favorite theory about photography based on the special photograph of his mother. In case readers of *L'Image fantôme* might not make the connection, Guibert placed the article about the retouch artist in close proximity to the chapter entitled "The photograph, as close to death as possible," where he describes his attempts to take a photograph of Barthes and his mother.[15] It seems that Guibert's conflict with Barthes was destined to continue even after he and his beloved mother were in their graves. If a touched-up photograph can make the dead walk, then the logical conclusion is that photography is just as fictional as writing! Even the sacred Photographie du Jardin d'Hiver may have been the handywork of some clever retouch artist, which means that the umbilical link described – and which Barthes needed so desperately to hang on to in order to avoid the work of mourning – may not exist. Typically Guibertian is the idea implicit in his article that Barthes's theory about photography may have been based on a trick photo!

In September 1981 *L'Image fantôme* was published. The book is made up of sixty-four fragments, which corresponds to the age of Barthes when he died, no doubt Guibert's way of acknowledging his debt to him. In fact, *L'Image fantôme* could be considered as Guibert's continuation of and riposte to *Camera Lucida*. I have already described two fragments, but there are many other traces of Barthes in Guibert's first autobiographical text.

---

15 "La retoucheuse" is the fifty-second fragment, "La photo, au plus près de la mort" the fifty-sixth, in *L'Image fantôme*.

The Deaths of Desire

The second chapter of *L'Image fantôme*, one of the longest, picks up where Barthes left off: "La photographie est aussi une pratique très amoureuse" (*IF*, 11) ("Photography is also an act of love" [*GI*, 10]). Guibert describes how, at age eighteen, he took a photograph of his mother. But this was no ordinary photo, for he began by remaking his mother if not in his own image then in an image that pleased him instead of his father. In fact, he begins by getting rid of his father:

> La première chose que je fis fut d'évacuer mon père du théâtre où la photo allait se produire, de le chasser pour que son regard à elle ne passe plus par le sien, et par cette demande d'apparence, donc en fait de la libérer momentanément de toute cette pression accumulée pendant plus de vingt ans, et qu'il n'y ait plus que notre connivence à nous, une connivence nouvelle, débarrassée du mari et du père, juste une mère et son fils (n'était-ce pas en réalité le décès de mon père que je voulais mettre en scène?). (*IF*, 12)

> The first thing I did was to remove my father from the scene where the photo was to be taken, to expel him so that her expression would no longer be transmitted by his, through his insistence on appearances, so that she was thus temporarily freed of all the pressure that had built up over more than twenty years, so that there was nothing left but our own complicity, free of husband and father, just a mother and her son (Wasn't it in fact my father's death that I wanted to stage?) (*GI*, 11; trans. alt.)

Although Guibert cannot make the twenty years of his parents' marriage disappear, he does the next best thing by establishing a special complicity between the mother and her son in the physical and symbolic absence of the father. The theatrical element of this Oedipal drama is emphasized by the use of *théâtre, mettre en scène*, which reminds us that Guibert wrote a version of *Oedipus Rex* in 1972 (*MP*, 63–80), just one year before the episode of "L'image fantôme." This time, however, Hervé is no longer just a dramatist but also actor, director, stage manager, and producer all rolled into one.

After his father's departure, Guibert washed his mother's hair in order to rid her of the hideous hairdo that heretofore had prevented him from wanting to photograph her. As her appearance changes, she seems to relax, and the tense wrinkles around her mouth disappear. Preparing his mother like a model or a corpse – she seems completely passive – involves removing every possible trace of his father and the time that the couple spent together. Even distracting objects are removed from the living room by the conscientious stagehand. Finally, he is ready to take the photograph of his mother, with her wrinkle-free face, her newly done hairdo, wearing only a slip, and sitting majestically, as Guibert describes her, like some queen about to be executed. Bathed in sunlight, she seemed to savor – *jouir*, "to enjoy" *and* "to have an orgasm" is the verb used – this shared moment of glory with her son in the absence of her husband:

> En fait, c'est ça: l'image d'une femme qui jouit, qu'elle ne pouvait jamais avoir, censurée par son mari, une image interdite, et le plaisir d'elle à moi était d'autant plus fort que l'interdit volait en éclats. Ce fut un instant suspendu, un instant sans inquiétude, rassérénant. (*IF*, 14–15)

> In fact, that's it: the image of a woman coming, one she could never have, censored by her husband, a forbidden image, and the pleasure between us was made even greater as the forbidden burst into pieces. It was a moment suspended in time, a moment of peace and serenity. (*GI*, 13; trans. alt.)

Mother and son are united in incestuous union, as if it were the first time she was ever allowed to know true sexual pleasure, a pleasure forbidden by both society and the father. Projecting onto the body of this mother his own homoerotic desire, the eighteen-year-old Guibert even goes so far as to coif her with a straw hat, an allusion to Tadzio, the beautiful teenager in Visconti's film version of *Death in Venice*. This moment of complicity, intimacy, and intense pleasure also has a confessional mode, as though Guibert were showing his mother the image of his own desire for an androgynous boy such as the one Thomas Mann wrote about in his novella.

Later on, the father returns, the mother puts on a dress, does her hair up as she always did, and Hervé – with his father's help – develops the photos just taken. The moment of revelation comes just as the mother is removing the makeup put on by her son: but what happens? The subversive image doesn't exist! The film had not been put into the camera correctly; as Guibert writes, "j'avais photographié à vide. A blanc" (*IF*, 16) ("I had photographed nothing. Blank" [*GI*, 15]), as though he had shot off his gun – his load – without any amunition. The scene of incest must remain symbolic, for it can neither be seen nor spoken about. But although the "ghost image" of his mother is invisible as well as inaudible, it can and does lead to writing. In fact, had the photograph turned out, there would have been no text, no book, so that the work we are reading is the product, like a child of Oedipus and Jocasta, of forbidden intercourse. This explains why there are no illustrations: "Donc ce texte n'aura pas d'illustration, qu'une amorce de pellicule vierge. Et le texte n'aurait pas été si l'image avait été prise ... Car ce texte est le désespoir de l'image, et pire qu'une image floue ou voilée: une image fantôme ..." (*IF,* 17–18; second ellipsis original) ("So this text will not have any illustrations except for a piece of blank film. And the text would not have existed if the picture had been taken ... For this text is the despair of the image, and worse than a blurred or foggy image – a ghost image ..." [*GI,* 16; trans. alt.]). The "ghost image" corresponds directly to the book we are reading, as inevitably as a tragic flaw leads to a fall from grace.

For readers familiar with Barthes's book on photography, *L'Image fantôme* reminds us that *Camera Lucida* is also based on an absent photograph, the famous Photographie du Jardin d'Hiver taken in 1898 when Henriette was five years old. Just as Barthes was obliged to construct his whole theory of photography on an absent photo – not because it did not exist but because it would say nothing to us – so too the cornerstone of Guibert's essay on the same topic will also be built on or around an invisible image. But the younger writer goes one step farther, for unlike Barthes he includes no photographs in his book. Indeed, it is the very lack or impossiblity of photographs – for whatever reason – that Guibert seeks to address. The visual and the textual are demonstrated to be not complementary, as some might have thought after a cursory glance at his photo-roman *Suzanne et Louise,* but mutually exclusive, the one foreclosing the other. Here, as elsewhere, Guibert has taken the "lesson" of Barthes and applied it literally, pushed it to the nth degree. It is as if Guibert must outdo Barthes in describing the link between an invisible photograph of the writer's mother and the essence of all photography and/or writing about photography. We realize that the episode of the ghost image is a textual allegory for all of *L'Image fantôme,* a work that displaces another parental figure, Roland Barthes himself. Where Barthes can speak only with longing melancholy of another's photograph of his mother, Hervé can speak firsthand of the staging of his incestuous intimacy with his mother. The link between the two mothers, and hence between the two writers, is literally highlighted by the fact that both Barthes and Guibert emphasize the importance of light. The old photograph of Barthes's mother is remarkable for the brightness of her eyes, just as Guibert takes care to mention the presence of a special luminosity in the room where the phantom image took place. Not only does the ever-Oedipal Guibert symbolically kill his biological father by having him leave the scene of the forbidden image even before the preparations begin, he also murders his intellectual father by writing a book on the essence of photography in which he seeks to go farther in circumscribing the topic. *La Chambre claire* has been replaced by the sunlit living room of Guibert's mother just as *L'Image fantôme*, by its literal inscription of what remains figural in Barthes, has displaced the former work from its unique status. Invisibility, like filial love, has been taken to new heights, thereby rendering the older writer's work if not useless then at least "redundant."

There are other passages in *L'Image fantôme* that illustrate Guibert's attempts to outdo Barthes. For example, Guibert does not hide his homosexuality:

> Ce n'est pas que je veuille la dissimuler, ni que je veuille la ramener avec arrogance. Mais c'est la moindre des sincérités. Comment voulez-vous parler de photographie sans parler de désir? Si je masquais mon désir, si je lui ôtais son genre, si je le laissais dans le vague, comme d'autres l'ont fait, plus ou moins habilement, j'aurais l'impression d'affaiblir mes récits, de les rendre lâches. (*IF*, 89)

> It's not that I want to dissimulate it, or that I want to boast about it arrogantly. But it's the least I can do in the way of sincerity. How can you speak of photography without speaking of desire? If I mask my desire, if I deprive it of its gender, if I leave it undefined, as others have done more or less cleverly, I would feel as if I were weakening my stories, making them flabby. (*GI*, 83; trans. alt.)

It would be hard to be more direct without naming Barthes outright. We remember the coquettish way he played with the topic of homosexuality in *Roland Barthes by Roland Barthes* as well as the kind of genderless love he describes in *A Lover's Discourse* where the third-person masculine pronoun used to refer to the beloved could be interpreted as a neutral "one"-type pronoun in French. It is true that in *Camera Lucida* Barthes did include a self-portrait of the young Robert Mapplethorpe. But in no other text published before the posthumous *Incidents* did Barthes speak as openly of same-sex desire as he did in that short work. Guibert continues in the confessional mode of the same fragment:

51   The Deaths of Desire

> Ce n'est même pas une affaire de courage (je ne milite pas), il en va juste de la vérité de l'écriture. Je ne saurais pas vous dire cela plus simplement: l'image est l'essence du désir, et désexualiser l'image, ce serait la réduire à la théorie ... (*IF*, 89; original ellipsis)
>
> It's not even a matter of courage (I'm not a militant), it has to do with the truth of writing. I don't know how to put it more simply. The image is the essence of desire and if you desexualize the image, you reduce it to theory ... (*GI*, 83; trans. alt.)

Theory for Guibert, who wrote this before the advent of queer theory, of course, represents all that is wrong with the nonself-disclosing character of writing by a theorist such as Barthes. Of course, today a younger gay man might reproach Guibert for his lack of militancy, or for the fact that the fragment on homosexuality bears no title!

Another example of Guibert trying to outdo or just plain "out" Barthes is to be found in the fragment where he explains the difference between an erotic photograph and a pornographic one. To be sure, Barthes does evoke these two types of photography, but he does so very briefly. Guibert, by contrast, devotes several pages to the same topic. Reading these pages, one is conscious of what seems to be a deliberate attempt to write in a manner like Barthes, to write the pages that might be construed to be lacking in *Camera Lucida*:

> Le corps érotique est une bonne pâte: je le malaxe comme je veux, je l'inverse, je lui fais dire autre chose que son texte, je le double, et il n'a pas de fatigue, il se décolle du papier pour emplir ma tête, je fais un bout de chemin avec lui, il fait tout ce qu'on lui dit. Le corps pornographique ne fait que ce qu'il veut, et ce qu'un metteur en scène peut-être abruti a voulu qu'il fasse. Alors j'enrage de retrouver mes fantasmes dans les revues pornographiques: ainsi donc mes fantasmes sont des modèles déposés, et imposés, et depuis des siècles sans doute. Je ne fais que les reproduire, je n'échappe pas à ce conformisme du plaisir. (*IF,* 103–4)
>
> The erotic body is easily handled, like good dough. I can knead it as I please, I can turn it over, I can make it articulate something other than its text, I can bend it in two, and it never tires, it detaches itself from the paper to fill my head, I can accompany it for a short distance, it does everything I tell it to. The pornographic body does only what it wants, or what some mindless director wanted it to do. So, I'm furious when I dis-

cover my fantasies in pornographic magazines. It means that they have been patented and prescribed in advance, and probably for centuries. All I do is reproduce them. I can't escape the conformity of pleasure. (*GI*, 95; trans. alt.)

Guibert adopts a typically Barthesian way of approaching a problem. First, begin with a general truth, which is therefore written in the present tense: "la limite entre l'érotique et le pornographique est plus trouble, elle touche au commerce: on peut faire passer du pornographique pour de l'érotique, rarement l'inverse" (*IF*, 103) ("the boundary between the erotic and the pornographic is more problematic; it has to do with commerce. Pornography can be made to pass for eroticism, rarely the opposite" [*GI*, 94–5]). Then illustrate the general truth with a personal example, which though particular continues to be applicable, true, and therefore can be written in the present tense also. In the rest of the paragraph, develop the two opposing terms of the binary opposition that you have "coined," as Barthes would say, but avoid using words such as *whereas, although, though*, since it is better to let readers perceive the fundamental difference for themselves. As well, do not forget to use a creative metaphor, preferably from a domain that is totally different, for example, by using a word from the language of recipe books: The erotic body, like good dough, allows itself to be kneaded, it does not tire, it does all that one wants it to do. But the pornographic body only does what it wants to, which leads to frustration and even anger as Guibert realizes that his own desire only reenacts age-old fantasies. Although he does not mention the Barthesian opposition of *plaisir* versus *jouissance* outlined in *The Pleasure of the Text*, it is clear that the pornographic photograph is on the side of the former and the erotic one is on the side of the latter. Clearly, Guibert has Barthes in mind when he wrote these lines; indeed, as already stated, it is as if he were writing the text that Barthes would have liked to but dared not write.[16]

In the penultimate chapter of *L'Image fantôme*, "L'image cancéreuse," Guibert tackles Barthes's ideas about referential emanation or radiation head-on. We remember that for Barthes the *noème* of photography is the direct link between the person looking at a photo, the Spectator, and the person portrayed, the Spectrum. To be sure, there might be a genetic or affective link, but this is not what the theorist cum memorial-

---

16 My recipe for writing a typically Barthesian fragment is, of course, an allusion to *Le Roland-Barthes sans peine* by Michel-Antoine Burner and Patrick Rambaud.

The Deaths of Desire

ist is talking about, for the link in question is present and operative even when we do not know the identity of the person portrayed. This link, according to Barthes, is based on the transmission of light from the Spectrum to the camera and therefore onto the photographic plate and its attendant chemicals, from which the negative and then the positive image will be developed. In looking at a photograph, we see a kind of ghostly remnant of the light from the original subject. Thus Spectrum and Spectator are viscerally linked, across the years, by a direct, umbilical-like ray of light.

Guibert will take this theory, turn it upside down, literalize it, and incorporate it in a narrative full of homoerotic desire. He begins poetically: "Longtemps, je n'ai gardé qu'une seule photo chez moi: la photo d'un garçon que je n'ai jamais connu, prise par un photographe inconnu dans un lieu inconnu" (*IF*, 165) ("For a long time I kept only a single photograph at home: the photograph of a boy I never knew, taken by an unknown photographer in an unidentified location" [*GI*, 154]). Up to the first time the word *photo* is used, the French sentence has the same number of syllables as a classical alexandrine. Thus the end of the first clause, "chez moi," could be interpreted as a kind of poetic enjambment. The repetition of *connu, inconnu, photo* is also poetical. Does not poetry continually refer to its own past phonetically, rhythmically? What is more, picking up the intertextual echoes in *Camera Lucida*, Guibert begins on a Proustian note since the first part of this first sentence of the fragment is a rewrite of the first sentence of *À la recherche du temps perdu*, "Longtemps, je me suis couché de bonne heure" ("For a long time I used to go to bed early"), a sentence Barthes used as the title of a lecture given in 1978.[17] Whereas Proust used his famous sentence to open his great novel, Barthes used it to announce a novel that was about to be written but which never was. Guibert intertextualizes the Proustian sentence at the outset of the second-to-last fragment of *L'Image fantôme*. Whereas the eponymous second chapter looks backward, "L'image cancéreuse" looks forward to some of Guibert's later works, including his first two novels, *Voyage avec deux enfants* and *Les Lubies d'Arthur* – published respectively in 1982 and 1983 – as well as *Vice* and even *À l'ami qui ne m'a pas sauvé la vie*.

---

17 The famous lecture was both critical and autobiographical in its analysis of writing a novel, a task that Barthes had embarked upon upon when he died. Guibert refers to Barthes's lecture in a text written in 1983 entitled "Le roman fantôme" that was first published in 1994 (*PA*, 129–32).

In this seminal chapter, Guibert describes how at first the photograph of an attractive young man aged between sixteen and eighteen seemed impervious to the passage of time. The young man refused to age, and the photograph didn't deteriorate, at least at first. Guibert kept it for seven years, not knowing if its Spectrum was alive or dead, or even who he was. At that point, the photograph finally began to show the passage of time, since little spots appeared on the young man's face: "Il était vérolé. L'image était cancéreuse. Mon ami malade" (*IF*, 167) ("He looked syphilitic. The image was cancerous. My friend sick" [*GI*, 156]). *L'Image fantôme* was published the same year that Guibert heard about a "'cancer that would hit only homosexuals'" (*Ami*, 21; *Friend*, 13), so that it seems likely that this is the first reference, however indirect, to AIDS in his oeuvre.[18] At first, Guibert does nothing to save his friend with the telltale spots that make him look as if he has a sexually transmitted disease: "Il était comme un pauvre tapin miné par la vérole" (*IF*, 167) ("He was like some poor hustler riddled with syphilis" [*GI*, 156; trans. alt.]). After considering various options, including burning the photograph, Guibert puts it under his mattress, then under his pillow, but the image continues to live, if only in Hervé's dreams. After this, he decides to wear the photo on his person, to be precise on his torso, to which he attaches the photo with elastic bands.[19] Finally, Guibert decides to detach himself from the image of the young man, only to discover that the photograph is as blank as the one he attempted to take of his mother. But this time the ghostly image continues to endure in the pigmentation of his own skin:

> Dans une glace, je vérifiais qu'elle avait adhéré à ma peau, comme un tatouage ou une décalcomanie. Chaque pigment chimique du papier avait trouvé sa place dans un des pores de ma peau. Et la même image se recomposait exactement, à l'envers. Le transfert l'avait délivré de sa maladie ... (*IF*, 169; original ellipsis)

> In a mirror, I verified that it had stuck to my skin, like a tatoo or a decal. Each of the paper's chemical pigments had found its place in the pores of my skin. And the same image formed itself identically in reverse. The transfer had saved him from his illness ... (*GI*, 158)

---

18 Ross Chambers has analyzed the link between "l'image cancéreuse" and Guibert's video *La Pudeur ou l'Impudeur* (*Facing It: AIDS Diaries and the Death of the Author*, 37, 56).
19 Let us remember just how affectively charged the word *torse*, "torso," is for Guibert on account of his concave chest.

The text must be read with *Camera Lucida* in mind. In *L'Image fantôme* the idea of referential radiation has permutated into a physical transfer from one body to another. As in Barthes, there is a direct link between the Spectrum and the Spectator, but Guibert has taken Barthes's theory one step farther by incorporating or literalizing the link of light in the form of a sort of tattoo since the chemicals responsible for the "cancerous image" have now impregnated his own skin. The process of transference carries with it images of Christian iconography – the Shroud of Turin – and Freudian overtones – psychoanalytical projection and fixation on the authority figure of the analyst, the quasi-paternal figure of Barthes – as well as the idea of the transmission of illness, an eerie premonition of HIV and AIDS, for now it is Guibert who inevitably must be the bearer of the "gay cancer" from which the young man suffered.

We can now jump to 1986 when Barthes was once again on Guibert's mind. In March his autobiographical work *Mes parents* was published. Predictably much of the book is devoted to Guibert's negative comments about his parents, for example, their stinginess. But his mother's mastectomy in 1981 is the occasion for a reconciliation, as he realizes for the first time just how vulnerable she is. The most blatant allusion to Barthes occurs in Guibert's description of his mother's room in a clinic: "La nouvelle *chambre, claire,* spacieuse: l'intervention de la lumière, qui rend supportable la situation [non plus la lumière caverneuse de l'hôpital]" (*Mes*, 145; my emphasis) ("The new bedroom, light and airy; the introduction of light making the situation bearable [no longer the cavernous light of the hospital]" [*My*, 132]). The room filled with light recalls *La Chambre claire*, but the citation is also an indirect allusion to the other sunlit room in which Guibert attempted to take his mother's photograph eight years earlier, the photo that resulted in a "ghost image." Whereas he felt no desire to take his mother's photograph when she risked becoming a "real" ghost in the cavernous hospital room, in the sunlit room of the clinic to which she was transferred three weeks after the operation, he once again had the desire to capture her image. As he was to write in the introduction to his album of photographs, *Le Seul Visage*:

> Et tout de suite cette lumière m'a réconcilié avec ma mère, ou plutôt avec l'image de ma mère, et avec mon espoir qu'elle reste en vie. J'ai eu envie de la prendre en photo. Je lui ai dit qu'elle était belle et je le pensais. Pour la première fois j'ai pensé qu'elle allait vivre: la lumière sur son visage, le renouveau de l'attrait photographique s'en portaient garants. (*SV*, [7])

> And immediately this light reconciled me with my mother, or rather with the image of my mother, and with my hope that she would remain alive. I felt like taking her photograph. I told her she was beautiful, and I believed it. For the first time I thought she was going to live: the light on her face, the renewal of the desire to take a photograph guaranteed it.

This time intertextuality functions not as an attempt to test the validity of Barthes's ideas; on the contrary, these ideas – about the necessary connection between photography and light, as well as the visceral link between a son and his mother – serve as a guarantee of the mother's ongoing recovery.

"Fragments pour H." was published on 19 March 1986, one day after the "achevé d'imprimer" of *Mes parents*. Given the evolution of this ongoing relationship with Barthes, the man he intended to be his mentor, the synchroneity of the two publications, Guibert's autobiography and Barthes's letter to Guibert, seems more intentional than coincidental. This is not the explanation, however, given by Guibert. In *L'Homme au chapeau rouge* he wrote, "I had given (Michel Butel) an unpublished letter by Barthes against the express wishes of his literary executors" (*MRH*, 64). Guibert felt beholden to Butel because he gave him a job working for *L'Autre Journal*, a monthly magazine, after he left *Le Monde*. Of course, an action can have more than one motive: it is entirely possible that Guibert wanted to exorcise the memory of the painful incident, and that his position at *L'Autre Journal* simply gave him the opporunity to do so. Indeed, just as he doesn't spare the readers of *Mes parents* painful scenes where his own conduct is not above reproach, his introduction to the letter is sufficiently ambiguous to allow one to interpret his actions here as a gesture of would-be atonement with Barthes, similar to his reconciliation with his mother at the time of her illness.

The publication of Barthes's letter to Guibert was certainly not seen in this way by Renaud Camus, a gay man, a prolific writer, and a friend of Barthes. Claiming not to know the identity of "H.," Camus expresses sympathy for his old friend, who apparently was under no illusions concerning the death of desire where he was concerned: "Barthes was, as he used to say, the first to know that he wasn't desirable, and he acknowledged it in terms much more brusque and more cruel that anything this man might have found to hurt him. The horrible thing was the will to hurt ..." (*Journal romain*, 261). As much as Renaud Camus sets high store on self-knowledge and lucidity, he deplores "the will to hurt" someone, which is how he interprets the actions of H. that resulted in Barthes's writing the letter he did. I shall return to Camus in another chapter, but for now let us get back to Guibert.

One reason why Guibert probably thought a lot about Barthes in the mid to late 1980s is that he found himself in a relationship with a younger man to whom he devoted numerous entries in his diary. He would later extract these entries and publish them in a slightly fictionalized version – the entries are printed in reverse chronological order, for example – entitled *Fou de Vincent*. Since I shall be devoting an entire chapter to Guibert's complicated textualization of this friendship, suffice it to say here that in this other relation he found himself in the position of the older man.

There is further proof that Barthes continued to be on Guibert's mind. His play *Vole mon dragon* (written in 1987 but not published until 1994) contains a scene in which a would-be lover asks a young man to put his fingers in his mouth, and another in which the character of the Man ends up eating one of the detached fingers of the young man. Guibert was to reprise this episode in a short story included in the collection *Mauve le vierge* published in 1988 under the title "Le citronnier." I believe that both the dramatic and narrative versions of this odd act of cannibalism can be traced back to the scene described by Barthes in his "Fragments pour H." The passage of time and Guibert's fascination with all things corporeal, not to mention his fertile imagination and a strong penchant for the grotesque, have now transformed the scene of the refused kiss – itself based on a reenactment of Werther's stolen kiss – into something quite different. Once again, he seems to have managed to out-textualize Barthes. *Mauve le vierge* is better known for "Les secrets d'un homme," the first text written by Guibert (other than his diary) about Foucault's final illness and death. It is not difficult to conceive of this collection of short stories as an ellipse, the two centers of which are these texts inspired by Guibert's relations with two of the most famous gay men of the period. Whether or not we can or should read the character Lulu in "Le citronnier" as modeled on Barthes – Lulu probably owes as much or more to Guibert himself – there is incontrovertible evidence that the young writer was definitely thinking of Barthes in the following passage taken from the 1988 novel *Les Gangsters*:

> Au moment de quitter ce garçon, je m'agenouillai pour baiser ses doigts, rien que cela, rien de plus. Cela m'amusait de repenser que l'écrivain R.B., quand j'avais dix-huit ans et qu'il en avait soixante, me baisait ainsi les mains, et, un soir, devant un arrêt d'autobus, me pria

d'apposer mes lèvres sur ses paupières fatiguées. J'avais trente ans, mais je me satisfaisais avec les jeunes garçons comme un homme de soixante ans ... (*G*, 84; original ellipsis)

At the moment of leaving this young man I knelt at his feet to kiss his fingers – nothing more, only that. It amused me to think how, when I was eighteen and he was sixty, the writer R.B. kissed my hands in this way and, one evening, at a bus-stop, asked me to touch my lips to his tired eyelids. I was thirty, but here was I indulging myself with young men like a man of sixty ... (*Gang.*, 82–3; trans. alt.)

As is typical of Guibert, he has changed certain details – in 1977 Guibert was twenty-two and Barthes sixty-two; an age difference of forty years has now grown into one of forty-two years – while retaining important elements from the real-life situation. No doubt he wanted to accentuate the age difference in order to make the passage more dramatic. But according to this version, Hervé did allow Barthes to kiss his hands! Is it wishful thinking on Guibert's part, or is it simply an example of his tendency to rework, refashion reality? Or is he perhaps rereading a more distant past through memories of the recent past? Whatever the case, he finds himself in the place of Barthes, as though the thirty-year old Guibert could no longer expect to inspire any sexual desire. And like Barthes, he indulges himself in a reenactment, either of the earlier episode, itself a reenactment as we recall, if not of what actually happened, then of what Barthes desired.

In *L'Incognito*, published one year after *Les Gangsters*, a fragment of Barthes's letter to Guibert is quoted, although its author is described only as "one of my masters."[20] Barthes also appears briefly in the guise of Roland Tarbe. Once more it is the context of a gay man finding himself too old to inspire any desire on the part of the other. As the thirty-four-year old Guibert says, "La trentaine, c'est l'âge où il faut se mettre aux

---

20 "Je repense à cette phrase d'un de mes maîtres, dans cette longue lettre de reproches qu'il m'avait adressée: 'Que quelqu'un accepte de poser la main sur moi est toujours de l'ordre du miracle'" (*I*, 177) (I remembered that sentence of one of my mentors in the long letter of reproach that he sent me: "That someone should accept putting his hand on me is always a kind of miracle"). Guibert seems to be quoting from memory; the actual sentence reads as follows: "Que quelqu'un accepte de me toucher est toujours pour moi de l'ordre du *miracle*" (*OC*, 3:1297) (That someone should accept touching me is always a kind of *miracle*).

tapins, j'ai un peu trop tardé. Roland Tarbe m'avait raconté qu'il s'y était mis très jeune, vers vingt-cinq ans, c'est plus astucieux, comme ça on ne lie pas ça à la défaite de l'âge" (*I*, 53) (The thirties are when you have to take up with hustlers, I had put it off too long. Roland Tarbe told me he had started very young, around twenty-five, which is more astute, that way you don't link it with the defeat brought on by age). Better to pay for sex long before one needs to in order to avoid having to confront "la défaite de l'âge," after which one must pay. Like many gay men, Guibert was tormented by the thought of aging, a process that was accelerated by the onset of AIDS. As for what he says about "Tarbe," it is difficult to distinguish between fact and fiction here, as in all of Guibert's novels, especially since *L'Incognito* is one of the most ludic of all his books. On the other hand, it is possible that what Guibert says about Tarbe may be an accurate reflection of something that Barthes told the young writer during one of their dinners in 1977. In Barthes's melancholic diary entry for 17 September 1979, he wrote: "Nothing will be left for me but hustlers" (*OC*, 3:1285; *Incidents*, 73). While it would appear that Barthes was used to paying young men for sex, such adventures certainly did not satisfy him, and the list he gives of young friends, including "R.L., too brief, B.M. and B.H., no desire" (ibid.), is imbued with sadness; like some anti–Don Juan, Roland Barthes declines a litany of failed relationships. As he wrote in the same entry:

> Une sorte de désespoir m'a pris, j'avais envie de pleurer. Je voyais dans l'évidence qu'il me fallait renoncer aux *garçons,* parce qu'il n'y avait pas de désir d'eux à moi, et que je suis ou trop scrupuleux ou trop maladroit pour imposer le mien ... (*OC,* 3:1285; my emphasis)
>
> A sort of despair overcame me, I felt like crying. How clearly I saw that I would have to give up young men, because none of them felt any desire for me, and I was either too scrupulous or too clumsy to impose my desire on them ... (*Incidents,* 73; trans. alt.)

French is a bizarre language: usually it is praised for its lexical precision and a rigorous syntax that imposes "logical" thinking. And yet the word *garçon* is often, as in this context and the passage quoted earlier from *Les Gangsters,* quite ambiguous. One's first reaction would be to translate it as *boy* (as did Richard Howard), but in fact that would be incorrect. Here the word would be translated more properly by *young man*, for in the context it refers to males in their early twenties.²¹ There is nothing pedophilic about such same-sex desire, although it does bring to mind the pederasty of the ancients. Today, especially in North America, intergenerational sex is the subject of a blanket condemnation, since little or no difference is made between men who sexually abuse children – pedophiles – as opposed to men who find themselves attracted to young men. No doubt such condemnation is part and parcel of individual and institutionalized homophobia still so characteristic of our society; one need only think of all the beauty contests in which young women of a similar age are allowed to pass as objects of desire in the eyes of older men to realize how different the standards are for straight and gay men!

Although Barthes is not mentioned in À *l'ami qui ne m'a pas sauvé la vie*, one episode recalls "Fragments pour H."²² When Muzil, the character who at once is and is not Foucault, is in hospital with the AIDS-related opportunistic illness from which he was shortly to die, Guibert visited him every day. One day, he tells us,

> j'étais seul dans la chambre avec Muzil, je pris longuement sa main comme il m'était parfois arrivé de le faire dans son appartement, assis côte à côte sur son canapé blanc, tandis que le jour déclinait lentement

---

21 This usage of *garçon* for *homme* is attested by *Le Grand Robert de la langue française*; after the example *garçon de vingt-trois ans* (a boy twenty-three years old), one finds the following remark: "The word implies either an absence of consideration due to age or familarity, and can in that case be used to describe mature men when the speaker is himself as old or older" ("Garçon," 1987 ed.). Renaud Camus has addressed the French preference for *garçon*, "boy," over *homme*, "man," in one of the published volumes of his diary: "I write 'a handsome boy' because of the exteme difficulty in writing 'a handsome man,' although the latter would be more appropriate. Some time ago a reader reproached me, and all [French] homosexuals along with me, with a kind of infantilism by saying *boy* for *man*. I wouldn't say he is wrong, far from it. American homosexuals ordinarily say *man*. But I find the word *man* very delicate to use. On the other hand, when one is dealing with a man of, yes, thirty-five, perhaps ..." (*Vigiles*, 148).

22 In the *Adultes!* manuscript Guibert takes literary encoding and re-encoding to new heights when he describes a novel by a certain Sonnlos in which the death of Thess (Barthes) is described (f. 150). It is an obvious reference to Werth, the character based on Barthes in Philippe Sollers's *Femmes* (145). Clearly, Guibert continued to be preoccupied by Barthes, his memory, and another writer's perception of him. If "Thess" does not appear in *L'Ami* I think we can safely presume that Guibert did not want to distract the reader's attention from the central figure of Muzil who, in common with Hervé, has HIV and AIDS.

> entre les portes-fenêtres grandes ouvertes de l'été. Puis j'appliquai mes lèvres sur sa main pour la baiser. (*Ami*, 101)

> Alone in the room with Muzil, I held his hand for a long time, the way I sometimes had in his apartment when we used to sit side by side on his white couch, while the sun slowly set, framed by the French windows standing wide open in the summer air. Then I pressed my lips to his hand in a kiss. (*Friend*, 91)

By now Guibert has learned the importance of a kiss, but this will not be the end of his feelings of guilt, as we shall see in another chapter. More than the actual events (how are we to know what "really" happened?), what is truly extraordinary is the series of textual and intertextual transformations that translate the evolution of Guibert as a writer.

Although there is no overt reference to Barthes in Guibert's second AIDS novel, there are two passages in *Le Protocole compassionnel* that indicate that Barthes was still on his mind in the last years of his life.[23] The first is a reference to the *Meditations* of Marcus Aurelius (121–80 CE), according to whom there is an age when a man must give up the pleasures afforded by young men: "Ai-je atteint cet âge-là? ça dépend peut-être si j'ai trente-cinq ans comme sur mon passeport, ou quatre-vingts comme dans mon corps" (*PC*, 88) ("Have I now reached that age? That depends on whether I am thirty-five as on my passport or eighty as in my body" [*CP*, 73]). Guibert now finds himself in the shoes of a man of eighty as a result of HIV and AIDS.[24]

The second reference to Barthes in *Le Protocole compassionel* is a moment of dense intertextuality:

> moi je ne pense pas que mes livres sont méchants. Je sens bien qu'ils sont traversés, entre autres choses, par la vérité et le mensonge, la trahison, par ce thème de la méchanceté, mais je ne dirais pas qu'ils sont méchants au fond. Je ne vois pas de bonne oeuvre qui soit méchante. Le

---

23 It is possible that this was triggered by Calvet's biography of Barthes published in the fall of 1990, i.e., between the publication of *L'Ami* and *Le Protocole compassionnel*. Guibert is not mentioned in the biography.
24 *Vole mon dragon* contains a similar passage about Marcus Aurelius, without the AIDS reference however (*VD*, 50). In his *Meditations*, the Roman emperor thanks his father for having taught him, among other things, when it is time to give up love affairs with adolescents (*Pensées pour moi-même suivies du Manuel d'Épictète*, 35 [1.16]).

> fameux principe de délicatesse de Sade. J'ai l'impression d'avoir fait une oeuvre barbare et délicate. (*PC*, 112–13)

> I myself do not think my books are unkind. I certainly feel that they are shot through by – among other things – truth and falsehood, treachery, by this theme of unkindness, but I would not say they are fundamentally unkind. I do not think any good work of art can ever be unkind. Sade's celebrated principle of delicacy. I have the feeling I've created a work both barbarous and delicate. (*CP*, 95–6)

The truth and lies mentioned are an allusion to Orson Welles's film *F for Fake*, the French title of which was *Vérités et Mensonges*. However, the Sadean allusion is more intriguing. Guibert is probably alluding to a passage taken from one of Sade's letters to his long-suffering wife.[25] While it is entirely possible that Guibert read Sade's correspondence, it seems more likely that he found the allusion to "le fameux principe de délicatesse" in Barthes's writing about the Divine Marquis. As is typical of Barthes, he has taken the "principle of delicacy" out of its original context and applied it back, so to speak, to a reading of Sade's own works:

> Le *principe de délicatesse* postulé par Sade peut seul constituer, dès lors que les assises de l'Histoire auront changé, une langue absolument nouvelle, la mutation inouïe, appelée à subvertir (non pas inverser, mais plutôt fragmenter, pluraliser, pulvériser) le sens même de la jouissance. (*OC*, 2:1162)

> The *principle of delicacy* postulated by Sade can alone constitute, seeing that the judgment of History will have changed, an absolutely new language, the unheard-of mutations, destined to subvert (not invert, but rather fragment, pluralize, pulverize) the very meaning of orgasm. (*Sade, Fourier, Loyola*, 171; trans. alt.)

---

25 "Charming creature, you want my dirty linen, my old linen? Do you realize that is of a rare delicacy? You see how I sense the worth of things. Listen, *my angel*, I would really like to satisfy you about this, for you know that I respect *tastes, fantasies*: however strange they may be, I think all of them are respectable, and since we are not the master of them, and since the most singular and the most bizarre of any of them, when properly analyzed, is always due to a principle of delicacy" (23–4 Nov. 1783, Letter 169 in *Oeuvres complètes du Marquis de Sade*, 12:412).

By using such a highly charged word as *délicate* in *Le Protocole compassionnel* to describe his own works, I believe Guibert is telling us not that he believes them to be like some delicate hot-house flowers but rather that he believes he has fulfilled Barthes's prophecy of a new type of writing that was yet to come in 1971, texts of readerly bliss in which meaning is as subversive, as fragmented, and as protean as is human sexuality itself. Desire may die in the flesh, but it lives on in the works. Surely Guibert has learned well from his writing master, even if his mentor was somewhat loath to give him lessons!

Le Protocole compassionnel was published in February 1991 and in July 1991, while he was working on his last book, *Le Paradis*, his interview with Didier Eribon, "Hervé Guibert et son double," was published in *Le Nouvel Observateur*. The title was well chosen, for Guibert's double can be read as Foucault or Barthes, not to mention one of the characters in his so-called *roman cocasse*, *Mon valet et moi*, published in September by Les Éditions du Seuil, Barthes's publisher.

Seuil was also to publish Guibert's *Cytomégalovirus* written between 17 September and 8 October 1991. Although Barthes is neither mentioned nor alluded to in this short book, it does recall one of his works, "Incidents."[26] Both works were published posthumously. The subject matter is different since Barthes's text is about a stay in Morocco, whereas Guibert is writing about the ordeals of a hospital stay. Nevertheless, it seems likely that Guibert had Barthes's text in mind when he wrote *Cytomégalovirus*. For example, in one fragment he writes: "Un séjour à l'hôpital, c'est comme un très long voyage ..." (*Cyto.*, 20) ("A hospital stay is like a long voyage ..." (*CMV*, 12)). Both works take the form of a diary (Guibert's is dated, Barthes's is not). The adventures of a person in a foreign environment – Morocco for Barthes, a hospital located near the *boulevard périphérique* in Paris for Guibert – are described in haiku-like fragments, often without verbs. In both works blindness is a leitmotif: Oedipus-like beggars in Barthes; Guibert's preoccupation with losing his sight in one eye. Colors are mentioned frequently in both texts, black and white being the dominant ones in the hospital diary. For example, Guibert wonders if his blindness will be total (black) or partial (white). Homoerotic desire plays a prominent role in "Incidents" as Barthes notes the hard-ons of the young men he meets, as well as their

---

26 "Incidents" is the second text included in *Incidents* (*OC*, 3:1255–72). First published in 1987, it was probably written in 1969–70 while Barthes was teaching at the University of Rabat.

quaint vocabulary for all things sexual, for instance, *rêver* ("to dream") for "to have an erection," *éclater* ("to burst") for "to come." In *Cytomégalovirus*, by contrast, Guibert has reached a stage where sex is a thing of the past. As he says, "qu'est-ce que j'ai à foutre de foutre à présent" (*Cyto.*, 92) ("I don't give a fuck about fucking right now" [*CMV*, 80]). Finally, "Incidents" is made up of 122 fragments, *Cytomégalovirus* of 221, which may be just a coincidence. I would interpret it rather as Guibert's homage to his former "master," as he described Barthes in *L'Incognito*.

Hervé Guibert was to die on 27 December 1991, thirteen days after his thirty-sixth birthday, in the same hospital depicted in *Cytomégalovirus*. As we know, he did not die of AIDS-related illness, but as the result of an attempt to commit suicide. Lawrence Schehr has written, "since AIDS assures death, Guibert's literature will reinscribe that eventual death as a dramatic, suicidal, or pathetic figure of his own textuality. No one can take that literary death away from him; no one can reinscribe his death in an other-than-literary fashion if he chooses to be the new Werther" (*Alcibiades at the Door*, 180–1). Perhaps we should interpret even Guibert's attempted suicide, at least in part, as a tribute to Barthes. The younger man finally understood the literary allusion to Goethe's Romantic novel, *The Sorrows of Young Werther*, that the critic and theorist had presumed (wrongly as it turned out) he knew if not directly then at least indirectly from *A Lover's Discourse*. More than fourteen years have passed, and now Hervé can justifiably claim his right to a literary death! Four years later, in 1995, the third and final volume of Roland Barthes's Complete Works, including both "Incidents" and "Fragments pour H.," was published.

Roland Barthes and Hervé Guibert had many things in common, such as their interest in theater, photography, and language, as well as young men. Despite the maturity of Guibert's writing in *L'Image fantôme*, it lacks the polish and the poignancy of *Camera Lucida*. But the former was Guibert's second book, whereas the latter was Barthes's last. Still their works – like their lives and their deaths – intertwine, forming a unique tapestry of late-twentieth-century intertextuality. It is certain that there was rivalry on the part of Guibert, a fact about which he was perfectly cognizant and up front (witness the direct and indirect references to Oedipus and the attempts to out-perform his former mentor). But one must not forget that there was also a great deal of admiration for Barthes's writing on the part of Guibert. He tended to read and appreciate authors who were not French, such as Thomas Bernhard and Kafka. Guibert found it impossible to write without a model; often this model, as is the case of Barthes, ended up playing an even larger role, as a character or as the source of intertextual allusions. We should also remember that Guibert's relationship with Barthes continued to evolve after the death of the critic and theorist. From the mid-1980s to the end of his life, Guibert seems to have come to a new stage in his relationship with the memory of his erstwhile friend. Indeed, one has the impression that had Barthes lived another five or six years, Guibert would have been able to identify more with the man and not just his works, as he too was to know the drama of the older gay man who finds himself confronted by the absence of desire on the part of the other. In any case, the death of same-sex desire continues to inform our readings of these two oeuvres, for desire dies not only as many times as it is inscribed but also as many times as that inscription is decoded by the would-be lover or his substitute, the reader.

Chapter Three

The Pursuit of Pleasure

[Les fauves] exècrent la foule qui s'échauffe à leurs attouchements, ils trouvent son odeur puante.

Vice, 60

The wildcats hate the crowd that gets excited when they touch each other, to them the people stink.

On leaving the gym early one evening, I discovered in a vacant lot between two old hotels better known for things other than the quality of their rooms – the famous Cecil known for its strippers and the older Yale known for its music – a brightly painted trailer and a dilapidated white Cadillac, both of which apparently belonged to Miss Sandy Smith, a stripper of some renown, according to a banner waving in the breeze. Between the trailer and the old limousine, a small crowd of people had gathered around something or someone. With their hands in their jeans pockets, these men – for all of them were men, probably heterosexuals who had just left a strip show in one of the hotels – were looking in silence at Miss Smith's companion and fellow traveler: a magnificent tiger walking in a circle between the trailer and its mistress's Cadillac. Now, I should tell you that the city where I live is probably one of the least interesting in the world as far as the unforeseen goes, since everything is always very clean and very proper. Not that sexuality is totally absent from this city: the three parallel streets in the old warehouse district frequented respectively by female, male, and transsexual prostitutes from dusk to dawn attest to a certain libido on the part of its citizens. But sex is always contained within well-delineated boundaries that are as respected as the "fourth wall" that separates the audience from the young and not-so-young bodies exhibited on the small, off-limits platforms of the various strip shows that dot what is sometimes called the tenderloin district. So when I saw the animal turning in small circles in an area circumscribed by bands of yellow plastic of the same kind that police put up around a crime scene to prevent onlookers from approaching too near, I realized I was witnessing a spectacle much more interesting than that of all the Mr or Miss Smiths of this city, one that Hervé Guibert no doubt would have appreciated, a scene of veritable vice.

Published in 1991, *Vice* was the second-to-last book by Guibert that appeared during his lifetime. However, according to the chronology at the end of *Photographies*, *Vice* was written in 1979, that is, between *La Mort propagande* and *Suzanne et Louise*. According to Guibert, after reading the manuscript of *Vice*, one publisher said, "that guy will never write a book!" (Interview with Garcin, 109). One may suppose that the young author, shaken by such a categorical judgment, set the manuscript aside for a dozen years or so. Only in the last years of his life, during that period when Guibert engaged in a race to write and publish as much as humanly and even superhumanly possible, did he find a publisher willing to publish this series of short texts that are roughly contemporaneous with the genesis of *L'Image fantôme*.[1] Unfortunately, *Vice* seems to have suffered from being compared to a text written by Guibert more than ten years later but published about the same time, *Mon valet et moi*, since there are more reviews of the latter than the former, and several of those that do treat *Vice* are unfavorable. For example, one journalist wrote that "Guibert should have kept silent rather than publish this manuscript" (Charrière, 4). I believe, on the contrary, that *Vice* has a crucial role to play in his oeuvre, since it demonstrates some of his ongoing obsessions, as well as some of his first advances in the direction of writing fiction.

The book is made up of three parts: the first, entitled "Articles personnels" – about thirty pages – describes objects from daily life like ear swabs and fly paper – and the last one, "Parcours" (Journeys) – fifty or so pages – presents a series of strange locales – from a children's cemetery

---

1 The intertextuality that links *L'Image fantôme* and *Vice* can be detected by allusions in the former to themes and motifs found in the latter, such as the zoo at the Jardin des Plantes (*IF*, 130 [*GI*, 120]; *V*, 59–60) and the theme of a man carrying a child in his arms (*IF*, 123 [*GI*, 113]; *V*, 56–8).

to the museum attached to a school of veterinary medecine. In between these two sections of short texts, the middle part is made up of nineteen photographs without dates or captions. The book's make-up is rudimentary since all of the photographs are between pages forty and forty-one. There is no attempt to exploit the relationship between the textual and the visual, except in the most conventional of formats: a simple gallery of photos without interpretation or captions inserted into a collection of texts. Although there is no text about the Musée Grévin, the Paris wax museum that was long to haunt Guibert's imagination, several photographs show its storage vaults. Thus, *Vice* can be read along with other texts, such as "Au Musée Grévin" and "La tête de Jeanne d'Arc," as discussed in chapter 1. Photographs in the last phototext illustrate these other works, even if they were actually written later. Other photographs, however, do reproduce the cavernous spaces that are described in the third part of the book, such as museums of natural history. While the descriptions of the first part rarely go beyond a somewhat derivative *choisisme* that recalls Francis Ponge more than Alain Robbe-Grillet, the last part of *Vice* tips the textual balance in favor of the fantastic, thereby marking the passage from "purely" descriptive writing to narrative, and hence the beginning of Guibert's fiction-making.

The back cover of *Vice* introduces it by quoting a passage in *La Mort propagande et autres textes de jeunesse*: "Il marchait dans la rue. Il voulut tout à coup être transplanté dans un bain de vice (décors et actes). Il était prêt à payer pour pénétrer dans une ambiance vicieuse, mais le cinéma porno lui semblait indigent" (*MP,* 324) (He was walking down the street. Suddenly he wanted to be transported to a den of vice [decors and actions]. He was prepared to pay in order to penetrate a vicious ambience, but porn films seemed to him a poor substitute). Vice is associated with penetration, but it does not refer to penetrating actual bodies, at least not at this stage. Pornographic cinemas, which might seem to be one of the most obvious of places to seek vice and or at least its representations – and we shall see how the two are related – are perceived to be artificial betrayals of authentic desire for vice. Where then to find a den of vice? Are there special locales where the spectator can observe or participate in the portrayal of vicious acts? What would such places be like? A first answer is to be found in the opening text of the third part, "Regulation" [1].[2] In this text of some twenty lines Guibert

---

2 The numbers in brackets refer to the order of the chapters, which are not numbered in the book.

describes a journey through a hypothetical urban space in search of vice, surely that most necessary of ingredients to any truly civilized city: "La ville, l'État devront désormais ménager un certain nombre de lieux vacants, dans le seul but de petites actions vicieuses, libertines, proprement luxueuses dans les pertes de temps qu'elles occasionneront aux citoyens" (*V*, 43) (Henceforth the city, the state will be obliged to arrange for a certain number of vacant places for the sole purpose of libertine acts of vice, truly luxurious in the waste of time that they will afford the citizens). From the outset, this utopian project emphasizes the public necessity of setting aside particuliar locales, whether permanent or temporary, where city dwellers could allow themselves to be caught willingly in "traps of pleasure." Although no specific space is described, the text states that vice must be multiple and varied, omnipresent but hidden, both open and secret, and especially free. In this idyllic city, designers of vicious architecture and machines will be crowned with glory. Each and every citizen is free to imagine the most extravagant of acts and decors, the best of which the state will reward with a prize or fellowship of Vice! The spaces set aside for such pursuits ("empty lots, houses in the process of demolition, theaters that are falsely or secretly abandoned") will allow citizens in need to follow a "ludic itinerary [that is] excessively mobile." This project – worthy of an eighteenth-century philosopher (the subtitle of the first part of *Vice* is "Inventory of the suitcase of Bougainville the traveler"), of a Sadean master of ceremonies, or of a Walter Benjamin roaming the *passages* of Paris in search of *realia* from the previous century – forms the link between the short paragraph on the back cover describing the frustration of worthy citizens wanting to plunge themselves into some pool of vice but who disdain pornography, and the examples following the Regulation, which will approximate an ideal journey. This trek for vice will take us to real places as witnessed by the photographs, so that "Journeys" realizes the hypothetical project by allowing us to enter buildings and spaces we pass all the time in our daily lives without being aware what vicious activities go on inside.

The seventeen texts following the introductory fragment, which vary in length from five lines to six pages, all treat bodies, animal and human, living and dead. It is in the problematic but fascinating passage from the ordinary to the extraordinary, from the monstrous to the "normal" that is to be found the real interest of this collection of texts that successively seek to circumscribe vice by coming at it from different angles of approach. One of the shortest texts appears to be the most obscure, since it merely describes a skein of wool destined to make clothes for human bodies. Surely no vice here! But read in the light of another text by Guibert – one that was as yet unpublished in 1979 but familiar to readers in 1991 – we realize the vicious potential of "The wool store" [3], for it rekindles memories from the past when young Guibert – he was four or five at the time – had recourse to textiles in order to stimulate himself.[3] As for the other texts, I will hazard the following taxonomy: spectacles for children ("The planetarium" [4], "The palace of mirages" [5]); spectacles of living animals ("The zoo" [7], "The crocodile bar" [10]); cemeteries of various kinds ("The children's cemetery" [6], "The cemetery of the Capucins" [15], "The chamber of relics" [14]); methods of preserving bodies ("The workshop of a taxidermist" [8], "The new embalming method of Professor Boitard" [17]); museums and museum storage rooms ("The gallery of zoology" [9], "The anthropology laboratory" [13], "The museum of the school of veterinary medicine" [11], "The museum of the School of Medicine" [16]); and places where men are confined in small spaces ("The steam room" [2], "The box with a double bottom" [12], and finally "The palace of desirable monsters" [18]).

There would be little point in following the complete itinerary made up of all these spaces, or of commenting on each of the individual texts. Furthermore, one can imagine two entirely different itineraries. If we read *Vice* as a discursive work like one of Foucault's books, our itinerary will correspond to the order in which the spaces of vice are presented. In this case, one notices that spaces that seem to have the least potential for vice, such as "Le planétarium" or "Le palais des mirages," are among the first, whereas others that describe cut-up or monstrous bodies tend to come near the end of the textual itinerary. On the other hand, if we read *Vice* as a fragmentary work like so many of Barthes's books, one can imagine numerous itineraries that would allow new meanings to be produced by juxtaposing noncontiguous texts. The synoptic table sketched out in the last paragraph corresponds to one of these nonlinear actualizations of the work. My object, here, will be to do justice to the variety of states, transformations, and locales in which Guibert places the bod-

---

3 "[J]e peux chaparder à ma mère ses pelotes de laine, les poser comme par mégarde auprès de mon lit et, quand la lumière est éteinte, en retenant ma respiration, faire passer la pelote sous les draps et y câliner mon sexe à l'intérieur" (*Mes*, 23) ("I can steal my mother's balls of knitting wool, put them, as if inadvertently, next to my bed, and when the light is turned out, holding my breath, slip the ball of wool between the sheets and fondle my sex with it" [*My*, 14; trans. alt.]). Cf. *MP*, 194 and *MV*, 14.

ies he describes and which create an "effect of fiction," to use Raymond Bellour's expression ("Guibert ou l'indécidable," 80). Our "journey," which will follow a progression that is partly linear and partly associative, will lead us to a definition, or several, of what constitutes vice in the Guibertian universe.

The first state of the human body described is one in which it is wounded. After recounting a visit to a steam bath where, despite all the heavy breathing of barely restrained sexual desire, nothing ostensibly "happens," the narrator tells us how he managed to become a "wounded man," to quote the title of a self-portrait by Courbet (Derrida, *Memoirs of the Blind*, 81) and the scenario that Guibert co-authored with Patrice Chéreau:

> [The visitor] se décide à en acheter une [eau de Cologne] que la caissière lui tend, la plus discrète, de Pompéi, et une fois rentré chez lui, il se blesse, comme délibérément, pour ouvrir la petite capsule d'acier qui ferme le flacon, en plusieurs endroits de sa main, il entaille sa peau, l'acier rentre sous son ongle. (*V,* 48)

> The visitor decides to buy one of the bottles of eau de Cologne held out to him by the cashier, the most discreet one – Pompeii – and when he gets home, he cuts his hand, opening the steel stopper that closed the little bottle, as though deliberately, in several places, he incises his skin, the steel goes beneath his fingernail.

The visitor, who was content to remain in the position of voyeur while walking around the bathhouse in order to get a good look at all the men who wait there for their sexual Messiah, as he says, is nicked, and therefore marked by the place where sexual activity appeared to remain so contained, so restrained, so tame. The banal event that closes this first text of the itinerary per se (it follows the Regulation) reveals that in order to experience vice, one need not limit it to "depraved or degrading behavior," since the word also refers to a defect, an imperfection, or an infirmity, as well as an irregularity in a judicial or some other official procedure. Nothing within the bathhouse penetrated the visitor's intact body, but nevertheless vice there is, since the fateful bottle of cheap cologne purchased ends up cutting open the voyeur's body: a graze for a gaze. He has gotten off neither unaffected nor unscathed: his virginal-like body is now soiled goods since it suffers from what in French is called a *vice de forme*, a defect or infirmity.

Another body state is, of course, illness. In this work dating from the beginning of Guibert's career, the sick body is not human. In this case, the sickness is, nevertheless, a serious matter, for the malady affects the brain of a machine that allows us to see the whole universe:

> La machine vrombissante continuait à ruer, et nous entendions les roues du chariot se cogner à l'enceinte de protection ... Je me demandais si cette calotte sphérique qui nous abritait n'était pas en fait une calotte crânienne, et ce spectacle les effets d'une embolie, d'un caillot soudain formé dans un des hémisphères ... (*V*, 51)

> The loudly humming machine continued to hurl itself about, and we could hear the wheels of the carriage hitting the walls ... I wondered if the spherical calotte that sheltered us was not really the top of a skull, and this spectacle the effects of an embolism, of a blood clot that had suddenly formed in one of the hemispheres ...

This passage is eerily premonitory of "Les secrets d'un homme" in *Mauve le vierge* and *À l'ami qui ne m'a pas sauvé la vie*, in which the brain of a great philosopher suffering from the final stages of AIDS-related illness has to be opened up. In this early version of a sick brain, the vice or imperfection is already apocalyptic even if it is only an electronic brain.

The body state most often described in *Vice* is death. But it seems as if death must be embellished or disturbed, thereby making it seem more pathological than an ordinary demise. Take, for example, the figure of the prophetess who performs a cabalistic dance in a dark and empty Palais des mirages. Is she a wax statue or a ghost? The answer is not clear, for we are between a dead body and a live body, between a real body and a represented body, between the ordinary and supernatural, as is characteristic of fantastic literature. The transformation that is death is made more complicated by other processes that seem never-ending, as though death were but a first step in a series of on-going processes. For example, in "The children's cemetery," a child disinters the body of a child almost as big as he. But the dead child, who drowned a few days earlier, was buried with his father so that by disintering the child, the young delinquent finds his double and the double of that double, the father who adored his son so much that he asked to be buried with him, with the result that their bodies are entwined together in the grave. The couple of father and son, of the father who carries his son in his arms even in death can be read as one of the key images of Guibert's entire oeuvre.[4]

Death is duplicated in other ways, for example when a dead body is preserved, either intact or in pieces, whether for scientific purposes or not, that is, as a specimen or relic. "The new embalming method of Professor Boitard" explains how a scientist managed to keep the body of a three-year-old child in a state of perfect preservation before he was buried several years later, like the other child, with his father. Where an earlier text on taxidermy emphasizes the violations of the body – nothing is respected, the animal's body is pierced, violated, lacerated with knives, scissors, axes, and saws – this text is remarkable for the delicacy of the means used by Boitard, for he worked with straws and special liquids. However, in both cases the objective is to duplicate as closely as possible a living body. The *simulacrum* reproduces the original, and the best "copy" – such as the body embalmed by Boitard – will be impossible to distinguish from the original, except for one thing: the life force. Like photography, the arts of the taxidermist and the embalmer allow one to tame or domesticate death: one could keep such bodies at home, as has been done. Preservation borders on reproduction and representation since it involves a transformation of the original "model." The more accurate the copy, the less important the passage between life and death becomes. The result is that the vice at work here, which might have been considered total, is only partial since it is dependent on the number and state of the substituted parts more than anything else. From this point of view, it is when a body has been so reworked that it becomes a statue – rather than a mummy or a relic that has managed to avoid substantial reworking – that vice takes over both the process and the product that results from it. In other words, it is mimesis itself that is truly vicious. Or perhaps I should say it is the passage from mere *duplication* – a kind of idyllic preservation of the body without human intervention – to the stage of *representation* that marks what is the most insidious in Guibertian vice.

---

4 In interviews Guibert described this recurring image: "I always depict the same positions (whether erotic or not). If there were only one tableau, it would be of my father and me" (Gaudemar, "Les aveux permanents," XII); "it comes from the relationship of unforgettable tenderness that, as a child, I had with my father. A man and a child is my image, a pictorial image. Some of my books are just a pretext for getting to that picture ... *The man who carries the child*, I have shown it in my own way ... A tumultuous image, nothing like Saint Christopher" (Interview with Jonquet, 109). On the theme of the *pédophore* (he who carries a child), see Michel Tournier, *Le Vent Paraclet* (123–5), as well as his magnificent novel *Le Roi des Aulnes*.

Here the intertext is to be found in a story entitled "History of a saint" included in the second edition of *La Mort propagande*. Although the saint in question is Guibert's great-aunt Louise, the following passage describes what happened to Saint Teresa of Avila:

> Les vrais ossements de Thérèse ont été transférés dans la chapelle du Carmel ... Avec ton teint de rose, tes paupières à peine fermées, tu sembles encore respirer. *Les touristes croient voir un travail d'embaumeur, mais ce n'est qu'une statue de cire. L'imitation, la représentation.* (*MP*, 162; my emphasis)

> The real bones of Teresa have been transferred to the Carmelite chapel ... With your rosy complexion, your barely closed eyelids, you seem to breathe still. *The tourists think they are looking at the work of an embalmer, but it's only a wax statue. An imitation, a representation.*

The fatal fraud and the devious vice perpetrated by the church take the form of a substitution: where gullible tourists think they are contemplating an embalmed body, in fact they are looking at a mere statue made of wax. One can easily imagine what the next stage will be: the inevitable postcard of the saint's statue purchased at the gift shop! Considering that *Vice* is a photo-text, this next level or supplement of vicious representation is all the more pertinent. This would be the case, for example, of the photographs showing statues of the anatomical exhibitions from the Specola Museum in Florence. While no chapter of *Vice* is devoted to this particular museum (cf. *AS*, 33), passages describing wax copies of anatomical parts in the Musée de l'École vétérinaire or the Musée de l'École de médecine, do recall these photographs. On the other hand, there are photographs in *Vice* that do reproduce dead bodies – stuffed birds, skeletons of dwarfs, and a mummified child – all of which add a strange uncanniness to the death-like character of all photography. As Barthes writes in *Camera Lucida*: "In Photography, the presence of the thing (at a certain past moment) is never metaphoric; and in the case of animated beings, their life as well, except in the case of photographing corpses; and even so: if the photograph then becomes horrible, it is because it certifies, so to speak, that the corpse is alive, as *corpse*: it is the living image of a dead thing" (78–9).

But one need not have recourse to photography in order to supplement what is essentially vicious in showing a body: other levels or stages of vice may be added to the preserved body itself. Such would be the case of certain false relics manufactured from "chair recueillie des mendiants lépreux, ou même de viande de cochon recolorée, en y apposant de faux scellés, de fausses digitales, de faux parchemins qui certifient le passage des objets de mains en mains" (*V*, 80) (flesh collected from leprous beggars, or even from tinted pork, stamped with false seals, false finger prints, false parchments certifying the transmission of such objects from hand to hand). A body can be preserved and then cut up into pieces; artificial parts can even be substituted for the original organs to which are attached supposedly divine or quasi-divine powers. But that is not the end of human vice. Take the case of the king who owned a collection of relics and who stipulated that after his death his body was to be "remis à des embaumeurs qui le découpent et le partagent secrètement en autant de parties saintes, de reliques qui seraient exposées au public encerclées de joyaux sous les faisceaux de lumière, dans sa chambre noire ..." (*V*, 81) (sent to embalmers so that they could cut it up, secretly making of it so many saintly portions, relics encased in precious stones that could be exposed to the public under beams of light, in his darkened chamber). Thwarted by his confessor who smelled a tinge of heresy in such a request, the king had the priest murdered, all of which goes to prove that it is unwise to frustrate human need for vice, even when it is a desire to be dead, embalmed, cut up, and exposed to spectators in search of would-be pious pleasures!

Another form of secondary or tertiary vice pertaining to dead bodies is, of course, the inevitable decomposition and rot that await all bodies, whatever the extent of attempted preservation. Some museums are noteworthy for the excellent state of their artifacts, even when it is based on "scientific" cheating, for example, the "penises injected with wax" at the School of Medicine (*V*, 87). Ironically such formal "defects" aping perfection are to be found in the museum of a university, that institution which prides itself on authenticity and truth untainted by any kind of make-up, whether ideological, factual, or material! On the other hand, some museums let their collections deteriorate. Such is the case of the zoological gallery where damage caused by a Second World War bombing raid and the rain of many years has left the animals in a lamentable state. Falling to pieces, it is as though they were sick:

> il se peut que ce visiteur, s'il est seul, se perde à jamais, après avoir par mégarde heurté du pied la tête d'une girafe détachée de son cou, qu'on le retrouve précisément, des années plus tard, étouffé dans l'étoupe poussiéreuse d'une carcasse, recroquevillé, ou alors, s'il parvient à quitter la galerie impunément, la gale a eu le temps de sauter sur lui, et il se

> gratte, sa peau en certains endroits se durcit et se recouvre d'écailles, une mousse verte y croît et disparaît aussi subitement, ses pieds se palment ... (*V*, 65–6; original ellipsis)

> if he is alone, the visitor might get lost forever after carelessly stumbling against the head of a giraffe detached from its neck; he might be found years later all curled up, suffocated by the dusty stuffing of a carcass, or if he is able to leave the gallery unharmed, mange will have had the time to get hold of him, he scratches, his skin has hardened in certain places and is covered in scales, a green moss grows on the surface and then disappears just as quickly, his feet become webbed ...

This time the vice in question risks contaminating the visitor if he dares penetrate this veritable cabinet of curiosities.[5] There is still another stage of vice: this old museum filled with moldy specimens stuffed according to old-fashioned methods of taxidermy includes a room that is never visited. Only the narrator has access! Here is to be found the special collection of animals thrice dead, since they are the deceased and decomposing representatives of extinct species. But such a state of things is too perfect a portrait of human vice for Guibert. When faced with the terrifying prospect of being shipped to a modern museum full of fancy, brand-new dioramas, the animals decide to rebel in what is the ultimate evolution of vice after an employee accidentally sets on fire the condemned gallery and its collections:

> En trois minutes toutes les collections étaient détruites, et, trois minutes plus tard, la charpente en fonte avait entièrement fondu: les yeux de verre des grands carnassiers jetaient une foudre ultime avant de couler le long de leurs joues avec un rictus de plaisir. Les lions rugirent encore,

---

5 This text, entitled "La galerie de zoologie," appeared initially as an article in *Le Monde* ("Le jour où les animaux empaillés se révoltèrent"). It should be read along with "L'image cancéreuse" in *L'Image fantôme*, since the preserved animals correspond to the photograph of the handsome young man, just as the festering skin in the photographic image will correspond to what happens to the bodies exposed in the condemned museum. At one point, Guibert considered having recourse to a kind of photographic taxidermy since he thought "injecter sous la photo, en la décollant légèrement avec des pinces, au moyen de petites poires, de compte-gouttes ou d'instillateurs, des acides supplémentaires, un vitriol plus net, plus franc que la colle" (*IF*, 168) ("that by carefully detaching the picture with tweezers, [he] could inject, using small syringes, medicine droppers, or instillators, additional acids, a vitriol more pure, more immediate than the glue" (*GI*, 157; trans. alt.]).

The Pursuit of Pleasure

> les cous des girafes s'enlaçaient, l'employé juste avant de suffoquer vit à tous ces animaux des ailes, des émanations diaboliques qui faisaient éclater la verrière en les emportant au-delà. (*V*, 67)

> In three minutes flat the entire collection was destroyed and three minutes later the iron structure had completely melted: the glass eyes of the big game animals gave one last terrible glance before flowing along their cheeks in a mocking grin. The lions roared again, the necks of the giraffes wound around each other; just before suffocating, an employee saw all the animals grow wings, and accompanied by diabolical radiations they burst through the glass roof, traveling to the great beyond.

The animals' revenge takes the form of an animation or reanimation as afterlife becomes the metamorphosis of death and what followed. Here we can appreciate the verve of Guibert, who can't seem to help himself from playing with all these bodies and their transformations. Like the outsider he was, he mocks the scientific establishment and the fate it has reserved for bodies, whether animal or human.[6] For the reader who has already read the later works, including *À l'ami qui ne m'a pas sauvé la vie*, there is a strange effect of déjà-vu, since this tale of a disaffected museum and its dilapidated specimens conjures up images of a semi-abandoned hospital and ailing human bodies seeking professional help amid the ruins of nineteenth-century dreams of hygiene and the preservation of life. From the zoological gallery to the Claude-Bernard Hospital described in the first AIDS novel, we have switched Paris *arrondissements*, but not the death of a dream. In the late twentieth century, the search for knowledge is unmasked for what it is: a project of unbridled ambition – essentially vicious – doomed to fail. The reanimation of animals hunted to death and extinction, "sick" with mold and rot, is just another turn of the screw in that vicious circle that Guibert likes to display and illustrate for the benefit of readers willing to look behind the walls of supposedly sage establishments (see figure 11). Neither the revenge of the animals nor his own prose is anywhere near as grotesque as the march of so-called civilization and progress that he so aptly and so concretely deconstructs. The bodies of the animals triumph over death, wreaking vengeance on the institution that emprisoned them and their life force.

---

6 See *Suzanne et Louise*, in particular the description of what will happen to Suzanne's body after her death.

There are other episodes that one could mention, such as the hair and the fingernails that continue to grow on dead bodies, which would constitute, supposedly, a kind of deathly defect. But let us leave the dead for the living denizens who inhabit "The box with a double bottom," which refers not to a box but a gay night club situated in the port district of a city that could well be New York. Here men engage in "water sports" by urinating on "victims" attached to wooden pegs that penetrate a certain body orifice, while others squirm and groan in bathtubs filled with blood and urine:

> les corps ne sont pas en position verticale, il sont pendus à l'envers à des crochets de fer, les cuisses comprimées dans des anneaux, les membres ligotés à des trapèzes écartés, à des équerres, ils se font piétiner, on pisse au-dessus de grandes baignoires à l'émail rongé par les traînées ocres de l'acide urique, sur des formes vivantes qui grouillent et qui gémissent, sur les dos qui ondulent comme pour se mettre au plus près des jets chauds qu'on leur délivre, mais ici tous les corps restent inertes, ils ne bougent plus aux trapèzes et aux anneaux, leur anus labourés par des points innombrables laissent retomber la masse souple démêlée de leurs entrailles qui se collent aux portiques, leurs visages à l'envers, voilés par les cheveux, collés par une pellicule de bave, répandent dans l'obscurité des lueurs bleuâtres fantômatiques, exhalent encore un semblant d'âme, les corps trop bondés par les chaînes et les lanières ont suffoqué ... (*V*, 73–74)

> the bodies are not in a vertical position, they hang upside down from iron hooks, their thighs tightly contained in rings, their limbs tied to widely spread trapezes, to braces, they are trampled on, guys piss down into huge bathtubs whose enamel has been eaten away by ochre streaks of uric acid on living forms that swarm and moan, on backs that undulate as if trying to get closer to the warm streams of urine directed toward them, but now all the bodies are inert, they no longer move about on the trapezes and rings, their anuses furrowed by innumerable stitches letting fall the soft untangled mass of their entrails that glue themselves to the crossbars, their upside down faces hidden by their hair, glued together by specks of spit, shed ghostly blue glimmers of light, exhaling still the semblance of a soul, the bodies too tightly packed together by chains and straps have suffocated ...

One recognizes textual motifs that will find their way into *À l'ami qui ne m'a pas sauvé la vie,* since the dungeon in *Vice* reminds us of the saunas visited by Muzil in San Francisco. Composed of two sentences, the first of which takes up a page and a half, this chapter has a unique status in the book, due as much to the maturity of the style as the subject. Unlike the chapters about museum collections, this one is about live men and their sexual "vices." As such, it is a sort of animation of the scene in the steam room where men had to be satisfied with looking at each other. Are we then to understand that sexual desire becomes vicious when it leads to action, or when it takes place in certain places, or with the aid of specific "props"? It would be difficult to reconcile such a point of view with Guibert's writing, both in *Vice* and his other works. Real vice, the kind that is of interest to Guibert and his readers, is of an entirely different order than sexual union. But the story continues. The men having sex end up dying for the sake of love – another premonition of AIDS, which indicates that in all probability not all of this book was composed in 1979. Then, their bodies were preserved by a kind of varnish. This *vernissage*, which means both "varnishing" and "preview of an exhibition," should preserve them for all eternity, surely a museologist's dream! In fact, the vice squad does transform the former night club into a museum of exhibits. So popular was the museum with tourists, however, that it had to be closed because of the damage caused by the hoards who came to gawk at the positions (the stations) of homoerotic "vice."

When the bodies are mummified, the text breaks loose from the restraints of realism for the artistic freedom afforded Guibert by the realm of the fantastic. The gay men are twice immobilized, first by death, second by a kind of three-dimensional photograph that "mortifies" their bodies. Then comes the stage of exhibition as the former pleasure palace is transformed into a "museum of vice" until it is forced to close because of damage to the exhibits caused by the crowds of people come to see and wonder at the different forms that sexual desire takes.[7] Where then are we to locate vice? In the activities that went on in the night club? In the conservation of their bodies? Or the deterioration of the museum's holdings and its subsequent closing?

At this stage in my research, it became clear to me that vice should be

---

7 Guibert may have been thinking of the wax museums created in the nineteenth century to exhibit the numerous ill effects that masturbation was supposed to have on the body. Foucault referred to these museums in his lecture at the Collège de France on 5 March 1975 (*Les Anormaux*, 221; 244n16).

sought not on the part of what is looked at – the *Spectrum*, to use Barthes's term referring to the photographic subject – but rather on the part of the visitors to museums of natural history and other institutions, such as the prisons and insane asylums described by Michel Foucault that used to offer up bodies for public display. Two chapters are significant in this regard: "The zoo" and "The crocodile bar." They have in common the fact that this time the animals are alive rather than more or less well-preserved bodies. But as in museums, the animals in "La fauverie" are locked up so that they can be observed by visitors. One thinks of the steam room as well as the night club and the men in those close confines, but let us not forget that they chose to exhibit themselves and, what is more, they were showing themselves to each other, at least before the vice squad became involved. Furthermore, the animals are housed in cages constructed according to the panoptic principle so that the public can see them all at once with the least effort: "La fauverie est un espace circulaire, un hémicycle de rouille et de ciment" (*V*, 59) (The cage for the wildcats is circular, a hemicycle of rust and cement). The allusion to Foucault is thus double: the animals, like prisoners, are housed in a panoptical space that takes the form of a half-circle, not unlike the *hémicycle* at the Bibliothèque Nationale where Foucault did his research for so many years (Macey, *The Lives of Michel Foucault*, 49). Long before its use in the construction of prisons conceived by Bentham, the panopticon was first seen in a menagerie built by LeVau for Louis XIV at Versailles as described by Foucault: "The Panopticon is a machine for dissociating the see/being seen dyad: in the peripheric ring, one is totally seen, without ever seeing; in the central tower, one sees everything without ever being seen" (*Discipline and Punish: The Birth of the Prison*, 201–2). Arranged by species, as in the Museum of Natural History, the animals must spend the rest of their lives in small, confined spaces open on one side for the enjoyment and edification of the public, just like a prisoner condemned to life imprisonment in a cell in full view of guards and other prison personnel:

> Les fauves sont ainsi isolés dans des cages étroites, bordées d'un système de grilles, de portes coulissantes par lesquelles on les chasse successivement pour leur délivrer la viande, laver le sol à grande eau, les accoupler, ou aérer leur fourrure mouchetée. (*V*, 59)
>
> The big cats are isolated in narrow cages, surrounded by a series of bars, sliding doors through which they are driven in turn to give them meat,

wash the ground thoroughly, get them to mate, or air out their speckled fur.

The animals' tortured existence is rendered all the more poignant by the raucous cry of the lions, whose roar is more like "un spasme, un étranglement, comme s'ils avaient avalé un gros caillou qu'ils tenteraient de recracher" (ibid.) (a spasm, a strangulation, as though they had swallowed a big pebble that they were trying to spit out). Here, vice pertains to the captivity in which the animals are held, which amounts to a long and painful life (death) sentence, *and* the public exhibition to which they are subjected.[8] One small example, typically Guibertian, sums up the horror of their incarceration: the animals' existence is made even more uncomfortable by the odors of the hordes of people come to look at them!

A variant of the same scenario is provided by a scene that takes place in Africa: "the lodge of the Samburu camp, in Africa, is one of the great decadent spectacles in the western world" (*V*, 68). As is the case with the gay men in "The box with a double bottom," vice might appear to be found in a scene perceived as "odd" or "different" but which presents nothing inherently vicious, here the spectacle of crocodiles eating putrid flesh. True vice enters the picture, however, when we are told about the audience of blasé English tourists who have traveled to Africa in order to satisfy their hunger for the exotic. When the guide says to them, in Swahili, "'Take care *smelly beasts* that the crocodile doesn't snap shut his teeth on you'" (*V*, 69), we understand where lies real vice. As in "The zoo," vice is to be found not in the "subject," whatever it may be, but in the spectators' supposedly superior position and attitude.

The final stage of vice is described in "The palace of desirable monsters," the last chapter of the book. At first, one might think that human beings with the head of a wolf or a dog are a new variation on the motif of vice since these hybrids would appear to be both abnormal and dangerous. But given Guibert's almost storybook-like fascination with animals, we can dismiss the first reason to attribute any vice to these monsters. And as for the second, it can also be eliminated, for we are told that they are "nevertheless very gentle" (*V*, 97). Perhaps then the vice is metonymic, since the scales and mosses growing on the monsters' bodies could conceivably contaminate Guibert's visitor: once again an

---

8 "The prison, the place where the penalty is carried out, is also the place of observation of punished individuals" (Foucault, *Discipline and Punish*, 249).

eerie anticipation or premonition of what medical authorities once thought about the dangers of simply being in the presence of persons with AIDS. But we are expressly told that the first-person narrator was spared any such contamination. What is more, not only are the monsters' bodies harmless, they are in fact quite pretty, "reflecting hues of silver and gold" (*V*, 96). Perhaps then vice is to be found in the very size of some of these creatures, a monstrosity so painful to behold that they must be hidden from public view, as is the case of the man "whose head was four times bigger than his body." But instead of insisting on the deformity of the hydrocephalus – something he would be quite capable of describing if he chose to – Guibert focuses on the point of view of this particular monster, emphasizing his suffering:

> Quand la nuit tombait, il perdait connaissance, chaque soir il se croyait devenir aveugle. On disait que le calvaire de cet homme était immense, mais il n'avait jamais vu d'autre être humain, la nourriture lui parvenait par une trappe percée dans le plafond, il croyait que la main qui maniait cette trappe et qu'il apercevait parfois était celle de Dieu ... (*V*, 97; original ellipsis)

> When night fell he lost consciousness, every evening he thought he was going blind. It was said that the suffering of this man was immense, but he had never seen another human being, food was delivered to him by a trap door in the ceiling, he thought the hand that worked the trap door which he sometimes caught sight of was the hand of God ...

The passage quoted, which concludes the final chapter, gives us the key to the book. Vice need not be attached to a specific form, whether dead or alive, of a body. To be sure, it can result from putting a body on exhibition but in the case of the gentle monster, no one seems keen on showing him off; in fact, he is hidden from public view. Vice pertains, as was the case of the zoo and the gay bar transformed into a museum, when a body has been isolated, confined, and locked up, whether in a cell, a cage, or a museum case especially built for that purpose.

Deprived of human company, the monster whose head was four times as big as his body – a metaphor for all those who have been labeled "abnormal" and confined in public institutions – has never known another human being, with the result that he supposes that the hand of the guard who feeds him is the hand of God. Like the so-called crazy person in the "garden of species" about whom Foucault wrote so eloquently, this "monster" has experienced neither love nor friendship; he has been shut up so long that he is unaware of his own humanity. And since he has not had the opportunity to take measure of other people, he neither understands nor even knows of their alterity, or their mores. Surely, real vice is what truly vicious people have done to this "desirable monster," as Guibert describes him.[9] For vice lives wherever there is enclosure and confinement, and some times there aren't even any walls, as was the case of the hungry crocodile dependent on eating in public before drunken tourists. Vice takes many forms, but the notion and practice of what Claude Simon has called the "carré carcéral" (carceral square) (*Album d'un amateur*, 9) defines vice in its essence, whether we are dealing with bodies that are supposed to be beautiful or ugly, dead or alive, intact or cut up, animal or human, for all these binary oppositions are erased by the practice of vice seen through the eyes of Guibert. Vice pertains to the fetichization of the object congruent to every collection. In other words, vice is represented in both senses of the term – illustrated and put on display – by the several centuries' old project of the *cabinet de curiosités* and its subsequent incarnations.[10] Didn't Guibert write in *L'Image fantôme*: "I'm suspicious of the collector's passion – I'm afraid that it will turn into a petty obsession, a form of mechanical accumulation" (*GI*, 112)?

It was at this point that I remembered that there used to be a polar bear in the zoo in my city. Like Miss Smith's tiger he turned in circles, until his keepers were obliged to shoot him after he became too sick to show to the public. Exhibited and punished because of who he was, he was at once strong and weak, like all those who are accused of vice in the first degree. For monsters are "different" and it is for that reason – and only for that reason – that we feel the need to study them, to keep them

---

9 I hear an echo of Foucault's preoccupation with monsters and other supposedly undesirable individuals. I'm thinking in particular of the case of Charles Jouy described at length in one of Foucault's 1975 lectures at the Collège de France. Arrested in 1867 for having allowed himself to be masturbated by a young girl who would play the game of "curdled milk" with village boys, Jouy, a simple-minded farm hand, was subjected to every imaginable form of scrutiny and analysis, including measurements of his skull, available to nineteenth-century psychiatrists. He was put on trial and acquitted, but ended up being committed to a hospital for life. Nonetheless, even the doctors who examined and studied Jouy were obliged to note that he was mild and gentle (*doux*), not unlike Guibert's "monster" (Foucault, *Les Anormaux*, 283). Foucault refers to Jouy in the first volume of his *History of Sexuality* (31–2).

10 See Douglas Crimp, *On the Museum's Ruins*, in particular the chapter entitled "This is Not a Museum of Art."

on public view, to emprison them in various types of panoptical spaces for taxonomic ends or our own perverse pleasure, which no doubt are one and the same. As Foucault said of the so-called insane, they remain monsters because they are worth showing (*montrés*) (*Histoire de la folie à l'âge classique*, 162).

What is fundamentally vicious in the museums and other similar institutions described in *Vice* is not the internal defect or *vice de forme* but rather what might be termed *vice de montre*, the evil inherent in display, and the concomitant *vice d'enfermement*, the perversion of the lockup, that precedes and makes possible all forms of exhibition. As such, both underscore the numerous echoes of the eighteenth century in *Vice*: in its own unique manner, Guibert's book describes and puts on stage for all to see the failure of the epistemological project of the Enlightment in two of its goals, on the one hand, a perfect representation of reality and, on the other, progress by the study and eventual elimination of various forms of deviant behavior and innate degeneracy.[11]

Here we would do well to remember how Guibert felt about his own "monstrous" body on account of the deformity in his chest. As he tells his readers in the last chapter of *Vice*, the reason he knows about the "desirable monsters" is that either he broke every law in the land to get into the place where they are kept, or he escaped from the home of his "brothers" (*V*, 96). In other words, Guibert is either a curious vice tourist or a curiosity so monstrous that he himself was once shut up by the authorities whose role it is to decide who is "normal" and who is not. This alternative we readers are given resumes and rehearses the *parcours* we have just undertaken, a voyage of discovery that has allowed us to pass from the outside to the inside of what is considered and constructed as vice in our society. In the end, we identify with the exhibits themselves, with all the "desirable monsters" who have been legally shut up in public institutions. As a result, *Vice* is well and truly a literary work, for it performs that which it describes and narrates: the ramblings of a

---

11 "The possibility of a perfect representation of Nature rests then on a complex series of metonymies and metaphors bridging the gap between the natural object and its representation. Assuming such a *continuous* representation the Enlightenment could then originate the idea of giving an ordered representation of Nature in various botanical gardens. It is in this idea of an ordered spectacle of Nature, supplemented by an ordered language that would describe the spectacle, that the idea of the *Museum* was born" (Donato, "The Museum's Furnace," 226–7). On the link between the notion of degeneracy in the eighteenth and nineteenth centuries and the advent of Nazi racism in the twentieth, see Foucault, *Les Anormaux*, 298–301.

solitary *promeneur* in Rousseauian terms or Baudelaire's *flâneur* who, having set off in search of vice, ends up finding himself on the wrong side of the bars, whether in a zoo, a museum, or an asylum. In the textual mirror that *Vice* holds up, inevitably it is our own image we see reflected.

Chapter Four

Memories of the Blind

> Sur le frontispice de la rue le directeur avait fait graver cette prohibition: "Défense aux visiteurs de laisser échapper des expressions de pitié."
> *Des aveugles*, 28

> Over the gate to the street the director general had had this warning engraved: VISITORS ARE FORBIDDEN TO GIVE WAY TO EXPRESSIONS OF PITY.
> *Blindsight*, 16–17

One can easily imagine the condescending paternalism of the sighted director general of the Institute for the Blind that prompted him to have engraved above the main entrance such a ban on expressions of pity. But in *Des aveugles* sighted people are just as likely to express a cry *for* pity as a cry *of* pity, for Guibert's blind are perfectly "normal": theirs is a world filled with love, compassion, and kindness but also lies, sadism, and murder. Translated as *Blindsight*, the French title of *Des aveugles* is even richer in meaning, since the first word can be interpreted as "on," "some," or "from." The first reading would be an appropriate title for a work of a nonfiction "about or on the blind," an echo of many of Montaigne's titles – not to mention those of Cicero; the second would refer more appropriately to a work of fiction entitled *The Blind*, whereas the third could refer to a letter sent "from the blind," or "from [the kingdom of] the blind" to us readers. Whichever way one interprets the title, it alludes to a work that clearly influenced Guibert, Diderot's 1749 *Lettre sur les aveugles à l'usage de ceux qui voient*, known in English as *Letter on the Blind*.

As for the title to this chapter, if we were studying Latin, it would be interpreted as either an objective or subjective genitive, which is another way of saying it can refer to the memories someone else has of blind people or to the remembrances of the blind themselves.[1] The former is appropriate, for Guibert's novel was based on real-life experience: in 1983 he researched and wrote several articles on the Institut des Jeunes Aveugles in Paris, and subsequently, he worked there as a volunteer reader.[2] As for the second meaning, memory is of course essential to blind people's ability to negotiate their way around a room, the institute itself – a large asylum-like building constructed in the nineteenth century – or in the streets of Paris, a city many sighted people find difficult to get around in, given the trees and café terraces that dot the sidewalks, the maze-like streets and irregular blocks, the human and vehicle traffic, not to mention the ubiquitous dog poop. In *Des aveugles* memory is essential; even the briefest of memory lapses can prove dangerous, perhaps fatal.

Made up of eighty-seven unnumbered fragments[3] separated by blank spaces that remind one of blind spots or the blink of an eye, *Des aveugles* was written to appeal to young blind people and at the same time to give a sighted person the opportunity to experience what it is like to be blind: "With this novel my fantasy is to have blind readers. It's because I would like to please them, to seduce them that I tried to write a horror story that, in fact, ended up becoming something quite different" (Interview with Francblin, 45). This explains the tale-of-terror ambiance, for the young blind people in Guibert's novel adore horror films: how could a story of sexual jealousy and a murder in an institute for the blind not intrigue them? On the other hand, most of the novel is not written from the perspective of a blind person.[4] Rather, Guibert chose

---

1 My title pays homage to Jacques Derrida's magnificent *Memoirs of the Blind: The Self-Portrait and Other Ruins.*
2 Guibert's *reportage* takes the form of several articles published in *Le Monde* on 14 July 1983 under the general title of "Les jeunes aveugles et la culture."
3 In the English translation, the fragments have not been printed in the same way, with the result that there are fewer of them. All references to fragments here will be to the original French version published by Gallimard.
4 *Point of view* and *perspective* – like *déjà vu*, *insight*, and *hindsight* – betray our culture's prejudices in favor of sighted people. Even an apparently neutral term such as *mode* in Gérard Genette's narratological scheme of things is based on the question "Qui voit?" Why not ask who is listening, touching, tasting, smelling? Guibert plays with both narrative mode and narrative voice: most of the chapters are narrated by a third-person narrator, except chapter 66, a long monologue by Taillegueur, and chapter 86, in which Robert recounts a dream to Josette. On the other hand, several chapters do give us the perceptions of a blind person: Robert in chapter 76, Josette in chapter 87, Taillegueur in chapter 78, and Kipa in chapter 24.

to give us the point of view of a sighted narrator who is something of a voyeur. Not only do we learn about the blind at work and play, their education, and general mores, we also get to read some highly suggestive descriptions of what happens in the institute's gymnasium when Taillegueur and Josette meet there for their adulterous trysts. In fact, the novel is full of visual terms: there are innumerable references to colors; odd objects of various sizes and shapes; bizarre, complicated spaces; human bodies in various types of garb, including outlandish disguises, engaged in all sorts of activities and positions. As well, there are many rare words that readers may never have seen before. All of this doesn't make the novel easy to read. In fact, by emphasizing the visual, Guibert paradoxically gives us a hint of what it is like to be blind. It is as though he were saying to his sighted readers, "You have eyes to see, well then, read!" At the same time, we have difficulty imagining – "seeing" – exactly what it is we are reading about. Take, for example, the following extract about a costume party:

> Ils étaient parés de robes incolores, de calottes de diable à cornes molles, de masques sans relief et sans trait, de capes informes qui n'étaient que le crissement virevoltant de leurs plis, de loups non échancrés, de diadèmes de lave et de collerettes de glace, d'inutiles azurs brodés, de pyjamas de soie rouge trompette et bleu violon, d'autres bleus mous et de verts irritants, de bruns indistincts, de brassards et de couronnes de grelots, ils ne représentaient pas des hommes mais des rayons de lune, des rivières, des arbres de foudre, des éruptions, des ténèbres phosphorescentes les encerclaient en crépitant de doigt en doigt comme des feux magiques ... (*Av.*, 11)

> They were arrayed in colorless robes, devil-caps with floppy horns, blank featureless masks, shapeless cloaks that existed only in the whirring rustle of their folds, eyeless dominoes, diadems of lava and ruffs of ice, superfluously embroidered azure fabrics, pyjamas of blaring red or violin-like blue silk, others a mellow-sounding blue, a screeching green or a toneless brown, brassards and crowns of bells: they represented not men but shafts of moonlight, rivers, forked lightning, eruptions, phosphorescent shadows encircling them, sparking from fingertip to fingertip like magic fire ... (*Bl.*, 1; trans. alt.)

Even before we get to the part of this run-on sentence where Guibert describes the blind rinsing out their eyes with alcohol, he provides the reader with clues about the revelers' blindness, such as the fact that the masks are featureless, the cloaks shapeless, and the dominoes without holes for eyes. As for the costumes, initially described as colorless, some of them, it turns out, are as garish as the vivid sound imagery used of necessity to describe them. Blindness is thus encoded in the text from the outset, even if at first the reader may remain blind to what is strangely obvious. Nevertheless, when we read this passage, we have the impression that our "mind's eye" is not working properly, since we have difficulty imagining the colors, as well as the shapes and the designs, of the costumes described. Guibert has managed to write prose that turns the reader, especially the sighted reader, into one who feels – and probably is – blind throughout much of the reading experience.

Guibert tells us that the blind are "habitués à l'idée du double, elle faisait partie de l'apprentissage" (*Av.*, 58) ("accustomed to the idea of a double, it was part of their apprenticeship" [*Bl.*, 44]). Certainly, many different types of doubling processes are to be found in the novel. One thinks of the disguises mentioned in the first fragment of the novel that both hide and "duplicate" the bodies wearing them; of the various couples portrayed, whether gay or straight; of the inevitable sensory substitutions to which blind people have to resort to perceive the world about them; of reproductions such as photographs and miniature models; of mirror, memory, and dream images; and, of course, of language and the always problematic relationship of words and things. Published just a year after the death of Michel Foucault, *Des aveugles* is dedicated "To the dead friend," the author of *Madness and Civilization* and *Discipline and Punish*, both of which express ideas that seem to have influenced Hervé Guibert.

A DISCIPLINARY SPACE

The institute forms a kind of parallel or alternate universe that remains foreign territory to sighted people, even though they may visit it on special occasions: "rares et louches étaient les relations d'un monde à l'autre" (*Av.*, 28) ("relations between the two worlds were infrequent and suspect" [*Bl.*, 16]). When sighted people do come to the institute, it is to take vicious pleasure in spying on the blind, whom they suppose will be poorly dressed and outright filthy. In fact, of course, the inhabitants of the institute are impeccably groomed, the cleanliness of the blind serving to "excuser leur infirmité auprès de ceux qui en jouissaient comme un spectacle (de la ville on se déplaçait pour venir *voir* les aveugles, les autorisations se disputaient)" (*Av.*, 29) ("excuse their infirmity in the eyes of those who enjoyed the spectacle they provided [people arrived from the city to *see* the blind, visiting permits were eagerly sought]" [*Bl.*, 17]). Those who read *Des aveugles* when it first appeared in 1985 could not have understood the clear allusion to the still-unpublished *Vice* and its denunciation of showing off "monsters" to the public. More familiar would have been the emphasis on the seemingly paradoxical cleanliness and good grooming of the blind, which echoes Diderot's famous *Letter on the Blind.*

Located between the city and the countryside, the institute constitutes a unique space where the blind are educated, work, and live out almost all of their lives:

> On ne rejoignait le monde des voyants qu'à la toute fin de sa vie, et rares étaient ceux qui arrivaient au grand âge, car l'Institut rejetait ses vieillards, ils étaient placés dans des hospices communs. On redoutait beaucoup, parmi les aveugles, cette intrusion tardive dans le monde des voyants, qu'on appelait, sinistrement, le Paradis. (*Av.*, 47)

> They did not enter the world of the sighted until right at the end of their lives, and it was rare for anyone to reach a great age, for the Institute threw out its old people – they were sent to old people's homes. The blind greatly dreaded that belated entry into the world of the sighted, which was given the sinister name of Paradise. (*Bl.*, 34)

Paradise is also the name of the pet store where Josette buys four more or less white mice (as the clerk explains to her, true white does not exist in nature). The mice, which soon begin to multiply in almost geometrical progression, can be considered to stand for or represent the four blind characters who play principal parts in *Des aveugles*: Josette, Robert, Tailleguer, and Kipa. When we learn that a blind researcher, an astronomer, believes that there are two suns, we begin to realize how important parallel structures, even – as opposed to odd – numbers, and symmetry are in this universe.

Guibert's institute for the blind is one of the many collective spaces established to house and confine within their walls a particular group of people: barracks for soldiers, boarding schools for students, hospitals for the sick, insane asylums for those perceived to be crazy, sanitoriums for people with tuberculosis, orphanages for illegitimate and other unwanted children, as well as institutes for the deaf and for the blind.

91   Memories of the Blind

Based on even older collective spaces represented by convents, monasteries, and leprosaria, the institutions constructed in the eighteenth and nineteenth centuries all had in common a prison-like environment characterized by extremely rigid control of time and space. Just as the inmates' time was governed by timetables that divide the years, months, and days of their lives, so too space, whether in the form of cells or common areas, remained under the constant control and surveillance of guards or other authority figures such as teachers and nurses. Like so many others, the blind were to be segregated and regimented, supposedly for their own good as much as for the welfare of society. Guibert ironically describes how benevolent the world is nowadays because "il n'exterminait plus les aveugles mais les enrégimentait dans de grandes maisons sûres" (*Av.*, 37) ("it no longer exterminated the blind but instead regimented them in big secure houses" [*Bl.*, 25; trans. alt.]). Of course, the irony here belongs to our own postmodern, early-twenty-first-century world. It would have been totally lost on yesterday's well-meaning souls, that is, the disciplinarians – whether civil servants or parents – of earlier centuries and a large part of the twentieth century. It is only recently and in the light of the extermination of millions of human beings believed by some to be inferior that we have begun to question so many of the assumptions regarding institutions that were once taken for granted.

Like so many other institutional spaces, the great building housing the blind is constructed on the basis of a symmetrical apportionment of space:

> Les bâtiments, plantés dans un jardin entouré d'un très haut mur, formaient une croix: l'aile nord, sur son deuxième étage, accueillait le dortoir des petits et sur son troisième étage celui des grands; les filles étaient de même disposées dans l'aile est. Sur son deuxième étage l'aile sud était réservée aux couples adultes, et l'aile ouest aux adultes célibataires. (*Av.*, 24–5)

> The buildings, set in a park surrounded by a high wall, formed a cross: the north wing's second floor housed the dormitory of the youngest and the third storey the older boys'; the girls were similarly confined to the east wing. The second floor of the south wing was allocated to adult couples and the west wing to unmarried adults. (*Bl.*, 13; trans. alt.)

Guibert will describe the institute in much greater detail, so that what at first seems clear becomes progressively less clear as he adds a library here, storage rooms, and an infirmary there, not to mention the offices of the dentist, the doctor, and the ophthalmologist, the steam room, the gymnasium, cafeterias, the director's office, and finally but not least the observatory where Crogius, who is as blind as Galileo was at the end of his life, and his assistant Bernus live![5] Guibert seeks to lose us in the labyrinthian corridors of the institute just as his first-person narrator will get lost there the day of the masked ball. Once more, a plethora of detail makes visualization of the actual fictive referent difficult. We are meant to suppose, however, that the building is symmetrical with two exceptions. The building takes the form of a cross at the center of which – on the ground floor but rising another story in height – is to be found the monumental music room also used as a chapel. Beneath it, in the basement, is a huge star-shaped public bath. One wonders if, in emphasizing symmetry, Guibert was thinking of Diderot's *Letter on the Blind*, in which he wrote: "Our blind man is an excellent judge of symmetry" (812).

The institute for the blind is housed in a prison-like building that inevitably recalls the words of Foucault in *Discipline and Punish*;[6] it conjures up similar images for Kipa, a loveable youth whose parents will not acknowledge his blindness. Since they have never allowed him near the institute, his first approach gives us the perception of someone who is both blind and unfamiliar with a Foucauldian "disciplinary space":

> La première fois qu'il [Kipa] l'aborda [the institute], le secret se dressa devant lui sous la forme d'une forteresse, en levant la tête il évalua la hauteur des murs qui le coupaient du bain d'air qui s'était raréfié à son approche, il vit la bâtisse avec des tourelles, de hautes cheminées fumantes, des drapeaux flottants: était-ce une prison, un bastion de l'armée, un crématorium? mais en même temps des bruits de musique lui parvenaient, des bouffées de rires de jeunes filles s'échappaient

---

5 One is reminded of Robert Pinget's novel *L'Inquisitoire*, near the end of which one learns of the existence of a "new" character, an astronomer named Monsieur Pierre, who lives in part of the chateau the reader heretofore didn't know existed.

6 "In short, its task was to constitute a prison-machine with a cell of visibility ... and a central point from which a permanent gaze may control prisoners and staff. Around these two requirements, several variations were possible: the Benthamite Panopticon in its strict form, the semi-circle, the cross-plan, the star shape" (Foucault, *Discipline and Punish*, 249–50). Note that the Institute would remind a French reader of the Abbaye de Thélème, a utopian anti-monastery, described by Rabelais in *Gargantua*.

d'une fenêtre et il se demanda s'il n'y avait là ce qu'il avait entendu appeler une maison de plaisirs. (*Av.*, 50)

> The first time [Kipa] went there, the enigma rose up before him in the shape of a fortress. Raising his head he measured the height of the walls that cut him off from the bath of air that had thinned out at his approach, he saw a building with turrets, tall chimneys smoking, flags flying; was it a prison, an army bastion, a crematorium? But at the same time sounds of music reached him, bursts of girlish laughter came from an open window, and he wondered if the place was what he had heard described as a "house of pleasure." (*Bl.*, 36–7; trans. alt.)

Kipa soon figures out what this apparent "house of pleasure" cum prison really is; and he manages to get himself hired as postman and guide. Gifted with the insight so often attributed to the blind, such as the Theban seer Teiresias, he tricks the inhabitants of the institute into believing that he is sighted. For Kipa to be in the company of other blind people represents a kind of paradise, a garden of Eden.[7] Kipa distributes the mail, "reads," or rather invents the letters received by the blind, and takes them on walks and even rides on a tandem bicycle. When he has accidents, he buys the goodwill of his charges by giving them items stolen from his parents' stationery shop, but God, good luck, or "blindsight," to use the expression of Guibert's translator, James Kirkup, protect him and his friends most of the time during these mad sorties.

Unlike prisoners, the blind are allowed out of the institute. With Kipa, a blind person truly can lead another blind person, despite what the Bible says (Luke 6:3), even though it is not clear who is in charge when he and Robert set out on an expedition to the pastry shop – to "look" at all the goodies in the window – and a local bookstore – to touch and smell the volumes. Kipa represents a freedom reminiscent of the ship of fools described in such loving detail by Foucault in *Madness and Civilization*. The *Narrenschiff*, which predated the great confinement of the seventeenth century, was believed to have freely roamed the waterways of Germany and Flanders. As mentioned by Foucault, there are numerous

---

7 In his article on *Des aveugles*, Richard Smith has described the institute as a kind of ghetto given the Jewish resonance of Kipa's name, which means "yarmulke" in Hebrew (18–19). Kipa "passes" for a sighted person among the blind, just as a Jew might pass for a gentile, or a homosexual for a heterosexual.

representations, literary and pictorial, of such ships. For example, Hieronymus Bosch painted a satirical *Ship of Fools* lambasting gluttony (1490–1500, Louvre; figure 12).[8] As for *Des aveugles*, freedom is associated with water (in the basement swimming pool and steam bath), to be sure, but it is also associated with Kipa. Wherever Kipa goes, he is not a guard of the blind but their guardian, their kindly keeper, hence the name. And as such, he presents a freedom and equality among peers that supposedly characterized the preclassical ship of fools.

Guibert's novel describes an institutional space in which the young and their elders, men and women, gays and straights cohabit. They live, eat, work, sleep, and make music as well as raise general havoc together. No wonder that Kipa perceives the institute as an idyllic space. Its dual character presents a symmetry – like the symmetrical wings of the building called "North Pole," for the children, and "Tropics," for the adults – making it a kind of Edenic prison. But then we know what happened in Eden.

RELATIONSHIPS

Among the adults who have lived most of their lives in the institute are Josette and Robert, a married couple. Josette, who is totally blind, lost her sight at age two, whereas Robert was blind at birth. He is not totally blind, however, for he has pinhole vision, which is as useless as it is distressing, light being experienced as searing pain, in fact, a kind of ocular rape. Although still young, Josette and Robert have outgrown each other, having reached the stage where they seek distractions from beyond the walls of the institute. Robert, for example, buys a leather biker outfit that proves doubly useless since he doesn't possess a motorcycle and instead of rekindling the sexual passion in their marriage, it turns Josette off. The only activities that the couple still enjoy together are playing pickup sticks and improvising concertos for harp and musical saw. Josette seeks substitutes for the children she has never had by buying her more-or-less white mice. She then proceeds to gouge out the eyes of her favorite one, whom she names Josette, intending the mouse to be her companion, her double. After becoming as blind as her mistress, the mouse, who is in fact a male, begins to copulate madly, the

---

8 See also Brueghel's *Dulle Grete* mentioned by Foucault. Cf. "The Ship of Fools: *Stultifera Navis* or *Ignis Fatuus*" in which the authors, Maher and Maher, claim that the ship of fools was purely allegorical, never a real historical phenomenon.

result of which is a population explosion that stands in sharp contrast to Robert and Josette's childless marriage. She even engages in a kind of sexual foreplay with her mice, although she will lose all interest in them when she discovers the pleasures of extramarital sex.

Apart from the mice, the mirror image of this relationship is the passionate affair Josette has with Taillegueur, a newcomer to the institute where he is hired as a masseur. Like Josette, Taillegueur was not born blind, but in constrast to her loss of sight, which remains a medical mystery, Guibert hints at the fact that Taillegueur was the victim of a terrible case of child abuse: his father allowed his son to play with a grenade, knowing that it would blow up in his face and make him blind, in order to receive a government pension. From their first meeting, Josette is drawn to Taillegueur by his intriguing aroma, a smell that Guibert describes as red with a tinge of wood, wool, and tobacco. Taillegueur and Josette meet for acrobatic sex in the older boys' gym, but Taillegueur's seductive qualities are based as much on his seemingly infinite knowledge as on his equally boundless sexual prowess. Not only does he know all the vices of the sighted – their cult of physical beauty, their bizarre admiration for bits of paint on canvas, their love of the sun that gives them cancers – he also knows the history of the blind across the centuries and in various cultures. Taillegueur's knowledge is truly encyclopedic in scope:

> Sais-tu qu'un gouffre nous était destiné où nos pères devaient à notre naissance nous jeter? Sais-tu que nous avons été adjoints à des cohortes de boiteux, de lépreux, de sourds et de fous? Sais-tu que nous avons dû partager le sort des imbéciles et des culs-de-jatte? ... Sais-tu que les bagnards ont été nos concurrents quand nous avons tissé le fil? (*Av.*, 112–13)

> Do you know that we were destined for a pit into which our fathers were supposed to cast us at birth? Do you know that we were lumped in with hordes of the lame, the lepers, the deaf and the mad? Do you know we had to share the fate of the feeble-minded and the legless cripples? ... Do you know that convicts were our competitors in rope making? (*Bl.*, 92–3; trans. alt.)

The lepers, mad people, and convicts are clear allusions to Foucault's work on the construction of insanity in the seventeenth century and the treatment of criminals in eighteenth- and nineteenth-century France. So complete is Taillegueur's knowledge of how the blind have been treated by the sighted throughout history that it is clear Guibert must have done extensive research on the topic.⁹ Indeed, one could well imagine a companion volume to *Madness and Civilization* and *Discipline and Punish* devoted to the history of blindness. Just as some critics perceive *À l'ami qui ne m'a pas sauvé la vie* as a supplement to *The History of Sexuality*, I read *Des aveugles* as a companion volume to the two earlier works.

Seeking to get rid of the inconvenient cuckold, Josette and Taillegueur plan to murder Robert in the auditorium. Their intent is to exchange or remove one of the miniature models that maps the great hall's complexity, so that Robert will make a fatal mistake. What happens is that Josette detects a smell of cock in Taillegueur's mouth, becomes jealous of her lover, and denounces him and the plot to her husband. Taillegueur ends up falling to his death, much to the satisfaction of both Robert and Josette, who love each other more than ever before at that point. Homoerotic love leads to death, just as it does in the scenario of *L'Homme blessé* coauthored by Guibert and Chéreau.¹⁰ The question we ask ourselves is with whom has Taillegueur been having sex? Josette surprised the couple *in flagrante delicto* but was not able to identify her male rival by sound or touch. Nevertheless, there is a clue. Taillegueur, who is new to the institute, seems very interested when he first learns about Kipa, and Josette's alert tongue detected the taste of a boy on her erstwhile lover's breath. Kipa's age – like that of the other characters in *Des aveugles* – is never divulged by the otherwise omniscient narrator. Clearly, Guibert wants to raise the possibility that Taillegueur's sexual partner was Kipa. When we remember that love, like Kipa, is blind, and that Cupid himself falls in love in many an antique conceit, the evidence seems as conclusive as things get in Guibert's elusive universe.

We now arrive at other same-sex couples, the first of which is Crogius and Bernus. The sexuality of the astronomer and his assistant is not described by the narrator. All we know is that they live and work together. But their twin beds have been pushed together, like those of Josette and Robert, and the symbolism of Bernus helping his friend put

---

9 In his interview with Catherine Francblin, Guibert said, "In order for fiction to interest me, it must not remain in the domain of pure fabrication [*affabulation*]; it must contain elements of truth. That is why I did a lot of research on the blind" (46).

10 In "Les escarpins rouges," a text dating from 1983, Guibert describes how the title of the film is based on Gustave Courbet's 1854 *Auto-portrait*, also called *L'Homme blessé* (*PA*, 138). Derrida includes a reproduction of the painting of the man with closed eyes in *Memoirs of the Blind* (81; cf. 72).

on the thick-lensed contraption that allows him to see – or to think that he sees – the night sky is clearly sexual:

> Bernus aidait Crogius à enchâsser ses lunettes, les fixant à un casque noué sur la nuque, et qui avaient déjà l'épaisseur et le poids de ces plus grandes lunettes astrologiques dans lesquelles elles s'encastraient. Il ressemblait ainsi à un insecte géant qui accomplit une intromission ou une ponte. (*Av.*, 43–4)

> Bernus helped Crogius to put on his spectacles, attaching them to a helmut tied at the nape of his neck; they were as thick and heavy as the big astronomical telescopes into which they were fitted. He thus resembled a gigantic insect laying eggs or caught in the act of intromission. (*Bl.*, 31; trans. alt.)

As already mentioned, Robert and Kipa form another couple. Of the various couples, this one seems to be the most successful. They form a symbiotic unit, Kipa "leading" Robert through the city. When they go out together, Kipa places his hand on Robert's shoulder in a gesture of childlike affection. Robert is touched by the gesture of this supposedly sighted child who in fact is neither, since he is a blind adolescent, while at the same time it feels proper for him as the adult to guide the "child." As with Josette and her mice, the blind inevitably make mistakes, but in this case, the error seems strangely appropriate. After all, the figure of a man and a male child linked by intense feelings of friendship, and possibly more, is frequent in Guibert, whether it be father and son or some other couple. As Jean-Pierre Boulé puts it, "the love story is perhaps also the one between Robert and Kipa, described as the adult and the child, that dares not write itself" (*Voices of the Self*, 129):

> Kipa vint chercher Robert. Comme toujours ils n'avaient aucun but, ensemble ils aimaient s'égarer. On ne pouvait pas savoir, lorsqu'on les voyait, lequel des deux guidait l'autre: Kipa était assuré que c'était lui le plus agile mais par gentillesse il posait sa main sur l'épaule de Robert, comme pour s'en faire guider. Et Robert, qui ne soupçonnait pas la supercherie, se disait qu'un voyant avait de bien gracieuses attentions et, de plus, d'une façon plus générale, plus symbolique, que c'était à l'adulte de guider l'enfant dans la vie. (*Av.*, 66)

> Kipa came to get Robert. As usual, they had no fixed destination, they

liked to wander aimlessly. Watching them, it was impossible to know which of the two was leading the other; Kipa was convinced he was the more nimble but out of sheer kindness he would put his hand on Robert's shoulder, as if to let himself be guided by him. And Robert, who did not see through the trick, thought that the sighted were so gracious and helpful and, moreover, in a more general, symbolic fashion, that it was after all up to the adult to guide a child through life. (*Bl.*, 51; trans. alt.)

Although most of the novel is narrated in the third person, Guibert appears as a first-person narrator in the guise of a man with a complex about his beauty – hence the attraction of being with the blind – who becomes a reader at the institute. During his visits, the man spies on a blind youth to whom he is sexually attracted. Things come to a head the day of the carnival, when some of the blind youths set a trap for the volunteer worker: "Le jour de leur carnaval, ils me tendirent des pièges: je revenais de la lecture, je ne les vis pas, je ne les entendis pas, ils s'étaient bien cachés, c'est moi qui étais aveugle, leurs masques leur donnaient la vue, l'agilité, la méchanceté" (*Av.*, 134) ("On the day when they held their carnival, they played tricks on me: I was going home from the reading, I didn't see them, I didn't hear them, they were well hidden, it was I who had become blind, their masks lent them sight, nimbleness, maliciousness" [*Bl.*, 112–13; trans. alt.]). But that is not all, for the attack is orchestrated by the blind youth so admired by the Guibert-like narrator. Having trapped the volunteer worker, he then proceeds to mutilate him:

> je sentis autour de l'aine une cassure d'écartèlement et soudain mes yeux virent sous eux l'éclat mat de la cuvette d'émail qui les attendait, mon favori s'approcha et les décapsula, il me dit à l'oreille, tout doucement: nous les grefferons à un chien enragé. (*Av.*, 134–5)
>
> I felt something wrench and crack round the groin and suddenly my eyes saw underneath them the dull surface of the enamel pan that awaited them, my favorite approached and popped them out, he said in my ear, quite softly: we'll graft them on to a rabid dog. (*Bl.*, 113; trans. alt.)

Symbolic castration takes the form of what Derrida calls "its abocular metonymies" (*Memoirs of the Blind*, 41) in this intratextual replay of Josette's gouging out the eyes of one of the male mice. The narrator's body is wounded, although not fatally, with the result that although he can no longer see the one whom he desires – or anything else – he will still be able to write. Thanks to the criminal actions of the blind youth fed up with being leered at, the voyeuristic volunteer joins the illustrious company of writers like Homer, Milton, Joyce, and Borges. As such, blindness is the price he must pay for having his eyes opened to the truth about unreciprocated sexual desire (on the part of the other), the crimes that can be perpetrated in an institute for the blind, as well as the connection between testicles and eyeballs. Here the intertext is clearly Georges Bataille's *Histoire de l'oeil*, in which various body parts of humans and animals are subjected to different types of textual mutation (metaphor and metonymy). Bataille was one of the writers whom the precocious Guibert read while still a teenager. And Bataille's famous novella about eyes and other globular objects including eggs and testicles (based on the phonetic transformations *oeuf, oeil, couille,* "egg," "eye," "ball"), which was the subject of a well-known article by Roland Barthes, "La métaphore de l'oeil," is clearly alluded to when a ball that Robert played with when he was a child is transformed into a kind of magical eye that captures an image of sexual union.[11]

Males usually have two eyes and two testicles, and in case there is any doubt about the significance of textual doubles in *Des aveugles*, we must not forget that Guibert splits himself in two, so to speak. Not only does he appear in the guise of a volunteer soon to be enucleated (fragments thirty-six and eighty-five), he also appears in the guise of another young man, a reclusive aesthete, who lives with a wax figure representing the head of Joan of Arc. Josette visits him along with Taillegueur, and at one point she threatens the young man with gouging out his eyes, although he doesn't take the threat seriously. To gouge or put out someone's eyes in French is *crever les yeux*, an expression that has two very different but related meanings since it denotes what happened to Samson (see Derrida's reading of Samson as a phallic figure in *Memoirs of the Blind*, 104–6), as well as signifying something that is self-evident, staring you in the face. Here it is as plain as day that same-sex love is the second principal theme underlying the novel's economy.

---

11 Castration is also symbolized by the musical saw played by Robert whose small cock will be replaced first by Josette's mice and then by the sexual organ of the well-endowed Taillegueur who plots to kill off Robert. Literal castration will appear in *Vous m'avez fait former des fantômes* when Mickie meets Bobo "le châtreur" (109–12).

SUPPLEMENTS FOR SIGHT

Sensory correspondences play an important role in the novel, as sight is replaced by hearing, touch, smell, and taste. For example, one day Josette is surprised and hurt by the "bruissement arrogant et blanc d'un col de dentelle" (*Av.*, 30) ("arrogant white rustling of a lace collar" [*Bl.*, 18; trans. alt.]) worn by another girl who flaunts her new dress by making a noise with the lace. Compared to her own dull gray – and no doubt soundless – smock, the other dress seems like the worst of insults, and Josette reacts by hurling the contents of a bottle of ink in the direction of its wearer. We never get to know who the other girl was; indeed, that is not important. What is important is that the rustling of the lace is described as arrogant *and* white in the original version. Colors become sounds, represent emotions – arrogance, humiliation – and can lead to acts of violence. Clearly, there is no lack of action, human interaction, and emotion in the institute for the blind.

For example, one of the teachers, a certain Mlle Keller, who is both blind and deaf, is brimming with words and ideas. Like Helen Keller, she has learned to talk, but the fingers of Guibert's character are never at rest, as though everything she wants to communicate were at their tips:

> le bout des doigts de Mlle Keller était pris, quand elle parlait comme lorsqu'elle se taisait, d'une myriade de fourmillements, comme s'ils picotaient, les faisant tressaillir, bondir comme des puces, éléments presque autonomes, distincts de ses mains. En public, si elle se savait observée, elle tâchait de les tenir morts, de les faire taire, mais ils gagnaient toujours, ils étaient si bavards, ils abondaient et ils débordaient de mots. (*Av.*, 39–40)

> the tips of Mademoiselle Keller's fingers, whether she was speaking or keeping silent, were possessed by myriad pins and needles, as if they were being pricked in a way that made them tremble and twitch like fleas, almost like autonomous elements distinct from her hands. In public, if she knew she was being watched, she would try to keep them quiet, but they always won out, their words welled up and overflowed. (*Bl.*, 27; trans. alt.)

Combining or "condensing" Diderot's imaginary blind philosopher, who situated his soul in his fingers, and Miss Sullivan's pupil, Guibert has recycled the information in the most concrete manner possible. There is no longer any talk about the soul of the blind person, and the importance of fingers as instruments of perception is translated by metaphor: Mlle Keller's fingers quiver with the pleasure of perceiving and describing the world about her, they even flit about like fleas!

Mlle Keller's vocabulary is full of references to colors and odors: she renames her students "cherry, hops, wool, burnt sugar, sawdust" (*Bl.*, 28), and in her classes the traditional French course about practical life (*leçon de choses*) becomes a sensuous experiment in perceiving the different fragances of her "perfume bank." Her teaching is based on synaesthesia, as is clear in the following passage that echoes a line from Baudelaire's famous sonnet "Correspondances," "Il est des parfums frais comme des chairs d'enfants ...": "Dans le parfum des jeunes gens, dit Mlle Keller, qui donnait son cours d'odorat, il y a quelque chose d'élémentaire, quelque chose qui tient du feu, de l'ouragan et du flot marin; les petits enfants, quant à eux, ont tous le même parfum, un parfum pur, simple, indéchiffrable ..." (*Av.*, 39) ("Mademoiselle Keller, who gave lectures on the sense of smell, said that in the odour emitted by young people there was something elemental, something suggesting fire, hurricanes and briny waves; on the other hand, little children all have the same perfume, a perfume that was pure, simple, indecipherable ..." [*Bl.*, 26]). And as we had occasion to remark, Josette is initially seduced by Taillegueur's odor as much as his voice: "cette odeur de sueur rousse, de laine et de bois. Bonjour, dit l'homme, et la voix était comme l'odeur, et comme la main: rude, mais chaude, puissante, enveloppante, un peu roublarde" (*Av.*, 83–4) ("that odour of foxy sweat, of wool and wood. Good morning, said the man and his voice was like his smell, powerful, overwhelming, a little suspect" [*Bl.*, 67]). The world of the blind in Guibert's novel is as full of sensuous plenitude as is Diderot's text.

REPRODUCTIONS

Two types of reproduction intrigue the blind in Guibert's novel: photography and models. The first does not frighten them: it just baffles them, for they cannot understand how a machine can "see," while they cannot: "Comment une machine pouvait-elle procéder, alors que leurs yeux en étaient incapables? Ne devait-on pas plutôt greffer ces machines à la place de leurs yeux?" (*Av.*, 68) ("How could an apparatus work thus, when their own eyes were incapable of doing so? Should they not rather graft on these machines in place of their eyes?" [*Bl.*, 53]). But references to photography are not limited to "lens-envy." For example, Robert seeks to protect himself from the painful flashes of light that he perceives through two tiny holes in his eyes by wearing dark glasses, which causes a sighted man to complain loudly about his "hypocrisy." The only time the *sténopées* – a term usually reserved for the small hole that replaces a lens in a *camera obscura* – are useful is when Robert manages to perceive something of his rival's fatal fall. One can well imagine how fascinating it must have been for Guibert the photographer and photography critic to research and write about people with little or no vision. As he said in his interview with Antoine Dulaure, "I never stopped making lists of problems relating to their perception of distance, transparency, infinity, light and shade, all of them a photographer's questions" (56). In the case of Robert, his eyes are as dysfunctional as a defective camera lens, which no doubt explains, as much as his loving friendship with Kipa, why Guibert writes of him with such tenderness. After all, didn't the novelist sometimes have problems with cameras too?

Although the institute possesses globes and other teaching devices donated by airline companies (another echo and update of Diderot's *Letter on the Blind*, which also describes maps for the blind), the most useful way to teach a blind person geography is to mold the shapes of countries and continents in the wet sand of the sandbox that also proves helpful when one wants to arrange an assignment.[12] Then there are the plaster-cast models – of teeth, spiders, human brains, and prehistoric animals – that are part of the teachers' regular pedagogical aids. Even more useful are the miniature models placed by all the doors in the institute so that the blind can figure out each room's configuration:

> Pour se repérer dans les espaces, à l'orée de chaque pièce dans laquelle ils pénétraient se trouvait une petite maquette en bois qui représentait la pièce à son échelle la plus réduite, ils l'exploraient d'un doigt pour vérifier qu'elle ne comportait aucune traître dénivellation ... (*Av.*, 58)

12 Hervé Guibert described how the geography teacher at the Institut des Jeunes Aveugles showed him the sandbox that the novelist was to put to use for more than pedagogical purposes in his novel: "In the geography class the teacher told me that, rather than globes in Braille, the best teaching tool is a sandbox. He showed me how he wet the sand in which he traced a map in order to get the pupils to follow it with their fingers before he rubbed it out and got them to reproduce it. It seemed to me both very simple and moving, and I immediately saw that this sandbox would be useful to me in my story as a means to convey messages" (Interview with Dulaure, 56).

In order to help them find their way, at the entrance to each room there was a little wooden model representing the room on a very reduced scale and they would explore it with a finger to make sure the room had no treacherous change of levels ... (*Bl.*, 44; trans. alt.)

These models, which can be read as self-reflexive *mises en abîme* of all the doubling techniques in the novel, can be as life-threatening as they are life-saving. When Taillegueur and Josette plot to kill Robert, they decide to switch one of the models so that the *terzo incommodo* will make a fatal mistake. In the end, of course, it is Taillegueur who will make the mistake, having been lured into a trap by the newly reconciled couple.

Wanting to test her young daughter's ability to function on her own, Josette's mother once shut her up in a lighted room supposedly filled with obstacles but which in fact contained only three cardboard models: a pyramid, a ball, and a cube. Much to her mother's astonishment, Josette survived the educational experiment, having successfully navigated her way around the room and the objects: she ended up sitting on the cube, wearing part of the pyramid as a hat, and clutching the ball in her hands! Once again Diderot's text about the blind comes to mind, on account of his discussion about how a person who regained his sight might distinguish cubes and spheres without touching them. This old debate about reality and the perception we have of it, which goes as far back as Plato's cave, was a topic of intensive discussion in the eighteenth century. Diderot's letter, which hardly seems subversive today, although it and several other works earned him a three-and-a-half-month prison term at the Château de Vincennes, carries on the debate about idealism engaged in by Locke, Condillac, and Molyneux.[13] There is another echo of the *Letter on the Blind* in the pyramid-like model constructed by Josette's mother, since it recalls what Diderot wrote about the work of the English mathematician Saunderson as well as his praise of Sophie Volland's niece, Mélanie de Sallignac. (I am thinking particularly of her description of a cube divided into pyramids). Although Guibert is not interested in rekindling an old philosophical debate, it is clear that in his own way he is as much of a materialist as Diderot, attaching the

13 D'Alembert made extensive use of Diderot's *Lettre sur les aveugles* in the article "Aveugle" in the *Encyclopédie*, although for fear of censorship he does not use Diderot's name. In his article about the Institut des Jeunes Aveugles, Guibert refers to an edition of the *Encyclopédie* open at this article, and in the novel there is a statue of a man with his hand on the head of a young beggar boy who is holding open an encyclopedia written in raised points, presumably Braille (*Av.*, 27).

greatest importance to sensory perceptions in the origin of ideas. However, as we leave the domain of models for the realm of images, the doubling process in *Des aveugles* becomes even more complicated.

IMAGES

Although several of Guibert's characters mention mirrors, it is Robert who is the most fascinated by them. For example, he is never without a tiny mirror that he keeps in a pocket. He caresses its cold surface, as though it were some talisman. And when everyone at the institute figures in a group photo, Robert imagines the camera must be a kind of mirror, an idea put to use in the photograph *La main de l'aveugle* (figure 13). In this picture Guibert has captured the specular or mirror image of the blind person's hand, thereby removing the viewer one more step from the reality invisible to the person whose photograph is being taken. As for Robert, he even imagines his brain as a miniature cave lined with mirrors: "Il était toujours captivé par les miroirs, il s'était assuré qu'il en avait doublé l'intérieur de son crâne, et qu'ils reflétaient à l'infini un lac sombre dans une grotte ..." (*Av.*, 69) ("He was always captivated by mirrors, he was sure that he had lined the interior of his skull with mirrors, and that they reflected to infinity a dark lake in a cavern (...)" [*Bl.*, 54]). Robert's version of the geography of the human brain anticipates Guibert's description of the magnificent – although slightly flawed – brain of the philosopher in "Les secrets d'un homme," which was written while he was working on *Des aveugles*. As well, Robert's image uncannily foreshadows the numerous references to MIRs, dysfunctional brains, and insanity in Guibert's last novel, *Le Paradis*. Although he has one of the more lowly positions in the institute – he is a dishwasher – perhaps Robert should have been a philosopher. Echoing Plato's cave, Stendhal's description of the novel as a mobile mirror, as well as modern theories about perception and writing, those of Maurice Merleau-Ponty and Claude Simon, for example, Robert's image of his brain also recalls Foucault's *Archéologie du savoir*. After all, who but an archaeologist would be competent to study the human brain conceived of as an underground cavern lined with mirrors?

In Guibert's novel, even more important than mirrors and their reflections are memory images. One kind of memory, located in the fingertips of the blind, is tactile. But the other senses also can provide them with "memories of signs," as Guibert says. Not wanting to disappoint his parents, who cannot accept the fact that their son is blind,

Kipa develops an elaborate mnemonic system in order to recognize the things – a giraffe, a church, a construction crane – they point out to him: "Il établit lui-même secrètement un système pour les reconnaître, mémoire de signes au croisement des odeurs et des sons, des échos, des vibrations" (*Av.*, 48) ("He himself secretly devised a system to recognize them, a memory-bank of signals produced by the interplay of smells and sounds, echoes, vibrations" [*Bl.*, 35; trans. alt.]). But it is Taillegueur who is most often associated with memory. For example, it is he who possesses the collective memory of the history of the blind, a memory that he seeks to share with Josette: "quelle mémoire as-tu de notre empire ...?" (*Av.*, 111) ("what memories have you of our empire ...?" [*Bl.*, 92]). And when he plots to kill Robert, Taillegueur follows him around the institute, "noting and memorizing areas of easy circulation" (*Av.*, 126; *Bl.*, 105). It is therefore all the more ironic that his death should be caused by a momentary lapse of memory when he forgets that the auditorium is asymmetrical in shape; the flash of false memory that makes him certain he can take five more steps in one direction proves fatal.

But it is to Robert that we return. While he is not as gifted for music as Josette, he is nonetheless able to learn and remember tunes:

> il lui suffisait de lire une fois, de la main gauche, sur la partition aux points saillants, la partie de la main droite, de la jouer aussitôt et d'enchaîner de la main droite avec la partie gauche pour les mêler et les mémoriser, par phrases courtes de quatre ou cinq mesures. (*Av.*, 54)

> with his left hand he only had to read once the score for the right hand, on the raised points of the music, in order to play it straight off and to proceed with the right hand to decipher the score for the left hand so as to memorize and mingle them in short phrases of four or five measures. (*Bl.*, 40-1)

Here memory serves Robert well, even though he doesn't like the piano. As a result, he deliberately makes mistakes, feigning forgetfulness! As with Taillegueur, memory does not always work, not just because we are prone to forget, but also because there are times when memory cannot replace sight. The most pathetic example of this took place when Robert was a young boy. Seeking to see himself in a mirror, he tried to reconstitute his image by memorizing a series of partial reflections:

> Une fois, quand il était enfant, il avait essayé de déchiffrer son visage, par un formidable effort de mémoire, comme un peintre au souvenir d'une figure défunte dont il lui faut reconstituer les bribes: mais sa tête avait tant et tant de fois roulé sur elle-même, devant le miroir, et de plus en plus vite, comme la mécanique endiablée d'un planétarium dont toutes les lucarnes, sauf une, seraient obstruées, au point de se cogner la tête, à toute volée, contre la glace, se rompant le cou. (*Av.*, 19)

> Once, when he was a child, he had attempted to decipher his features by a formidable feat of memory, as a painter recalls a forgotten face that must be reconstituted from a few scant recollections; but his head had rolled round and round in its orbit so many times in front of the looking glass, ever faster and faster, like the mechanism of an out-of-control planetarium all of whose skylights but one are blocked, that in the end he had flung his head full tilt against the mirror and broken his neck. (*Bl.*, 8)

The passage recalls several in *Vice*, notably those describing the broken planetarium and the man whose head was larger than his body, although this time Guibert stops just short of the fantastic. Forever fascinated by images, Robert attempts the impossible: to see with his eyes, or rather with his memory's eye. It is an ingenious attempt, but it is to no avail, and this would-be Narcissus almost dies in the process.

Dream images are much more satisfactory; whether recounted in the third or first person, they bear witness to Robert's active night life. Here the images become much more vivid as though we were seeing what is actually reflected in the mirrors of the subterranean cave. For instance, in the first dream that we learn about, Robert rides a horse, is accosted by a brigand, escapes, gets thrown off his mount, and finally arrives at a castle. As blind in his dream as he is in real life, Robert strikes his forehead on the walls of castle, but he soon regains his senses and is able to avoid the moat and negotiate the drawbridge. Eventually he meets the castle's inhabitant, an angel with black wings who predicts his future – he will die in Venice – before disappearing.

His second dream, which Robert describes to Josette in the penultimate chapter, begins with an image of light that gives Robert his sight. This leads into a narrative about a reception held for the institute's benefactors – they wear name tags indicating how much money they have given to help the blind – and ends with the description of a child sleeping on a slide, "un enfant s'était endormi sur le toboggan, la chute des lattes épousant parfaitement celle de son dos" (*Av.*, 137) ("a child had fallen asleep on the slide, the curve of its wood perfectly accommodating his back" (*Bl.*, 115; trans. alt]). As Robert points out to Josette, she is nowhere in the dream, which is itself prophetic, for in the last chapter she is eaten up by a monster in the basement. Guibert gives no explanation why Robert is still in an institute for the blind if he is not blind, but it is not difficult to decode the entire dream sequence as a lead-in to the image of the sleeping child that ends the chapter. As such, it conjures up images of other couples formed by an adult and a child. The boy in the dream is as much the child Robert and Josette never had as he is a younger incarnation of Kipa. From the initial dream image of light to that of the sleeping child over whom Robert stands protective guard, the entire chapter is a vision of a fairyland where people dance beneath illuminated garlands, a dreamed-of paradise that stands in sharp contrast both to the real institute and the nightmarish prediction according to which Robert is destined to die in Venice.

WORDS AND THINGS

Des aveugles provides us with a mini-course on the evolution of language. For example, the most simple kind of communication takes the form of mimicry, as when Taillegueur imitates an owl:

> il aimait entendre les cris des garçons, le bruit lancinant de leurs pas qui tournaient en rond, leurs chuchotements, et leurs échauffourées, leurs cavalcades, les hurlements de ceux qu'on prenait plaisir à brimer, il se ressouvenait de jeunesses qu'il n'avait pas eues, il était en train d'inventer celle du pensionnat, au cas où, un jour, un de ses mensonges l'amènerait à devoir la raconter. Du haut de son deuxième étage, avec son sifflet, il imitait le bruit de la chouette ... (*Av.*, 99)

> he liked to hear the boys' shouts, the piercing sound of their feet pounding around, their whisperings and their scuffles, their races, the howls of those who were favorite butts of practical jokes, he would recall youthful experiences he had never known, he was busy inventing the one about boarding school, in case one day one of his lies led him to tell it. From his second floor lookout he would imitate the sound of an owl with his whistle ... (*Bl.*, 81; trans. alt.)

In this passage, which anticipates Taillegueur's brief encounter with "his" Kipa, the young man attracts the attention of blind youths by whistling at them. He then graces them with a wad of his spit. It seems fitting that it should be Taillegueur, the character most in touch with his origins, who should resort to mimicry. In doing so, he reenacts not just the story of other blind people across history, but also the history of human language and indeed prehuman communication itself.

Another old form of communication takes place in the sandbox where first Josette and Robert and later Josette and Taillegueur leave written messages for each other in the wet sand. As Guibert says, "Des motifs simples furent dessinés. Puis, au cours des ans, l'exploration mutuelle prenant des formes différentes, des orgies abstraites comme des géométries apparurent et disparurent dans le sable" (*Av.*, 63) ("Simple patterns were designed. Then, as the years went by, mutual exploration took on different forms, and abstract orgies like geometric shapes appeared and disappeared in the sand" (*Bl.*, 48]). It is not difficult to interpret this orgy of activity as a kind of abstract sand sculpture or even a form of primitive hieroglyphics; in either case, the characters in the sand represent the writing of the novel or just plain writing in general. Later on, Josette and Taillegueur agree on a similar form of communication. After she explains how a T can represent the trampoline on which they have sex, or an arch of triumph, a pair of shorts, Taillegueur's reaction demonstrates his enthusiasm: "We'll have to extend the system" (*Av.*, 106; *Bl.*, 88). No doubt if he and Josette had continued their affair long enough, they would have had occasion to reinvent the entire history of writing from the Ancient Egyptians down to the present!

At the time when *Des aveugles* was published in 1985 most writing still took the form of printed letters, *le noir*, as it is called in the institute. While the blind have access to Braille, in *Des aveugles* they show little love for reading: "Ils méprisaient décidément la lecture qui était, disaient-ils, faite pour les voyants, et qui devenait un labeur sous leurs doigts, une longue énigme hostile et ricanante ..." (*Av.*, 35) ("They quite definitely despised reading, they said it was for the sighted, and it became hard labor under their fingertips, a long, hostile, and mocking enigma" (*Bl.*, 23; trans. alt.]). Robert and Josette, for example, never read, preferring to "watch" television or horror movies on video. No wonder when one considers that a dictionary in Braille is ten times the length of the version for sighted people! In the library of the institute, "les manutentionnaires en blouses grises poussaient des brouettes pleines de livres gaufrés et ondulés, reliés au gros fil" (*Av.*, 37–8) ("the assistants in gray overalls pushed trolleys laden with embossed and corrugated books, bound with coarse string" (*Bl.*, 25]). In a scene reminiscent of some medieval monastery, writing appears less as a lost art than a cumbersome burden. Every person living in the institute has a little machine with six keys that allows him or her to write in Braille, but as Guibert points out, more often than not the machine remains unused.

The drama of language, for the blind, is that most of the words used "represented things they had never held in their hands" (*Bl.*, 23), just as Diderot points out in his *Letter on the Blind*. I believe this explains why Guibert has included rare words and descriptions of complicated spaces that are hard to visualize: he is attempting to give sighted readers an experience of what it is like to be blind. But if words refer to things, they can also refer to each other. Here blind and sighted readers are on a level playing field, for the wordplay that is an integral part of the text's economy is equally perceptible, or conversely, invisible, to all since it is a question of actualizing the potentialities programmed into the text. Some examples of wordplay are straightforward, and it is these that alert readers to the existence of more "subterranean" effects. For example, when Josette wants to mock Robert, she calls him Bébert. He retaliates by calling her Zézette. Taillegueur points out to Josette that his name is Tiger, which goes well with the color red associated with him. Some of the sighted, *voyants* in French, are also *voyeurs*, such as the narrator. Josette buys a supposedly white mink coat to please Taillegueur. In fact, just as the mice were pink or gray, the coat is anything but white since it is green. More important, mink is *vison* in French, *vision* minus an *i*!

Such wordplay is reminiscent of the French New Novel of the 1960s and 1970s, as well as the fiction of Georges Bataille, especially his seminal *Histoire de l'oeil*. But it also recalls the work of Raymond Roussel, about whom Foucault wrote a book. Based on elaborate systems of anagrams and verbal transformations, Roussel's writing was explained by the author himself in a posthumously published work entitled *Comment j'ai écrit certains de mes livres*. Foucault discusses this metatextual work in the first chapter of his book: "Finally giving us the key, the last text, which is like a first rereading of the work, has a double function: to open up in their most exterior architecture certain texts, and also to show that they and the others require a series of keys, each one of which opens its own box ..." (*Raymond Roussel*, 14–15). As it happens, a key figures prominently in the last chapter of *Des aveugles*. When the monster is about to eat Josette, she offers it a key as a kind of peace offering, although to no avail:

> Josette n'avait plus que sa clef, qu'elle tendit vers l'animal. Mais c'était trop tard: elle fut éblouie par une tache verte et grise, horriblement fétide, et geignante, qui la propulsait vers le ciel tout en la broyant, et la déchirait, la labourait, mais en même temps l'aimait et la mangeait. Le lagodon, en effet, l'avala tout entière. (*Av.*, 141)
>
> Josette had nothing left but her key, which she held out to the animal. But it was too late: she was dazzled by a gray-green splash, horribly foul-smelling and whimpering, that propelled her into the sky as it crushed, rent and pounded her, but at the same time loved her and devoured her. The *lagodon*, in fact, swallowed her whole. (*Bl.*, 119)

Theorists have taught us, among other things, not to feel sorry for characters in novels, and in this case I believe they are right, although for the wrong reasons. We need not feel pity for Josette: after all, in Guibert, being eaten is more of an act of love than anything else. And we also know that Guibert's monsters are kindly creatures, and this one clearly loves Josette. But that is not all, for I propose to read the monster as the key to the novel. Like Roussel, Guibert provides us with a "solution" to his text, although in this case the key is to be found within the confines of the work itself. As Richard Smith has pointed out, *lagodon* is an anagram of *gondola*. One could add that the name of the monster recalls *lagoon* (*lagune* in French), another word associated with Venice. Smith also underlines the Flaubertian intertext of Josette's demise, comparing it to the apotheosis in "La légende de saint Julien l'Hospitalier," a text that greatly impressed the young Guibert. The death of Josette, as she is propulsed through the air towards the sky, provides the novel with a fantastic end.

Robert's death, as we have seen, is foretold in a prophecy within a dream; appropriately enough for this dishwasher, his nightmare conjures up images of dirty cold water, as his body is supposedly destined to be dumped into a canal in Venice. A closer look at Robert's first dream, linked to Josette's demise by the Venetian theme, reveals that he will be exploited by a mean *gondolier*. The gondolier can be interpreted as a older and much nastier version of Kipa, just as the sleeping child in the second dream can be interpreted as a younger and more innocent incarnation of the same character. We know that the first dream is a nightmare that represents some of Robert's worst fears, such as running into the walls of buildings, exploitation, death, and finally expulsion from a safe place. Being thrown out of the gondola is like being expelled from the institute, as will inevitably happen to him when he reaches a certain age. And if Kipa becomes a nasty gondolier, then Robert will have truly lost his keeper.

Taillegueur's death is the only more or less realistic one in the novel. After his funeral, which is probably based on Foucault's, he is buried in the earth, a fitting end for such an earthy character. How is Taillegueur's death related to the others? Earth, air, and water, to be sure, provide a symbolic link. But there is more, for once again the Venetian theme appears. In Robert's dream, the gondola in the dream prophecy is described as a *nacelle*, a small boat with oars:

> [Robert] la gagnerait [his livelihood] en mendiant, en chantant de tristes romances, rançonné par un gondolier qui lui ferait chèrement payer sa place, debout au-dessus des amoureux, ses os humides tanguant en équilibre sur la funèbre *nacelle*. (*Av.*, 121; my emphasis)

> [Robert] would gain a living by begging, by singing romances, be fleeced by a gondolier who would make him pay through the nose for riding standing up behind the lovers, his humid bones swaying as he kept his balance on the funeral craft. (*Bl.*, 101)

The word *nacelle* is appropriate here; indeed, if one looks up *gondolier* in *Le Robert*, one of the most complete of French dictionaries, the meaning of the word is illustrated by a quotation from Chateaubriand's *Mémoires d'outre-tombe* in which a gondolier pilots a gondola or *nacelle*. Therefore, it is not surprising that when we later come to the description of Taillegueur's funeral, we read the following:

> et quand parfois d'un même accord [the funeral procession] s'interrompait, le frottement léger du bois contre les épaulettes, que des crampes faisaient rouler, puis la dégelée des courroies qui laissaient glisser la *nacelle* au-dessus du vide, cela faisait penser au jeu lancinant d'une bouée contre une coque ravi [*sic*] par la dégringolade d'acier de l'ancre quand on la mouille ... (*Av.*, 133; my emphasis)

> and, when sometimes of a common accord they stopped for a moment, the rubbing of wood against their shoulder-pieces could be lightly heard as cramps made them fidget; then the release of the leather straps permitting the coffin to slide into the empty grave made a sound like a buoy scraping against a hull and being ravished by the steel torrent of an anchor chain when it is dropped ... (*Bl.*, 111; trans. alt.)

This time the skiff is metaphorical since it refers to the coffin in which Taillegueur's body is encased. Lost in the translation, the mention of a boat triggers, generates, and justifies the rest of the maritime imagery, which appears arbitrary in English.

The word *nacelle*, which is quite rare in this sense, is derived from a diminutive for the Latin *navis*, "boat," a word that has also given *nef*, "boat," or "nave." Foucault used both words to describe the ship of fools that predates the great enclosure of the seventeenth century when eccentrics and other supposedly crazy people were locked up in hospitals. I described the excursions of Robert and Kipa as voyages of a kind of ship of fools. And it is certainly not by chance that Taillegueur is associated with the word *nacelle*. It recalls the following sentence, for example, "C'est vers l'autre monde que part le fou sur *sa folle nacelle*; c'est de l'autre monde qu'il vient quand il débarque" (*Histoire de la folie*, 22; my emphasis) ("It is for the other world that the madman sets sail in his fools' boat; it is from the other world that he comes when he disembarks" [*Madness and Civilization*, 11]). But why does Foucault use this particular word when the more usual expression is *nef des fous*? (The word *nef* is used three times in the same section of his monumental work, whereas *nacelle* occurs four times in the space of a few pages.) Apart from the poetic sound of *nacelle*, I believe that Foucault chose to use it because the word can designate a cradle (*berceau en nacelle*), or a bed (*lit en nacelle* or *nacelle* by itself). In a note omitted in the English translation, Foucault draws a parallel between the "le fou sur sa folle nacelle" and an abandoned child, "l'enfant interdit et maudit, enfermé dans une nacelle et confié aux flots qui le conduisent dans un autre monde" (ibid.) (the child, banned and cursed, is enclosed in his cradle and entrusted to the waves that will take him to another world). The "fools," like the unwanted child, are at once protected in their ship and condemned to the vagaries of the waves and the currents.[14]

I believe that Guibert uses the same word for many of the same reasons. A *nacelle* protects one from the outside world and from the foul night air. Unlike the walls of a prison or an asylum, freedom is associ-

---

14 In *Le Protocole compassionnel* one can find a sentence that echoes both Foucault's description of the *nacelle* and Guibert's use of the image in *Des aveugles*: "J'aime les petits cercueils près du corps, fragiles comme des embarcations incertaines, qui voguent sur des mers vides" (*PC*, 122) ("I like those little coffins just big enough for the corpse, fragile as unseaworthy vessels drifting on empty oceans" [*CP*, 105]). Interestingly enough, his friend Gustave anticipates a clandestine ceremony for Hervé's burial "with the complicity and the big arms of Taillegueur" (ibid.)!

ated with it, for while a bed, a cradle, and even a nacelle (in English, as in French, the word is used to refer to the basket of a hot-air balloon) contain and protect a human body, they do not emprison it. There could be no greater homage that Guibert could pay his former master than by describing the burial of the most Foucauldian of his characters – Taillegueur shares his model's encyclopedism and activism – in a metaphorical *nacelle*. It is as though Taillegueur were doubly protected, both by the thing and by the word used to describe it figuratively.

We are now able to take better stock of the ending of Guibert's novel. As we have seen, all three deaths are associated explicity or implicity with the image of a boat, since even the monster is an anagram of *gondola*. Josette will be as protected as Taillegueur, the only difference being that she is within the insides of a living form that is the result of a series of verbal transpositions that link it to a protective *nacelle*, the crucial link in the chain of words that joins the three passages. And as Richard Smith points out in "Humour et politique dans *Des aveugles*," all three are linked by the Venetian theme. Venice is associated, to be sure, with gondolas and other boats, lagoons, water, but also homoerotic desire. After all, in *L'Image fantôme* did not Hervé dress his mother up in a hat to make her look like Tadzio, the beautiful adolescent in *Death in Venice*? Whether it be Thomas Mann's novella, Visconti's film, or a video such as *Voyage à Venise* by France's premier director of homoerotic films, Jean-Daniel Cadinot, Venice has often been associated with same-sex desire.[15] As well as death, Venice is also associated with the disguises, the masks, and the tricks that accompagny the carnival, all of which make us think of various sequences of *Des aveugles*.

Thus we are better able to take measure of how the creative process works in Guibert's writing. Based as much on productive intertextuality as on creative wordplay, his novel is not "just" a fantastic tale. It is also a well-crafted textual artifact into which he has carefully incorporated

---

15 Cadinot's video, translated as *Carnival in Venice*, was released in 1986. Synchroneity plays odd tricks: did Guibert see an advance copy of this film in which outlandish costumes play such a large part, or is it a question of two creative minds working independently with similar images? It is also possible that Guibert may have heard about the carnival in Musterlingen that Foucault witnessed in 1952: "It was the custom for inmates [of the psychiatric hospital] to spend much of the spring making large, ornate masks to be worn in a procession" (Macey, *The Lives of Michel Foucault*, 61). Athough Foucault's own attempts to film the procession failed, Georges Verdeaux did make a short film of it. More than twenty years later Foucault was to speak of this "atrocious" spectacle in an interview (*Dits et écrits*, 3:62).

numerous allusions, a winking of the authorial eye, so to speak, to other writers. If we return once more to Robert's dreams, we can see that they must be read together, for as much as the first dream represents a hellish view and a watery end, the second one provides an Edenic perspective with an open-ended future. Protection is provided by Kipa or his dream substitute in the space of a virtual *nacelle* represented, for example, by the tandem bicycle on which the two friends take rides. Robert and Kipa figure the quintessential couple; they represent *en abîme* and therefore stand in for other pairs (of writers): Roussel and Foucault, but also Diderot and Guibert, Flaubert and Guibert, Bataille and Guibert, Roussel and Guibert, as well as Foucault and Guibert.

Chapter Five

Searching for Vincent

> Penché sur lui, et aussi bas que possible ..., je lui dis: "tu es le plus bel enfant de la terre," il me répondit: "et toi tu es le plus bel adulte de la terre et de la gadoue."
>
> *Voyage avec deux enfants*, 40–1
>
> Leaning over him, and as softly as possible ..., I said to him: "you are the most beautiful child on earth," he answered me: "And you are the most gorgeous adult on earth, and on muck."

Among Hervé Guibert's many obsessions was that of returning to the same characters, putting them on "stage" in more than one text. Sometimes the character's name changes from one work to another: for example, the reader recognizes T. or Thierry, as he is called in some texts, under the name of Jules in *À l'ami qui ne m'a pas sauvé la vie* and *Le Protocole compassionnel*. But this kind of "transfer" from life to writing was not new in Guibert's approach to writing. He never attempted to hide how he used (or abused, as some would have it) reality: "In order to write fiction I need a pedestal of truth. On this pedestal I like to let flow particles of lies, like a transfusion, a surgical stitch. Like the editing of two different images in a film, I like to make people think there is only one image" (Interview with Gaudemar, "Les aveux permanents d'Hervé Guibert"). I do not intend to follow every meandering path of reality in Guibert's fiction but rather to examine how the adventure of writing leads to one of his characters reappearing in texts that span his *oeuvre*, from almost the very beginning of his creative output to the final blank of death. Vincent appears, for the first time, in *Voyage avec deux enfants* (1982) and in *Le Pro-*

tocole compassionnel, the penultimate novel published during Guibert's lifetime, nine years later. Guibert himself wondered about the status of this reappearing character in his works: "Qu'est-ce que c'était? Une passion? Un amour? Une obsession érotique? Ou une de mes inventions?" (*FV*, 8) (What was it? Passion? Love? An erotic obsession? Or one of my inventions?). No doubt the answer to these questions is that Vincent is all of the above, and probably something more as well.

BIRTH OF A CHARACTER

Voyage avec deux enfants represents his first attempt at what was to become his favorite mode of writing – fictionalized autobiography or *autofiction*. *La Mort propagande* and *L'Image fantôme* were closer to autobiography, whereas *Voyage avec deux enfants* is at once a story invented from scratch *and* a travel tale based on a real trip to Morocco. The first part of the novel describes the journey as Guibert imagines it before it takes place, the second "what really happened," and the third narrates a kind of epilogue, bringing the characters back to Paris. Vincent is mentioned for the first time in the first part, which "normally" would give him a fictional quality from the outset. On the other hand, since his appearance is tied to a diary entry, the reader is tempted to consider him "real":

> Le soir de notre rencontre, et alors que rien ne pouvait laisser prévoir notre voyage, j'avais écrit dans mon journal: "des deux enfants j'irai vers celui dont le charme est le moins évident, et je baiserai le naevus de son oeil, sa paupière droite qui ferme mal, toutes les taches de ses hanches et de sa nuque." (*Voy.*, 28)

> The evening of our meeting, and while nothing could have led one to foresee our trip, I wrote in my diary: "of the two children, I will go towards the one whose charm is the least obvious, and I will kiss the naevus of his eye, his right eyelid which doesn't close properly, all the freckles of his thighs and the nape of his neck."

Thus Vincent, who will not be named until seventy pages later, makes his first appearance in the works of Hervé Guibert via a quotation taken from his diary if we are to believe him. It should be made clear from the outset that neither of the so-called children in *Voyage avec deux enfants* is a child: the fact that Guibert prefers to use this word is in itself an indication of the fictional status of a book that poses as a "real" travel diary, at least in part. The two young males are fake children, since both are adolescents, as becomes increasingly clear. By comparing a later book with Guibert's first, one can determine Vincent's age in the *Voyage*: sixteen (*PC*, 49). Typically Guibert leads us astray regarding the age of the teenagers, thereby accentuating the gap between them and their adult companions, whereas he does not seek to camouflage his own feelings. Already one can see how closely linked sexual desire and writing are: a strong desire for "the one whose charm is the least obvious" is implicitly coupled with the desire to inscribe this attraction, first in the diary, and then in the novel whose genesis is told here. The diary extract itself textualizes Vincent in the form of a memory, as will be the case also in the third part of the novel where the autodiegetic narrator describes how much he misses the "parrot child." But the rest of the novel's first part is a kind of futuristic novel of proleptic fragments narrating a dreamed-of and fantasized trip to Morocco. The entries of this fictional diary – fictional to the second degree, as is so common in Guibert – correspond to the dates of the supposedly real trip described later, in the second part, so that the two parts function as a diptych of contrasts:

> J'ai pris huit feuilles en haut desquelles j'ai marqué une des dates de la semaine prochaine, comme des cases qu'il me reste à remplir, en prospection du voyage ... Ce sera la première partie du livre: un premier voyage se déroulera d'ici, de ce bureau calme qui donne sur ces maisons blanches et grises, sur cette grue qui grince un peu en pivotant, parmi mes livres, mes dossiers, dans ma quiétude, dans mon isolement. La seconde partie du livre sera le journal du vrai voyage, la palinodie se fera dans des alternances de lumière crue et d'ombre fraîche, dans le bruit, et dans la proximité bruissante des enfants, leurs rires, leur odeur ... si la première partie doit être le récit du plaisir, la seconde partie menace déjà d'être le récit de la souffrance. (*Voy.*, 32–3)

> In anticipation of the trip I took eight sheets of paper, at the top of which I put the dates of next week, like empty boxes that remained to be filled ... This will be the first part of the book: the first journey will start here, from this calm study that looks out on these white and gray buildings, at that crane that creaks slightly when it moves, among my books, my files, in my tranquillity and isolation. The second part of the book will be the diary of the real trip, the recantation will take place between harsh light alternating with cool shadows, amid the clamor and the noisy

proximity of the children, their laughter, their odors ... if the first part is to be a tale of pleasure, the second one already threatens to become a tale of suffering.

Comparing the two parts of the *Voyage*, one is immediately struck by the difference in styles. As much as the first part drips with a heavy, sensual orientalism, the second part is the banal narration of the excursions of four travelers, their nights in various hotels, the games of the so-called children, and so forth. In the first part of the novel, however, the narrator throws himself blithely into the writing of a transgressive text – transgressive not only because he is writing without the knowledge of T., the other loved one, but also because he is inventing, fabulating without the prop and support of reality as had been his practice up until then.[1]

Scarcely has the ungainly child entered the space of Guibert's new writing style when the character is imagined to have fallen sick, bitten by an insect or by a dead person according to the sorcerer whom the adult travelers consult. The old man tells them that if the "parrot child" is to get well, a dance must be performed by the other child in front of a cobra and in the presence of the other travelers (the two adults and the sick child) in order to cleanse Vincent's body of an evil spirit. In a passage reminiscent of another dance before a snake, in Flaubert's *Salammbô*, Guibert eroticizes the body of the other "child" and the effect on the snake. The passage ends with a double ejaculation: the semen that will make the snake go crazy, and then its spurting blood, since it must be killed before it strangles the orgasmic adolescent:

> Petit à petit, à chaque note, à chaque souffle produit par la gorge de l'enfant, la bête fondait sur son corps, elle devenait plus liquide, plus chaude, elle s'écoulait, le frôlait, léchait plus particulièrement son ventre, la fente de ses fesses. L'enfant dansait dans sa stupeur, il cinglait l'espace de gestes cabalistiques dont le sorcier résolvait au fur et à mesure les équations. Alors on vit la fontaine de l'enfant s'agiter toute seule et cracher sur son ventre trois quatre jets blancs laiteux, mais la première semence d'un enfant rendait dément le naja à deux têtes ... Lorsqu'ils virent la semence jaillir, avant même qu'on leur en donne l'ordre, et alors que la bête encore molle ne l'avait pas encore reniflé, les

---

[1] Although T. will figure as Vincent's foil, Jean-Pierre Boulé's conclusion that "*Voyage avec deux enfants* is above all a book about 'T.'" (*Hervé Guibert: Voices of the Self,* 97) seems somewhat of an exaggeration.

deux gardes Nubiens dégainèrent leur sabre et sur l'enfant décapitèrent la bête, puis cisaillèrent son étreinte jalouse et avide autour des jambes, autour du ventre, c'est une seconde danse que produisaient les Nubiens aux pieds de l'enfant sur lequel le sang bleu glacé jaillissait en épousant la semence tiède. (*Voy.*, 57–8)

Little by little, at each musical note, at each breath produced by the heaving breast of the child, the beast's body seemed to melt, it became more liquid, warmer, it flowed as it lightly touched his body, licking his stomach, the crack in his butt. The child danced in a stupor, he whipped the space around him with cabalistic gestures the equations of which the sorcerer solved in sequence. Then we saw the child's fountain burst forth, spitting on his stomach three or four milkish spurts, but the first semen of the child was already driving the two-headed cobra crazy ... When they saw the semen burst out, even before the order was given, and before the still soft beast could even smell it, the two Nubian guards drew out their swords, decapitating the snake on the child, then, chiseling its jealous, eager grip away from the legs and stomach, the Nubians enact a second dance at the feet of the child on whom the frozen blue blood shot forth and mingled with the warm sperm.

The narrator projects first on the snake and then on the Nubian slaves the desire he feels, not for the beautiful child, but for the other one, the one with whom he will try to make love on the real Good Friday, whereas the dance with the cobra takes place on the fictitious Good Friday. But the second scene is barely erotic, and certainly not *jouissif* or blissful in writerly terms. The fictionalization of an absent Vincent, of a Vincent dreamed or fantasized, or even of his metonymic substitute – not his twin, just a fellow traveler (*coéquipier*) as Guibert calls him in the novel's dedication – must take a back seat to banal reality. In any case, the travel tale continues, the plan to write is realized, although the style is completely different from the Flaubertian pastiche of the first part. Things begin to change in the hard light of Morocco; for example, physical appearance and gender are transformed, for now it is the more or less chaste "child" who appears more handsome, while at the same time he is feminized.

Hervé falls in love with the boy who said he didn't want "to sacrifice his virginity in the arms of a man" (*Voy.*, 93). But on the narrator's return to Paris the beloved becomes "un venin, un sortilège qu'il était impossible d'extraire, ou même d'affaiblir" (*Voy.*, 115) (a poison, a piece of witchcraft it was impossible to extract or even to lessen). The last part of the novel is the narrative counterpart to the first, in particular the description of the fictitious bite and the double orgasm of semen and blood, as the narrator falls victim to the spell of the man-child whom he calls both his son and his daugther. The second part of the novel is supposed to tell the "real" trip (see figure 14), but it would have little or no meaning without the other two parts of this novel. This is made clear at the end of the book by the description, *mise en abîme*, of a letter Vincent sends Hervé. The letter describes another journey, a short trip taken by the teenager to the Paris suburbs. Suddenly and *in extremis*, all becomes clear: Vincent is not exactly a child, whatever he may look like. He smokes, drives a car, thinks about having a trade. Hervé falls in love but the "virgin child" (*Voy.*, 50) was always already an invention, a fiction, a kind of lie. The moments of greatest sexual desire correspond to two absences: the literary fantasy of anticipation in the first part of the novel and the dream delirium of memory in the last. In order for writing and love to work, the loved one must be unavailable, off stage. This absence/presence which is at the basis of all desire – one thinks of how Proust's narrator gets to the point of wishing his mother would come and give him his good-night kiss as late as possible so that the waiting game and desire itself can be prolonged almost but not quite infinitely[2] – is intimately linked with the birth of the writing project in Guibert, just as it is in Proust. In *Voyage avec deux enfants* the homoerotic games of the narrator with the child, so called, but in fact an adolescent, are less significant in and of themselves than is the fact that the writer loses his textual virginity, whence the fear of T.'s jealousy. The young novelist – he was only twenty-seven at the time – is both drawn to and repulsed by the writing of fiction as though he were already fully aware of all the dangers posed by writing just beyond the pale of the very reality without which there can be no autobiographically inspired text. A great love has been born, and this love verges on insanity as the narrator fictionalizes – in the first, in the second degree – that which already passes for a fantastic fabrication. As lucid as Phaedra in her folly, the narrator claims to be equally afraid of writing and the madness to which it is linked (*Voy.*, 62).

2 "[C]e bonsoir que j'aimais tant, j'en arrivais à souhaiter qu'il vînt le plus tard possible, à ce que se prolongeât le temps de répit où maman n'était pas encore venue" (Proust, *À la recherche du temps perdu*, I:13) ("I reached the point of hoping that this good night which I loved so much would come as late as possible, so as to prolong the time of respite during which Maman would not yet have appeared" [*Remembrance of Things Past*, 1:13–14]).

A DRAMATIC RETURN

The publication in 1994 and 1995 of three works written some ten years earlier ("L'ours" in *La Piqûre d'amour*, *Lettres d'Égypte: du Caire à Assouan, 19..*, and *Vole mon dragon*) confirmed how interrelated Guibert's books are. The extent to which the character of Vincent was caught up in the creative process of Guibert's writing became clearer also.

In "L'ours," one of the rare texts where Guibert speaks about his own books, he describes the genesis of his second novel, *Les Lubies d'Arthur*. This picaresque tale, which owes more to *The Golden Legend* than to Jules Verne, relates the adventures of Bichon, a young man, and Arthur, his adult soul mate. As Guibert says: "It was the first time since the fiction of the first part of *Voyage avec deux enfants* that I had invented a story" (*PA*, 143). As is so often the case with Guibert, a writing project is linked with a desire to leave the city, to go on a trip with the blessed "child" – this time to Spain – since Paris is associated with sterility and a life without love: "Je me retrouvai sans amour et me demandai si cette activité de l'écriture, à laquelle je l'avais tant lié [l'enfant], n'était pas morte à jamais" (*PA*, 139) (I was without love and wondered if the activity of writing to which I had so closely associated the child was forever dead). Another incarnation of Vincent, Bichon is dressed in women's clothes by his friend Arthur and one day he even finds himself pregnant! Once again, the character of the young man plays the role of muse. In *Voyage avec deux enfants*, Guibert lamented the fact that his notebook became an obstacle between him and Vincent; this time, however, he is determined not to repeat the same error: "I knew that this time writing could not come between us" (*PA*, 140). But the presence of the so-called child puts the writer in the writing mood: "The child had put me back in the mood to write ..." (*PA*, 142). Again, childhood – or what passes for it – and creativity are linked, for it is Vincent who first realizes that his friend's feverish note-taking will eventually lead to a new book.

The theme of travel is associated with Vincent once again in *Lettres d'Égypte*. This short work is made up of letters written by Guibert to his friends in Paris. Although the year of the trip is not indicated anywhere in the book, external evidence indicates it took place in 1984 (cf. "Repères biographiques" in *Photo.*, n.p.). Once again the thin line between fiction and reality tends to disappear, since the letters remain unmailed. They knit together, forming a collection of impressions, memories, and anxious thoughts that are to be read against the backdrop of the Egyptian countryside seen in the photographs of Hans Georg Berger that make up the other part of this photo-text. The journey to Egypt of a writer and a photographer is, of course, a kind of postmodern reenactment of the journey of Gustave Flaubert and his friend Maxime du Camp to Egypt, a journey in which homoeroticism also played a role. As one can imagine, one of Guibert's letters is addressed to Vincent. In it, the writer describes a diadem, seen in a Cairo museum, that was made for another young man, Tutankhamen. Since he cannot give Vincent the actual diadem, Guibert can only write about it: "Seul m'importe, désormais, qu'il soit fait tien par mon imagination ..." (*Let. É.*, 49) (All I want is that henceforth it become yours through my imagination). There are several intertextual echoes of *Voyage avec deux enfants*. For the second time, Vincent is associated with a country in Africa; in other texts it is Morocco, the Congo, and Mali. (Africa incarnates an intriguing mystery for Guibert, an unreality similar to that Barthes associated with being in love, and an omnipresent danger even before the AIDS-theme kindles a new fear of the continent.) In *Voyage avec deux enfants* Hervé wrote about crowning Vincent his son and described him as a "child king" (*Voy.*, 78). Bit by bit, text by text, we see how the figure of the other is constructed in Guibert's writing, whether he be perceived as a child (in contrast with the adult), a king (as opposed to the commoner writer), or an absent friend. Vincent continues to represent the person on whom desire fixates, the unattainable other, the reward that threatens to remain forever beyond the lover's grasp.

Guibert's frustration with Vincent's refusal to allow himself to be "possessed" is thematized next in the play *Vole mon dragon*. We know that Guibert worked with Patrice Chéreau on the scenario of *L'Homme blessé*, for which they received a César, France's equivalent of an Oscar, in 1984. Guibert adapted his novel *Des aveugles* for a stage version produced by Philippe Adrien.[3] Apparently, the last project that Guibert worked on was a film based on the same novel (Mazureck, 23). But apart from his early work "La pièce d'Oedipe," written when he was seventeen, *Vole mon dragon* is his only play to which we have access. Finished in 1987, it was not published until 1994. (I have learned of no stagings of this play to date.) Now that most of Guibert's works have been pub-

---

3 Richard Smith has addressed the links between *Des aveugles* and *Fou de Vincent*, such as the fact that Robert, like Vincent, buys a brightly colored biker's suit, as well as their patent lack of realism. But Taillegueur also presents certain similarities with Vincent, for example, his ability to give massages and his freckled body ("Humour et politique dans *Des aveugles*, 21-2).

lished, we can appreciate how important is the process of intertextual allusion and citation. For example, in order to be understood fully, *Vole mon dragon* – the title means "Make me come" (*VD*, 59) – must be read along with *Mauve le vierge* and *Fou de Vincent.*

In *Vole mon dragon* the role of the Young Man corresponds to Vincent, and that of the Man to Guibert. According to the list of characters, the former is between sixteen and eighteen, the latter thirty. Although the couple is somewhat older, the age gap remains constant. Inevitably, the one who used to be described as the child has become a young man. And for the first time, a clear and evident atmosphere of danger surrounds the Vincent-like character. For example, the two characters meet in front of the window of an arms merchant, and the Young Man will lose two fingers in an accident.

Once again, writing intervenes between these two new incarnations of Vincent and his friend. But this time, the stakes are higher since writing is no longer an activity that distracts or diverts: now it is portrayed as a potentially poisonous *pharmakon* that can be used to reply to the other's indifference, whether feigned or real:

> LE JEUNE HOMME, *en jouant.* Qu'est-ce que tu as écrit? (*Il parvient enfin à lire:*) "Hymne à la pluie. Hymne au tissu. Hymne à la délicatesse." (*Il rit.*) Ils sont écrits, ces hymnes?
> L'HOMME. Non. Ils restent à écrire ...
> LE JEUNE HOMME. Quand est-ce que tu écris?
> L'HOMME. Pas tout le temps.
> LE JEUNE HOMME. Alors tu n'es pas écrivain?
> L'HOMME. Je suis écrivain comme l'animal venimeux pique, de temps à autre, quand on le provoque, quand on lui marche dessus, quand on l'attire. Le venin peut être un suc amoureux ... (*VD*, 39–40; original ellipses)

> THE YOUNG MAN, *play-acting.* What have you written? (*He finally manages to read:*) "A hymn to rain. A hymn to fabric. A hymn to delicacy." (*He laughs.*) Are they written, these hymns?
> THE MAN. No. They're to be written ...
> THE YOUNG MAN. When do you write?
> THE MAN. Not all the time.
> THE YOUNG MAN. Then you're not a writer?
> THE MAN. I'm a writer in the same way a poisonous animal bites from time to time, when you provoke it, when you step on it, when you attract it. Poison can be a lover's juice.

The intertextuality at work here is remarkable, since an almost identical passage can be found in *Fou de Vincent*:

> Voyage avec Vincent. Ces notes dans la voiture, tandis que nous fumons, que je prends sur le petit reçu de la banque:
> Hymne à la pluie.
> Hymne au tissu (je viens de palper sa cuisse à travers le pantalon).
> Hymne à la délicatesse.
> Invention de l'amour.
> Le (un) travail de la littérature: apprendre à se taire. (*FV,* 73–4)
>
> Trip with Vincent. While we smoke, I write down these notes on the little bank receipt:
> A hymn to rain.
> A hymn to fabric (I have just felt his thigh through his pants).
> A hymn to delicacy.
> Invention of love.
> The (a) work of literature: learning to keep silent.

In *Fou de Vincent* Guibert has removed both Vincent's laughter and his replies, whereas the context of the conversation – a car trip during which they both smoke grass – and the caress are not in the earlier text. In the dramatic version, by contrast, the Barthes-like aphorism about literature and silence is missing. This metatextual commentary replaces the line of dialogue in the play where the writer angrily answers the Young Man's questions by claiming to resemble a poisonous animal, one that bites. This is an intertextual echo of the bite suffered by the fantasized-about Vincent in the first part of *Voyage avec deux enfants*.

But there is more. In the last part of the same novel, the narrator wrote that Vincent "était dans le sang qui continuait de passer par le coeur un poison, un venin" (*Voy.,* 115) (was in my blood that continued to pass through my heart, a poison, a venom). The image has had a far-reaching intertextual resonance.[4] Love has become a poison, as in the

---

4 In *Vous m'avez fait former des fantômes* (1987), one of the characters tells the would-be "infantero" – the entire novel is an elaborate conceit in which children are substituted for bulls in corridas that are hardly any more grotesque than the real thing – to avoid the "mortal poison" of children's saliva and especially the look in the eyes of a child about to be put to death (*Vous,* 110–11). This passage is premonitory of Guibert's AIDS fictions, while at the same time it incorporates the early theme of love as poison: "c'est leur regard, s'il te touche au moment où tu mettras à mort l'enfant, tu es fait toi aussi,

eponymic short story of *La Piqûre d'amour*. Later, Guibert will describe his dream of sharing a needle with Vincent as the ultimate proof of love: "Je voudrais connaître le flash avant de mourir, le flash avec Vincent" (*PC*, 106) ("I'd like to experience a drug addict's rush before dying, a rush with Vincent" [*CP*, 90; trans. alt.]). If the lover has been "pricked," then he may well jab the unwilling beloved in return, the writer's "venom" taking the form not of semen but its replacement, the ink used to write the Barthes-like haikus that celebrate the other's unfeeling incomprehension. The Young Man a.k.a. Vincent must be ousted in the flesh so that writing can begin. As such, the body of the beloved plays a similar role to the photographs that block and impede the writing process in *L'Image fantôme*. And what better way to compensate for the other's absence than by taking immediate revenge in the "dangerous supplement" that constitutes writing?

FROM PARANOIA TO CANNIBALISM

Les Gangsters tells the story of Hervé's two grand-aunts who lose a large sum of money to rip-off artists masquerading as kind and thoughtful housepainters. More important is the fact that this novel is the first one in which the first-person narrator is sick. All of the subsequent novels will be written under the sign of illness, especially AIDS, although in *Le Paradis*, the last one, Guibert "lends" the syndrome to someone else. This time, it is a painful case of shingles that aggravates Hervé's dealings with his relatives, the police, Vincent, who always seems to be either absent or asleep, and, what is more, a panic fear that permeates the narration just as it will in the later novels, *L'Incognito* and, especially, *À l'ami qui ne m'a pas sauvé la vie* published a year later, after the diagnosis of the narrator's positive HIV status was confirmed.

---

il y a dans ce regard une mélancolie qui rend fou, c'est là le vrai poison, il réside bien sûr dans ces glandes qui tapissent leurs bouches, et qu'on peut aussi extraire de leurs aisselles, mais *des chimistes sont sur le point de trouver la formule d'un décapant qui parviendra à anéantir la lèpre au moment où par le relais de la salive elle se mêle à notre sang*, et la vraie peste, je te le jure, c'est le regard, ne regarde jamais un enfant quand il meurt!" (*Vous*, 111; my emphasis) (it's their gaze, if it catches you when you put a child to death, you're done for too, there is a melancholy in their gaze that can drive a man crazy, that's the real poison, it comes, of course, from glands in their mouths; it can also be extracted from their armpits, but *chemists are on the point of discovering the formula for an acid that will destroy the leprosy the moment it mixes with our blood by way of saliva*, but the real plague, I swear, is the gaze, don't ever look at a child when he is dying!).

In *Les Gangsters* the figure of Vincent still appears as a possible consolation for the many ordeals that Hervé, like a knight of old, must undergo if he is ever to become worthy of the loved one. Hence the project of another trip with Vincent, this time to the Vendée.[5] But when Hervé is able to be with his friend, he seems strangely distant, unavailable; Hervé is not at all consoled by the presence of the one so desperately sought after as a balm for his suffering body and mind. On the contrary, desire for the other has become fear of the other. For example, Hervé seems to suspect Vincent of wanting to destroy the manuscript of the new book under way ("the book's at his mercy" [*Gang.*, 103]). And at the very end of the novel, when they visit the Atlantic coast, Hervé is uncertain of the other's intentions: "je sens les mains de Vincent dans mon dos. Est-ce qu'elles me poussent ou est-ce qu'elles me caressent?" (*G*, 109) ("I feel Vincent's hands on my back. Are they pushing me [into the chasm] or are they caressing me?" [*Gang.*, 107]). On a symbolic level, this passage reveals the narrator's desire for anal penetration, for it is he who has led Vincent to the Trou du Diable as the chasm is known, even if this desire can only be articulated subtextually for the moment.

The same atmosphere of danger that permeates *Vole mon dragon* can be found in *Les Gangsters*. Hervé's desperate appeals for help or consolation are answered nastily or not at all by his friend. And even when they are together, all Vincent does is sleep! Some measure of how much things have changed since *Voyage avec deux enfants* can be understood by the way in which the theme of the child-carrying man, which continued to fascinate Guibert to very end, has been transformed. Instead of Hervé carrying a child, as he both dreamed of doing and actually did in the *Voyage*, now it is a man of stone who gets to carry a child on his shoulders: "Plus loin à l'angle de la baie, surgit à contre-jour la silhouette d'ours de l'homme qui portait un enfant sur ses épaules, quelle masse de pierre *bouleversante*!" (*G*, 106; my emphasis) ("Further off, at the turn of the bay – what an overwhelming mass of rock it is! – the silhouette of a bear of a man, carrying a child on his shoulders, stands out against the light" [*Gang.*, 105]). Hervé's dismay and disarray are aptly expressed in that last unhappy adjective.

The insanity that Hervé feels coming on him is articulated openly: "j'ai senti cet épuisement nerveux proche de la folie" (*G*, 100) ("I've felt this nervous exhaustion getting on for madness" [*Gang.*, 99]). The

---

5 In another text, Guibert tells of an intervening journey to Spain (*PA*, 140–3).

effect of this alienation, which has been linked from the very beginning of this *amour fou* to the writing of autobiographical fiction, is made all the worse by physical illness. But Hervé continues to need the company of someone whom he insists is literally driving him crazy. That the causes of his pain, complaints, and fears may be imaginary doesn't change anything since we know how thin or even nonexistent is the line between reality and fabrication: within Guibert's fictive universe a troubling sense of unreality rubs off on all that is supposedly "real."[6]

But exactly why does Hervé need this other person so much? The reason why he is still so keen on Vincent is apparently very simple: it is because of the way he sleeps:

> [Vincent] s'endort sur le dos, et son poignet gauche, orné de la cordelette de tissu barriolé, se casse mollement au-dessus de son torse, déliant ses doigts dans une féminité inconsciente, qui le frôlent à peine, suspendus comme par un charme. J'ai regardé Vincent dormir quand il était encore enfant, j'ai parfois le soupçon de ne l'aimer qu'à cause de ce geste de sommeil, ce petit tableau que j'ai peint mentalement, et qu'il ne pourra jamais voir. (*G*, 100)

> [Vincent] falls asleep on his back and his left wrist, adorned with a multicoloured cloth bracelet, is bent limply above his torso, so that his fingers, loosened in an unconscious femininity, suspended as if by magic, barely touch it. I've watched Vincent sleeping when he was still a child. I sometimes suspect I love him only because of this configuration of his when he's asleep, the little picture I have painted in my mind and which he'll never be able to see. (*Gang.*, 98–9; trans. alt.)

Absent, Vincent is a perpetual source of anxiety, as Hervé tries by every possible means to get hold of him. And when physically present Vincent is perceived to be disagreeable or perhaps even dangerous. Once asleep, however, Vincent again becomes the "child" of the *Voyage avec deux enfants*, almost a woman, and in any case the only being in the world who can calm Hervé's distress. But Hervé can enjoy the presence of this person and the calm that he brings him only when Vincent is asleep. We recognize the soothing effect of Albertine on Marcel, especially in the

---

6 In an interview Guibert described the last part of *Les Gangsters*, the trip to the Vendée, as "entirely false" (Gaudemar, "Les aveux permanents").

famous description of his captive's sleep.[7] And when the other is asleep, what else is there to do but write about Vincent's sleep? As in Proust, the "illness" that is love comes with its own remedy!

Mauve le vierge is known especially for "Les secrets d'un homme." But one can measure just how important the Vincent character was in Guibert's imagination by the fact that two stories in the same book star him. The first, "Le tremblement de terre," describes the aftermath of catastrophic earthquake in an unnamed city. The narrator of this nightmarish tale wants to find one of his friends. Not knowing if the friend is dead or alive ("Je n'imagine ni sa mort ni sa survie" [*MV*, 116] [I can't imagine either his death or his survival]), he is sure, however, about what he will do if he finds the body: "je sais que de tous ces membres je ne pourrais rien reconnaître de Vincent et que si j'avais le soupçon d'une reconnaissance je cracherais sur le membre désigné et passerais mon chemin ..." (*MV*, 119) (I know that in all those body parts I won't be able to recognize anything of Vincent and if I suspected I did I would spit on the designated part and continue on my way). The narrator seeks to take vengeance on the other, as though he has been the victim of some terrible wrong, a wrong that is not stated in the short story, although we can supply it in light of the intertext. The end of the tale is especially curious, for just as the narrator finds himself caught up in a

---

7 "J'ai passé de charmants soirs à causer, à jouer avec Albertine, mais jamais aussi doux que quand je la regardais dormir ... Elle avait posé sa main sur sa poitrine en un abandon du bras si naïvement puéril que j'étais obligé en la regardant d'étouffer le sourire que par leur sérieux, leur innocence et leur grâce nous donnent les petits enfants. Moi qui connaissais plusieurs Albertine en une seule, il me semblait en voir bien d'autres encore reposer auprès de moi" (Proust, *À la recherche du temps perdu*, 3:579–80) ("I spent many a charming evening talking and playing with Albertine, but none so delicious as when I was watching her sleep ... She had laid her hand on her breast with a droop of the arm so artlessly childlike that I was obliged, as I gazed at her, to suppress the smile that is provoked in us by the solemnity, the innocence and the grace of little children. I, who was acquainted with many Albertines in one person, seemed now to see many more again reposing by my side" [*Remembrance of Things Past*, 2:65–6]). Cf. "Par moments je regardais l'enfant endormi, tourné vers moi, ou retourné sur le ventre, découvrant entre le drap les lignes fines de ses omoplates, son poignet est orné d'un mince cordelet, et à chaque fois la position du poignet abandonné relève d'une grâce extrême, non pas la mollesse, mais une noblesse inconsciente, une féminité bouleversante" (*Voy.*, 77–8) (From time to time I would watch the sleeping child, turned towards me, or turned over on his stomach, revealing above the sheet the delicate lines of his shoulder blades, his wrist adorned with a thin bracelet, and each time the position of the drooping wrist was a demonstration of extreme grace, not softness, but rather an unconscious nobility, a deeply moving femininity).

crowd of people milling about in the gardens of the morgue, he thinks he sees Vincent:

> c'est de leur côté [with the bodies of the young girls and boys lying on the grass] que je voudrais m'agenouiller ou m'évanouir, ce sont eux que je voudrais fouler comme par mégarde pour en emporter quelque chose sous mes chaussures; en se croisant dans l'interminable labyrinthe les deux tortillons de la foule se cognent, s'invectivent comme deux colonnes ennemies, s'écrasent les pieds, s'ignorent en se lançant des coups de coude, c'est à ce moment que je crois voir le visage de Vincent rire tout près du mien. (Ibid.)

> it's with them [the bodies of the young girls and boys lying on the grass] that I would like to kneel or faint away, they are the ones I would like to tread upon as though by chance in order to take away something of them under my shoes; in the interminable labyrinth, as the two twisting parts of the crowd pass by, they bump into each other, hurl abuse at each other as though they were two enemy columns, crushing each other's feet, ignoring each other, giving each other shoves. At that moment I thought I saw Vincent's face laughing right next to mine.

The short story, whose meaning might seem so ambiguous, so encoded as to be indecipherable, is in fact not as obscure as it appears. The narrator goes looking for Vincent; if he intends to spit on Vincent's dead body, it's because he won't even be able to look at his friend sleeping! It will be the end of a relationship on which the narrator no longer seems keen. But at the same time, Vincent's laughter reminds one of *Voyage avec deux enfants*, and *mutatis mutandis* with the euphoric experiences of travel, love, and painless writing associated with a faraway time and place. "Les secrets d'un homme" is followed immediately by "Le tremblement de terre": the former recounts the death and burial of a great philosopher, whereas the latter tells of the possible disappearance of a young man. The two short stories can be read as a diptych on the loss – past or future, and possible or certain – of a friend who is dear.

In "Le citronnier," the second short story in *Mauve le vierge* that is pertinent for our purposes, Lulu, the character who corresponds to the Man in *Vole mon dragon*, ends up obtaining what he longs for from his beloved Cistrou, albeit in a rather bizarre fashion, since he eats one of the beloved's cut-off fingers that had been buried at the foot of a lemon tree! The desire to approach the other – to the point where one does not just penetrate but actually ingurgitates him – leads to a scene of cannibalism and quasi-necrophilia in which the unmentionable penis has been replaced and displaced by the precious digit that the lover recovers. This time the friend of the younger man does not spit on his body or its parts: instead he devours it greedily, and having done that, he has nothing more to say, either to the beloved or to us, since that is how the short story and the book end! Cistrou's reaction to the cannibalistic acting out of his friend ("He's crazy! I love you! You're crazy!" [*MV*, 156]) reminds us of the fear of madness described in *Voyage avec deux enfants* and *Les Gangsters*, all the while anticipating the madness in *Fou de Vincent*, in which the same reappearing character will be afraid to "confier sa bite à ma bouche, de peur qu'une folie soudaine me la fasse dévorer" (*FV*, 40) (entrust his cock to my mouth, afraid that sudden madness might make me devour it). We also remember the Barthesian intertext about a hand kissed or a hand denied. The other older man has by now been condensed with a projection of the older Hervé, whereas Cistrou or the Young Man, however he is called, has taken on the role of the younger Guibert. The roles have been inverted by the passage of time, and the change of actors, but the scenario remains essentially the same – unshared or at the very least misunderstood homoerotic desire of an intensity that is both unbearable and unbeatable.

HE'S DRIVING HIM CRAZY

Fou de Vincent, a series of extracts supposedly taken more or less directly from Guibert's diary and arranged in inverse chronological order, begins (or culminates, depending on how you look at it) with Vincent's accidental death caused by jumping out of a fourth-story window.[8] At the end of the novel we arrive at 1982, the year of the trip to Morocco described in *Voyage avec deux enfants*. Thus *Fou de Vincent* ends well, even if this happy ending is really a (false) beginning, for we are supplied with a crucial piece of the puzzle that was missing in the previous work: "'J'avais décidé de ne plus aimer les hommes, mais toi tu m'as plu'" (*FV*, 86) ('I'd decided not to love men any more but I liked you'). Play with

---

8 According to Jean-Pierre Boulé, "the fact that the narrator describes [Vincent] as dead on the very second page of the book certainly proves my hypothesis about the need for Guibert to write *Fou de Vincent* so as to put to death this character swamping the diary and his other books, to finish him once and for all, to expell him through literature, to stop being obsessed with Vincent" (*Hervé Guibert: Voices of the Self*, 168).

narrative time and blatant intertextuality both work to lift this diary from the plane of the quotidian, making it into a literary text.

Fou de Vincent explicitly thematizes intertextuality: "Relu hier soir avec émotion, en attendant Vincent, des *Fragments d'un discours amoureux*: l'impression que je poursuis souvent des choses indiquées par Barthes" (*FV,* 51) (Yesterday evening while waiting for Vincent I reread with emotion parts of *A Lover's Discourse*: impresson that I am often doing things indicated by Barthes). The long time spent waiting by the diarist, his anxiety, his impression of falling victim to an ever-increasing insanity and of living a human drama of total moral and physical solitude, as well as the fragmentary form – these all call to mind Barthes's most famous book. "J'aime Vincent, c'est ça le problème, et ma vraie solitude? Bernard me dit qu'il est impossible de faire partager l'emballement qu'on nourrit pour quelqu'un" (*FV,* 36) (I love Vincent, that's the problem, and my real solitude? Bernard tells me that it is impossible to get another person to feel how carried away you can be for someone). Even Guibert's title seems to come straight out of the other book. Didn't Roland Barthes say: "I am mad to be in love" (*A Lover's Discourse,* 120) and "the other attempts *to drive me mad*" (ibid., 125)? Whereas before it was Guibert who refused the advances of an older man – Barthes himself, as we recall – now it is Hervé who is the object of a certain refusal on the part of a younger man. How ironic then that in the 1980s Hervé's own body would be as undesirable to another person as Barthes's was to him in the 1970s! The crisscross effect of age differences and of the relationship between life and writing leads to an ironic pathos that underpins each and every page of *Fou de Vincent.*

A more deeply encoded form of intertextuality leads us to Proust. An important fragment in *Fou de Vincent* reminds the reader of a key scene in *À la recherche du temps perdu*. The context is Vincent turning up at a concert at the Saint-Louis-les-Français church in Rome when Hervé thinks his friend is aboard a plane taking him back to Paris. This sudden and unexpected arrival takes the narrator by surprise; he imagines that he is seeing not Vincent but Vincent's ghost. But the Proustian echo is less in this mini-drama in and of itself, although one could draw a parallel with Marcel's perception of his grandmother as a ghost,[9] than in the subsequent commentary of a friend of Hervé's:

---

9 "On a emmené Hector à un concert de Rameau à Saint-Louis-les-Français, je m'ennuie, j'imagine Vincent dans l'avion, on décide de partir à l'entracte. Vincent débouche de derrière une colonne. À la première seconde c'est un revenant" (*FV,* 10–11) (We took

Hector me prend à part et me demande: "Mais c'est qui?" Je dis: "C'est Vincent." Il s'exclame: "C'est lui, Vincent?" Le ton veut dire: "*C'est ça, Vincent!*" (*FV*, 11; my emphasis)

Hector takes me to one side and asks me: "But who is he?" I say: "It's Vincent." He exclaims: "He's Vincent?" The tone means: "*That's* Vincent!"

This passage reminds me of one in *La Fugitive* where Robert de Saint-Loup reacts to a photograph of Albertine when Marcel is trying to use his friend as an emissary to get his girlfriend back to Paris:

"*C'est ça*, la jeune fille que tu aimes?" finit-il par me dire d'un ton où l'étonnement était maté par la crainte de me fâcher. (Proust, 4:21; my emphasis)[10]

Hector to a Rameau concert at Saint-Louis-les-Français, I'm bored, I imagine Vincent in the plane, we decide to leave at the intermission. Vincent appears from behind a column. For the first second he's a phantom); "Hélas, ce fantôme-là, ce fut lui que j'aperçus quand, entré au salon sans que ma grand-mère fût avertie de mon retour, je la trouvai en train de lire" (Proust, 2:438) ("Alas, it was this phantom that I saw when, entering the drawing-room before my grandmother had been told of my return, I found her there reading" [2:140]).

10 "Ce qui avait décontenancé Robert quand il avait aperçu la photographie d'Albertine était ... le saisissement ... qui fait dire: 'Comment, c'est pour ça qu'il a pu se faire tant de bile, tant de chagrin, faire tant de folies!'" (Proust, 4:22) ("What had struck Robert when his eyes fell upon Albertine's photograph ... may be expressed by: 'What, it's for this that he has worked himself into such a state, has grieved himself so, has done so many idiotic things!'" (3:446). Guibert's "C'est ça" also reprises Barthes's "c'est ça" when he describes the power of a photograph to designate reality by comparing it to "the gesture of a child pointing his finger at something" (*CL*, 5). Claude Simon has intertextualized the same Proust passage in his novel *Les Géorgiques*: "un homme en train de raconter la passion qu'il a eue pour une femme et dont il sait bien qu'elle est incompréhensible à tout autre qu'à lui-même, prévoyant le sursaut réprimé, l'acquiescement poli, stupéfait, du confident auquel il montrera la photographie ..." (348) ("a man describing the passion which he felt for a woman and which, as he is well aware, is incomprehensible to anyone but himself, anticipating the stifled jump, the polite, amazed acquiescence of the confidant to whom he is going to show the photograph ..." [*The Georgics*, 235]). While Simon retains the gender of Proust's character, he uses the scene in a metaphoric manner to describe the future incomprehension of Orwell's readers when they come across the word *magic* used to describe the time he spent in Spain during the civil war. Guibert, by contrast, changes the gender of Proust's character and transforms the scene of the photograph into a living tableau, a metamorphosis typical of his writing on photography.

"*That's* the girl you love?" he said at length in a tone in which astonishment was curbed by his fear of offending me. (3:445; trans. alt.)

What happens at the church in Rome is a kind of living photo, like the many examples of photographic tableaus in *L'Image fantôme*. Hector's surprise reminds the reader of Saint-Loup's reaction, the "*C'est ça ...*" of Proust echoing intertextually in the literal repetition in French of "*C'est ça ...*" in Guibert. The lover's seemingly unreasonable and even blind attraction for the beloved leads to a friend's stupefaction when he sees for whom the lover is tearing himself apart. It is a love story that is literally unsayable, for it cannot be expressed orally. If Hervé were to talk about what attracts him in the other, or what the other is doing to his peace of mind and sanity, no one would believe him. As in Proust and Barthes, only writing can give even a small idea of the lover's torments. Guibert will write: "Parfois je redoute la nécessité d'une notation ... mais l'écriture fait aussitôt tomber ce qui en elle s'annonçait de tortueux: l'indicible" (*FV*, 46) (Sometimes I am afraid of having to write something down ... but immediately the writing removes what was going to be tortuous: the unsayable).

Readers of *Fou de Vincent* once again find themselves in Proustian territory when Hervé, who is waiting for Vincent, is on the lookout for a ray of light under the door, the sign of the other's arrival, just as Marcel waited for a similar sign that would announce the arrival of Albertine: "Ce sera un rai de lumière sous la porte, je le guette, et je guette les pas qui dépassent mon palier en effaçant provisoirement ma tension ..." (*FV*, 52) (There will be a strip of light under the door, I'm watching for it, and I'm waiting for the sound of footsteps on the landing).[11] One also thinks of what Barthes wrote about waiting in *Fragments d'un discours amoureux*: "The lover's fatal identity is precisely: *I am the one who waits*" (*A Lover's Discourse*, 40). As for Guibert, he will say that he "loves to wait" (*FV*, 52) and even that to "wait for him is delicious" (ibid.).

If Vincent assumes the identity now of Albertine, now of the beloved in *Fragments d'un discours amoureux*, he also brings to mind the Christ figure in "La Légende de saint Julien l'Hospitalier" by Flaubert. In *Mes parents* Guibert quotes a long passage describing the leper's kiss (*Trois*

---

11 "Si tout d'un coup cette raie devenait d'un blond doré, c'est qu'Albertine viendrait d'entrer en bas et serait dans deux minutes près de moi ..." (Proust, 3:126) ("If, suddenly, this strip turned to a golden yellow, that would mean that Albertine had just entered the building and would be with me in a minute ..." [2:755]).

contes, 107–8). How then can we not think of Flaubert when we read a fragment such as the following?

> Vincent à son retour d'Afrique: un lépreux. Les trous dans sa chair, sur les doigts, sur le menton. La dépigmentation de certaines zones de son dos. Il fait peur. Il me demande de dormir avec moi. Pour la première fois, il me caresse. (*FV*, 80)

> Vincent after his return from Africa: a leper. The holes in his flesh, his fingers, his chin. The depigmentation of certain areas of his back. He is a fright to behold. He asks to sleep with me. For the first time he caresses me.

A new element is added to Hervé's torture: *Fou de Vincent* is the first book, along with *L'Incognito*, to mention AIDS openly. (In "Les secrets d'un homme" Guibert wrote that "above all you weren't supposed to pronounce the name of the leprosy" [*MV*, 108].) The fear that Hervé feels for Vincent is now associated with the fear of getting AIDS: "Vincent s'est assis sur le lit, je lui dis: 'Fais voir tes pieds,' il refuse, il dit: 'Je te cache quelque chose.' Je dis: 'Quoi?' Il dit: 'J'ai le sida'" (*FV*, 71) (Vincent sat down on the bed, I said to him: "Show me your feet," he refuses, he says: "I'm hiding something from you." I say: "What?" He says: "I have AIDS"). But this is far from certain: after all, the Guibertian narrator glibly admits to making Vincent perform many different roles in his life: "Tant de peaux que j'ai voulu faire endosser à Vincent: celle du putain, celle de l'enfant, celle du voyou, celle du sadique, celle du premier venu" (*FV*, 35–6) (I've made Vincent wear so many costumes: hustler, child, street kid, sadist, anybody who just happens to come by). The *role* – and the word is important here – of potential PLA can now be added to this list of dramatic parts played by the beloved, for let us not forget that Hervé cannot *not* fabulate, fabricate, or prevaricate about Vincent, so it would be more accurate to say that his friend plays the role here of a late-twentieth-century Everyman suffering not from AIDS but from the fear of AIDS.[12]

Again we wonder just why Hervé keeps on seeing or trying to see Vincent. The diarist asks himself the same question: "Quand est-ce que je le rayerai de la carte, ce minable petit con?" (*FV*, 34) (When am I going to scratch him off the map, that pitiful little dummy?). To be sure, one can

---

12 James Kirkup "diagnoses" a case of chronic athlete's foot (*MRH*, 13; translator's note).

invoke various reasons: Vincent represents a link with the narrator's own young adulthood, Vincent's presence allows Hervé to get a restful night's sleep, waiting for Vincent is sweet torture, but the most important reason is that this *crazy love affair is the best source of inspiration for the lover*: "Écrire sur lui est un assouvissement" (*FV*, 41) (Writing about him is satisfying), writes Guibert in what must be the biggest understatement of his oeuvre. Hervé is conscious of the link between his addictive love for Vincent and the fictionality that is part and parcel of the tale he is both living and telling: "Obsession (toujours la verge de Vincent, comme une folie, comme une fiction)" (*FV*, 79) (Obsession [always Vincent's dick, like folly, like fiction]). His body is so intimately linked to the writing project that it would not be stretching a point to say it is with the fantasized about and fictionalized body of Vincent that Hervé writes. On the one hand, the love Hervé feels for Vincent seems as unreal ("Douleur à l'irréalité de cet amour" [*FV*, 85] [The pain of the unreality of this love]) as a piece of fiction, a photo of a photo, or a hologram. On the other, this love is destined to be made concrete by the materiality of the language used to represent its unreality, especially, I would argue, in the frequent repetition of words containing the letter *V*, for example, "la verge de Vincent," "je vois la veine," "les naevi de son visage," "voyage avec Vincent," "voir Vincent danser sur ses vagues," "Vincent: misère de son visage, de ses vêtements, de sa vie," "voir Vincent le soir est une joie dès le réveil, dès la veille au soir," "il se love contre moi," and so on. The sensuous vibrating of the *v*, that labiodental consonant that appears in the first names of the two friends – Hervé and Vincent – incarnates and "literalizes" the act of kissing the other. Just to say Vincent or even to pronounce the initial letter is like intoning a mantra, or better still, it is as if one were putting the beloved in one's mouth to eat him, to swallow him, to assimilate him – entirely or in part – into one's own being, as in "Le citronnier."

Fou de Vincent is the most important of Guibert's works in which Vincent appears. In fact, it would not be an exaggeration to say that this little book – eighty pages – is the key to the entire oeuvre, underscoring the link between love and writing, insanity and fiction, the unreality of obsession and the materiality of language. It is certainly not by chance that intertexuality plays such a prominent role in this book, for it is one way of warding off the spell of mimetic desire as the beloved becomes a pre-text, a "the symbol or the phantom of love" (*FV*, 62). *Fou de Vincent* or the story of an insane love: it had to be written in fragments, in detached pieces, for these inverted anamneses allow us to live the violence of desire, the waves of love and hate that intersect, crisscross, coil and uncoil in the insides of Hervé Guibert's writing.

THE LAST TIME, ALMOST

With the exception of *Le Protocole compassionnel*, Vincent appears only briefly or not at all in the other AIDS fictions.[13] Such an absence seems surprising on the part of a character who "haunted" so many of Guibert's other works. Has Vincent's fall from a fourth-story window erased all memory of him, or has it simply entailed a concomitant fall from grace?

Although *À l'ami qui ne m'a pas sauvé la vie* removes Vincent from the story, nonetheless there are numerous links with *Fou de Vincent*. For example, the chronologies of the two narratives overlap and both works owe much to Guibert's diary. In the AIDS novel the narrator wants to leave the five ex-votos that in his mind represent Jules, Berthe, Titi, Loulou, and himself in a Lisbon church named Saint-Vincent, an episode that happens at the end of 1988, just after Vincent's death in November of the same year. The fatal fall with which *Fou de Vincent* opens is supposed to have happened during the night of 25 November, which corresponds to one of the worst moments in the life of the narrator of *À l'ami*, for it was then that his T-cell count plunged and the results of the anti-AIDS vaccine turned out to be less than encouraging. As well, Vincent's leap into the dark is supposed to have happened exactly one month before the narrator of *L'Ami* began to write his first AIDS narrative, another type of leap in the dark. In both books, Hervé mentions giving a lamp to Vincent after learning about his positive HIV status. The shingles that plagued Hervé in *Les Gangsters* are mentioned in *L'Ami*. Hervé's sojourns in Rome appear in both works. Finally, in *L'Ami*, Guibert speaks of having left a manuscript in which he talks about AIDS with his publisher. Such a work could be *L'Incognito*, where we find the sentence "I was persuaded I had AIDS" (11), or *Fou de Vincent*: "I'm persuaded I'm infected" (81). Both books appeared in 1989, the year before *À l'ami qui ne m'a pas sauvé la vie* was published.

The first AIDS novel is devoted largely to two friendships: Hervé and Muzil, on the one hand, and Hervé and Jules, on the other – all three of whom are seropositive. While it is true that the friendship of Hervé and

---

13 In *L'Incognito*, there are several brief references to Vincent: 117–18, 139, 196. In *L'Homme au chapeau rouge*, Vincent is only mentioned in relation to a "portrait présumé," which in fact dates from the 1920s: 27, 32, 35 (*MRH*, 13, 18, 20).

Muzil mirrors to a certain extent his relationship with Vincent, there is no indication that sexual desire had any part in his relations with the great philosopher. But in terms of being an older friend who can give advice to and calm the panic of a younger friend, Hervé finds himself in a situation similar to that of Muzil vis-à-vis a younger man, that is, himself several years earlier.

> Je me sens être mon père face à moi. J'essaye de faire revenir à toute allure, à sa place, Michel en moi, et sa sûreté, son sens de l'équité. L'ami mort parle par ma bouche pour réconforter Vincent, pour chasser la panique. (*FV*, 70–1)
>
> It feels like I'm my father facing me. In his place, at top speed I try to bring back Michel in me, his assurance, his sense of equity. The dead friend speaks through my mouth in order to comfort Vincent, to drive away the panic.

Vincent had to be excluded from *À l'ami* so that Hervé can retain his role as the younger man. Another example is also pertinent: in *Fou de Vincent* Hervé ends up playing the role of Saint Julien l'Hospitalier with a "leprous" Vincent (*FV*, 80). In the 1990 novel Muzil writes an article on Manet using the pseudonym Julien l'Hôpital, a fact that is all the more ironic since he will die in a Paris hospital where he is treated like a leper, given the lack of knowledge about AIDS in 1984 – for example, Hervé and other friends are required to dress up in special astronaut-like clothing in order to avoid a possible "contamination" from Muzil! If Hervé plays "le beau rôle" in relation to Vincent and his many troubles, the narrator of *L'Ami* gives himself a less than glorious role in relation to Muzil. Finally, we know that T., or Jules as he is later called, is Vincent's sexual and textual rival since *Voyage avec deux enfants*. In *Les Gangsters* Hervé describes T.'s jealousy (*G*, 69; *Gang.*, 68). Thus, given the important part of Jules in *L'Ami* – he and Hervé live their AIDS-related infections like two mirror images of each other, which only adds to their tourment – there simply is no room for Vincent in the first AIDS fiction. He has become the *terzo incommodo* who must be thrust aside, all the more so since he is not a member of the "Club des 5" for the PLAs, whether actual or potential, of Hervé's inner circle. By removing Vincent from the scene of the fiction in *L'Ami*, Hervé guarantees his friend's survival. Vincent, in short, has no business here.

The literary stakes are high, and the situation complex. For example, one of the themes of *L'Ami* is insanity, which – as we know – has long been associated with the relationship of Vincent and Hervé. But in *L'Ami* madness is different, for it is linked, on the one hand, to excruciating pain, and, on the other, to the insane love that Hervé feels for his new "friend," that is, the manuscript of his first AIDS fiction. Vincent has disappeared since he isn't even responsible for the birth of this new narrative, an engendering role that heretofore was his. Let us remember that the narrator compared his love for Vincent to a hologram. I believe that if Vincent is to be found at all in *L'Ami*, it is as a kind of subtextual hologram or cipher. In *L'Ami*, as in *Fou de Vincent*, the letter *V* is remarkable for its constant repetition, not just in the abbreviation HIV, but also in words such as *vie*, "life," and *victoire*, "victory," a word used by Hervé's publisher to describe his first AIDS narrative, a use that his friend David disapproves of:

> C'est quand j'écris que je suis le plus *vivant*. Les mots sont beaux, les mots sont justes, les mots sont *victorieux*, n'en déplaise à David, qui a été scandalisé par le slogan publicitaire: "*La première victoire des mots sur le sida.*" (*PC*, 124; my emphasis)

> It's when I'm writing that I feel most alive. Words are beautiful, words are just, words are victorious, whatever David says, who had been scandalized by the publicity slogan for my book: "The first victory of words over Aids." (*CP*, 106)

After all, the name *Vincent* means "he who hangs on to victory," whereas *Hervé* means "active in combat."[14] So, even though Vincent is ostensibly absent from *L'Ami*, his inter- and subtextual presence continues to haunt its pages.

Whereas we thought Vincent died on 29 November 1988, he reappears alive in the second AIDS fiction, *Le Protocole compassionnel*, where he is mentioned for the first time in a paragraph dated 29 June 1990 (*PC*, 30). In fact, an entire chapter of this novel is devoted to Vincent: he and Hervé spend an unforgettable evening together. Not only does he turn up, he even arrives on time! He is full of kindness, good thoughts, and positive "vibes" about his friend's prospects for survival. Furthermore, he confirms and authenticates their relationship, which probably means

---

14 The meaning of *Hervé* is taken from *Les Gangsters* (23), that of *Vincent* from Voragine, *The Golden Legend* (1:105).

more to Hervé than anything else that Vincent could say to him: "[Vincent] disait: 'Notre histoire,' pour la première fois. Il disait: 'On a quand même baisé ensemble pendant sept ans,' alors qu'il avait toujours réfuté qu'on ait eu ces rapports-là" (*PC,* 143) ("He said: 'Our story,' for the first time. He said: 'We've been fucking together for seven years,' whereas he had always denied that we'd had such a relationship" [*CP,* 123; trans. alt.]). He encourages Hervé in his fight against AIDS:

> Vincent me disait: "La dernière fois, j'ai eu les boules quand je t'ai vu. Tu m'as fait peur. Mais aujourd'hui c'est différent, je suis sûr que tu vas t'en sortir. Tu vas rester parmi nous, Hervé, je le sens. Je crois au magnétisme ..." Je me sentais au plus mal avant que Vincent n'arrive, épuisé, à bout de tout, tout au bord de la mort, au plus près d'elle comme jamais, et maintenant Vincent me faisait oublier ma fatigue. (*PC,* 143; original ellipsis)

> [Vincent] added: "The last time, I felt really pissed off when I saw you. The sight of you scared me. But today is different, I'm sure you'll pull through. You're going to stay with us, Hervé, I can feel it in my bones. I believe in magnetism ..." Before Vincent arrived I had been feeling very low, worn out, at the end of my tether, on the brink of death, closer to it than ever before, and now Vincent was making me forget all my weariness. (*CP,* 123; trans. alt.)

To see Vincent again, to hear him speak such words is almost as if Hervé were miraculously cured; in fact, the last evening with Vincent, which corresponds to a time when Hervé was feeling at his worst, is a kind of proleptic leap forward to when he will feel much better after beginning to take the ddI of the dead dancer. No longer does Vincent represent a definite or even a possible danger; on the contrary, he is the messenger sent to deliver the good news, even if the reader knows that the news will end up being false.

Present, attentive, tender, reassuring: what more could one ask of the loved one? All of this is the absolute opposite of absence and folly. Instead, a calm joy, a feeling of well-being and contentment in the presence of the beloved. But of course, it is too much to last:

> Dans l'appartement, il venait s'asseoir exprès à côté de moi, alors que d'habitude il s'esquivait ou le feignait quand je revenais à la charge pour atteindre son corps sur ce même canapé ... Mais là je n'arrivais pas à le

toucher. Je ne savais même pas si j'en avais envie, ni si Vincent en était dépité ou soulagé ... je le caressais par-derrière, ça ne me faisait presque plus rien. Je connaissais son corps par coeur. Il s'était imprimé à l'intérieur de mes doigts, je n'en avais plus besoin pour de vrai. J'aimais toujours Vincent mais ça ne me faisait presque plus rien de retoucher son corps, cette anomalie était apparue en moi, comme la difficulté à me relever de mon fauteuil ou à monter la marche de l'autobus. Nous nous quittâmes sur un petit baiser sur la bouche, comme nous en avons le secret ensemble. (*PC*, 144–5)

In the apartment, he deliberately came and sat beside me, when usually he would turn away or pretend to whenever I'd tried to get at his body on this sofa ... But now I couldn't bring myself to touch him. I didn't even know if I wanted to, whether Vincent was put out or relieved by this ... I caressed him from behind, it had almost no effect upon me. I knew his body by heart. It was imprinted indelibly on my fingertips, I no longer needed the real thing. I still loved Vincent but touching his body now meant almost nothing to me, this anomaly had turned up in me, just like the difficulty I have getting up out of my armchair or stepping onto the bus. We parted with a little peck on the lips, our own private code. (*CP*, 124; trans. alt.)

Hervé no longer needs Vincent in the flesh. No doubt one could explain this by invoking fatigue, loss of energy, but there is something else here. Hervé knows Vincent's body by heart, so that he no longer has an obsessional need for it, as he did in the past. One might say that for Hervé, at this stage, his friend has already become a memory. In this regard, the use of the word *imprinted* in the passage quoted is significant, for it reminds us that the narrator has progressed from the stage of agonizing feelings to a calm imprint, whether that imprint be in his memory or on the printed page.[15]

---

15 Later in the same novel, Hervé thinks of Vincent when he is in Morocco: "J'étais grisé par l'océan, par ces immenses rouleaux blancs aplatis et violents, qui déferlaient régulièrement, et sur lesquels Vincent aurait aimé faire du surf. Je ne regrettais pas de ne pas être avec lui, mais je pensais toujours tendrement à lui" (*PC*, 187–8) ("I was hypnotized by the ocean, by these enormous white rollers, broad, violent, unfurling with a regular pounding, and on which Vincent would have loved to go surfing. I did not feel any regret at not being with him here, but I kept thinking of him tenderly" [*CP*, 162]). We recognize the surfer from *Fou de Vincent* and *Vole mon dragon* who believes in nothing but the beauty of a wave.

PARADISE LOST

Le Paradis, the last novel, tells a strange tale, or several, about the travels and loves of the narrator with a woman called Jayne Heinz. The descendant of the inventor of ketchup, Jayne begins by dying, her stomach ripped out of her body by a coral reef while she was surfing in Martinique. The rest of the novel is a mishmash of trips to Africa – Mali – and Bora Bora, the misnamed paradise. Jayne, a former model, was working on her doctoral dissertation on Nietzsche, Strindberg, and Robert Walser. She was tall and beautiful, aged twenty-six or twenty-seven when she died, all of which appears fairly straightforward. However, there are problems: Jayne never existed, for when the local gendarmes do a police check on her identity after the swimming accident, they can find no trace of such a person in either the nineteenth or twentieth century! "La femme que j'aimais était un fantôme?" (*P,* 33) (Was the woman I loved a ghost?), wonders Hervé, thereby echoing *L'Image fantôme* and the eponymous text about his mother's photograph. The fact that the narrator does not have AIDS and that he is a failed writer may lead us to believe that, unlike so many of Guibert's other novels, this one is a "real" fiction. But *Le Paradis* is also – at least in part – an autofiction in the tradition of *Le Protocole compassionnel* and *L'Homme au chapeau rouge*. For example, the narrator is sick, his name is Hervé Guibert, his great-aunt Suzanne dies. More important, the folly that waits in the wings of so many of Guibert's texts makes its inevitable – and final – appearance on stage. And this time it is not just a subject for a student cum surfer writing a thesis: it is also a very real neurological threat faced by the narrator, a painful MRI (magnetic resonance imaging) session having detected "espèces de constellations, de lunules, de tout petits points blancs" (*P,* 67) (kinds of constellations, half-moons, all sorts of little white spots) in his brain:

> J'ai pris entre mes mains un photomaton de Suzanne jeune, un craquement dans le bois s'est fait entendre, le tic-tac de l'horloge translucide aux pulsations de rubis et d'argent me maudissait à jamais et me hantait pour la vie, mon singe vert empaillé qui a transmis le sida à l'homme s'est mis à bondir vers moi. J'étais fou. (*P,* 121)

> I picked up a photo of Suzanne taken when she was young, there was the sound of cracking wood, the ticktock of the translucid clock with its ruby and silver pulsating mechanism would curse me forever and haunt me

for the rest of my life, my stuffed green monkey which transmitted AIDS to man began to jump towards me. I was crazy.

On ne revient jamais d'Afrique, voilà la vérité. Je resterai fou, fou et amnésique ... (*P,* 136)

You never come back from Africa, that's the truth. I will remain crazy, crazy and amnesic ...

As far back as *Voyage avec deux enfants,* insanity was linked with the project and practice of writing. Many times it is love that drives Hervé crazy. At other times pain does so, especially in *À l'ami qui ne m'a pas sauvé la vie.* Now in *Le Paradis* the narrator keeps coming back to the insanity he can feel invading his brain as he begins to hallucinate. The last novel is certainly the most disturbing of all of Guibert's books, since the theme of insanity is reproduced *en abîme* in the writing of the novel. It is impossible to determine in what order the journeys to Bora Bora, Martinique, and Mali were made, since what little there is left of a chronology makes no sense. There are contradictions – for example, the narrator, who hasn't published any books, remembers them anyway – as well as a radical change in style and tone in the last twenty-six pages of the novel, where the fragments are shorter, the tone more anxious, and the theme of insanity more personal.

As for Vincent, he is nowhere to be seen. However, we do hear intertextual echoes of him. For example, on the second page we read the following sentence: "Aucune vague ne me fera jamais peur" (*P,* 12) (No wave will ever make me afraid). One could well imagine Vincent saying the same thing.[16] When Jayne drives with the narrator, he uses the verb *brinquebaler,* "to joggle," to describe how he feels (*P,* 15), just as he did when Vincent was driving (*FV,* 22). In *Le Paradis* Jayne is the same age as Vincent (*P,* 20; *PC,* 49). The narrator accuses Jayne of having made love

---

16 Cf. "Pendant une heure, Vincent me parle d'une vague – de la façon de la prendre, de s'en jouer ou de s'en meurtrir, de faire corps seul avec elle – ; je tremble de peur, sentant la mort se lover entre nous" (*FV,* 80) (For an hour Vincent talks to me about a wave – about the way to take it, to play with it or get hurt by it, to form a single body with it – ; I tremble with fear, feeling death coiling itself between us). In *Vole mon dragon,* the young man, who as we have seen is another incarnation of Vincent, tells the older man: "Je ne peux croire, et encore à peine, qu'à la beauté de la vague sur laquelle je surfe ..." (49) (I believe only, and just barely at that, in the beauty of the wave on which I am surfing ...).

with Blacks in Africa, which is almost a literal repetition of an earlier passage – except the gender of the beloved's supposed African lovers has been changed (*FV,* 76; *P,* 113). Vincent's travels to Africa are reprised by the narrator's own in Guibert's last novel. Finally, in *Fou de Vincent* did Guibert not announce his intention to write a novel somewhat like *Le Paradis*?

> Depuis deux trois jours je pense à un autre livre (c'est toujours assez joyeux d'entrevoir un livre nouveau), alors que je me disais que je ne serai plus fichu de rien faire: un faux journal de voyage, ou un faux roman, un tour du monde en Camper avec Vincent, une arme, et peut-être Vincent deviendrait une femme dans le récit, s'appellerait Jane? Comme Jane [*sic*] Mansfield. (*FV,* 16)

> For two or three days I have been thinking about another book (it's always a joy to be thinking of another book) just when I thought I was incapable of doing anything: a fake travel diary, or a fake novel, a trip around the world in a camper with Vincent, a firearm, and perhaps Vincent would become a woman in the story, a woman named Jane? Like Jayne Mansfield.

In Guibert's last novel, a revolver plays a prominent part in the lovers' sex life, and what is *Le Paradis* if not a kind of "fake travel diary"?

Guibert appears to have transformed Vincent into Jayne, a sex change that reminds us of Proust's transformation of Agostinelli into Albertine, a character who – as we have seen – is not unlike Vincent. Guibert always mixes truth and falsehood, "reality" and fiction, his texts and other authors' texts in a series of ever-changing permutations. He even raised the subject of transsexuals in *Le Protocole compassionnel.* Waiting to leave for Morocco where he is to see a faith healer, the narrator writes: "Parce que Casablanca évoquait encore les opérations clandestines de transsexualité, j'avais aussi dit en riant, à qui voulait bien l'entendre, que j'y allais pour me faire opérer, afin de plaire enfin à Vincent" (*PC,* 176) ("Because Casablanca still evoked clandestine surgery on transsexuals, I had told all and sundry, as a joke, that I was going there to have myself 'altered,' in order to please Vincent" [*CP,* 152; trans. alt.]). With one of those inversions that are as typical of Guibert's prose as Proust's, the sex change will affect not Hervé but Vincent.[17]

17 Boulé believes that "[i]f one is determined to look for a character behind Jayne, it

This is the point I had reached in my thoughts about Guibert's most important reappearing character by the spring of 1996 when I was preparing my notes for this research project. Later when I went to the Institut Mémoires de l'Édition Contemporaine in July to take a look at the manuscipt of *Le Paradis*, I discovered two quite different versions of the novel: the longer one, which corresponds pretty much to the published version, is in three gray file folders, the shorter one, entitled *Congolo gâté (Roman fou)*, is housed in a single mauve file folder.[18] Initially, one might wonder which version Guibert intended to use. According to the dates on the manuscripts as well as the information of a close friend of Guibert familiar with his writing, Mathieu Lindon, it is the longer version that Guibert had typed up and then corrected ("Le coeur fatigué"). Be that as it may, I was happy that my theory about the novel based on internal and intertextual evidence was corroborated by its *avant-texte* or foretext. For in the manuscript of *Congolo gâté*, Vincent appears in the place occupied by Jayne in the published version: "Est-ce moi qui ai tué Vincent? Je l'ai déjà fait mourir et ressuscité dans plusieurs de mes livres, mais là il est carrément éventré, ça va être dur. Je me souviens de mes livres, c'est la seule chose la seule chose [*sic*] dont je me souviens précisément. Mais comment ordonner un livre. Le dater?"[19] (Did I kill Vincent? I already killed him off and resuscitated him in several of my books, but now that he is definitely eviscerated, it's going to be hard. I remember my books, that's the only thing, the only thing I remember precisely. But how to organize a book? Date it?).

As in the published version, time plays havoc with any attempt to tame the chaos of impending insanity, the mark of which – whether real or fictitious – is indelibly sketched into the fabric of the novel. Guibert's intent and desire to kill Vincent off are paralleled not only by Jayne's

---

would in [his] view be that of Gertrud in *L'Homme au chapeau rouge*... Gertrud, as it happens, is Dutch like Jayne, and they resemble each other physically to some extent" (*Hervé Guibert: Voices of the Self*, 252). Boulé may be right in his interpretation, but it does not exclude my own reading. Surely a character can have more than one model, whether she be real or "merely" literary.

18 According to Guibert, "congolo gâté" is how Africans refer to an insane person ("Le coeur fatigué"; cf. *P*, 34). The subtitle "Roman fou" (crazy novel) bears an uncanny resemblance to two of Renaud Camus's novels, *Roman roi* and *Roman furieux*. In the latter, Roman, the exiled king of an imaginary country in Eastern Europe called Caronie, gradually becomes more and more alienated from reality before becoming a "fou furieux" living in the United States.

19 *Congolo gâté (roman fou)* ff. 3–4, cited with the permission of Christine Guibert (cf. *P*, 115).

death in *Le Paradis* but also by the sex change to which he has been subjected. Hence, Vincent is thrice removed from his initial appearance in Guibert's oeuvre, for in the end he has become a dead adult woman, as opposed to a very much alive male adolescent in *Voyage avec deux enfants*. While it is true that *Le Paradis* portrays Jayne alive when she accompanies Hervé on his travels through the Caribbean, Polynesia, and Africa, all of these are played out, despite the narrator's failing memory, in flashback mode of events that predate her death and burial in Martinique as narrated at the outset. Clearly, in making Vincent into a woman, Guibert the writer of what are at least partially autobiographical fictions removes Hervé, his autodiegetic hero, from the "temptation" of homosexuality. And, of course, his or her death removes the writer from the possibility of sex, *tout court*, except as an act of memory, but then his memory is faulty ...

Guibert's state of sexless solitude at the end of a novel written in the last year of his life might seem less puzzling than his "conversion," as a writer, to the depiction of heterosexuality. True, the shift is foreshadowed in some of his other books. For example, in *Le Protocole compassionnel* Hervé claims that he can no longer stand men (*PC*, 226), and falls in love with his doctor, Claudette Dumouchel. In *Le Paradis*, there is an allusion to the narrator's youthful love affairs with young men (*P*, 73), but until Jayne's death he had an on-going and passionate relationship with her. As for the novel's title, Guibert explains it within the book: it refers to an island paradise that Jayne once heard about from a friend of the family (*P*, 49). But if we read the title in light of one of Guibert's other works, then a different interpretation becomes possible. In *Des aveugles*, he wrote of the alienation experienced by the older inmates of the Institute for the Blind who, in their last days, are expelled from the only home they have known and sent to hospices where they will have to cohabit with people who are not blind. Fearing this last-minute integration into the world of the sighted, the blind refer to these hospices ironically – "in a sinister way" Guibert says – as "Paradise" (*Av.*, 47; *Bl.*, 34). The *in extremis* conversion of Guibert's narrator to heterosexuality is therefore ambiguous: is paradise a south-seas island – although this is hardly corroborated by the "facts" as he describes his stay in Bora Bora – or an intimation of death? or perhaps something else? Are we dealing with the final textualization of the already feminine (but not effeminate) Vincent seen through the eyes of a homosexual? Does Guibert feel compelled to leave his homosexual "home," like the blind who at the end of their lives must go to "Paradise," because he too is near the end? Or because of a desire to appeal to a broader heterosexual readership, including women, after the success of *L'Ami* and *Le Protocole compassionnel*? Or is Guibert's attempt to leave the "confines" of homosexuality for the "paradise" of heterosexuality a form of self-inflicted exile, an ironic twist of fate, the ultimate turn of the screw in the vicious circles so endemic to his fiction? It is impossible to tell, for the conversions, inversions, and other permutations of the figure of the beloved make him a character almost as indecipherable as Proust's Albertine.

From the adolescence of the one Hervé calls "the graceless child" to the death of Jayne, former ABD[20] and would-be exegete of writers (almost) as crazy as the narrator, torn apart on a coral reef, Vincent accompanies the narrator from the first to the last novel. He plays many parts, but Vincent is above all the beloved – even if he doesn't always let himself be loved the way Hervé (his fellow traveler in the strongest sense of the term, as used in the dedication of *Voyage avec deux enfants*) would like, and it would be difficult to imagine Guibert's oeuvre without the presence/absence of this character. Vincent is the other who accompanies, as best he can, a writer who is less a polymorphous pervert than a fundamentally solitary being.

Vincent represents the intriguing but always disturbing sense of unreality that impregnates the pages where he appears, in whatever guise. Often when Hervé evokes the figure of the other, he or she is associated with an agonizing question: for example, is Vincent going to push Hervé into the ocean? what does he do while Hervé is waiting for him? who exactly is Jayne? did she in fact ever exist? These unsolved enigmas allegorize the freedom of this writer of fiction. He can kill off his characters, make them live again, even change their gender with a stroke of the pen. The fundamental doubt concerning Vincent is not really about an "eternal character" or the fundamentally unknowable nature of the other. Rather it is about the freedom that accompanies all fiction writing: What should one write? And then, what to say next? How does one link a word, a sentence, a paragraph, or a larger textual unit with some other word, sentence, or fragment? From this point of view, to write about Vincent is to write about fiction, or, rather, to write on the writing of fiction.[21]

---

20 All But Dissertation: a graduate student who has completed her course work and examinations for the doctorate but who has not yet completed her dissertation.
21 The exception that proves the rule is to be found in several fleeting references to a certain V. in *Cytomégalovirus*, which is not a fiction.

1. *Self-portrait*, 1986.

2. *Self-portrait with Suzanne and Louise*, 1979–80.

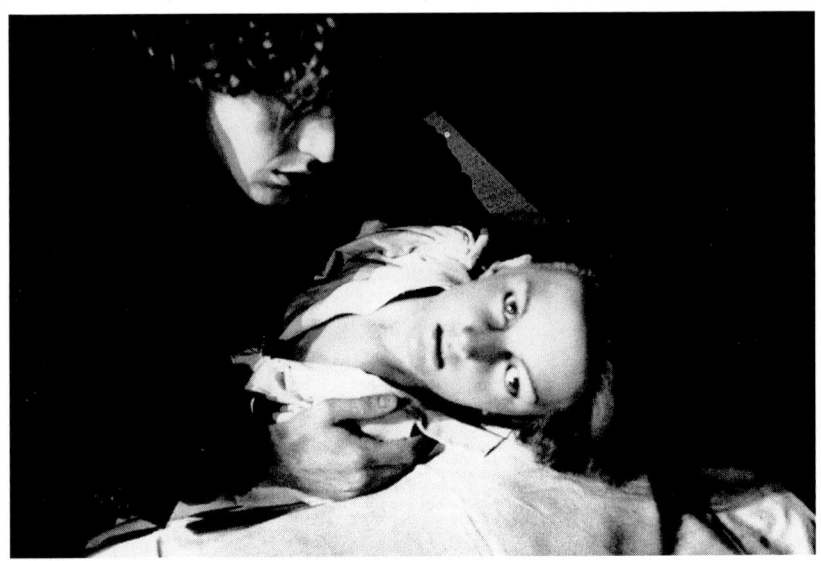

3. *Self-portrait, Grévin Museum*, 1978–9. Hervé and the head of Joan of Arc a.k.a. Louis XVII.

4. *Michel*, 1981. Multiple images of Foucault.

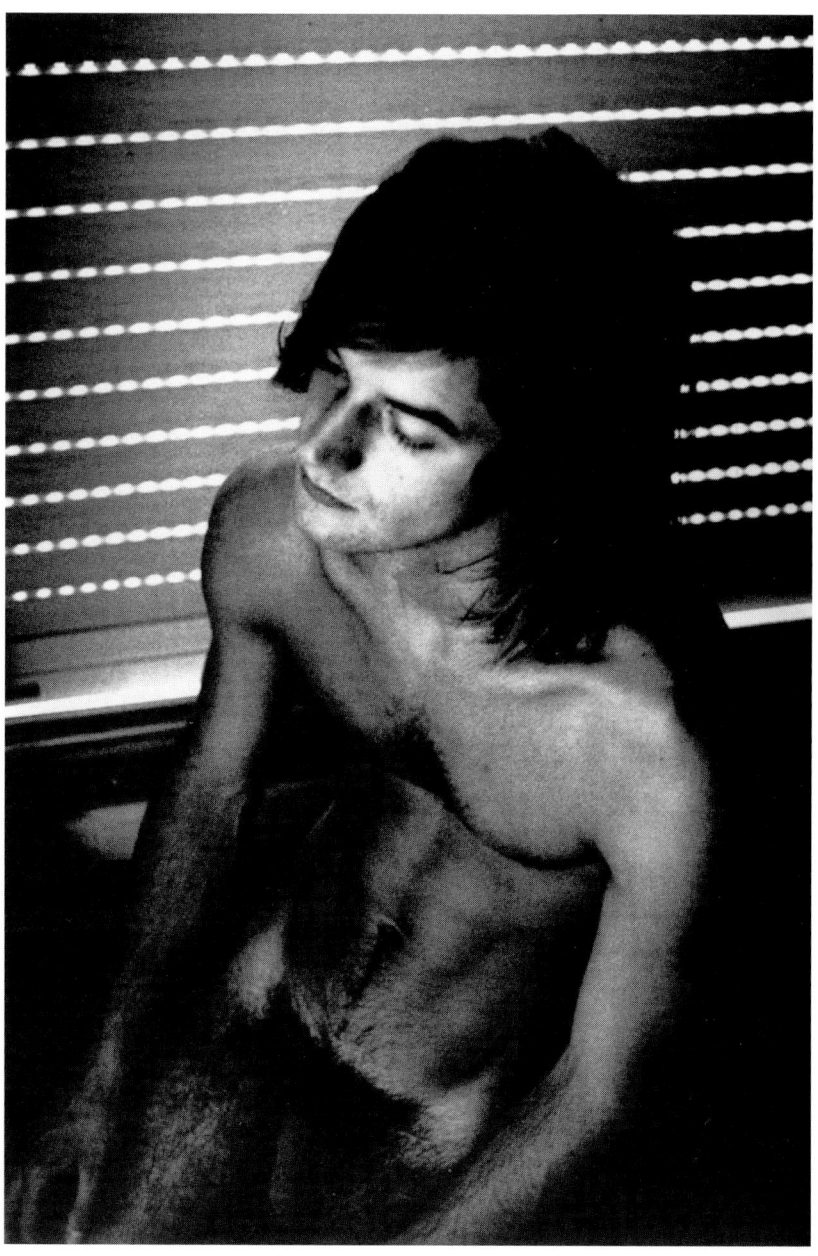
5. *T.*, 1976.

6. *Writing*, 1983. T. plays the writer.

7. *Rue de Vaugirard*, 1980. The death of the author.

8. *Villa Médicis*, 1987–8. "Luxe, calme et volupté," as Baudelaire wrote in "L'invitation au voyage."

9. *Reading*, 1979.

10. *Le Club des Cinq*, 1988.

11. Untitled, n.d. The animals before their ultimate metamorphosis.

12. *Ship of Fools*, 1490–1500. Painting by Hieronymus Bosch. The folly represented is gluttony and other forms of self-indulgence.

13. *The blind man's hand*, 1983. The last image in *Le Seul Visage*, the catalogue of the exhibition of Guibert's photographs held at the Galerie Agathe Gaillard in the fall of 1984. *Des aveugles* was published in March 1985.

14. *Voyage avec deux enfants*, 1982.

15. *Saint Sebastian*, 1528. Painting by Sodoma. This image of the "gay saint" appears on a banner that was used in times of plague.

16. *Self-portrait*, 1988. Copyright © 1988 The Estate of Robert Mapplethorpe.

17. *After the Duel*, 1872. Painting by Antonio Mancini. The enigma painting that so intrigued Guibert.

18. Untitled, 1987. Bookshelves with a well-used copy of a language dictionary, postcards of Rembrandt's self-portraits, and a photograph of Jean Genet.

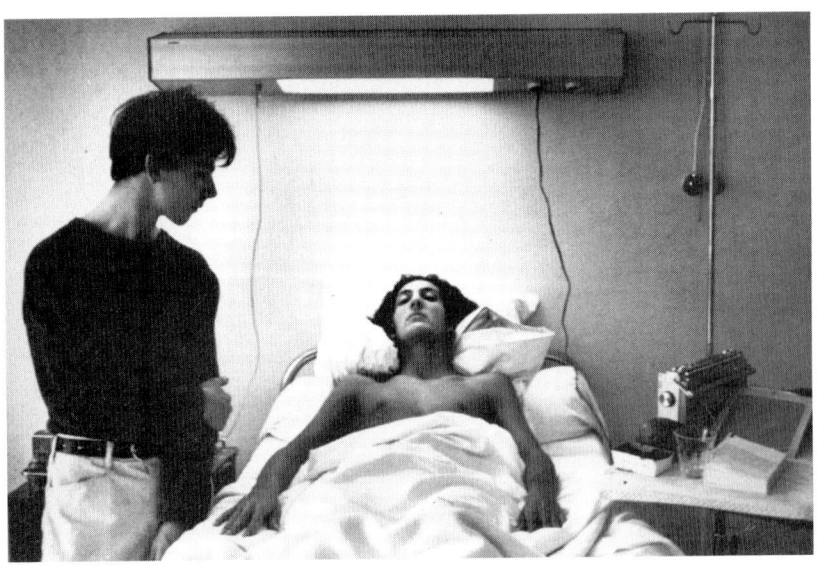

19. *Friends*, n.d.

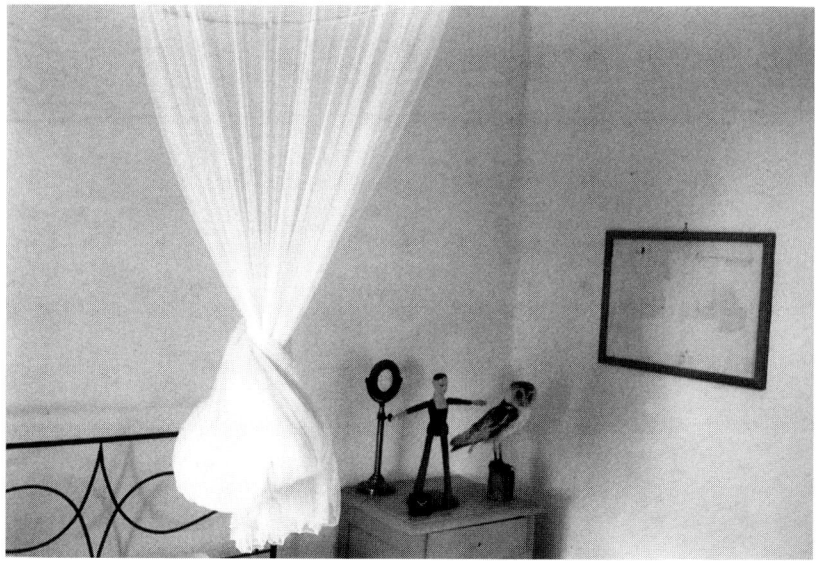

20. Untitled, 1989. Mosquito net and miscellaneous objects, including a stuffed owl, on the Island of Elba.

21. *Self-portrait*, 1982(?).

For Hervé Guibert, to write meant entering a transgressive space, returning to a time when every childish prank – whether naughty or nice – when every touch and glance – whether randy or not – was allowed. Writing for Guibert meant leaving Paris, the world of adults and work to play hooky. (In reality this usually meant traveling to the Island of Elba in order to stay with his friend Hans Georg Berger.)[22] Several of Guibert's works of fiction resemble children's stories, in particular *Les Lubies d'Arthur* but also *Voyage avec deux enfants* and *Les Gangsters*, at least in part. Since Vincent incarnates this freedom associated with childhood, he is at once the character, the symbol, and the ideal addressee of these fictions in which figure love and hate, desire and pain, characterized by an almost endless series of vertiginous permutations, in short, the staging of that crazy freedom that is novel writing. This explains why Vincent reappears in so many texts of an author whom we have scarcely begun to understand. The lives of Vincent and Hervé are thus forever entwined in a universe of innocence and fantasy where the figure of the other is a key player in the twin games of love and textuality.

CODA

My search for Vincent finally led me to meet, in the flesh, the model for this character. Before leaving for France, I was not at all sure I would succeed, less because of the detective work that would be involved than because of Guibert's particular blend of fact and fiction. After all, it would not have been presumptuous to conclude from the works themselves that Vincent, like Jayne, was dead. But apparently one can indeed survive jumping out of a window. Should I add that he was generous enough to give me one of Guibert's letters to him? That, unlike me, he and his nephews are very good at *pétanque*? That he and his family were perfect hosts? No doubt the best thing is to return to Guibert's writing, which I shall do by quoting two extracts about Vincent, the first from *Les Gangsters*, the second, not included in *Fou de Vincent*, from the manuscript of that book: "Un jour Vincent m'a dit: 'Je suis content de te faire écrire, que tu écrives grâce à moi'" (*G*, 71) ("One day Vincent said to me: 'I'm glad to be making you write, that you're writing thanks to me'" (*Gang.*, 71); "Il me dit, il y a peut-être un an: 'Si tu n'avais pas ce trou en plein milieu de la poitrine, tu n'aurais pas été aussi sensible, tu n'aurais

---

22 Godard, "Dialogue sur l'île d'Elbe," 32; interview with Jonquet, 108; *PC*, 129–30.

pas écrit tes livres.' Chacun de ses mots me reviendra un jour" (Ms. of *Fou de Vincent*, f. 6; quoted with the permission of Christine Guibert) (He told me perhaps a year ago: "If you didn't have that hole right in the middle of your chest, you wouldn't have been so sensitive, you wouldn't have written your books." Each one of his words will come back to haunt me some day). I would like to thank Vincent for agreeing to speak with me about Guibert and other subjects. I could have written this chapter without contacting him, but as Guibert himself wrote, "an evening with Vincent cannot be refused," and this reader too found it hard to resist meeting a figure so central to an entire oeuvre, however much the author has reshaped reality for his own purposes.

Chapter Six

For an AIDS Aesthetic

> AIDS is not only a medical crisis on an unparalleled scale, it involves a crisis of representation itself ...
>
> Simon Watney, *Policing Desire*, 9

> If Aristotle was correct, then the artistic representation of human suffering shouldn't make us depressed. Rather, it is the avoidance of genuine tragedy and the substitution of glib sentimentality that diminishes us.
>
> Judith Pastore, Introduction to *Confronting AIDS through Literature*, 2

In "AIDS Writing and the Creation of a Gay Culture," Michael Denneny has spoken about the "essential vulgarity of [the] purely aesthetic response" to AIDS writing (50). According to Denneny, "Aesthetic appreciation is neither the intention nor the relevant response to such works" (45). And following Douglas Crimp's lead in advocating "activist responses to AIDS by cultural producers" ("AIDS: Cultural Analysis/Cultural Activism," 4), a Canadian academic who has written about AIDS literature, James L. Miller (not the same person as the author of *The Passion of Michel Foucault*), envisages a "Novel of Cultural Activism" whose hypothetical hero would be "a cultural activist whose agenda ... will provide the main impetus for the plot by opposing the agendas of fatalistic governments and fundamentalist bigots" ("AIDS in the Novel," 268). Miller's no doubt well-meaning prescriptions certainly do not apply to any of Guibert's writing in his trilogy: *À l'ami qui ne m'a pas sauvé la vie*, *Le Protocole compassionnel*, and *L'Homme au chapeau rouge*. On the contrary, AIDS activism is treated with biting irony in the first of these novels.[1] But to come back to the aesthetic element of AIDS writing, critics prominent in the field of gay studies would have us believe that such an element is incompatible with the subject matter. According to Lawrence Schehr, in reading AIDS fiction "we are being asked to suspend our aesthetic interest in favor of another pleasure of the text" (*Parts of an Andrology*, 201). He bases this opinion on the unpleasant medical interventions that typically constitute a large part of an AIDS narrative. Going even farther, Joseph Dewey describes Persons Living with AIDS (PLAs) in the final stages of the illness with incredible insensitivity: "As a genre, this body of plague literature, of course, has little promise – there is no aesthetic beauty in the caved-in, yellowed faces and skeletal figures in AIDS hospices ..." ("Music for a Closing," 24–5). As we shall see, Guibert will take a position diametrically opposed, for he beholds physical beauty in the person living with AIDS. But one does not have to take such an extreme position as Dewey's to deny the appropriateness of an aesthetic response to AIDS writing. Gregory Woods expressed the point most succinctly when he wrote that "aesthetics can wait" ("AIDS to Remembrance," 155). For some, the aesthetic dimension is seen as a luxury at best, as an impediment to communication at worst.

It is as though a work of imagination must suspend its literary, or to use Roman Jakobson's term, its poetic function, when it tackles a subject as delicate as Acquired Immune Deficiency Syndrome. To be sure, the stakes are huge, beyond even those of a cancer narrative, since the writer must cope not only with AIDS but also with the prejudices that still may attend his very existence, even on the part of the imagined reader. And like a cancer narrative, AIDS writing will inevitably confront the topic of pain that is unimaginable for those who have the good fortune to be seronegative. To be sure, pain is not a pretty thing, but that does not mean that the representation of suffering must depend on simple empathy, and much less on "glib sentimentality," as Judith Pastore has written in the passage quoted at the beginning of this chapter. And to exclude the aesthetic dimension from the AIDS narrative because some PLAs do not correspond to late-twentieth-century stereotypes about beauty is, I would say, truly obscene. Emily Apter has articulated the problem concisely: "How does one write pain so that

---

1 "AIDS became the social raison d'être of many people, their hope for public recognition and a position in society, especially for doctors who tried in this way to escape the boring routine of their medical practices" (*Friend*, 118).

it hurts the way pain hurts? ("Fantom Images," 91). I will argue here that Guibert's novel trilogy succeeds in representing the pain of living with AIDS, which goes beyond physical pain, precisely because of the aesthetic and rhetorical choices made. In other words, if an HIV-negative reader gets even a glimpse or a hint of what it meant to live with AIDS in France at the beginning of the 1990s – and these two provisos are crucial owing to the rapid development of new treatments, in particular combination therapy, as well as the country-specific culture of the world of medicine[2] – this comes about through our appropriation of texts that incorporate the frustration, the pain, the lows, and sometimes the highs that Guibert experienced during the last few years of his life. Writing was an integral part of Guibert's existence during this period, no doubt what kept him living though he makes no effort to hide the always possible option of suicide.[3] And while some of the elements that together make up what I call Guibert's AIDS aesthetic are to be found in earlier works, the literary configuration that I will analyze here under various rubrics – elegy and eulogy, indeterminacy, games of truth, transgression, and self-reflexivity – is most characteristic of the trilogy.

Douglas Crimp has argued that "AIDS does not exist apart from the practices that conceptualize it, represent it, and respond to it" ("AIDS," 3). As he goes on to say, "This assertion does not contest the existence of viruses, antibodies, infections, or transmission routes" (ibid.). What it does mean is that the representation of AIDS is a construct. And in the case of Guibert, we are dealing with literary artifacts "that attempt to write "the body in pain" from the inside where pain is visceral" (Cummings, "Reading AIDS," 159). Obviously, different writers will resort to various artistic choices in their attempts to write AIDS; and their works will have to be judged on their own merits. We would do well to remember, however, that no other work of AIDS writing in French has known the success that *À l'ami qui ne m'a pas sauvé la vie* has since it was published in 1990. Together with the other two novels of the trilogy, this novel illustrates just how powerful an "activist response to AIDS" can be when that response is anchored in the actual writing practice.

---

2 Boulé underlines the same important point (*Hervé Guibert: Voices of the Self*, 192).
3 Ross Chambers reminds us that Guibert was aware that "the attraction of suicide is not something that one puts behind one, once and for all, in order to write but a permanent temptation that continuously underlies, and so continuously valorizes, the choice to die writing" (*Facing It*, 40).

ELEGY AND EULOGY

Some Parisian journalists cried foul when Hervé Guibert published his first AIDS novel. For them what was most scandalous were not the terrible conditions he described in hospitals or the way his infamous friend Bill treated him by not living up to his promise to make an anti-AIDS vaccine available to him. What these journalists claimed to be shocked by were the revelations concerning Muzil's homosexuality and death from AIDS-related causes. What the journalists missed, obvious though it may seem to us now, is that À l'ami can be read as an elegy, a work of lament about a dead friend. In this, the novel can be situated in the long tradition of friendship elegies, "acts of homage to intellectual masters," about which Gregory Woods has written in his *History of Gay Literature* (418n9). In *L'Image fantôme* Guibert described the idea of the collection of mental images – slides, he called them – we all possess of those whom we know and love, a unique collection that disappears with each individual's death. Some idea of the importance of friendship for Guibert can be understood by looking at the portraits of his friends in *Le Seul Visage*, including the famous photo of Foucault discussed in chapter 1. It seems inconceivable that Guibert would have wanted to betray his friend; and certainly there is nothing particularly scandalous about Muzil in the novel. On the contrary, he is portrayed as an honest, hard-working intellectual with a sense of humor, as well as a faithful and considerate friend who sought to bolster his younger friend's morale when things were going badly for him.

Interestingly, the memorializing function of the AIDS creative work has been seen in almost as unpopular a light as is the notion of an AIDS aesthetic itself. Douglas Crimp has argued in favor of "a critical, theoretical, activist alternative to the personal, elegiac expressions that appeared to dominate the art-world response to AIDS" ("AIDS," 15). But if there is no room for elegy, what meaning would an interventionist activism have? Surely the fight to find a cure for AIDS, to improve the treatment, housing, and care of PLAs would have little meaning if the lives of the dead were not worth remembering and celebrating!

When the narrator of À l'ami was going through a bad period, Muzil gave him a copy of one his favorite books, Marcus Aurelius's *Meditations*, which starts out with a series of homages to his elders – members of his family and his masters – beginning with the dead: "Muzil, qui allait mourir quelques mois plus tard, me dit alors qu'il comptait prochainement rédiger, dans ce sens, un éloge qui me serait consacré, à moi qui sans doute n'avais rien pu lui apprendre" (*Ami*, 76) ("On that occasion Muzil, who was to die a few months later, told me that he planned soon to write my eulogy – even though I had probably never managed to teach him anything" [*Friend*, 67; trans. alt.]).[4] Muzil's unwritten encomium to Guibert is thus mirrored by the text of the novel, the elegiac element of which is, I would argue, crucial to Guibert's enterprise. For example, we are told of Muzil's extreme courage in the face not just of impending death but also of the humiliations inflicted upon him by his failing memory and a hospital establishment that seems to set higher priority on tidiness than anything else, as witnessed by the nurse who will not allow Muzil to keep copies of the two recently published volumes of his *History of Behavior* with him in his hospital room:

> [L'infirmier] dit qu'on n'était pas dans une bibliothèque, il attrapa les deux livres de Muzil que Stéphane lui avait rapportés de la maison d'édition et qui sortaient tout frais de l'imprimerie, et décréta que même ça on n'en voulait pas ici, qu'il fallait uniquement le corps du malade et les instruments pour les soins. Dans un regard Muzil me pria de ne rien dire, et de sortir, moralement aussi il souffrait atrocement. (*Ami*, 103)[5]

> The nurse announced that we weren't in a library, he grabbed the copies of Muzil's two latest books that Stéphane had picked up for him at his publisher's office, fresh from the printers, and decreed that even this stuff was not allowed in there, only the patient and what was necessary for his medical care. With a look, Muzil begged me to say nothing, and to leave; he was suffering atrociously in mind as well as body. (*Friend*, 92; trans. alt.)

---

4 The *Meditations* are bound in the same book as Epictetus's *Manual*. By this gift, Muzil reenacts the habit of General Gordon (1833–85) of presenting his friends with the works of both Marcus Aurelius and Epictetus ("Epictetus," *Oxford Companion to Classical Literature*). As we now know, like Muzil, Gordon was homosexual. This chain of gay stoicism is underscored by Guibert when he describes the fact that the Italian painter Antonio Mancini was buried with a copy of Epictetus's *Manual*.

5 On hospital workers' obsession with tidiness above everything else, Eric Michaels's AIDS diary *Unbecoming* offers a poignant deconstruction: "Tidiness inhabits and defines a 'moment,' but one outside time, ahistorical, perhaps the ancestral Dreamtime home of all 'life styles.' It is a perfect bourgeois metaphor. The tidy moment does not recognize process, and so resists deterioration, disease, aging, putrefaction. On this basis, it justifies an appropriate discourse to inflict on the diseased, the aging, the putrefying" (17). As Ross Chambers writes about tidiness in this context, "*homophobia, discrimination, bureaucracy*, would be one series of alternative names; *complacency, indifference, dismissal*, another" (*Facing It*, 98).

Muzil's stoicism is as evident here as when, shortly before, he continued to go to the library every day to work on the footnotes to his great book, right up to the day he passed out in his kitchen, where his friend Stéphane found him lying in a pool of blood. Foucault has been reproached for not speaking publicly about the fact that he had AIDS, which presumes that he knew; but Guibert gives a different interpretation. For him, the philosopher in his novel demonstrated great pride but also sublime generosity in not telling anyone that he was ill, "allowing friendships to live as light as air, carefree and eternal" (*Friend*, 7; trans. alt.). Indeed, the word that best describes Muzil is *friend*, as in the expression "that irreplaceable friend" (*Ami*, 90). Rather than betraying the memory of his friend, Guibert incorporated a homage to his mentor and intellectual master in his first AIDS novel. Most critics have not realized the fact that *À l'ami* belongs to the ancient and modern tradition of the friendship elegy. If AIDS itself is a relatively recent phenomenon, the lament for a dead friend of the same sex is not. As Gregory Woods has pointed out, the homosocial theme and the practice of elegy in literature have a long history, going all the way back to the Bible (David and Jonathan) and to the personal laments of the ancient and medieval worlds (Achilles and Patroclus, Roland and Olivier in *La Chanson de Roland* [*A History of Gay Literature*, 108–23]).

Guibert's AIDS fictions celebrate the living also. In this, they renew contact with another genre, that hymn of praise in honor not of a god but of a human, whether he be a warrior or an athlete, namely, the encomium. For Guibert the warrior of today is the doctor fighting alongside the PLA against illness and all the attendant discomforts of the body in dis-ease. It is true that not all the doctors described in the AIDS fictions live up to Guibert's high standards for caring professional conduct, but Claudette Dumouchel in *Le Protocole compassionnel* certainly does. In fact, this novel can be read as a "kind of Barthesian love affair" between Guibert the thirty-five-year-old PLA and the younger female doctor, as Emily Apter has pointed out in her article "Fantom Images: Hervé Guibert and the Writing of 'sida' in France" (94). Dumouchel reminds Hervé of his female classmates in high school ("Sometimes I get to thinking I've met an old classmate again" [*CP*, 192]); but she also shows all the tenderness that his father showed him when he was a child. Sensitive to her youth, her energy, her mocking sense of humor but also her beauty, Guibert describes his doctor in an extended metaphor that transforms her into a medieval lady:

> Pour la première fois j'ai remarqué ses mains. Très belles mains, fines et longues, blanches, soignées, racées, comme la brutalité de la palpation n'aurait pu me les faire imaginer, les mains d'autrefois d'une gente dame du Moyen Age, aptes à délacer sur son gantelet les serres d'un oiseau de proie apprivoisé. (*PC*, 221)
>
> For the first time I noticed her hands. Very beautiful hands, long and slender, white, cared-for, aristocratic, I'd never have imagined them from the roughness of her palpations, the hands of a grand dame of the Middle Ages, able to uncurl from her gauntlet the claws of a tame bird of prey. (*CP*, 193; trans. alt.)

Guibert's AIDS fictions contain hymns of praise for other friends: the writer Eugène Savitzkaya; Vincent; Yannis; and Gustave. One could also mention the faith healer called simply the Tunisian and his wife Lumière.[6] Finally, and certainly not least, there is Berthe, in whose honor Hervé began to compose an encomium similar to the one Muzil intended to write about him. In *Le Protocole compassionnel* we learn of Hervé's marriage to Berthe: "Pouvait-on dire que c'était un mariage d'intérêts? Non, bien sûr que c'était un mariage d'amour" (*PC*, 152) ("Could it be described as an arranged marriage for business reasons? No, of course it was a love-match" [*CP*, 130; trans. alt.]). Guibert is better known for betraying secrets than for loving the small group of friends close to him. It is true that he believed that secrets have to circulate (*IF*, 170; *GI*, 159), and in an interview he mentioned the high demands that he made on his friends by using them as models (Jonquet, "'Je disparaîtrai,'" 111). But circulating his friends' stories can be interpreted not as a form of betrayal but as a form of praise. I return to the image of the collection of pictures of the faces of those whom we have known in our lives: "Chaque mort provoquerait la destruction d'un fonds photographique qui repasserait une dernière fois, dit-on, dans un rayon de conscience" (*IF*, 144) ("Every death brings about the destruction of a photographic reserve that, it is said, reappears one last time in a corridor of consciousness" [*GI*, 133]). No doubt this sentence explains the elegiac and eulogistic dimensions of these novels. Writing in the face of

---

6 Savitzkaya (*PC*, 118 [*CP*, 101]); Vincent (*PC*, 143–5 [*CP*, 123–4]); Yannis (*HCR*, 69–70, 75, 109–10 [*MRH*, 46–7, 50, 76–7]); Gustave (*PC*, 121–2 [*CP*, 104–5]); and the faith healer and his wife (*PC*, 215 [*CP*, 187]).

imminent death – whether it be due to AIDS or the suicide that he envisages committing if the pain of living becomes too great – Guibert seeks to perpetuate his own particular "photographic reserve" of transparencies by sharing them with us. To write about AIDS is to bear witness, and while the AIDS fictions are read first and foremost as testimony about what it means to live with the syndrome, they must be read also as testimonials of friendship. The elegiac dimension celebrates past losses, whereas the encomastic dimension reminds us of the ever-present possibility of the loss not only of those praised but also of the one who sings their praise, the narrator, the friend with AIDS.

INDETERMINACY

The bewildering effect of reading Guibert's AIDS writing is caused first and foremost by not knowing exactly what we are reading. To be sure, the first editions of the three novels display their genre since the covers carry, as is the usual practice for novels published by Les Éditions Gallimard, the word *roman*, "novel." And yet we know that these novels are more than novels, for they are closer to autobiography than most. We know, for example, that he worked for *Le Monde*, as he describes in *L'Homme au chapeau rouge*. And we especially know that Hervé Guibert, as the first-person narrator of all three AIDS fictions names himself in the novels, had AIDS.[7] Perhaps the best way to resolve the dilemma concerning which genre Guibert's AIDS writing belongs to is to posit a new category, one that combines one better known in English-speaking countries – *AIDS fiction* – and a French one – *autofiction*, that is, factual fiction. Closer to autobiography than an autobiographically inspired novel (such as Proust's *Recherche*), autofiction nonetheless incorporates fictional elements.[8] I define an *AIDS autofiction* as *a work of literary creation in which the author describes, through a fiction, the physical and mental pain of*

---

7 Guibert was firm in his belief that his first AIDS novel was both a fiction *and* that it told his own story: "I am keen on the word *novel*" (Interview with Gaudemar, "La vie sida," 21). He admitted in an interview that he would have been quite capable of putting forth the fiction he had AIDS: "It's true that I could have written this book [*À l'ami*] based on the account of a sick friend. It would not have been impossible, neither especially mendacious nor far removed from the methods of writing I've used before, with a documentary or journalistic basis. But the fact is *this is really my story* [*c'est bien mon histoire*]" (Cherer, "Guibert gagne," 20).

8 On the notion of autofiction, see Philippe Lejeune, *Moi aussi*, 62–9; as well as two articles by Marie Darrieussecq, "L'autofiction, un genre pas sérieux"; and "De l'autobiographie à l'autofiction: *Mes parents*, un roman?" In the introduction to *Hervé*

living with AIDS based on direct personal experience; although such a work is fictional, it is nonetheless based on first-person testimony by a witness whose name is identical with that of the author. What is important is not to assign a mere label to Guibert's AIDS writings but rather to understand and appreciate just how indeterminate they really are. Now they tend to autobiography, now they tend to fiction, and never shall the twain be parted. As Emily Apter states, "[Guibert's] novels are neither fiction nor pure autobiography; combining elements of both, they resemble working notebooks dispatched from the land of ghosts" ("Fantom Images," 83).

Interesting as the generic ambiguity may be for literary specialists of literature,[9] I prefer to read this irreducible indeterminacy as a metaphor for another type of uncertainty, that is, the incertitude that accompanies Guibert the PLA regarding not just the length of time left but also day-to-day trials and tribulations, including battles with incompetent medical personnel, the vicious circle of blood tests, medical procedures, and new medications, not to mention the anti-AIDS vaccine that Bill alternatively promises and refuses Hervé and his friends. As a result, Guibert can imagine several scenarios and several endings to the story he begins to tell us in *À l'ami qui ne m'a pas sauvé la vie*:

Guibert: Voices of the Self, Jean-Pierre Boulé claims that I am wrong to speak of Guibert's autofictions (9–11), although he himself used the term in an earlier work (*Hervé Guibert: "À l'ami qui ne m'a pas sauvé la vie" and Other Writings,* 2). Boulé now prefers the notion of "a novel in which the *I* lies" (*Voices of the Self,* 269), a new genre he calls *le roman faux*. More helpful is Edmund White's brief but seminal article on gay autofiction, which he characterizes as "a convergence of two very different literary traditions, realism and the confession" ("On Gay Fiction," 7). He goes on to say: "The form, which is neither purely fact nor fiction, gives the writer both the prestige of confession (this is my story, only I have the right to tell it, and no one can challenge my authority in this domain), and the total freedom of imaginative invention (I'm a novelist, I can say whatever I please, and you can't hold me responsible for the opinions expressed by my characters, not even by my narrator" (8). White then wonders if "this doubleness reflects perhaps the unfinished business and ambiguous status of homosexual identity itself" (ibid.). Needless to say, what White says here applies as much if not more to Guibert's AIDS autofictions, where ambiguity and doubleness (cf. the so-called double blind) will play such important roles.

9   "The AIDS narrative of a PLA hovers between genres, between an (auto)biographical narrative and fiction, between a documentary and an intervention" (Schehr, *Alcibiades at the Door,* 156); "Is the 'I' of a PLA writing fiction, writing fiction about AIDS, or, for that matter, writing a diary about AIDS, still in position to distinguish between genres? Or, to ask a more radical question, does the 'I' of a PLA bring into question everyone's distinctions between genres? Can we be so sure now that our previous distinctions were correct?" (ibid., 159).

> J'entrevois l'architecture de ce nouveau livre que j'ai retenu en moi toutes ces dernières semaines mais j'en ignore le déroulement de bout en bout, je peux en imaginer plusieurs fins, qui sont toutes pour l'instant du ressort de la prémonition ou du voeu, mais l'ensemble de sa vérité m'est encore caché; je me dis que ce livre n'a sa raison d'être que dans *cette frange d'incertitude, qui est commune à tous les malades du monde.* (*Ami*, 10–11; my emphasis)

> I have a sense of the structure of this new book I've been harboring within myself all these last weeks, but I don't know how it will unfold in its entirety; I can image several endings, all of which fall for the moment under the heading of premonition or heartfelt desire, but the whole truth of it is still hidden from me, and I tell myself that this book's raison d'être lies only along *this borderline of uncertainty, so familiar to all sick people everywhere.* (*Friend*, 2–3; my emphasis)

This zone of uncertainty characterizes not just those who are ill but also the narrative itself. Because this AIDS fiction begins and ends *in medias res*, the narrative must remain open-ended. Indeed, all three AIDS fictions are incomplete, leaving the reader to wonder what happened next. To a certain extent, the final blank page of each book is filled in, so to speak, by the next work, so that *Le Protocole compassionnel* supplies details missing in *À l'ami* just as *L'Homme au chapeau rouge* "completes" the previous novel. Though *Le Paradis* marks a new beginning, there are elements in this book that fill in some of the gaps in *L'Homme au chapeau rouge*, in particular the story of Guibert's trip to Mali in early 1991. Nevertheless, the overall effect is still one of incompletion, which is the last word of the last AIDS novel: "De nouveau je pourrais appeler ce livre ... *L'Inachèvement*" (*HCR*, 154) ("Once more I would be able to call this book ... *Incompletion*" [*MRH*, 111; trans. alt.]).

The greatest uncertainty is, of course, now resolved, since we know that Guibert died, though not directly as a result of AIDS. Reading Guibert today is thus a different experience from reading the first two volumes of the AIDS trilogy in 1990 and 1991. For us today the uncertainty is no longer the final outcome of what will happen to Guibert himself. Lawrence Schehr emphasizes this point: "To read Guibert now means to read with him, even if our knowledge is always more complete than his own. For the first time in a long time we have the resurgence of a narrator who knows less than the reader, less than the literary structures imply, less than the real world ... If Guibert the man knows that he is dying, at the beginning of *À l'ami* at least, he is also the narrator who does not know to what extent he is dead" (*Alcibiades at the Door*, 164). But this does not mean that there is no more indeterminacy, since it continues to function at every level of these narratives. What excuse will Bill come up with not to give Hervé the vaccine? What will be the effect of ddI on Guibert's life and writing? Did Muzil know he had AIDS? These and many other specific examples of uncertainty still combine to form an overall effect that leaves readers feeling, like Guibert, that they are in "cet intervalle précis d'incertitude," even when the incertitude is perhaps feigned – for example, when Hervé and Jules wait for the results of their HIV tests.[10]

GAMES OF TRUTH

As Judith Pastore states in her introduction to *Confronting AIDS through Literature: The Responsibilities of Representation*, "One of the earliest tasks literary AIDS took on was combatting the multiple untruths and prejudices surrounding the disease" (3). Guibert himself will write that AIDS is surrounded by official lies: "je ne sais que trop, de sources sûres qui me parviennent des plus hauts niveaux, que le sida est pris dans une chaîne de mensonges" (*PC*, 86) ("I know only too well, from top-level sources, that AIDS is caught up in a whole chain of falsehoods" [*CP*, 71; trans. alt.]). Such a statement confirms the dynamic principle of what Foucault called "games of truth" in the writing of history:

> Not a history that would be concerned with what might be true in the fields of learning, but an analysis of the "games of truth," the games of truth and error through which being is historically situated as experi-

---

10 There is one counter-example that might seem to prove the contrary at first reading: "If life was nothing but the presentiment of death and the constant torture of wondering when the axe would fall, then AIDS, by setting an official limit to our life span – six years of seropositivity, plus two years with AZT in the best of cases, or a few months without it – made us men who were fully conscious of our lives, and freed us from our ignorance" (*Friend*, 164–5). The passage is curious, for it presupposes not only that there is a fixed limit to the length of time a person diagnosed seropositive will live, which we now know is false, but that Hervé knows when he was infected. Surely, the uncertainty that attends the future also impinges on the past. It is almost as though there were so much uncertainty in his life that the narrator wrote this passage as a way of assuring himself that some things at least are now more certain. Of course, today with the advent of new medications the lifespan of a PLA is no more reducible to a fixed term than that of any other human being.

ence: that is, as something that can and must be thought. What are the games of truth by which man proposes to think his own nature when he perceives himself to be mad; when he considers himself to be ill; when he conceives of himself as a living, speaking, laboring being; when he judges and punishes himself as a criminal? (*The History of Sexuality*, vol. 2, 6–7)

It is not a coincidence that this self-description of the Foucauldian approach to the past informs and influences so much of Guibert's writing. We know that Guibert refused to give a so-called factual account of the final illness and death of Foucault. In this, I believe he was remaining faithful to the principles of his friend, for it is in light of Foucaut's critique, in the first volume of *The History of Sexuality*, of various kinds of obligatory and supposedly factual confessions that I read Guibert's refusal to write about Foucault in any mode other than fiction and, what is more, autofiction. In fact, I believe we can go one step farther by positing a dual influence of Foucault *and* Barthes on Guibert's writing. It is full of "games of truth," most notable of which are the lies, the false clues (*leurres*), and the enigmas that are open-ended or partially resolved, all of which Barthes wrote about in his analysis of Balzac's novella *Sarrasine*, *S/Z*. There exists a convergence not just between the younger man's writing and the two theorists who had the greatest influence on him but also between that writing and the subject of AIDS itself. For Guibert, if there can be no writing without falsehoods, *a fortiori* there can be no writing about AIDS without lies. As Donna Wilkerson says in her article "Hervé Guibert: Writing the Spectral Image," "In this game of fake-real (which is also the game of writing), the reader learns quickly that she or he cannot trust anything" (283). Unlike Paul Monette, Guibert does not think it important to see through all the lies that surround the syndrome.[11] The French writer's solution, as we shall see, is to enter the space of the lie – not to get at the truth – but rather to *play with the idea of truth* in order to illustrate just how problematic such a notion is in this age of AIDS.

Falsehoods and lies abound in all of Guibert's AIDS writing, but

---

11 "'Will anyone understand what it was like?' It was curiously easy, perched on the mountain of death, to speak about the future when all of them would be gone. 'Maybe the gay ones will.' 'Yeah, but they'll have to see through all the lies'" (Monette, *Afterlife*, quoted by Denneny, "AIDS Writing," 42).

nowhere does the narrative hinge on them as much as in *L'Homme au chapeau rouge*. In fact, this novel can be read as Guibert's homage to Orson Welles, since it is a rewrite, to a certain extent, of his film about art forgery, *F for Fake*. According to Guibert, "On butait sur le problème du faux dès qu'on commençait à s'intéresser à la peinture, à vouloir en acheter ou en revendre" (*HCR*, 12) ("As soon as one began to take an interest in painting, wanting to buy or sell them, one came up against this problem of fakes" [*MRH*, 2]). At one point Hervé is supposed to accompany the painter Yannis to Madrid where some fake paintings imitating his style are to be destroyed. Within the fictive universe, counterfeit paintings seem to proliferate at a frightening speed, for they are everywhere – in art galleries, museums, auction houses, as well as private collections. The situation is made all the more complicated when Yannis discovers that one of the fake paintings is itself a chef d'oeuvre, a kind of "true" fake. Hervé enters the game by passing himself off as an American art dealer, by putting a false address on his checks, and finally by telling his friend Jules that he has been making love with Yannis: "Hier soir j'ai avoué à Jules que je baisais avec Yannis. C'est faux. Du coup nous avons rebaisé ensemble, Jules et moi, alors que nous ne baisions plus depuis au moins six mois. C'était étrange, habituel et intense" (*HCR*, 114) ("Last night I confessed to Jules that Yannis and I were fucking. It's not true. Then we started right away, Jules and me, fucking together all over again, when we hadn't been fucking for at least six months. It was so strange, so familiar and so intense" [*MRH*, 81]). As this passage demonstrates, a lie can have a happy result. It seems that to have AIDS is necessarily to enter a world of falsehood and lies. For example, the testing of new medications involves the double-blind protocol,[12] which can panic people so much that they are obliged to go to a laboratory in order to know whether they are taking a placebo, "ayant besoin de savoir coûte que coûte s'il était vrai ou faux" (*Ami*, 159) ("needing desperately to know whether it was real or fake" [*Friend*, 143]).

Even the HIV virus itself relies on a kind of lie to replicate itself:

---

12 James Kirkup describes the double-blind protocol as follows: "Unlike the more usual single-blind, in which the researchers but not the participant know who is receiving the experimental treatment and who is receiving the control treatment, a double-blind is one designed to eliminate false results in the protocol (or plan of the experiment), in which neither the researchers not the participants know the make-up of the test groups" (*CP*, 8; translator's note). On the similarity between the double-blind principle and the suicide experiment in *La Pudeur ou l'Impudeur*, see Chambers, *Facing It* (48).

> Bill m'a expliqué que le virus est si diabolique parce qu'il se divise pour mettre en jeu un processus de *leurre*, qui épuise le corps et ses capacités immunitaires. C'est l'enveloppe du virus qui fait office de *leurre*: dès que l'organisme décrypte sa présence, il envoie ses T4 à la rescousse, qui, massés sur l'enveloppe et comme aveuglés par elle, ne détectent pas le noyau du virus, qui traverse incognito la mêlée pour aller infecter les cellules. (*Ami*, 259; my emphasis)

> Bill explained to me that the virus is so diabolical because it splits in two, running a decoy operation that exhausts the body and its immune system. It's the viral envelope that functions as a decoy: as soon as the host organism detects its presence, T4 cells are sent to the rescue; it's as if, massed on the viral envelope, they are blinded to the presence of the viral core, which slips incognito through the fray and goes on to infect other cells. (*Friend*, 239; trans. alt.)

The word *leurre*, "decoy" or "lure," here refers not to the patient seeking to delude himself or herself, but rather to the virus's capacity to deceive the helper cells of the human body. But other lies are strictly human in origin – for example, Muzil's sister will not permit the hospital records of her brother to read "Cause of death: AIDS." The French medical establishment itself seems to have participated in these games of truth when dealing with a patient who has a fatal illness, if we are to believe the words Guibert attributes to Muzil:

> Muzil m'avait dit: "Le médecin ne dit pas abruptement la vérité au patient, mais il lui offre les moyens et la liberté, dans un discours diffus, de l'appréhender par lui-même, lui permettant aussi de n'en rien savoir si au fond de lui il préfère cette seconde solution." (*Ami*, 33)

> Muzil had said to me, "The doctor doesn't tell the patient the truth straight out, but he gives him the means and the opportunity, by talking in a roundabout way, to figure it out for himself, which also allows him to remain blessedly ignorant, if that's really what he wants." (*Friend*, 25)

Hervé willingly participates in such "games of truth." In the following passages, he tries to fool himself into believing that he is seronegative, even while he wisely conducts himself as if he were seropositive. It is significant that he uses the word *leurrer*, which I emphasize in the following quotations, since it is related to *leurre*, the term used to describe how HIV can camouflage its presence in the human body for years:

> [J'étais] persuadé de connaître le résultat du test sans avoir besoin de le faire, ou bien lucide ou bien *leurré*, affirmant en même temps que la moindre des moralités consistait à se comporter dans les relations amoureuses, qui avaient tendance à décroître avec l'âge, comme un homme atteint ... (*Ami*, 18)[13]
>
> I was convinced that I knew the results beforehand and didn't need to take the test, being levelheaded or just fooling myself, allowing at the same time that a minimum of moral decency required that one conduct one's love life, which tends to slow down with age, as though one were infected by the disease ... (*Friend*, 10)

The world of AIDS is demonstrated to be as Foucauldian as it is Guibertian by the very instability of the notion of truth. The truth, were it to exist, which is not often in this universe of quackery, fakery, forgeries, false clues, false hope, hoaxes, and pseudo-hoaxes, can only be approached indirectly, if at all. Given the important place of falsehood in the narratives, perhaps one should not even begin to ask what is true or not. And yet it is difficult to avoid asking oneself about the truth behind these autofictions. For example, Yannis is based on the Spanish painter Miquel Barceló;[14] Guibert visited him in Majorca, not Corfu; thirty-five counterfeit paintings really were destroyed in Madrid – all of these things are fairly easy to find out (*Miquel Barceló 1984–1994*, 94–6). It is less easy to determine if other episodes such as the trip to Moscow described in *L'Homme au chapeau rouge* are based on fact or not. One work may contradict another; for example, in *Le Protocole compassionnel* the narrator tells us he took neither his video camera nor the digitalin drops to the Island of Elba, which he visited in the summer of 1990 (*PC*,

---

13 Cf. "avec la complicité du docteur Chandi à qui j'ai laissé comprendre que je souhaiterais me *leurrer*, un brin d'espoir" (*Ami*, 68; my emphasis) ("with the complicity of Dr. Chandi, whom I've given to understand that I'd rather be taken in by my own charade, have a bit of hope" [*Friend*, 59; trans. alt.]); "Simplement [Dr. Chandi] devait m'entraîner, avec la plus grande douceur possible, tout en me laissant libre comme l'avait dit Muzil de savoir ou de me *leurrer*, vers un nouveau palier de la conscience de ma maladie" (*Ami*, 137; my emphasis) ("[Dr. Chandi] now had simply to lead me – as gently as possible, leaving me free all the while, as Muzil had said, to know the truth or to deceive myself – toward a new stage in my awareness of my disease" [*Friend*, 123; trans. alt.]).
14 Yannis is incorrectly identified as the Greek painter Tsarouchis in a translator's note in *The Man in the Red Hat* (1).

119; *CP*, 102).¹⁵ And yet as anyone who has seen the AIDS video *La Pudeur ou l'Impudeur* knows, the most powerful sequence in that film is the one where Guibert plays Russian roulette with the fatal medication. Clearly, the novelistic version is false, but that does not mean that the film is true, for it is possible that he did know whether the drops of the digitalis mixture were in the glass of water he drank on camera; "in fact," the person who edited the film claims that in this dramatic scene Guibert was miming his own suicide.¹⁶ But then we begin to wonder what it might be to mime a suicide just as the expression to *play Russian roulette* could itself be ambiguous. Neither visual images nor language itself can remove the fundamental falsehood that imbues story-telling. When the stories in question thematize lying, it becomes virtually impossible to determine where the lies begin. Indeed, it is like dealing with a set of Russian dolls, each one hiding another level of falsehood, the ultimate lie consisting of the camouflage that HIV resorts to in order to attack the body's immune system. Lies are anchored not just in storytelling, art, or language, but in the very substances that are at once part and not part of the body of the Person Living with AIDS. Perhaps all that can or should be determined with any degree of certainty is that in reading Guibert, we are dealing with not just fakery, but good fakery, like the good counterfeit paintings of his own work that Yannis discovered, because usually one cannot tell what is "false" from what is "true." The fundamental difference between the terms of such a binary opposition have been erased, made redundant by the writing of AIDS.

TRANSGRESSIONS

Guibert's AIDS writing is nothing if not transgressive. Sometimes the transgression goes against the grain of the heterosexist *doxa*, but at other times he managed to raise the hackles of gay activists, as was the

15 Ross Chambers has written about this contradiction: "[T]hese two texts, the video and the book, are in complementary relation with respect to Guibert's suicide attempt: one denies its possibility, the other documents it. Guibert is doubtless covering his tracks, but the two accounts thus also reproduce textually something like the double blind structure of the experiment itself, which will be either real suicide or a blank, and this in turn relates to digitalis's own well-known qualities as a *pharmakon* that, according to dosage, can kill or cure" ("The Suicide Experiment: Hervé Guibert's AIDS Video, *La Pudeur ou l'Impudeur*," 79).

16 "In the scene where he mimes committing suicide with Digitaline, he really put the drops in one of the glasses, and he played Russian roulette" (Mazureck, "'Sa façon de regarder un lézard,'" 23).

case with his video *La Pudeur ou l'Impudeur*. There can be no doubt that Guibert liked to shock his readers, and his AIDS writing in particular leaves little that is forbidden – to do, to say – unchallenged.

The writing of AIDS allows Guibert to take self-revelation to a new level: "De même que le sida ... aura été pour moi un paradigme dans mon projet du dévoilement de soi et de l'énoncé de l'indicible, le sida aura été pour Bill le parangon du secret de toute sa vie" (*Ami*, 247) ("Just as AIDS will have been my paradigm in my project of self-revelation and the expression of the inexpressable, AIDS will prove to be the perfect model for the secret of Bill's entire life" [*Friend*, 228]). Just as AIDS facilitates Bill's predilection for wrapping himself up in secrets, so too it becomes a kind of test case of Guibert's pet project; his *projet du dévoilement de soi*, as he calls it, is pushed to its logical extreme. Guibert had long been fascinated by Montaigne's conditional ambition to "se peindre nu" (to paint himself naked), if he lived in one of "those nations said to be living still in the gentle liberty of the first laws of nature." For Guibert now there is much more to reveal and the stakes are even higher, for there are medications, medical interventions, and tests to describe: no detail concerning his own body, however intimate, will be beyond the pale of what he will seemingly attempt to disclose. And even as his corporeal presence diminishes as he progressively loses weight and strength, Guibert will find ever more to say about his body, not to mention the bodies of others. As in the New Novel, the power of description is brought to bear on objects and our relationship to them, but now the "things" in question are no longer the ordinary objects of daily life but bizarre medical apparatuses, the whole *pharmakon* of chemicals that may kill as well as cure, not to mention the body's own liquids – semen, tears, sweat, and especially blood.

Echoing the title of Baudelaire's unfinished work "Mon coeur mis à nu," the narrator of *À l'ami qui ne m'a pas sauvé la vie* describes how he feels as if his entire body were exposed publicly:

> Bien avant la certitude de ma maladie sanctionnée par les analyses, j'ai senti mon sang tout à coup découvert, mis à nu, comme si un vêtement ou un capuchon l'avaient toujours protégé, sans que j'en aie conscience puisque cela était naturel, et que quelque chose, je ne comprenais pas quoi, les ait retirés. Il me fallait vivre, désormais, avec ce sang dénudé et exposé, comme le corps dévêtu qui doit traverser le cauchemar. Mon sang démasqué, partout et en tout lieu, et à jamais, à moins d'un miracle sur d'improbables transfusions, mon sang nu à toute heure, dans les

> transports publics, dans la rue quand je marche, toujours guetté par une flèche qui me vise à chaque instant. (*Ami*, 14)
>
> Long before my positive test results confirmed that I had the disease, I'd felt my blood suddenly stripped naked, laid bare, as though it had always been clothed or covered until then without my noticing this, since it was only natural, but now something – I didn't know what – had removed this protection. From that moment on, I would have to live with this exposed and denuded blood, like an unclothed body that must make its way through a nightmare. My blood, unmasked, everywhere and forever (except in the unlikely event of miracle-working transfusions), naked round the clock, when I'm walking in the street, taking public transportation, the constant target of an arrow aimed at me at every minute. (*Friend*, 6; trans. alt.)

The sensation that his blood is exposed to the other's gaze or even a wounding arrow (see figure 15) is how Guibert describes through metaphor the extreme vulnerability of the PLA to infectious diseases, not to mention his exposure to the glances and comments of passers-by.[17] In the heterosexist discourse of the media, the Person Living with AIDS has been constructed as a postmodern Typhoid Mary – the infamous "Patient Zero" (Treichler, *How to Have Theory*, 312–13, 360n7) – guilty of spreading a multitude of diseases to a healthy population of so-called innocent victims. Guibert deconstructs the stereotype by describing what it is like to feel as though he were flayed alive, his arteries and veins open to everyone's mocking or malevolent comment and action. There is a tragic irony in this because the situation described exacerbates one of Guibert's stated intentions. It is almost as if some cruel god said to him, "So you wanted to display yourself naked? Well, I'll show you." And show him he does, for the passage quoted could be considered as a rewriting or textual expansion of the French expression *avoir une sensibilité d'écorché vif*, "to be as sensitive as someone who has been skinned alive." In this new version of a project for a book that Edgar Allan Poe deemed undoable, "My Heart Laid Bare," the narrator takes on all the

---

17 The arrow mentioned in the quotation is a reference to Saint Sebastian. As Charles Clark explains in *AIDS and the Arrows of Pestilence*, "In the iconography of epidemic disease in western European art, the dominant plague figure is Saint Sebastian" (30); "St. Sebastian, the 'disease saint,' provided an opportunity for artists to explore male beauty and physique as he was the only male saint whose iconography permitted a nearly nude portrayal" (caption for plate 4).

characteristics of the flayed bodies painted by one of Guibert's favorite artists, Francis Bacon.[18] Not only are the body's vital organs exposed, but the very blood that is at once the life force as well as the seat and center of the terrible infection has been made visible. Hervé experiences this long before the diagnosis of his seropositive status. Everyone knows that such a diagnosis is determined by a blood test, and blood figures in the dreamed-for miracle by which all of his blood could be replaced by some improbable transfusion. Of course, this is not possible, precisely because HIV is not just some alien power attacking the human body's defense mechanisms: it has become an integral part of the body's new makeup. Uncovered, naked, exposed, and vulnerable – this is how Guibert feels about what is happening to him. By some cruel twist of fate, all of this seems perfectly logical – just as a tragedy is logical in its preordained chain of events – for someone as obsessed by self-revelation as Guibert. After all, did not his first published text, *La Mort propagande*, describe the dissection of his own body?

One could cite the many other self-revelations Guibert narrates in the course of the AIDS trilogy. Often these revolve around sexual desire. Hence, going straight from a painful operation on his throat to a restaurant, Hervé is bewitched by a young server's glance:

> Ce fut un jeune garçon que je n'avais encore jamais vu qui par hasard nous servit. Il m'observait à la dérobée avec des yeux innocents, ébahis et effrayés. Moi aussi je le regardai à la dérobée, j'avais envie de lui lécher le cul. Mais nous étions chacun pour l'autre déjà dans l'autre monde: séparés par une glace invisible qui est le passage de la vie à la mort, et qui sait de la mort à la vie. (*HCR*, 40–1)
>
> By chance a youth whom I had never seen before served us. He kept glancing sidelong at me from time to time, his innocent eyes wide with

---

18 Poe, *Complete Works*, 16.128. Poe's idea and title for a book "[n]o man dare write," "My Heart Laid Bare," inspired Baudelaire's "Mon coeur mis à nu" (*Oeuvres complètes*, 622), which in turn led to the guiding principle behind *L'Age d'homme* by Michel Leiris (*Manhood*, 158). Guibert's project of an unveiling of self appears to be underpinned not only by Montaigne (see introduction) but also by Poe, Baudelaire, and Leiris, who comes closest to realizing Poe's project. There are numerous passages in *L'Age d'homme* that anticipate some of Guibert's principal concerns, e.g., blindness, phantoms, a wounded man, *The Golden Legend*, as well as the dangers inherent in life writing, which is compared to bull fighting. On Guibert's fascination with Francis Bacon, see *L'Homme au chapeau rouge* (53–5 [*MRH*, 33–5]).

fright. I too was watching him sidelong, I longed to lick his hole. But we were already in different worlds: separated by an invisible glass barrier which is the passage from life to death, and who knows, from death to life. (*MRH*, 24; trans. alt.)

Sexual desire has not yet disappeared; but the two men might as well be on opposite sides of a glass partition, able to see and wonder about each other, although unable to touch in this world. Another revelation takes the form of the episode in which the narrator describes having sex with Jules, an image of sexual union made all the more remarkable since, like some Medieval dance of death, it pairs off "two sodomitical skeletons" (*Friend*, 141). Elsewhere, Hervé avows the erotic emotion kindled in him on seeing some young males in the street, just as he confesses to a desire to cannibalize the flesh of the half-naked workers seen on a construction site. Whether it be sexual practices that call to mind the originary sex scene never described, intergenerational sex, or the yearning to devour a worker's "raw, vibrant meat, hot, tender and filthy" (*CP*, 74), it is clear that Guibert always remains faithful to his project to describe the body, its desires, functions, and dysfunctions as it lives in the face of HIV and AIDS. To be sure, Guibert's project of self-revelation predates the AIDS fictions, but now there is much more to reveal. And as the stakes have risen, so too has the transgressive force of defying that which it is forbidden to do, to say, or to write.[19]

Guibert's revelations about Muzil's final illness and his own conduct at the time take the project of self-revelation to its logical extreme, for in this case not only are two bodies in question – Hervé's and Muzil's – but also the moral issue raised by revealing another person's secrets. In *À l'ami*, Hervé describes how, after each of his daily visits to the hospital, he noted down in his diary all the petty details concerning his friend's decline. He seems to be betraying the most intimate details of Muzil's private life. But there is much more. One day Hervé kisses Muzil's hand, thereby reenacting but reversing the role that Barthes would have liked him to play but which Guibert was not to perform in 1977. Any residual guilt about that earlier scene is soon erased by what follows:

---

19 I do not see Guibert's AIDS writing as vicious in the sense described in chapter 3. What is vicious (in the sense of a vicious circle) is the seemingly endless cycle of doctors' appointments, medical tests, as well as the truly horrifying violations to which the body of a PLA may be subjected, the worst of which, in Guibert's experience, amounts to oral rape (*PC*, 56–60; *CP*, 45–8).

169   For an AIDS Aesthetics

> Puis j'appliquai mes lèvres sur sa main pour la baiser. En rentrant chez moi, je savonnai ces lèvres, avec honte et soulagement, comme si elles avaient été contaminées, comme je les avais savonnées dans ma chambre d'hôtel de la rue Edgar-Allan-Poe après que la vieille putain m'eut fourré sa langue au fond de la gorge. (*Ami*, 101)
>
> Then I pressed my lips to his hand in a kiss. When I got home, I washed these lips with a feeling of shame and relief, as though they'd been contaminated, the way I'd washed them in my hotel room on Calle Edgar Allan Poe after the old whore stuck her tongue down my throat. (*Friend*, 91)

Here fear of AIDS drives Hervé to soap and water, thereby assimilating his friend and mentor with a female prostitute who French kissed him at a strippers' show in Mexico City. He is terribly ashamed of what he has just done, and yet what else can he do at that point but write it down in his diary? "Et j'étais tellement honteux et soulagé que je pris mon journal pour l'écrire à la suite du compte rendu de mes précédentes visites. Mais je me retrouvais encore plus honteux et soulagé une fois que ce sale geste fut écrit" (*Ami*, 101) ("And I was so ashamed and relieved that I got out my diary to make an entry, just as I had after all my other visits. But I felt even more ashamed and relieved after writing down this nasty gesture" [*Friend*, 91; trans. alt.]). Washing his lips may help him feel relieved, but it does not take away his sense of shame; and the subsequent writing about what he has just done makes him feel more shameful since this second (re)action seems to constitute an even worse betrayal of his friend. We see here how the mechanism of self-revelation works in Guibert. First, he performs the action for which he will soon be ashamed; then he expresses his shame in words, which is itself followed by increased shame. The process would appear to be circular and never-ending. But he does manage to break out of this vicious circle by reaching a third stage. At this point, he will be able to justify the inscription of his previous actions:

> De quel droit écrivais-je tout cela? De quel droit faisais-je de telles entailles à l'amitié? Et vis-à-vis de quelqu'un que j'adorais de tout mon coeur? Je ressentis alors, c'était inouï, une sorte de vision, ou de vertige, qui m'en donnait les pleins pouvoirs, qui me déléguait à ces transcriptions ignobles et qui les légitimait en m'annonçant, c'était donc ce qu'on appelle une prémonition, un pressentiment puissant, que j'y étais

> *pleinement habilité* car ce n'était pas tant l'agonie de mon ami que j'étais en train de décrire que l'agonie qui m'attendait, et qui serait identique, c'était désormais une certitude qu'en plus de l'amitié nous étions liés par un sort thanatologique commun. (*Ami*, 101–2; my emphasis)

> What right did I have to record all that? What right did I have to use friendship in such a mean fashion? And with someone I adored with all my heart? And then I sensed – it's extraordinary – a kind of vision, or vertigo, that gave me *complete authority*, putting me in charge of these ignoble transcripts and legitimizing them by revealing to me (so it was what's called a premonition, a powerful presentiment) that I was completely entitled to do this since it wasn't so much my friend's last agony I was describing as it was my own, which was waiting for me and would be just like his, for it was now clear that besides being bound by friendship, we would share the same fate in death. (*Friend*, 91)

In a passage reminiscent of the search of Proust's narrator for the memory that triggered the felicity associated with the *petite madeleine*, Guibert's narrator also experiences an epiphany. The difference is that in this case the moment of vision or vertigo leads to a premonition about the future rather than a clue about the past. But the experience is every bit as empowering, for Hervé comes to the realization that his writing project is legitimate. Rather than constituting a betrayal of Muzil, his diary entries are in fact proof that the two friends are linked not just by friendship but also by a similar spell, "the same fate in death." In describing Muzil's agony, Hervé is also textualizing his own, something that few writers have been able to do. Again one thinks of Proust, and the use that he made of his own experiences almost up to the day he died. It is typically Proustian that such material was oriented to the past, since he used his own experiences to describe the final illness of the fictitious writer Bergotte. Like Proust, Guibert establishes a link between two writers, Muzil and Hervé; but unlike Proust, the Guibertian narrator manages to anticipate his own death within the description of the first death, thereby fulfilling the challenge so many writers have faced of wanting to be able to write a sentence as impossible as "I am dead."

We would do well to remember the word that Guibert uses to describe this enablement or empowerment: *habilité*. This adjectival use of the past participle of the verb *habiliter* is related to the noun *habilitation*, "capacitation," a technical term used to describe granting official

For an AIDS Aesthetics

authority to undertake certain performative acts to someone who up until that point was not deemed worthy or capable of such acts. For example, after passing a second doctoral-like oral examination, a French university professor is *habilité* to direct PhD candidates. The *habilitation* takes place several years into the career of a new professor, and the examination is based not on his or her dissertation but on the publications record as well as a "thesis" analyzing the course and development of that body of research. In a similar manner, Guibert the writer is empowered to write about the final days of Muzil at a point in his life when he has already proven himself as a writer. He can now get on with the next stage in his career by writing about the death of his beloved friend. Like any nervous candidate, Hervé wonders if he is an impostor – hence the anxious questions at the beginning of the last quotation – but the adverb *pleinement*, "fully," used to describe *habilité*, "entitled," indicates that he knows that he has "passed." He is now empowered to write of the death of his master and mentor – his teacher – because his will be a similar death, thereby presupposing the seropositive diagnosis he will receive almost four years later, in 1988, the same year he began to write *À l'ami qui n'a pas sauvé la vie*, the novel in which he textualizes what I have just been discussing.

Transgression also takes the form of narcissism. Guibert was fascinated by postcards of Rembrandt's self-portraits, as described in *L'Image fantôme*: "Je les scrutai sans relâche, comme un miroir de science-fiction qui me renverrait tous les âges de ma vie à la fois" (*IF*, 64) ("I examined them incessantly, as I would a magic mirror that could reflect for me all the ages of my life simultaneously" [*GI*, 61; trans. alt.]). In terms of Guibert's own writing, there are numerous self-portraits in his books, going back to his autobiographical essay on photography discussed earlier. The AIDS trilogy continues this tradition of self-regard and self-description even as his body is prone to the opportunistic diseases that HIV allows to attack it.

Eventually Guibert was able to come to terms with his new self-image. First, however, when he looked at himself in the mirror, he saw only a skeleton. No doubt it was at this time that he refused to be photographed. But towards the end of *À l'ami*, his attitude changes:

> Je me suis vu à cet instant par hasard dans une glace, et je me suis trouvé extraordinairement beau, alors que je n'y voyais plus qu'un squelette depuis des mois. Je venais de découvrir quelque chose: il aurait fallu que

> je m'habitue à ce visage décharné que le miroir chaque fois me renvoie comme ne m'appartenant plus mais déjà à mon cadavre, et il aurait fallu, comble ou interruption du narcissisme, que je réussisse à l'aimer. (*Ami*, 242)

> At that moment I saw myself by chance in a mirror, and thought I looked extraordinarily handsome, when for months I'd seen nothing more in my reflection than a skeleton. I'd just discovered something: in the end, I would have to get used to this cavernous face that the mirror invariably shows me, as though it no longer belongs to me but already to my corpse, and I would have to succeed, the height or the renunciation of narcissism, in loving it. (*Friend*, 223; trans. alt.)

He learns to love the new image of himself, to see not what is no longer there – the flesh that has disappeared – but rather the beauty of what remains. Where a pre-AIDS aesthetic would teach us to find ugliness, Guibert realizes there is beauty to be found, and it is a beauty that he can and must love. Lee Edelman has written an eloquent commentary on this same passage in his book *Homographesis: Essays in Gay Literary and Cultural Theory*: "In the face of 'AIDS,' which [Guibert] will not allow to usurp his own face here, the narrator insists on the necessity of learning to embrace the body anew: on the need to love, not leave, the mirror, by rediscovering the luxury of narcissism from within an experience constructed on every side as a rupture in narcissism itself" (116). When one recalls that one commentator wrote that there could be nothing aesthetic about AIDS writing because the bodies of PLAs are ugly, it becomes clear just how transgressive are both Guibert's self-description and the commentary on it. As Edelman says, such self-regard and self-love are part and parcel of a "strategic mode of resistance" (116) that is every bit as political as activist interventions.

Traditionally gay men have been reproached for their passivity and their narcissism, although activism is seen by some as a means to get beyond these twin "weaknesses" (ibid., 117). Guibert writes about receptive anal sex acts, which are described in both *À l'ami* and *Le Protocole compassionnel*. But the self-love of a PLA raises the barrier of what cannot be felt and said even higher. He learns this lesson from two people: his friend and lover Jules, and the photographer Robert Mapplethorpe:

> Oui, il fallait trouver de la beauté aux malades, aux mourants. Je ne l'avais pas accepté jusque-là. J'avais été très choqué, l'été précédent, à la

> mort de Robert Mapplethorpe, que *Libération* publie en première page une photo de lui où cet homme d'une quarantaine d'années était devenu un vieillard émacié, ratatiné sur sa canne à pommeau de tête de mort, ridé et vieilli prématurément, les cheveux peignés en arrière, emmené en fauteuil roulant, disait-on sur la légende qui commentait cette ultime apparition en public, et accompagné d'une infirmière avec une tente à oxygène. Cette photo m'avait fait froid dans le dos ... Mais Jules, qui vit le journal en même temps que moi, commenta différemment la photo et s'étonna qu'elle me fit cet effet déplorable: "C'est absolument splendide, me dit-il, il n'a sans doute jamais été aussi beau." (*PC*, 115–16)

> Yes, it was necessary to see beauty in the sick, in the dying. Until then I had not accepted such a thing. I had been very shocked when the summer before, on the death of Robert Mapplethorpe, *Libération* published a photograph of him on its front page, showing this man in his forties as an emaciated old man, bent over his walking stick with its death's-head pommel, so wrinkled and prematurely aged, his hair combed straight back, being wheeled away in a wheelchair, as the caption informed us commenting on this final public appearance, accompanied by a nurse with an oxygen tent. This photo had sent shivers down my spine ... But Jules, who saw the newspaper at the same time as I did, interpreted the photograph differently and was astonished that it should make such a deplorable impression upon me: "It's absolutely splendid," he told me, "he has probably never been so beautiful." (*CP*, 98–9; trans. alt.)

About the same time that Hervé saw a photograph of Robert Mapplethorpe (cf. figure 16), a young woman in a bus tells him how handsome she finds him, and it is after this that he wrote the passage just quoted. Hervé is now able to go one step farther, and allows the painter Yannis to paint twenty-five portraits of him.[20] Just as Muzil taught Hervé that the relationship of the patient to his illness is one that evolves, so too his rela-

20 "This acceptance is a real turning-point at the level of self-identification. The narrator is now ready to face the ordeal of his own body, and it is in this sense that the projects of allowing himself to be painted in the nude by Barceló and of appearing naked on stage at a performance in Avignon should be interperted: they both betray a concern to 'aller au bout d'un dévoilement' ([*PC*,] p. 25) ('take an unveiling to its limit') ..." (Boulé, *Hervé Guibert: Voices of the Self,* 217). François Buot quotes fragments of an interview with Barceló in which the painter discusses his friendship with Guibert (*Hervé Guibert: le jeune homme et la mort,* 274–9).

tionship with his own body image continues to change throughout the AIDS trilogy: from grudging denial to what Foucault called *souci de soi,* "care of self," and then ultimately *maîtrise de soi,* "self-mastery." Roughly speaking, each of the AIDS novels corresponds to one of these successive stages, the final stage of stoic self-acceptance *and* self-control coinciding with the last AIDS fiction, *L'Homme au chapeau rouge.* At this point, Hervé's love of self allows him to love another person subliminally:

> C'était un amour d'une tension extraordinaire qui passait entre ces deux regards, de celui qui fixait en peignant, et de celui qui fixait en étant peint. C'était une activité physique qui aurait rendu dérisoire l'activité érotique, qu'elle comprenait sans l'exprimer il va sans dire. (*HCR,* 109–10)

> A love of extraordinary intensity passed between those two looks, the one that stared as it was painting, and the one that stared as it was being painted. It was a physical activity that would have rendered erotic activity ridiculous, and that it included without expressing it. (*MRH,* 77; trans. alt.)

This final passage about his self-regard allows us to realize just how far Guibert has progressed from the initial stages of refusing to allow his image to be "captured." And it is also this passage which allows us to appreciate how significant the "transgression" of narcissism is to the communication of bodies *and* souls.

Guibertian transgression often takes the form of what I will call superabundance. One could also call it *excess, surfeit, immoderation, overabundance, intemperance, overindulgence, piling it on, going too far, saying too much,* except that in each case the word or expression carries with it a negative connotation, since we tend to value economy, restraint, moderation, temperance. Language itself espouses a classical as opposed to a baroque rhetoric. Guibert is closer to the latter than the former. In his own way, he is writing carnivalesque texts in which "too much" is an integral part of the story. This is because if he is going to give readers even a hint of the pain and frustration that he is suffering, then they must experience that intimation of mortality *in the reading experience itself.* The text, as is the case in all literature worthy of the name, must not just tell but show, not just describe, but *perform.* In this case, it must perform a superabundance of just about everything.

It is crucial that Guibert "drown" the reader in a sea of details about what is happening to him, hence the emphasis on the innumerable medical tests, and what seem like mythical quantities of blood extracted from his hurting body. Life becomes a negative epic with Guibert at its center. There can be no doubt that sometimes Guibert does "exaggerate." For example, in the eerily mock epic tale of his experiences in getting to the Claude Bernard Hospital, the narrative folds back in on itself so that certain episodes that only happened once are repeated; the repetition serves to underline just how traumatic the subjective as opposed to the objective experience was.

In reading the AIDS trilogy, we have the impression that there is a surfeit of everything. There are too many blood tests, too many visits to doctors' offices, too many details about horrific medical interventions, whether tests or outright operations. And in stylistic terms, there are too many words, too many long sentences, too many commas – Guibert's favorite form of punctuation, which he uses instead of semi-colons and periods – in a word, too much of everything. We get a glimpse of what Guibert was attempting to accomplish in the following passage:

> David n'avait peut-être pas compris que soudain, à cause de l'annonce de ma mort, m'avait saisi l'envie d'écrire tous les livres possibles, tous ceux que je n'avais pas encore écrits, au risque de mal les écrire, un livre drôle et méchant, puis un livre philosophique, et de dévorer ces livres presque simultanément dans la marge rétrécie du temps, et de dévorer le temps avec eux, voracement, et d'écrire non seulement les livres de ma maturité anticipée mais aussi, comme des flèches, les livres très lentement mûris de ma vieillesse. (*Ami*, 70)

> Perhaps David hadn't understood that when I'd learned I was going to die, I'd suddenly been seized with the desire to write every possible book – all the ones I hadn't written yet, at the risk of writing them badly: a funny, nasty book, then a philosophical one – and to devour these books almost simultaneously in the reduced margin of time available, and to devour time along with them, voraciously, and to write not only the books of my anticipated maturity but also, like arrows, the slowly ripened books of my old age. (*Friend*, 61–2; trans. alt.)

Faced with what he believes is an imminent death sentence, the narrator feels the need to write, even if it means having to write badly, as many books as possible. The sentence itself is a mirror image of the Rabelaisian voracity that it describes, for Hervé must accomplish as much as possible and in as many different forms as possible; in other words, he feels compelled to condense a whole career, an entire oeuvre into what little time remains, just as he seems obliged to stuff as many words as possible into his often Gargantuan sentences.

It has been observed that artists trying to come to terms with AIDS have had to invent new forms, and that when they have espoused existing forms such as the novel, they have had to improvise new writing strategies, which often take the form of short books.[21] In fact, Guibertian superabundance is all the more noticeable because neither the books themselves nor the individual chapters are long. Thus, there is a discrepancy between the deluge of words and sentences versus the relative brevity of the works themselves as well as the chapters or fragments. The shorter units are stretched to the limit of comprehension, whereas the longer units are compressed; in some cases, chapters resemble Barthesian fragments more than chapters in a conventional narrative. It is as if Guibert were able to hype himself up to intensively detailed and labyrinthian writing of sentences – some of which constitute entire paragraphs and even chapters, such as the first one of *Le Protocole compassionnel* – whereas the books themselves are relatively short. Nonetheless, these works never appear simple or straightforward because of the elaborate use of the *montage* technique. What is remarkable in Guibert is that this neo-baroque impression of excess is created in relatively short narrative spaces. Hence, the superabundance is all the more remarkable because the texts themselves are compressed by the constraints of space and, especially, time.

One of the most ubiquitous forms that superabundance takes is that of numbers. Numbers are used to refer to the numerous medical tests and the results obtained, especially the all-important T-cell count, but they also chronicle the dates and times of appointments whether with

---

21 "HIV will be seen to have shaped, not only the subjects of gay art, but also its forms. Activist artists have had to develop new methods, new combinations of materials – I am thinking of the propaganda of ACT-UP, in particular. But even those who are working in traditional forms and genres – the novel, the elegy – have had strategies dictated to them by the state of their health. The simplest and yet the most extreme of these effects has been the need to trim one's artistic ambition to the possibility that one has not long to live. Many gay writers are writing short books ... [Proust] felt that he had time to indulge his expansive artistic integrity. AIDS literature, on the other hand, is generally still characterised by a sense of urgency" (Woods, *A History of Gay Literature*, 367).

specialists or friends, not to mention Hervé's weight. Throughout the AIDS trilogy, numbers serve to remind the reader just how quantifiable life becomes for a PLA, even for someone who heretofore lived in the realm of the arts and letters. It is as though people with AIDS must become scientists, their own medical researchers, a new and probably totally foreign career "choice." We have progressed into the aesthetic of the number, a kind of postmodern variant of Baudelaire's "Fusées," in which he wrote "*Tout* est nombre. Le nombre est dans *tout*. Le nombre est dans l'individu" (*Oeuvres complètes*, 623) (Everything is numbers. The number is part of everything. The number is in the individual).[22]

Guibert deals with this unbearable presence of all things numerical in two ways. First, he jumbles the chronology, so that it is almost impossible to follow his AIDS itinerary in the "right" order. Emily Apter has referred to a "dysfunctional chronology" ("Fantom Images," 85). Chapters do not occur in chronological succession; for example, the two fibroscopies described in *Le Protocole compassionnel*, which are separated by several months, are telescoped into adjoining chapters in order to emphasize the contrast between the first medical test, a barbaric act of oral rape, and the second one, not exactly a pleasant procedure but one done with care and respect by a doctor who is willing to listen to his patient. Another example is what Guibert calls the "Miracle of Casablanca," which fills the longest chapter in the same novel (*PC*, 174–217; *CP*, 152–89). It seems clear that the reason he chose to place this chapter towards the end of the novel, where it "normally" does not belong, is in order to juxtapose and highlight its positive atmosphere with the similar ambience of his stay on the island of Elba. The first occurred in April 1990, the second in July and August of the same year. By removing the Casablanca episode from its "proper" place in the chronological sequence, Guibert is able to camouflage the fact that the Moroccan faith healer's positive vibrations, good thoughts, and no doubt well-meaning send-off were all to naught, since Hervé finds himself at his lowest point after his return to Europe. It is only by attempting to reconstitute the chronologies – an impossible task – of this novel and the other AIDS fictions that one realizes just how much Guibert has doctored the narratives. In *Le Protocole compassionnel* he describes the process of textual montage and how he continues to work on his novel even when he is away from his writing instruments, lying in a darkened bed chamber:

---

22 Eventually in *Le Protocole compassionnel* the narrator gets to the point where he doesn't want to know the results of the medical tests he undergoes.

> Et j'écris mon livre dans le vide, je le bâtis, le rééquilibre, pense à son rythme général et aux brisures de ses articulations, à ses ruptures et à ses continuités, à l'entremêlement de ses trames, à sa vivacité, j'écris mon livre sans papier ni stylo sous le chapiteau de la moustiquaire, jusqu'à l'oubli. (*PC*, 153)
>
> I am constructing my book in the void, I'm building it up, adjusting its balance, thinking of its overall rhythm and the breaks in the cadences, the disruptions and the continuities, the interlacings and the interweavings, of its vitality, I write my book without pen or paper under the mosquito-net's big top, until oblivion descends upon me. (*CP*, 131–2; trans. alt.)

Another means that Guibert uses to deal with this avalanche of numbers is to treat them in a manner diametrically opposed to the way they are used in modern medicine, which is supposedly scientific. He thereby renews with a premodern tradition of alchemy by attributing a special meaning to certain "magical" numbers. Textual numerology is not unique to Guibert, for he has predecessors as illustrious as Plato and Milton, not to mention the Marquis de Sade.[23] What is unique to Guibert is the double use to which he puts numbers – both factual and symbolic – in the context of AIDS writing.

Five, as we know, has an almost magical resonance since it evokes the "Club des 5," Hervé's elective family. Seven is the number of letters in *Guibert*, but it is also the number of times the word *abîme*[*r*] is used in *À l'ami*,[24] whereas thirteen, a lucky number in the Guibertian universe, supposedly corresponds to the number of books the author had written by 1990. Just how important the number thirteen was to Guibert can be understood by the fact that he claims, contrary to fact, that *À l'ami qui ne m'a pas sauvé la vie* was his thirteenth book – in fact, it was his seventeenth book. In order to make *À l'ami* appear to be his thirteenth book-length publication, Guibert limited the list of his previous publications to twelve under the heading "By the same author," a lie made all the more obvious by the fact that within the fictive universe of his 1990 novel, he manages to describe *en passant* each of the works missing from the "official" list! The key to this positive symbolism of the number thirteen can be found in *Vous m'avez fait former des fantômes*, where Guibert describes how a character reverses certain superstitions: "Toi aussi, tu as

---

23 Cf. MacQueen, *Numerology: Theory and Outline History of a Literary Mode*.
24 *Ami*, 21, 36, 114, 169, 207, 226, 267.

des superstitions? commença-t-il. Bien sûr, répondit Rudy, mais je les brave, *je les utilise à l'envers* ..." (*Vous*, 181; my emphasis) ("Do you too have superstitions?" he began. "Of course," answered Rudy, "but I defy them, I use them in the opposite way"). As the narrator states at the end of *Le Protocole compassionnel*, "The number 13 brings luck" (*CP,* 199). The thirteenth unit in each of the AIDS novels is highly significant. For example, in *À l'ami* it is the chapter in which the narrator describes in loving and admirative detail the great work of his friend Muzil, the *Histoire des comportements* that stands in place of Foucault's *Histoire de la sexualité*. In *Le Protocole compassionnel*, chapter 13 is the one in which the narrator describes the first horrendous fibroscopy, which might seem an odd choice – given the symbolic signficance Guibert attributes to the number – until one realizes that he considers himself lucky to have lived through the experience. And in *L'Homme au chapeau rouge*, whose fragments, like the chapters of the previous novel, are not numbered – thereby adding to the camouflage of the encrypted message – the thirteenth fragment is the one in which the narrator describes how, under the influence of unbearable pain after an operation on his neck, he managed to write a text about the painter Yannis, his artistic double.

As for seventeen, one must remember the odd relationship Guibert had with Joan of Arc, or rather the wax representation of her head, which he claims to have stolen from the Musée Grévin. As described in chapter 1, Hervé fell in love with that androgynous head (figure 3), so we are not surprised to learn in the thirteenth fragment of chapter 55 of *Le Protocole compassionnel* that the Tunisian faith healer's mother thinks she is a reincarnation of Marie-Antoinette. "So maybe it's Louis XVII who has cured you ..." (*CP,* 187). Thirteen, seventeen, fifty-five: the numbers intersect at a crucial point in the narrative, with the result that this overdetermination of symbolic meaning should be a portent of good luck.

Fifty-five is the year in which Guibert and a number of his friends were born, a very good year, which corresponds to the number of chapters in *Le Protocole compassionnel*.[25] In the fifty-fifth chapter of *À l'ami qui ne m'a pas sauvé la vie* Guibert's writing blends and folds into that of Thomas Bern-

---

25 This is not clear in James Kirkup's translation, *The Compassion Protocol*. Not only have chapters 45, 46, and 47 been collapsed into one chapter, but chapter 18 (*PC*, 82–3), the one in which Guibert describes his attraction to women and ends up wondering if he will ever make love with a woman, has been omitted entirely! Even *Le Paradis* contains a numerical cipher, since the number of fragments (110) corresponds to 55 multiplied by two. No doubt this is a hidden homage to a friend or friends of Guibert's also born in 1955.

hard, so that it is impossible to tell them apart. Sixty-nine is an obvious sexual cipher, as well as the number of textual units in *Le Protocole compassionnel*, which is somewhat hidden since one of the chapters, the so-called Miracle of Casablanca, is divided into fifteen sections. Seventy-one is the number of fragments in *L'Homme au chapeau rouge*, a figure that seems to correspond to Guibert's age at the time the novel was composed – thirty-five – added to the age of his friend Thierry, who was a year older. There are one hundred numbered chapters in *À l'ami*, no doubt because one hundred is *cent* in French, a homonyn for *sang*, "blood."

Clearly numbers are not arbitrary in Guibert.[26] Rather they are redolent with meaning, even if much of it may remain unnoticed by the reader. The AIDS novels are traversed by "rules, secret laws, subterranean or celestial systems" (*MRH*, 41). In its context, this statement refers to the supernatural messages contained in our world according to the character Lena. I read it, however, as a *mise en abîme* of the fictive universe of Guibert and its encoded messages. Guibert believed that as long as he could keep writing he would continue to live, and that is why he included so many numbers in his novels, even if readers might be oblivious of their symbolic importance for him. Encrypted within the novels, which were published in thousands of copies, these numbers were like so many well-wishing prayers protecting him and those whom he loved. We know, for example, that he copied the calligraphy of ritual prayers during a visit to the Temple of Moss in Kyoto (*Ami*, chapter 43; cf. "L'autre journal d'Hervé Guibert," 76). In *L'Homme au chapeau rouge*, Hervé tells Lena that he is a nonbeliever, while at the same time admitting that he believes in the beliefs of others. Guibert was willing and able to try many things to obtain the hoped-for cure for AIDS: both scientific treatments of a highly technical character and prescientific practices of an equal but different complexity, whether it be faith healing or textual numerology.

---

26 Edmund White, while not addressing the use of numbers in the context of AIDS writing, does ponder their significance in relation to homoerotic desire: "Suddenly I thought how numerical desire is, all a matter of number of years, inches, dollars, and that lust, which would seem to the most concrete science, was actually a twin to mathematics, the most abstract ..." (*The Farewell Symphony*, 215). Read in this light, the use of numbers in Guibert could be interpreted as a new slant on the important role numbers can play in the life of a gay man: assignations, times, dates, addresses, as well as the numbers in sex advertisements mentioned by White. In Guibert these uses have been displaced by medical appointments, the results of tests, as well as the more esoteric or occult use to which he will put numbers in his AIDS fictions.

For an AIDS Aesthetics

In *Illness as Metaphor* Susan Sontag wrote that "the most truthful way of regarding illness – and the healthiest way of being ill – is one most purified of, most resistant to, metaphoric thinking" (3). In her subsequent work, *AIDS and Its Metaphors*, Sontag deconstructs certain specific metaphors about the syndrome, demonstrating how they often mask illogical thinking: "Such is the extraordinary potency and efficacy of the plague metaphor: it allows a disease to be regarded both as something incurred by vulnerable 'others' and as (potentially) everyone's disease" (64).[27] Lee Edelman has demonstrated how metaphor allows even scientific writers to naturalize that which is alien to the truth about the body (*Homographesis*, 91). To be sure, metaphor is slippery terrain, for AIDS is not like anything else, and the writer risks offending others by his or her choice of image. On the other hand, we know that metaphors can help a PLA, as Alain Ménil acknowledges: "It is understandable for people to use metaphors to describe the illness they are suffering from when the subjects of such discourse intend to underscore the subjective character of their relationship with the sickness: their words in the first person are meaningful since they are situated in the context of their relationship with their own selves (*une relation de soi à soi*) that the illness has transformed" (*Sain(t)s et Saufs*, 212–13). It is quite another thing for people speaking or writing in the third person, such as journalists, politicians, public servants, or clergy, to use metaphors to instill fear, guilt, shame, or hate (ibid.). In using metaphors to describe AIDS, Guibert is laying claim to his right as an individual and as a creative writer to the subjective perception of the illness and its effects on his body.

The first metaphor Guibert uses to describe AIDS is the most neutral. At the outset of *À l'ami*, he describes how the AIDS virus works by comparing it to the Pacman game.[28] Later he will make use of a military met-

---

27 "While Sontag is certainly correct in her assertion that the process of investing a disease with moral significance is potentially damaging to those who have the disease, and her desire to draw attention to this problem and to rectify it is undoubtedly admirable, the remedy that she offers is, unfortunately, highly problematic. Where are we to look for this 'most truthful way of regarding illness' that she proposes? Without relying on metaphors, how can we think about illness at all?" (Patton, "Cell Wars," in J.L. Miller, ed., *Fluid Exchanges*, 272). See also Alain Ménil, *Sain(t)s et Saufs*, 205–24; and Treichler, *How to Have Theory in an Epidemic*, 15, 170–3, 365n14.

28 "Before anyone had ever heard of AIDS, an electronic game invented for the amusement of adolescents portrayed the effects of the virus in the bloodstream. On screen, the circulatory system was a labyrinth through which roamed the Pacman, a yellow cartoon blob controlled by a lever; as it gobbled up all it encountered, stripping the various passageways of their plankton, Pacman was itself threatened by the sudden

aphor (*Ami*, chapter 22), a figure for which Susan Sontag has excoriated journalists and the authors of government propaganda. But it is the Holocaust metaphor that is most problematic. Judith Pastore has written about the rejection of the Holocaust image, since "using the vocabulary of other disasters betrayed the reality of the AIDS epidemic" (22), and Les Wright has devoted an article to the topic of "Gay Genocide as Literary Trope" in which he concludes: "Despite the ideology of resistance, the figural terms of gay genocide subsume the homophobic discourses embedded within the dominant cultural discourse" (67). Guibert's use of Holocaust imagery, however, does not take the form of a political statement about "gay genocide" in the 1940s as such, when he describes the look in his eyes by comparing it to the images of concentration-camp prisoners in Alain Resnais's at once magnificent and terrifying documentary film *Night and Fog* (*Ami*, chapter 4). And Guibert is reminded of his visit to Dachau as he approaches the almost abandoned Claude Bernard hospital where he is to undergo a series of blood tests. This reference is expanded then in *Le Protocole compassionnel* when Guibert refers to the Auschwitz death camp:

> Ce corps décharné ..., je le retrouvais chaque matin en panoramique auschwitzien dans le grand miroir de la salle de bains ... Cette confrontation tous les matins avec ma nudité dans la glace était une expérience fondamentale, chaque jour renouvelée, je ne peux pas dire que sa perspective m'aidait à m'extraire de mon lit. Je ne peux pas dire non plus que j'avais de la pitié pour ce type, ça dépend des jours, parfois j'ai l'impression qu'il va s'en sortir puisque des gens sont bien revenus d'Auschwitz, d'autres fois il est clair qu'il est condamné, en route vers la tombe, inéluctablement. (*PC*, 14–15)

> This shrunken body ... was the body I discovered every morning, an Auschwitzian exhibit in the full-length bathroom mirror ... This confrontation every morning with my nudity in the mirror was a primal experience, lived through again every day, I can't say the prospect helped me to extricate myself from my bed. Nor can I claim I've felt pity for the guy in the mirror, but it depends, some days I get the feeling he'll

---

appearance and proliferation of even more gluttonous red blobs. If you compare AIDS to the Pacman game, which remained popular for quite a long time, the T4s would stand for the initial inhabitants of the labyrinth, while the T8s would be the yellow blobs, themselves closely pursued by the HIV virus, represented by the red blobs and their insatiable appetite for immunological plankton" (*Friend*, 5–6).

make it, because people did come back from Auschwitz, at other times it is obvious he is condemned, that he is en route for the tomb, ineluctably. (*CP*, 6–7; trans. alt.)

Schehr speaks of "the frighteningly *unheimlich* nature of the metaphor [that] reminds us of the seeming inexorability of the death sentence" (*Alcibiades at the Door*, 175).[29] But Guibert does not compare himself to someone who died in a death camp; rather he compares himself to a potential Holocaust survivor. What I find especially interesting here is the distancing process; Guibert refers to himself in the third person. As we know, the third-person pronoun has been described as that of the nonperson by the linguist Émile Benveniste, an idea subsequently taken up by Barthes, who illustrated this in his "Fragments for H." The first-person narrator of *Le Protocole compassionnel* speaks of his reflection in the mirror as though it were of another person. AIDS has reduced him to the state of a nonperson, just as the Nazi death camps did for so many millions of Jews and others. The strangeness of the image, which is at once his own and yet seems to be that of another, is such that sometimes the narrator does not even feel any pity for himself. It is this loss of self-identity and self-pity that is no doubt the most difficult to bear, for it is difficult to have any self-regard when there is no self-image with which one can identify. One has to admire Guibert for having the courage to pursue this line of thinking so far, by incorporating within the narrative the alienation imposed upon the so-called nonperson.

Earlier I spoke of a healthy narcissism and the stoic acceptance that end up not just by allowing Hervé to love himself but also by allowing Yannis to paint portraits of him. The proof that Hervé has managed to get beyond this feeling of alienation is that some one hundred pages into *Le Protocole compassionnel*, he states quite matter-of-factly that his friend Jules calls him "Bébé-Auschwitz" (*PC*, 110; *CP*, 93). "A mere reference is enough; since the metaphor is transparent," writes Lawrence Schehr, "it can be introduced as speech in inverted commas: it becomes part of a gallows humor that no longer seeks to explain but to defy the situation at hand" (*Alcibiades at the Door*, 175). The humor at work here is made all the more poignant when one remembers that Jules is known as

---

29 Also uncanny is the textual reprise of the image of looking at oneself in the mirror and seeing the degradations brought on by the passage of time; just such a passage is to be found in a premonitory text written in the second person and dating from the early 1970s (*MP*, 99)!

Bibi in some of Guibert's texts; the Holocaust metaphor has been integrated into the idiolect or baby talk of the two friends. Hervé has indeed become a child again, as described by the ending of À l'ami qui ne m'a pas sauvé la vie: "J'ai enfin retrouvé mes jambes et mes bras d'enfant" (267) ("At last my arms and legs are once again as slender as they were when I was a child" [*Friend*, 246]). In the next AIDS novel, his friend Gustave is obliged to carry him to the beach just as his father used to when he was a small child: "J'ai besoin de m'agripper aux hanches de mon père pour qu'il me ramène à la plage" (*PC*, 150) ("I have to hold on to my father's hips so he can get me back to the beach" [*CP*, 128; trans. alt.]). At this point, the death-camp inmate and the young child – can one think of any image of more poignant disempowerment than that of a young child in a death camp? – have become one. Gustave has been transformed into the PLA's father, which is significant because, as described in *Mes parents*, one of Guibert's fondest memories is of being carried by his father, and it was from his father and mother that he first learned about Second World War atrocities. Now it is up to his friends Jules and Gustave to protect a childlike Hervé from the tortures of AIDS-related illness.

The last type of image used by Guibert to textualize AIDS is that of contagion. The image of a virulent type of infection is accompanied, as I shall explore in greater detail in the next chapter, by the practice of flagrant intertextual allusions, with the result that the metaphor for HIV becomes textually productive. Lee Edelman has described just how appropriate the image is: "this metastatic or substitutive transcription of the cell is particularly difficult to counteract to the extent that HIV, like metaphor, operates to naturalize, or present as proper, that which is improper or alien or imported from without. Subsequent to the metonymy, the contiguous transmission, of infection, the virus establishes itself as part of the essential material of the invaded cell through a type of metaphoric substitution" (*Homographesis*, 90). In fact, to speak of the same and the other is no longer pertinent, for contagion, like parody, has become legion. Just as the virus propagates itself by copying certain genetic information, so too intertextuality has become "simple" textuality (see Danthe, "Le sida et les lettres," 79–80).

We can now appreciate just how wrong Susan Sontag was to refuse AIDS writers the use of metaphor. To be sure, she wrote *AIDS and Its Metaphors* before Guibert's first AIDS fiction was published. But as he demonstrated, metaphor is central to his AIDS writing. Without it, À l'ami would not have the powerful impact on readers that it does. I would argue that by finding this metaphor of viral contagion and by transforming the metaphor into a writing practice, Guibert has found a way to represent the experience of living with AIDS at the level of both content and form.

From the most personal of self-revelations to blatant narcissism, from a superabundance of words and numbers to the use of metaphor and pastiche, Guibert has transgressed many of the rules of conventional discourse. One is not supposed to use more words than necessary, and, as we have seen, there are subjects that, according to some, are beyond the purview of metaphor. Guibert has transgressed many taboos, whether they be the prohibitions of polite bourgeois society or of high modernism. In fact, in preferring pastiche over originality, Guibert illustrates one of the main tenets of postmodernism: "Il est clair que je ne pouvais pas écrire sans admirer une écriture" (*PC*, 23) ("It was apparent that I could not write without admiring someone else's writing" [*CP*, 15]). At the same time, his use of an overpowering superabundance of details and tropes reminds us of a baroque aesthetic founded on the principle of *surcharge*, "excess." And it could be argued that his use of self-revelations and narcissism is a refusal of the heterosexist doxa according to which "real" men neither eat quiche nor engage in certain sexual acts. To embrace the image and the body of persons living with AIDS, to see in them a beauty that our present-day stereotypes about fitness and muscle would have us deny, is to posit a new aesthetic, one based on transgression of some of the most deeply encoded of cultural prejudices that our society has constructed. Thus Guibert's AIDS writing is, in its own way, a type of activist response. Its transgressive practices remind us that the death of the author is not just a hypothetical speculation about textual practices, as theorized by both Barthes and Foucault, but rather a very real possibility in the light of which Guibert has produced novels that can liberate us from several interdictions, some of which we probably didn't even know we shared before reading his work.

SELF-REFLEXIVITY

In reading Guibert, we discover that living with AIDS is like living in a gallery of mirrors, with the result that it is difficult if not impossible to determine when self-regard, self-revelation, and self-reflexivity interconnect, overlap, or end up meaning the same thing. This is a universe where writing goes hand in glove with reading. References to other writers may take the form of a list of authors admired: "Les écrivains morts faisaient la ronde autour de moi, une sarabande où ils m'entraînaient gentiment en me tirant par la main, le tourbillon de mes fantômes chéris" (*HCR*, 79–80) ("Dead writers danced in a ring all round me, in a saraband into which they gently drew me by the hand, the whirlwind of my beloved phantoms" [*MRH*, 54]), a clause followed by a long list: "Tchekov, Leskov, Babel, Boulgakov, Dostoïeski, Soseki, Tanizaki, Stifter, Musil, Kafka, Ungar, Walser, Bernhard, Flaubert, Hamsun." There are also numerous direct references to Guibert's other works, as well as the book that the reader is in the process of reading. In Eric Michaels's AIDS diary *Unbecoming*, he mentions that he was "warned against too much explicit reflexivity, a principle that I agree to, even as I sit here violating it" (19). Guibert, by contrast, often writes about writing, about its intoxicating ability to make him if not forget at least live through the pain: "It's when I'm writing that I feel most alive" (*CP*, 106). He also describes the kind of style he aspires to, a style quite different from the previous one: "J'avais envie d'une écriture gaie, limpide, immédiatement 'communicante,' pas d'une écriture tarabiscotée" (*PC*, 172) ("I longed to create a style that would be gay, limpid, immediately 'accessible,' not overloaded with ornamentation" [*CP*, 148]). In the last part of the sentence quoted Guibert seems to be referring to the ornate style used in *Des aveugles*. As for the adjective *gaie*, it probably does not mean "gay" in the contemporary sense – at least at the first level – since Guibert has not used the spelling *gay*, which is the most common one used in France when referring to gay liberation, for example. On the other hand, in other parts of the francophone world, such as Québec, where *gaie* has acquired the same meaning as in English since the 1970s, this sentence would be interpreted as a description of writing that is specifically homosexual, or better, *homophile*. But the two meanings are not mutually exclusive and, while not an gay activist, Guibert must have been sufficiently aware of current usage of the word *gay* in France to want to hint at the idea of same-sex love. Another example from the same chapter of *Le Protocole compassionnel* describes Guibert's use of *gai* to refer to the concept of an "open work," one in which the ending is neither predetermined nor even known: "cette marge d'imprévu réservée à l'écriture vivante, à l'écriture gaie" (*PC*, 173) ("that margin of the unpredictable that is the prerogative of living writing, writing that is gay" [*CP*, 149]). But one could also make the case that such unpredictability is one of the salient features of gay life, whatever style the person living it chooses to adopt.

Guibert even describes events about which it is impossible to write: "Il y a des événements qui résistent à leur tentative de restitution par l'écriture. Cela fait trois fois que j'essaie de raconter les séances de pose par Yannis, et trois fois sur plusieurs mois que j'ai senti la nécessité de déchirer immédiatement le papier" (*HCR*, 108) ("There are events that refuse to be reconstituted in writing. This is the third time I've tried to describe the sittings with Yannis, and over the past several months I've felt compelled to tear up the pages at once" [*MRH*, 76]). It is clear from these examples that the story of living with AIDS is, for Guibert, intimately connected with the experience of writing about that experience. However, such "explicit reflexivity," to use Michaels's term, is only part of the process of self-representation at work in Guibert's AIDS novels. Clearly, Michaels – or, as I suspect, his friends – and Guibert do not share the same aesthetic principles.

Self-reflexivity in the three AIDS fictions is not, however, limited to direct references to writing. In fact, all three novels are chockablock full of examples of *mise en abîme*, that technique by which a work refers to itself while at the same time designating some other form of reality proper to the fictive universe. In fact, each of the characteristics identified as part of Guibert's AIDS aesthetics is reflected within the novels themselves. These small-scale models of the larger phenomenon function as reading guides in a manner similar to the miniature three-dimensional models to be found at the door of each room of the school for the blind described in *Des aveugles*. For example, elegy and eulogy are anchored in the textual space of *À l'ami qui ne m'a pas sauvé la vie* in the form of Muzil's gift to Hervé of Marcus Aurelius's *Meditations* in which the Roman emperor pays homage to his ancestors and masters. Indeterminacy is mirrored not textually this time but in pictorial terms in a painting by an Italian artist (figure 17): "Le tableau n'avouait pas l'anecdote de son sujet pour le murer, comme j'aime toujours, sur une énigme" (*Ami*, 73) ("The painting didn't reveal the story behind its subject, and so remained an enigma, which I always like" [*Friend*, 64]).[30] As for incompletion, both *Le Protocole compassionnel* and *L'Homme au chapeau rouge* state that in the world of art, studies

---

30 The painting in question is *Dopo il duello* (After the duel) (1872) by Antonio Mancini (1852–1930). The narrator wonders if the young man represented in the enigmatic painting is the killer of an unseen victim, his second, his brother, his lover, or his son. According to Guibert, what we do know is that Mancini adored the model who posed for several of his paintings, a certain Luigiello. Mancini took his friend with him to Paris for his first big exhibition; but the painter's family pressured him into sending the young man back to Naples. Later they had Mancini interned in a psychiatric hospital (*Ami*, chap. 24). Cf. note 4.

are often more beautiful than completed paintings. The games of truth so essential to Guibert's AIDS aesthetic are to be found in the series of forged paintings in the last novel, but also in a simile in which Hervé compares himself to a pharaoh:

> préférant accumuler autour de moi des objets nouveaux et des dessins comme le pharaon qui prépare l'aménagement de son tombeau, avec sa propre image démultipliée qui en désignera l'accès, ou au contraire le compliquera de détours, de mensonges et de faux-semblants. (*Ami*, 213)
>
> preferring to accumulate new objects and drawings around me, like a pharoah preparing the furnishings of his tomb, with his own image multiplied over and over to mark the entrance, or on the contrary to obscure it with detours, lies, and simulacra. (*Friend*, 195)

The practice of self-revelation is mirrored by strippers seen in Mexico City and Montreal, the former female, and the latter male, just as Mapplethorpe's self-portrait is a reflection of the self-love that Hervé eventually discovers.

Even the process of self-reflexivity is itself mirrored by the use of the word *abîme* as in *mise en abîme*. Whether used as a form of verb *abîmer*, "to destroy," "to ruin," or as a noun, "abyss," Guibert uses the word seven times in *À l'ami*. The last example, on the last page of the novel, is the most interesting and also the most untranslatable: "La mise en abîme de mon livre se referme sur moi. Je suis dans la merde" (*Ami*, 267) ("My book is closing in on me. I'm in deep shit" [*Friend*, 246]). In typical Guibert fashion, he reanimates the figurative and rhetorical meaning of the expression by exploiting its literal sense, so often forgotten, since *mise en abîme* can be interpreted as "putting into the abyss" as much as "self-representation." Self-reflexivity becomes a trap for Hervé, a trap built by his own discourse as much as Bill's actions or rather lack of action. The AIDS autofiction comes full circle on itself as any difference between so-called reality and its reflections in the numerous textual mirrors in which Guibert has sought to capture it becomes indistinct. Self-reflexivity closes in on the narrator like the door of some crypt, like the literal door of his basement locker in *Le Proctocole compassionnel* in which he finds himself, like one of Poe's heroes, a prisoner.[31]

---

31 My thanks to Natasha Nobell for drawing my attention to the similarity between the episode in *Le Protocole compassionnel* (66–74; *CP*, 54–61) and Poe's tale "The Pit and the

Some of the traits I have characterized as representative of an AIDS aesthetic are to be found in Guibert's other works; for example, the autofictional element can be found in *Mes parents*, the self-reflexivity in his first novel, *Voyage avec deux enfants*. Nevertheless, we are dealing with an aesthetics that is based on unique human experiences and ethical choices revolving around the diagnosis of HIV and the experience of living with AIDS. Let us therefore attempt to bring some order to the question. There is writing about AIDS that corresponds to the AIDS aesthetics, such as the three AIDS autofictions: *À l'ami qui ne m'a pas sauvé la vie, Le Protocole compassionnel, L'Homme au chapeau rouge*. There is also writing in which AIDS is mentioned, for example, *L'Incognito* and *Fou de Vincent*, the difference between these texts and the trilogy being the degree to which AIDS is a secondary versus a primary concern and the presence of some as opposed to all of the characteristics studied. One could add the short story "Les secrets d'un homme" to this list. But there is also writing about AIDS that does not espouse this aesthetic: *Cytomégalovirus*, a hospital diary made up of raw material too close to the truth that, had he lived, Guibert might have turned into an AIDS autofiction. Finally, there is a video that espouses – at least in part – this aesthetic, *La Pudeur ou l'Impudeur*, which proves that it subsumes the difference between writing and film-making. Indeed, it is in the AIDS video that physical self-revelation reaches its logical but unbearable visual limit. As for the unfinished novel *Adultes!*, it did not espouse the AIDS aesthetic (the sentences are short, the style plebian, and the point of view that of a third-person narrator writing about a certain Gaspar). I believe this explains why the project was abandoned in the fall of 1987. The other crucial difference between the abandoned novel and *À l'ami qui ne m'a pas sauvé la vie* is that in the former, unlike the latter, Guibert was reluctant to come to terms with the subject of AIDS: he gets to the point of describing Gaspar's fear of being HIV-positive only on the last page of the typed copy of the manuscript: "Gaspar thinks he has AIDS" (*Adultes!*, f. 182, quoted with the permission of Christine Guibert). In *L'Ami* Guibert describes this failure to come to terms with

---

Pendulum" (1843). A close reading of both texts reveals a high degree of intertextuality, including use of the same words by Poe (or Baudelaire in the French translation) and Guibert. In "L'ours" (1983) Guibert describes reading "Les aventures d'Arthur Gordon Pym," the only text by Poe that he had *not* read when he was an adolescent (*PA*, 139–40).

AIDS in *Adultes!* as a refusal to validate, through writing, "la prémonition la plus injuste du monde" (*Ami*, 221) ("the most unjust premonition in the world" [*Friend*, 203]). As he goes on to say, in order for his book to see the light of day, he had to be able to write the following sentence: "Il fallait que le malheur nous tombe dessus" (ibid.) ("Disaster had to strike us" [ibid.]). In other words, unlike the successful trilogy of AIDS autofictions, *Adultes!* fails on the grounds of ethics as well as aesthetics.[32]

We must never forget the time element in considering the AIDS fictions of Hervé Guibert. There simply was no time (or the desire) to write a "roman bien fait" like a well-wrought play, no time to polish the punctuation or eliminate the repetitions, not that all – or any – should have been removed. This does not mean that the novels are without structure. Rather, the structure is always still evolving, based on a sense of urgency as the writing barely catches up with the living. In *Le Protocole compassionnel* Guibert comments on his preference for texts that are open-ended, subject to all the risks and hazards that turn up in the writing process. This postmodern project of AIDS autofictions is diametrically opposed to the jewel-like perfection attained by Albert Camus in his novel *La Chute*, or the structural triumph represented by *L'Emploi du temps* by Michel Butor. Of all the moderns, closest to Guibert would be Claude Simon. The latter's novels remind us of the etymology of the term *baroque*, "an irregularly shaped pearl."

It is, of course, impossible to convey totally the trauma of AIDS to someone who is not living with it. But Guibert does attempt to give us a picture of what he is suffering by finding various textual and rhetorical devices that correspond to his own experience. To be sure, there is nothing "politically correct" about this representation: Guibert's universe is not a collective one, for it is made up of individuals who must find their own ways through the labyrinth of mispresentations and lies that surround AIDS. Nevertheless, from time to time, there can be and there is real solidarity, such as that between Hervé and some of his doc-

---

32 There are also numerous references to the abandoned novel in *L'Incognito*, most of them negative (15, 20–4, 52–3, 61, 81, 132, 176–7, 180). It should be noted that in fact *L'Ami* does not begin with the sentence mentioned within the narrative space of the same text. Clearly, Guibert was more intent on beginning his first AIDS novel with the idea that he thought he had AIDS for a specific time – three months. In doing so, he avoids the idea of an inevitable death sentence in favor of the hope, uncertainty, and doubt that characterize a text in which ambiguity and ambivalence play such important roles.

tors or between Hervé and the other members of the "Club des 5." Finally, let us remember that, as Emily Apter has pointed out, Guibert avoids both sentimentalizing and politicizing the subject.[33]

Not all AIDS discourse has intrinsic aesthetic intent or merit: to begin with there is medical discourse. And even within the realm of works produced by creative writers, many of the attempts to write about AIDS – whether in the form of memoirs, activist texts, or fiction – do *not* seek to express this testimony, activism, or story in a unique form that is commensurate with the enormity of the subject and the ethical dilemmas and choices that it entails. Although it is a purely subjective impression, I will give it here: cultural producers working in the realm of the visual arts seem to have understood the need for new aesthetic forms earlier on than have writers.[34] To use the expression of Charlotte Delbo to describe her own writing about the Holocaust, Guibert's AIDS writing seeks to make us see (*donner à voir*), rather than just tell us about, what is at stake.[35] What is important in Guibert is not just that he wrote about AIDS or that he chose the form of fictionalized autobiography, autofiction, but that developing upon his earlier work he was able to produce an aesthetic that both captivates and frightens the reader, and thereby succeeds in textualizing the experience of living with AIDS. He succeeded in finding not an equivalent of but an aesthetically

---

33 On the supposedly African origins of AIDS, see *Ami*, 181, 223 (*Friend*, 164, 205). See also Sontag's *AIDS and Its Metaphors*, 50–1; Edelman, *Homographesis*, 258n18; Woods, "Ce pays de malheur"; Boulé, *Hervé Guibert: Voices of the Self*, 255–6, 304n43; Lévy and Nouss, *Sida-Fiction*, 32–4; and Treichler, *How to Have Theory*, 29, 101, 121, 320. Guibert's perception of Africa is one of a place of both real and imagined danger. It is also a place of loss: loss of innocence in *Voyage avec deux enfants*; loss of youth in *Fou de Vincent*; loss of the manuscript described at the end of *L'Homme au chapeau rouge*; and loss of memory about his trip to Mali in *Le Paradis*. While such a point of view might be seen by some to tie in with the agendas of certain right-wing politicians, I believe this is not the case. For example, Guibert's ongoing love affair with Morocco is clearly visible in *Le Protocole compassionnel*. Finally, we should not forget his complete contempt for French politicians' remarks about African immigrants to France: "Chirac's '[cooking] odors,' Cresson's 'charters,' Giscard's 'invasion': independent of my state, I will never vote again in my life" (*CMV*, 42 [trans. alt.]; *Cyto.*, 52).
34 See the scenario of Derek Jarman's *Queer Edward II* for an example of just how effective even typography can be as an eloquent form of protest against homophobia. For other examples of visual art about AIDS, see *Ecstatic Antibodies*, edited by Tessa Boffin and Sunil Gupta; *Don't Leave Me This Way*, edited by Ted Gott; and *Fluid Exchanges*, edited by James L. Miller.
35 Lawrence L. Langer, Introduction to Charlotte Delbo, *Auschwitz and After*, x.

valid representation of living with a body in pain.[36] By this I do not mean that Guibert's AIDS writing is "pleasing" in the traditional sense. Rather I use the word *aesthetic* as it pertains to "pure emotion and sensation as opposed to pure intellectuality" (*Webster's Unabridged Dictionary*). In *L'Homme au chapeau rouge*, playing on the French word for AIDS (*sida*) and the adjective *sidérant*, "staggering," he describes a terrible pain as a "douleur sidérante" (*HCR*, 14). I would describe Guibert's AIDS autofictions as *une écriture sidérante*, writing that causes us to stagger – emotionally, physically – as if we had been hit by a falling star.

---

36 In this Guibert's writing practice is diametrically opposed to what Thomas Couser has discerned in certain examples of life writing about AIDS: "The narrative of a late twentieth-century epidemic is simple a new version of the old. Rather than calling for new forms of autobiographical narrative, then, this new illness requires only the grace to see its underlying truth; once AIDS and homosexuality are rightly seen, autopathography virtually writes itself, following an eternal and literally canonical paradigm" (*Recovering Bodies*, 107).

Chapter Seven

Writing on Writing on ...

Écrire dans le noir?
Écrire jusqu'au bout?
En finir pour ne pas arriver à la peur de la mort?
Cytomégalovirus, 93

Writing in the dark?
Writing until the end?
Putting an end to it so as not to end up fearing death?
Cytomegalovirus, 81

"I had AIDS for three months." It is with these still impossible words that Hervé Guibert chose to open his 1990 novel, *À l'ami qui ne m'a pas sauvé la vie*, a work that is part autobiography, part fiction, and, as I will demonstrate, part document. But the subject of the book posed as much of a challenge to critics as did its generic ambiguity. When dealing with a life-and-death drama that was still being lived and written about by the central "character" when it was first published, one hesitated to treat this novel like any other text. As Lawrence Schehr wrote: "The risk of the AIDS-infected text is the loss of textual space, the loss of the text itself in favor of a sympathy that blinds the reader to what he or she is reading. 'AIDS' risks being the only readable signifier in a way that it becomes not a transcendental signifier but a transcendental signified ... Everything is AIDS" (*Alcibiades at the Door*, 162). On the one hand, the compassion that we feel for the protagonists of AIDS writings – most of which take the form of first-person narrations by the PLA – is such that we are tempted simply to see through such works as texts. No doubt this can make for a reading experience that is moving, but it can also lead to critical silence if the sympathy precludes any other type of readerly reaction. On the other hand, the opposite point of view, which would contend that a creative work about AIDS is still "just" a text, seems even more untenable.[1] This double bind was the situation in which I found myself when I was collecting information about and quotations of Guibert's works but before I actually began to write about them. A graduate student in linguistics who knew that I had amassed a lot of material asked me if he could use it as a corpus for a study on a particular morpho-syntactic structure – I forget which one, but let us say the expression *le fait est que* or some such other lifeless bauble. It was then that I realized that Guibert's works are not and can never be just a corpus like any other, which was why I refused the student permission to use the material for such a study, to his director's great surprise.

I realized that I had to find a way out of this critical impasse, since silence was not the solution. I was looking for a means by which to situate my own discourse somewhere between silent empathy and "pure" objectivity. Between these two zones of forbidden territory, I hoped to find my own discursive place, if necessary in no man's land. In order to tackle the problem, I decided to approach *À l'ami qui ne m'a pas sauvé la vie* using various concepts imported from narratology: paratext, mimotext, foretext, and intertext. My working hypothesis was that the conjuncture of these various types of textuality, which are not watertight compartments – far from it, since all of these categories can and do fulfill a metatextual or commentary-type function – might explain why Guibert's first novel about AIDS continues to have such an impact on readers such as myself mourning the death of an author who cannot and must not be forgotten. And what better way to help avoid such forgetting than by bearing witness to his most well-known work?[2]

---

1 According to Boulé, "it is ... not the role of the critic or the reader to enter into a 'compassion protocol' that will blur any critical judgment" (*Hervé Guibert: "À l'ami qui ne m'a pas sauvé la vie*," 4). He repeats this in his more recent work *Hervé Guibert: The Voices of the Self* (192).

2 Ross Chambers had described the link between reading and both mourning and witnessing with an economy of words that underscores their eloquence: "[C]riticism can thus be viewed as charged with significant responsibility for the afterlife of texts viewed as sites of discursive interchange, in which the death of the author requires both mourning for that death and continuation of the authorial project" (*Facing It*, 129).

PARATEXT

Although Guibert's 1990 novel has no dedicatee, its title takes the form of a dedication: *A l'ami qui ne m'a pas sauvé la vie.* In a work of fiction we usually suppose that there are at least two parts that are not part of the fictive universe: the names of the author and the dedicatee. On the other hand, we consider that the title is part and parcel of the text, some would say the first "sentence." Thus, a dedication that is a title or a title that takes the form of a dedication puts the fictivity of the work to test. If the title is well and truly fictitious, then it can be explained by something in the work. If, however, the author has simply moved the dedication from the inside to the outside, then we are dealing with a real dedication that has been "promoted" to the status of title. Such a case would be bizarre, but no doubt not unique in the annals of paratextual paraphernalia studied by Gérard Genette in *Paratexts: Thresholds of Interpretation* – titles and dedications, but also notes, introductions, and so forth. The case of *To the Friend Who Did Not Save My Life* appears all the more odd since, while one might easily conceive of such an inscription in the affirmative, the negation of the verb *sauver*, "to save," seems to run counter to common sense, unless, of course, the person was not capable of saving the life in question. To judge by the critical reception of this novel, most readers interpret the title as a dedication to Bill, a researcher in pharmacology working for a big American drug company, who alternately holds out and withdraws his promise of giving the autodiegetic narrator named Hervé a new anti-AIDS vaccine being tested in the United States. In the end, with quantities of the new drug severely limited, he chooses to give the vaccine – and the promise of life it represents – to someone who is younger, less ill, and more physcially attractive than his old friend Hervé. Thus the title should be read, according to this interpretation, as an ironic dedication, or a non-dedication, since the first word can be read simply as "To," as one might put on a parcel address, which would thereby erase any difference between dedicatee and addressee.[3]

---

3 See, for example, Bellour, "Trompe-la-mort," 54; Bernstein, "Hervé Guibert: À l'ami," 21; and Leclère, "Hervé Guibert: Les années sida," 25. More recently, Boulé has suggested that the title may be read as a sincere, i.e., non-ironic, dedication: "To the friend who did not save my life (Bill) but who nevertheless gave me a pretext for writing, particularly by his behaviour" (*Hervé Guibert: Voices of the Self*, 199). Boulé then goes on to say: "[I]t must not be forgotten either that *À l'ami* is a textual act of revenge on Bill" (ibid.). I find such ambivalence to be very faithful to Guibert's project.

In fact, the possible meaning of the title is even more ambiguous than one might suppose at first. Aside from Bill, four other friends of Hervé could be dedicatees of the novel. The first is Jules, the narrator's long-term friend and lover, who will find out that he too is seropositive, and can do little or nothing to help, much less save, his friend. Another possibility is Muzil, the friend who is Hervé's predecessor both as writer and PLA. Or, the friend in question could be the reader. After all, *Le Protocole compassionnel*, the next AIDS fiction, was dedicated to "all those men and women who have written to me about *À l'ami qui ne m'a pas sauvé la vie*. Every one of your letters has overwhelmed me." And in the second AIDS novel Guibert describes *L'Ami* as a kind of letter to his readers (*PC*, 121; *CP*, 104). Finally, another interpretation is that the eponymous friend is the book itself, considering that Guibert speaks about it in these terms:

> j'entreprends un nouveau livre pour avoir un compagnon, un interlocuteur, quelqu'un avec qui manger et dormir, auprès duquel rêver et cauchemarder, le seul ami présentement tenable. (*Ami*, 12)

> I'm beginning a new book to have a companion, someone with whom I can talk, eat, sleep, at whose side I can dream and have nightmares, the only friend whose company I can bear at present. (*Friend*, 4)

In short, the title may be fictitious, ironic, sincere, referential, self-reflexive; it may be addressed to characters as opposite as Muzil or his foil, Bill, just as it may be addressed to the reader, the sick friend, or even the book itself, since it risks displacing and maybe even replacing all of Hervé's other friends.

We can understand the importance of dedications for Guibert by the fact that four of them are quoted or referred to within the text of *À l'ami qui ne m'a pas sauvé la vie*. For example, one of them is destined to Bill: "En rigolant Bill lisait mon livre que je venais de recevoir de mon éditeur, et que je lui avais donné avec la plus réfléchie, la plus grave, et la plus affectueuse des dédicaces que je lui avais faites jusque-là, c'était sans doute rusé de ma part" (*Ami*, 193) ("Bill was chuckling over the book I'd given, which I'd just received from my publisher, and which I'd inscribed with the most thoughtful, serious, and affectionate dedication I'd ever written for him, which was probably very cunning on my part" [*Friend*, 175; trans. alt.]). An internal study of the chronology reveals just how ironic Guibert is being here, since the novel in question appears to be the one published in 1988, *Les Gangsters!* If Hervé wrote such an affectionate dedication to Bill, it's because he hopes to receive from him the anti-AIDS vaccine that has been promised him for several months. It seems that a dedication has a price even if it is the life of the author! Another inscription described in *L'Ami* is discovered by the narrator in the house where Muzil grew up: "'À Maman, le tout premier exemplaire de ce livre qui lui revient de droit et de naissance'" (*Ami*, 114) ("'To Mama, the very first copy of this book, which belongs to her by right and by birthright'" [*Friend*, 101]). This one demonstrates not the price but the necessity of certain dedications based, for example, on filial duty.

The situation becomes more complicated when we consider two other dedications mentioned in *L'Ami*:

> Quelques mois après que j'eus suscité ce fou rire chez Muzil, il s'abîma dans une sévère dépression, c'était l'été, je percevais sa voix altérée au téléphone, depuis mon studio je fixais avec désolation le balcon de mon voisin, c'est ainsi que discrètement j'avais dédié un livre à Muzil, "À mon voisin," avant de devoir dédier le prochain "À l'ami mort" ... (*Ami*, 21-2)

> A few months after I'd provoked Muzil's fit of hilarity, he went into a deep depression; it was during the summer, I could hear the change in his voice over the phone, I'd stare disconsolately from my studio apartment over at my neighbor's balcony (that's how I'd discreetly dedicated a book to Muzil, "To my neighbor," before having to dedicate the next one "To the dead friend" ... (*Friend*, 13; trans. alt.)

As is so often his habit, Guibert mixes different levels of the recent and more distant past in one sentence. In chronological sequence, these are: 1. Muzil's laugh in 1981 on being told by Hervé of the existence of a gay cancer that affected only homosexual men;[4] 2. Muzil's depression; 3. the first book dedicated to Muzil; and 4. the second book dedicated to Muzil after his death in 1984. In fact, these dedications exist: the first, "To my neighbor," is to be found in the collection of short stories published in 1982, *Les Aventures singulières*, and the second one, "To the dead friend," in the novel *Des aveugles* published in 1985. Of course, these books are

---

4 Foucault's laughter on hearing of a gay cancer is reprised in Edmund White's novel *Farewell Symphony*: "One evening I told Michel Foucault and the writer Gilles Barbedette about AIDS and Foucault laughed at me and said, 'Don't you realize how puritanical you're being. You've invented a disease aimed just at gays to punish them for having unnatural sex'" (380).

not actually dedicated to Muzil since the dedicatee in question was Michel Foucault, Guibert's friend and neighbor. The collapsing of reality and fiction within the space of the novel by the erasure of difference between a real dedicatee and a fictitious one allows us to realize just how complicated Guibert's universe is. One could also add that it is a universe populated by authors who do not stop writing – even in the face of impinging death – both books and dedications to their books. After all, the fundamental similarity between the "dedication of the work" (*dédicace d'oeuvre*) and the "inscription of the copy" (*dédicace d'exemplaire*), the terms Gérard Genette uses in *Paratexts* (117–37) to describe respectively the printed dedication and a dedicatory note written by the book's author, is that in each case we are dealing with a gift, whether real or symbolic, of that part of us we would like to be immortal.

Now we are better placed to appreciate the title of Guibert's first AIDS novel. It is the fifth dedication, just as we found five possible dedicatees and/or addressees of *À l'ami qui ne m'a pas sauvé la vie*. Five is a special figure for Guibert since not only are there five letters in the names of both *Hervé* and *Jules*, but their little family of PLAs, both real and potential, makes up the "Club des 5," as represented by the photograph of the five ex-votos that I described in chapter one. Five is full of symbolic signification since it represents the hoped-for cure of Guibert and his elected family. Five also corresponds to the number of stages through which Hervé progresses in relation to HIV and AIDS as recounted in *L'Ami*: 1. a time of total ignorance about the virus (until 1981);[5] 2. a period of growing awareness of AIDS in general and of semi-awareness of his own possible/likely HIV-positive status, a time that is characterized by denial, hope, and fear (1981–7);[6] 3. the three months mentioned in the first sentence of the novel when he believes that he is condemned to die of AIDS (December 1987 to March 1988); 4. a period of uncertainty and hope as he waits for Bill to get the miraculous vaccine that will save him and his friends

---

5 "C'est Bill qui le premier me parla de la fameuse maladie, je dirais en 1981" (*Ami*, 21) ("Bill was the first to tell me about this famous disease, it must have been sometime in 1981" [*Friend*, 13]).

6 "A toutes petites touches très subtiles, par sondes du regard qui devait tout à coup freiner ou reculer devant les cillements de l'autre, [le docteur Chandi] m'interrogeait sur ces degrés de conscience et d'inconscience, faisant varier de quelques millièmes de millimètres l'oscillomètre de mon angoise" (*Ami*, 137) ("With the smallest, most subtle touches, with probing looks that could stop or withdraw at the blink of the other's eye, [Dr. Chandi] questioned me about these degrees of awareness and unawareness, producing variations of a few thousands of a millimeter in the oscillometer of my anguish" [*Friend*, 123]).

(March 1988 to September 1989);[7] and 5. the final stage of despair accompanied by anger towards Bill after his "betrayal," which is how Hervé perceives his erstwhile friend's actual conduct as opposed to his life-giving but unfulfilled promises (October 1989).[8]

Thus it is not by chance, I believe, that there are five possible candidates as dedicatees, including Bill. As such they constitute a mirror image of the "Club des 5," both groups counting as one of their members the beloved Jules, and of the five stages of consciousness about HIV and AIDS that Hervé and Jules must live through. Where I disagree with some critics is in their attempt to identify the "correct" dedicatee of À l'ami as a specific character. The advantage of such an ambiguous title is that it allows us to enter that troubling zone of uncertainty where we must abide, at least for the time it takes to read this AIDS fiction. It is this incertitude that is significant, since it reproduces at the level of the reading experience the unknowable future that Hervé faces. Indeed, I would claim that it is one of Guibert's greatest discoveries. Hence, we must not attempt to reduce it by opting for one or another dedicatee, but rather read the title as an enigma for which there is no critical machine that will allow us to learn the truth. As we know, in a literary work, different meanings, different truths, accumulate; they are not mutually exclusive.

We have seen how easily Guibert mixes truth based on life experiences and fictional truth. But the paratext is not the only part of the novel that leads to this type of (con)fusion. The "fringe of uncertainty" (*Ami*, 11) described by the narrator affects not only characters but also readers, who like the former cannot stop wondering about where all of this is leading.

---

7 "J'entrais dans une nouvelle phase, de suspension, d'espoir et d'incertitude, qui était peut-être plus atroce à vivre que la précédente" (*Ami*, 177) ("Now I was entering a new phase, a limbo of hope and uncertainty, that was perhaps more terrible to live through than the one before" [*Friend*, 160]).

8 Note that the death of Muzil occurs during the second stage (June 1984), and that Hervé begins to write *Adultes!*, the novel that he will abandon, during the same stage (Fall 1987). He will begin to write *À l'ami qui ne m'a pas sauvé la vie* during the fourth stage (December 1988), which explains why the first sentence reads "I had AIDS for three months" and not "I have had AIDS for three months." The novel has two endings: the first (false) ending occurs in March 1989 when he is still in the fourth stage, whereas presumably he has been in the fifth stage for only a matter of days when he writes the final chapter. This explains why the novel could not end with chapter 77, i.e., at a time when Hervé already hates Bill but is not quite ready to give up all hope that his friend may save his life.

MIMOTEXT

Where *L'Ami*'s paratext dialogues with the novel's fictive universe, at the level of the writing, a process of stylistic imitation is at work, thereby making it a mimotext: "every imitative text, or arrangement of mimetisms" (Genette, *Palimpsests*, 81). As early as the third chapter, Guibert warns us that his book, which, supposedly, was to be rigorous, has become something else: "Mon livre, mon compagnon, à l'origine, dans sa préméditation si rigoureux, a déjà commencé à me mener par le bout du nez, bien qu'apparemment je sois le maître absolu dans cette navigation à vue. Un diable s'est glissé dans mes soutes: T.B." (*Ami*, 12) ("My companion, my book, which I'd imagined would proceed according to the original flight plan, has already begun to wrest the controls from my hands, even though I might appear to be the captain of this exercise in contact flying. There's a demon stowed away in my baggage compartment: TB" [*Friend*, 4]). On first reading, the meaning of this passage will remain obscure for another two hundred pages, especially since anyone reading the novel in the English-language translation might well presume that the narrator is referring to tuberculosis.

When describing a particularly troubling time for the "Club des 5," the narrator slips the following into a sentence: "I was obsessed, paralyzed by this image of Titi (one of the children of Jules and Berthe), unable to do a single thing, even to keep reading Thomas Bernhard's *Perturbation* ..." (*Friend*, 196). The rest of the chapter takes the form of a commentary on the style of Thomas Bernhard (1931–89), the Austrian writer who authored, among many other works, two novels about illness – *Der Atem: Eine Entscheidung* and *Die Kälte: Eine Isolation*. (Bernhard died while Guibert was in the process of writing *L'Ami*, as he underscores in chapter 76 of his novel.) According to one critic, there are "[s]imilarities (between Bernhard and Guibert) in the perception of illness, in the fundamental role of writing but also, much more disturbing, in their styles" (Sion, "Deux écrivains," 37). Among these similarities are repetitive constructions, lengthy sentences, and at the thematic level an obsession with illness, which becomes the prism through which the rest of world and the other characters of their respective authors are perceived. More than mere stylistic mimetism, we are dealing with outright pastiche. Furthermore, Guibert establishes a parallel between his own work, which seems to take on Bernhardian characteristics as though of its own free will, and HIV itself. Faced with these two virulent powers, he can do nothing but comment on his own imminent defeat:

> j'attends avec impatience le vaccin littéraire qui me délivera du sortilège que je me suis infligé à dessein par l'entreprise de Thomas Bernhard, transformant l'observation et l'admiration de son écriture ... en motif parodique d'écriture, et en menace pathogène, en sida, écrivant par là un livre essentiellement bernhardien par son principe, accomplissant par le truchement d'une fiction imitative une sorte d'essai sur Thomas Bernhard, avec lequel j'ai voulu rivaliser, que j'ai voulu prendre de court et dépasser dans sa propre monstruosité, comme lui-même a fait de faux essais déguisés sur Glenn Gould [*Der Untergeher*], Mendelssohn-Bartholdy [*Beton*] ou, je crois, le Tintoret [*Alte Meister*], et comme à l'inverse de son personnage Wertheimer qui renonça à devenir un virtuose du piano le jour où il entendit Glenn Gould jouer les *Variations Goldberg*, je n'ai pas baissé les bras devant la compréhension du génie, au contraire je me suis rebellé devant la virtuosité de Thomas Bernhard, et moi, pauvre Guibert, je jouais de plus belle, je fourbissais mes armes pour égaler le maître contemporain, moi pauvre petit Guibert, ex-maître du monde qui avait trouvé plus fort que lui et avec le sida et avec Thomas Bernhard. (*Ami*, 216–17)

> I impatiently await the literary vaccine that will deliver me from the spell I purposefully cast upon myself through Thomas Bernhard, transforming the observation and admiration of his writing ... into a parodic motive for writing, and into a pathogenic threat, into AIDS, thus writing a book that is essentially Bernhardian in its essence, a work of imitative fiction that is actually a kind of essay on Thomas Bernhard, with whom I have tried to compete, whom I've tried to catch unawares, unprepared, to outdo him at his own monstrosities, the way he himself wrote fake, disguised essays on Glenn Gould [*The Loser*], Mendelssohn-Bartholdy [*Concrete*], or Tintoretto [*Old Masters*], I think it was, and I did not lay down my arms in recognition of a superior genius (unlike his character Wertheimer, who gave up his ambition to become a piano virtuoso the day he heard Glenn Gould play the *Goldberg Variations*), on the contrary, I rebelled against the virtuosity of Thomas Bernhard, and I, poor Guibert, I tried even harder, I pulled out all the stops to make myself the equal of this modern master, I, poor little Guibert, ex-master of the world who found himself bested by both Thomas Bernhard and AIDS. (*Friend*, 198–99; trans. alt.)

The Wertheimer character in Bernhard's novel *Der Untergeher*, translated as *The Loser* in English and as *Le Naufragé* in French, is a pianist who cannot stand being second best to Glenn Gould: "But everything about him [Wertheimer] was pure cowardice toward Glenn's triumph with the *Goldberg Variations*. How can I perform in public now that I've heard Glenn, he often said, while again and again I tried to make him understand that he played better than all the others, *although not as well as Glenn*, which I didn't say to him but which he could intuit in everything I said" (*The Loser*, 105). Consequently, Wertheimer ends up by killing himself, and this "loser," as the Canadian pianist is supposed to have called him, becomes the foil of Guibert's narrator in *L'Ami*. Contrary to the suicidal perfectionist who wasn't up to scratch, Hervé has the courage and the unmitigated gall to try to compete with a genius, or rather with several.

According to the afterword by Mark M. Anderson that follows the American edition of *The Loser*, "Bernhard's genius consists in his ability to vary the main themes and settings for his work, which function as an analogue to his own writing ... Here it is Bach's *Goldberg Variations*, played by Glenn Gould, that provides as it were the basso continuo for Bernhard's own deliberately droning repetitions and variations" (187). Perhaps then we should consider *L'Ami* as a mimo-mimotext, that is, as a mimotext of Bernhard's novel, which is itself a mimotext of the famous piece of music by Bach, the *Goldberg Variations*, as well as Glenn Gould's (first?) interpretation of them. The fact that Bernhard dared write about a semi-fictitious Glenn Gould, as well as the style of his novel – a monologue composed of long sentences that as often as not lack logical transitions – remind us of Guibert's novel. As for the comparison of Guibert's variations with those of Bach and Bernhard *en passant* ... only an interdisciplinary study could determine if a musical style – or more appropriately styles – can be textualized in words. No doubt it would be a fascinating study to undertake, made all the more difficult by the fact that the *Goldberg Variations* are based, as we know, on both difference and identity. All of this is made even more complicated by the fact that Guibert read Bernhard's novel in the French translation, which adds another level of textual transcendence to the processes involved.[9]

But Guibert does not limit himself to imitating Bernhard's style, for he also comments on it: the mimotext includes a metatextual-type commentary. In short, Guibert's novel becomes a kind of imitative essay when he begins to comment on both the Austrian novelist's writing and

---

9 On the musicality of Bernhard's prose, see Michael P. Olson's article, "Thomas Bernard, Glenn Gould, and the Art of the Fugue: Contrapuntal Variations in *Der Untergeher*."

on his own folly of trying to compete with someone who is "stronger than he." Writing in the shadow of Thomas Bernhard, Guibert finds himself imitating the other's style in order to purge himself of it. (One is reminded of the therapeutic function played by Proust's pastiches of L'affaire Lemoyne.) But the problem is that the literary infection is propagating itself at such speed that the autodiegetic narrator cannot *not* write in the manner of the author whose writing style is both obsessing and destroying him. Any voluntary effort at the outset to create a work that was in part a mimotext has gotten totally out of hand by now. The only way to get out of this mimetic melee is to articulate the experience of writing in the style of someone else in order not to cure the malady, which is uncurable, but to soothe the pain that the work we are reading describes and re-presents. In short, all that can be hoped for is to transform the mimotext into a metatext that is not critical but fictional. (It is here that we can appreciate just how impossible it is to separate the various textual categories postulated when dealing with a real text!)[10] But there is more, for Guibert's novel becomes a textual allegory of what ails him:

> La métastase bernhardienne, similairement à la progression du virus HIV qui ravage à l'intérieur de mon sang les lymphocytes en faisant crouler mes défenses immunitaires, ... parallèlement donc au virus HIV la *métastase* bernhardienne s'est propagée à la vitesse grand V dans mes tissus et mes réflexes vitaux d'écriture, elle la phagocyte, elle l'absorbe, la captive, en détruit tout naturel et toute personnalité pour étendre sur elle sa domination ravageuse. (*Ami*, 215–16; my emphasis)

> The Bernhardian metastasis, *in a manner similar to the progress of the HIV virus* as it slashes its way through the defensive ranks of my lymphocytes ... this Bernhardian *metastasis* has spread just like the HIV virus at Top Speed capital T capital S through the vital tissues and reflexes of my writing, imprisoning it, absorbing it, gobbling it up, destroying all its personality and natural qualities with its ravenous domination. (*Friend*, 198; my emphasis)

10 "If one views transtextuality in general not as a classification of texts (a notion that makes no sense, since there are no texts without textual transcendence) but rather as an aspect of textuality, and no doubt *a fortiori* of literariness, as Riffaterre would right put it, then one should also consider its diverse components (intertextuality, paratextuality, etc.) not as categories of texts but rather as aspects of textuality" (Genette, *Palimpsests*, 8).

This passage reminds us of the one in which Guibert establishes a parallel between continuing to read dangerous texts and the reinjection of the AIDS virus: "Je me suis arrêté de le lire [Thomas Bernhard] pour stopper l'empoisonnement. On dit que chaque réinjection du virus du sida par fluides, le sang, le sperme ou les larmes, réattaque le malade déjà contaminé, on prétend peut-être ça pour limiter les dégâts" (*Ami*, 12) ("I've stopped reading these pages to keep the poison from spreading. It's said that each reintroduction of the AIDS virus through bodily fluids – blood, semen, tears – renews the attack on the already infected patient; perhaps they're just saying that in an effort to contain the damage" [*Friend*, 4]). The problem is that it is already too late. Just as HIV is replicating itself in the narrator's body at superhuman speed, so too the style of the other writer is taking up all the textual space, infiltrating every sentence, so that Guibert's has no literary defense mechanisms to ward off the powers of the text that is invading and even becoming his own. (In narratological terms, Bernhard's text is the *hypotext*, Guibert's the *hypertext*.) As with the AIDS virus, Guibert can no longer distinguish between what is foreign – Bernhard, HIV – and himself. Thus, it is not surprising that he uses the word *metastasis* to describe the process by which his writing and his body are colonized to the extent that he loses control of both. We know that metastasis refers to "the transference of disease-producing organisms or of malignant or cancerous cells to other parts of the body" (*Webster's Unabridged Dictionary*). Certainly, the term does not seem too strong to describe what is happening to the narrator and his prose, and we recall with bitter irony Foucault's laughter upon learning of a so-called gay *cancer*. But we must not forget that the term *metastasis* has another meaning in classical rhetoric: "After an opponent has solidly established the facts, a speaker responds by placing the blame elsewhere" (Dupriez, *A Dictionary of Literary Devices*). The two meanings of *metastasis*, the medical and the rhetorical, are both equally appropriate to what Hervé is living and describing. Bernhardian metastasis must be understood in the strongest sense of the term, that is, as a fatal syndrome for which there is no vaccine, and as a process of self-replicating contagion the result of which is that human and textual bodies become resistant to both will power and medications. There is no better therapy available to the writer of fiction whose body is in such "dis-ease" than the possibility of inscribing his pain, and "placing the blame elsewhere," in short, by becoming part and parcel of a process of literary metastasis the mimetic function of which does not exclude its role as textual *phamarkon*, at once poison and remedy.[11]

FORETEXT

Some critics reacted very negatively to the fact that Guibert dared to speak of the death of a philosopher whom they identified as Foucault. "If Foucault didn't want to broadcast his private life, should we do so now by relating conversations he thought were intimate, sealed by the secret of friendship, by relaying, without any embellishment, the painful details of his mortal agony?" (Braudeau, "Écriture contre la montre," 30). Another critic managed to denounce Guibert and at the same time gleefully uncover the "real" identity of Muzil, as though there were no difference between a character in a novel and a real person: "By describing the sexuality, then the illness, and finally the agony of a famous man of whom he was the intimate friend, Guibert has violated the law as much as the memory of the departed, who is none other than Michel Foucault" (Garcin, "Hervé Guibert raconte l'agonie de Michel Foucault," 80). Not every critic cried scandal, however. For example, the following judgment is more nuanced: "This position as 'traitor' chosen by the author leads to a second error of interpretation, probably deliberate, in a society always on the lookout for more or less scandalous anecdotes: reading the novel for no other reason than to identify the real-life people behind the characters and feeding on the indiscreet secrets that the narrator divulges ... But the 'revelations' concerning the death of Foucault will only be revealing to those who feigned ignorance about the illness he was suffering from and perhaps also those who will be jubilant at the idea that his work is contaminated or even devalued by the life of this thinker" (Czarny, "La 'maladie' acceptée," 9). Since the time of Foucault's death rumors had circulated about the cause. In fact, *Libération*, went so far as to include an unsigned insert in its twelve-page supplement published on 26 June 1984 denouncing "'the viciousness of the rumor [which] remains astounding. As if Foucault must have died shamefully'" (quoted by James E. Miller, *The Passion of Michel Foucault*, 21; cf. Eribon, *Michel Foucault* [1991],

11 "In once again comparing what happens to his body with a literary metaphor, the colonisation of his prose by that of Bernhard, the narrator enters a new phase of acceptance of his illness. Literature here transcends its function of mimicking reality and becomes a mediator between Guibert and his non-fictive self" (Boulé, *Voices of the Self,* 202).

350–1). Today it seems incredible that the left-wing newspaper that Foucault had helped found would publish such a piece of hateful nonsense. No doubt we must remember the context. It is certain that since 1984 attitudes about AIDS have changed in France, thanks in part to Guibert.

When he was asked about writing a fiction based in part on his dear friend, the novelist replied that he never claimed to possess the factual truth about Foucault's death: "I would also like to clarify that I have never had the impression of saying the truth about the death of [Foucault]. I don't possess it" (Interview with Lançon, 83). In another interview, Guibert articulated a more sophisticated position in relation to "truth" that is written down:

> AIDS has allowed me to make even more radical certain narrative techniques, the relation to truth, the staging of myself beyond what I had ever thought possible. I speak of truth and all that can deform it through writing. It is [precisely] for that reason that I am keen on the word *novel*. My models exist, but they are characters. I stick to the truth to the extent that it allows me to transplant particles of fiction like pieces of film with the idea that it be as transparent as possible. But there is also the powerful incentive to lie [*des grands ressorts de mensonge*] in this book. (Interview with Gaudemar, "La vie sida," 21)

It is neither necessary nor possible to determine with any exactitude what is factual and what is fictitious in *L'Ami*, as Foucault's biographers have discovered.[12] Macey concludes his lengthy tome by telling us that Foucault himself probably would have preferred Guibert's novel to an "objective" biography! Undoubtedly, the truth that Foucault would have preferred is poetic or literary truth, the same truth that pertains in Guibert's statements.

If this truism applies to the novel as a whole, then it applies equally to its metatextual dimension. For the metatext, which here is fictional despite what Genette has to say on the subject ("the metatext is by essence nonfictional" [*Palimpsests*, 397]), must be read as kind of fictional truth. In *L'Ami* Guibert's writing becomes metatextual – as well as mimotextual – when he describes Thomas Bernhard's writing synchronically, whereas the metatext of the other writer's book describes it in its diachronic dimension. The book in question, which reminds us of Fou-

---

[12] See Eribon, *Michel Foucault* (1991), 347–55; Miller, *The Passion of Michel Foucault*, 354–74; and Macey, *The Lives of Foucault*, 470–80.

cault's *History of Sexuality* (1976–84), is one on which a philosopher worked for ten years, in fact right up to the day he fell sick: Muzil's *History of Behavior*. The theories developed in this work are not described, since Guibert preferred to concentrate on its problematic genesis. I quote the passage in its entirety because its length is part and parcel of its significance:

> Engagé au premier tiers d'un chantier dont il avait dessiné le plan, *les pylônes et les arêtes*, les zones d'ombre aussi, et les passerelles de circulation, selon les règles du système qui avaient fait leurs preuves dans ses livres précédents, qui lui avaient valu sa réputation internationale, le voilà saisi d'un ennui, ou d'un doute terrible. *Il arrête le chantier, raye tous ses plans, stoppe cette histoire monumentale des comportements* ordonnée par avance sur le papier à musique de ses dialectiques. Il pense d'abord reporter à la fin le deuxième volume, le laisser en tout cas en attente, *pour prendre un autre angle d'attaque,* décaler les origines de son histoire, et inventer de nouvelles méthodes d'exploration. *De déviation en déviation, axé sur des voies périphériques, des excroissances annexes de son projet initial qui deviennent à elles seules des livres en soi plus que des paragraphes*, il se perd, se décourage, détruit, abandonne, *rebâtit*, regreffe et se laisse peu à peu gagner par la torpeur excitée d'un repli, d'un manquement persistant de publication, *en butte à toutes les rumeurs, les plus jalouses, d'impuissance et de gâtisme, ou d'un aveu d'erreur ou de vacuité,* engourdi de plus en plus par le rêve d'un livre infini ... L'assurance de sa mort prochaine mit un terme à ce rêve. Une fois le temps compté, il entreprit de réordonner son livre, avec limpidité. (*Ami*, 36; my emphasis)

Committed to the first section of a project for which he had drawn up the plans, designed *the framework and vaults*, sketched in connecting passage-ways and areas of shadow, following the rules of a system that had already proven its value in his previous books and won him his international reputation, he was now struck with boredom, or some terrible misgiving. *Everything comes to a halt on the building site, the plans go out the window, and he stops working on this monumental history of behavior* already plotted out on his dialectical graph paper. At first he intends to move the second volume to the end of the series, or at least to set it temporarily aside, so that he can *approach the subject from another angle*, shift the beginning of his study back in time, and invent a new methodology of exploration. *Following peripheral roads from detour to detour, supplementary paragraphs burgeon into something more like complete books*, he becomes lost, discouraged, destroys pages, abandons efforts, *rebuilds*, rearranges, slowly falling prey to the insidious lassitude of withdrawal, of persistently avoiding publication, and is *exposed to the most jealous of rumors of all kinds, accusations of impotence, senility, his silence interpreted as an admission of error or vacuity, seduced more and more by the dream of an endless book* ... The certainty of his approaching death put an end to this dream. Once his days were numbered, he began to reorganize his book with absolute clarity. (*Friend*, 27–8; trans. alt.; my emphasis)

Such is the homage that Guibert pays to his friend's masterly work. Of course, the sentence that I have just written is ambiguous, since the novel's autodiegetic narrator is named Guibert and the friend in question could be either Foucault or Muzil, according to the interpretation one wishes to give to the tribute paid to an older friend, whether real or imaginary. I prefer to retain this ambiguity, for by now it has become clear that it is neither pertinent nor possible to distinguish between the two in our reading of *L'Ami*. In fact, the novel teaches us to be wary of such drastic distinctions. What is significant is the fact that Guibert's novel describes with so much brio – and admiration – the conception, planning, fleshing out, and rewriting of another work.[13]

The narrator of Guibert's novel describes a truly Proustian enterprise that only the impending death of the researcher/writer forces him to bring to a close. Guibert makes use of engineering metaphors to explain how Muzil's orginal project grew: "framework and vaults," "building site," "peripheral roads," "rebuilds." On the other hand, he also has recourse to critical terms to demonstrate the processes of research and rewriting: "the rules of a system," "approach the subject from another angle," "supplementary paragraphs burgeon into something more like complete books." And he does not refrain from reminding his readers of the vicious gossip so characteristic of intellectuals

---

13 Guibert's homage to Muzil's final research project can be read as a rewriting of what Foucault himself said about the long gestation of *The History of Sexuality* after the publication of the first volume: "The risks [of this long detour]? First, there was the likelihood of delaying and upsetting the publication schedule that I had projected. I am grateful to those who followed the advances and detours of my work ... As to those for whom to work hard, to begin and begin again, to attempt and be mistaken, to go back and rework everything from top to bottom, and still find reason to hesitate from one step to the next – as to those, in short, for whom to work in the midst of uncertainty and apprehension is tantamount to failure, all I can say is that clearly we are not from the same planet" (*History of Sexuality*, vol. 2, 7).

whether they live in Paris, Berkeley, or Toronto: "exposed to the most jealous of rumors of all kinds, accusations of impotence, senility, his silence interpreted as an admission of error or vacuity."

Rather than the end product, Guibert emphasizes the *process* by which this great project evolved into something quite different from what was originally intended when the first volume was published in 1976. Muzil had to reconceptualize his initial research project in a different manner: he found himself obliged to conceive, construct, and utilize new approaches to a problematic that was evolving constantly in his mind and in his notes. I believe that the passage quoted is a better description of intellectual work than what one finds in many a work of criticism, precisely because the repetitions, the parallel and subordinate constructions, as well as the almost unbearable length textualize just how frustrating, exhilarating, and captivating a research project can become. Guibert's prose becomes truly mimetic here by the perfect symbiosis of the work commented upon but not cited and a metatext that seems to push mimetism to its extreme limit, since Guibert's sentences follow the sinuous, even tortuous course taken by the thought processes involved in this almost infinite project. The Bernhardian metatext was full of rivalry and jealousy, but in describing Muzil's work there is nothing of the kind. But we would do well to remember that even while paying tribute to Muzil, Guibert's writing imitates not Foucault's but Bernhard's style! It is as if the pastiche form has become so internalized that it continues to function, to hold sway, in fact to reign supreme even when it comes time to describe another text, a friendly text, so that the new text produced is already another manifestation of textual metastasis.[14]

INTERTEXT

One of the most important forms of intertextuality in Guibert's works is that which links *À l'ami qui ne m'a pas sauvé la vie* and a short story written by Guibert the day after Foucault's funeral (Interview with Jonquet, 110), "Les secrets d'un homme," published four years later in 1988 (*MV*, 101–11).

14 Bernhard's eponymous loser also worked on an infinite project, revising it until there was nothing left but the telltale title: "[Wertheimer] wanted to publish a book, but it never came to that, for he kept changing his manuscript, changing it so often and to such an extent that nothing was left of the manuscript, for change in his manuscript was nothing other than the complete deletion of the manuscript, of which finally nothing remained except the title, *The Loser*" (*The Loser*, 53–4).

As mentioned in chapter 1, James E. Miller attaches great importance to the short story, in particulier three secrets that Foucault is supposed to have shared with Guibert in the days leading up to his death (*The Passion of Michel Foucault*, 364–74). In fact, it seems likely that the so-called secrets were overdetermined by some typically Guibertian concerns. For example, the shed where a woman was held captive in Poitiers reprises André Gide's text *La Séquestrée de Poitiers*. It is possible that Foucault's father took him to see an operation, but the detail could just as easily be a transformation of one of Guibert's personal memories, for example, of being taken to the slaughterhouse where his father worked (*MP*, 232; *Mes*, 56 [*My*, 47]). Finally, the young student jealous of the Parisians who "invade" his school before disappearing in the Holocaust recalls – and inverts – the disdain of one of Guibert's characters for his fellow high school students in La Rochelle (*MP*, 107). Even if all three "dioramas" were loosely based on conversations that Foucault had with Guibert, one still cannot base any theories about Foucault or his sexual practices on the basis of such a fanciful short story. To do so is as unfair to Guibert as it is to Foucault. Miller himself acknowledged this in a endnote: "The specific details about the death and burial in the short story ... are often pure fantasy – naturally casting into doubt the verisimilitude of the 'secrets' discussed later in this chapter" (*The Passion of Michel Foucault*, 463n33).

We must remember that "Les secrets d'un homme" is part of a collection of short stories in which fantasy and imagination play havoc with factual truth. This is not to say that there is no relation whatsoever between Guibert's real-life experiences and *Mauve le vierge*. However, I think it is safer and more profitable to compare this book to Guibert's other works instead of using it as a key to someone else's life. In the case of "Les secrets d'un homme," the intertextual link to *L'Ami* is provided by a passage describing the great book of the unnamed philosopher:

> Il lui fallait finir ses livres, ce livre qu'il avait écrit et réécrit, détruit, renié, redétruit, repensé, refabriqué, raccourci et rallongé pendant dix ans, ce livre infini, de doute, de renaissance, de grandiose modestie. (*MV*, 108)

> He had to finish his books, that book he had written and rewritten, destroyed, repudiated, redestroyed, rethought, rebuilt, shortened and lengthened for ten years, that infinite book of doubt, rebirth, and grandiose modesty.

Although shorter than the corresponding passage in *L'Ami* already discussed, we can see the germination of Guibert's tribute to his friend's great research project. Whereas the emphasis here is on the series of verbs used to describe the philosopher's "infinite book," in *L'Ami* Guibert will expand the description by resorting to an extended metaphor in which the book becomes a construction project of some huge expressway or even an entire town. Two verbs in the longer version echo this first attempt to write about another's writing: "rebâtit" and "regreffe" (*Ami*, 36; *Friend*, 28), the prefix *re-* serving to remind us of the Sisyphus-like task involved in the rethinking of the original project. One could compare this first textual tribute to a study or sketch on which a later painting will be based. For example, although the word *sida*, "AIDS," is used in *L'Ami*, all that is or can be said in the earlier work is a euphemism, "leprosy" (*MV*, 109) and an anagram of *sida*, "se vida" (emptied) (*MV*, 107) that also carries with it an echo of the word *suicide*. Alternately, one could consider that despite its brevity, the short story does sketch in certain details to which Guibert will not return, such as the long Rabelaisian description of the philosopher's brain (*MV*, 104–5). In *L'Ami* only a brief mention is made of the operation, presumably because the first version removes the necessity for such a detailed textualization that, given its fanciful treatment of the subject – complete with Rabelaisian echoes of Pantagruel's mouth – was more appropriate to a short story.

Those who read *À l'ami qui ne m'a pas sauvé la vie*, *Le Protocole compassionnel*, and *L'Homme au chapeau rouge* when they were first published will never forget their unique impact. They were like faxes sent directly to thousands of readers, as Guibert described in his second AIDS novel: "En fait j'ai écrit une lettre qui a été directement téléfaxée dans le coeur de cent mille personnes, c'est extraordinaire. Je suis en train de leur écrire une nouvelle lettre. Je vous écris" (*PC*, 121) ("In fact what I wrote was a personal letter faxed directly to the hearts of a hundred thousand readers, it's something extraordinary for me. I am busy writing them a new letter" [*CP*, 104]). Of course, once the books were published, they became part of a larger circle of "texts" – reviews and interviews attracting as well considerable attention from the nonprint media, such as Guibert's appearances on French television in 1990 and 1991. The success of *L'Ami* meant not only that this novel was read by thousands of people but also that his earlier works were also discovered by the reading public:

> Mon treizième livre officiel, *À l'ami qui ne m'a pas sauvé la vie*, m'a porté

> chance. Il a connu un succès qui m'a réconforté au moment *ad hoc* de ma maladie, je l'ai porté en moi comme un talisman, avec la chaleur des réactions. Il a été accepté par la communauté des malades et de leurs soignants, et j'en ai été très soulagé parce que je craignais beaucoup qu'ils ne le rejettent ... Après ce livre-là et son acceuil, je ne pouvais pas écrire une pochade, je me sentais une responsabilité par rapport à ces inconnu(e)s que j'avais ému(e)s. Le succès aussi m'a paralysé. J'étais parvenu à mes fins, dans tous les sens du terme: me faire entendre, et faire lire mes autres livres, faire lire tous mes livres à la fois comme la plupart des lettres en témoignaient ... (*PC*, 171)

> My thirteenth official publication, *To the Friend Who Did Not Save My Life*, brought me luck. It had a success that comforted me at an intermediate stage of my illness, I wore it like a talisman, together with all the reactions to it, that warmed my heart. It was accepted by the vast community of the sick and their attendants, I felt very relieved because I had very much feared they would reject it ... After that book and the welcome accorded it, I could not dash off something lightweight, I felt I had a responsibility to those unknowns whom I had moved so much. Success also paralysed me. I had attained all my ends, in all senses of the term: to let my voice be heard, and to have my other books read, to have all my books read all at once as the majority of the letters proved they had been ... (*CP*, 147)

This passage in *Le Protocole compassionnel*, like the dedication in the same book to the readers of his first AIDS fiction, refers directly to *L'Ami* and its reception not by journalists but by ordinary readers, many of whom – including myself – wrote to Guibert at the time. Once again the text takes on the appearance of a letter describing both the positive and negative effects that writing a bestseller can have on its author. This "letter" is as metatextual as it is intertextual, and as such must be read in conjunction with the earlier novel.

There is, however, another work in which intertextuality with *L'Ami* functions: *Cytomégalovirus*, a series of fragments named for CMV, an opportunistic infection that can cause blindness.[15] Written between 17 September and 8 October 1991, the fragments number between one and twenty-two per day. That Guibert was able to continue writing at a

---

15 On *Cytomégalovirus*, see Murray Pratt's article "'A Walk along the Side of the Motorway': AIDS and the Spectacular Body of Hervé Guibert," in *Gay Signatures*.

time when he was threatened with blindness and when conditions of treatment and even simple hygiene were far from optimal offers proof of how much survival depended on writing. And as the writing, which includes passages of black humor like the following, goes on, so too allusions to other books continue to weave a textual tapestry of ever-increasing detail:

> Fond d'oeil sous dilatation sans apposition du verre sur la cornée, maintenant que je n'en ai presque plus peur. Apparemment pas d'amélioration, elle [ophtalmologist] réclame dix jours de plus de traitement d'attaque. Je lui donne mon livre, *Des aveugles*, avec cette dédicace: "L'explication d'une hantise?" Je lui demande si la cécité provoquée par le mégalo est une cécité blanche, ou noire. Elle répond: "ça bouge en fonction de l'avancée du virus." (*Cyto.*, 82)

> The fundus of the eye under dilation without having the glass attached to the cornea, now that I'm almost no longer afraid of it. Apparently no improvement, [the ophthalmologist] wants ten more days of aggressive treatment. I give her my book, *Des aveugles*, with the dedication: "Explanation of an obsession?" I ask her if blindness provoked by CMV is partial or total. She answers, "It changes as the virus advances." (*CMV*, 70; trans. alt.)

A paratextual inscription creates another intertextual link that is all the more moving when we recall that *Des aveugles* was dedicated to Foucault. Furthermore, this was the book that Guibert was in the process of writing while his friend was dying (*Ami*, 105). Now it has become uncannily premonitory, since Guibert, like the characters in *Blindsight*, must come to terms with blindness.

Among the entries detailing the small as well as the horrendous events of a hospital stay, the anticipation and the memory of pain, Guibert inserts several references to "M.," Michel Foucault. What is important is that several of these allusions refer directly to events narrated in *L'Ami*. For example, in the novel we read the following sentence: "Le jeune médecin, il l'avait rapporté à Stéphane, passait de longs moments dans la nuit à discourir avec Muzil" (*Ami*, 107) ("The young doctor told Stéphane he spent long hours talking with Muzil during the night" [*Friend*, 94; trans. alt.]). And in the hospital diary, Guibert returns to these nighttime conversations in a longer development (*Cyto.*, 40–1; *CMV*, 31). Between the hospitalizations of Foucault and Guibert, many things have happened, but at the end of their journeys (or almost), the two friends find themselves in the same situation, in an anonymous hospital bed, where the patient loses his identity, becomes a case, a tag with names and numbers, a body which no longer enjoys either freedom or human dignity:

> Muzil passa une matinée à l'hôpital pour faire des examens, il me raconta à quel point le corps, il l'avait oublié, lancé dans les circuits médicaux, perd toute identité, ne reste plus qu'un paquet de chair involontaire, brinquebalé par-ci par-là, à peine un matricule, un nom passé dans la moulinette administrative, exsangue de son histoire et de sa dignité. On lui glissa par la bouche un tube qui alla explorer ses poumons. (*Ami*, 32)

> Muzil spent a morning in the hospital having tests done, and told me he'd forgotten how completely the body loses all identity once it's delivered into medical hands, becoming just a package of helpless flesh, trundled around here and there, hardly even a number on a slip of paper, a name put through the administrative mill, drained of all individuality and dignity. They slid a tube down his throat to examine his lungs. (*Friend*, 23–4)

The same painful medical procedures that were performed on Foucault await Guibert, as he will recount in *Le Protocole compassionnel* and *Cytomégalovirus*. Words that were written supposedly about Muzil echo throughout this book: "[J]e repris les mots de l'unique testament autographe de Muzil: 'la mort, pas l'invalidité.' Pas de coma prolongé, pas de démence, pas de cécité, la suppression pure et simple au moment adéquat" (*Ami*, 152) ("I used something Muzil had said in his sole handwritten will: 'Death, not invalidism.' No prolonged coma, no dementia, no blindness, pure and simple suppression at the appropriate moment" [*Friend*, 137; trans. alt.]).

Between the two books the intertextual links are so strong that one could consider the hospital diary to be the continuation of the novel. What cannot be said in the diary – because of a lack of time, energy, or sight – has already been said in *À l'ami qui ne m'a pas sauvé la vie*. In short, the 1990 novel is to *Cytomégalovirus* what the diary is to *Des aveugles*: both inter- and metatext. It might seem peculiar to describe the earlier work as a commentary on a later one. And yet in this case, it is perfectly clear that the scenes in *L'Ami* giving detailed descriptions of the death of an author[16] in a hospital, with all that implies in terms of both anonymity – and worse, banality – can be inserted between the pages of the diary. The novelist was indeed correct when he had that terrible intuition that his fate was to be similar to Muzil's (*Ami*, chap. 34). By writing about his friend's death, Guibert was inscribing his own in a work that is about life and death and the passage between the two. Paradoxically, the present is (re)written by the past, and fiction becomes a commentary on nonfiction, thereby creating the "extraordinary coherence of an oeuvre placed under the sign of the body" (Jonquet, "'Je disparaîtrai,'" 104). But the body must also be understood as a body of works, a corpus, the writing of which – whether diary or novel – never ceases to quote and to comment upon itself in an oeuvre that is as metatextual as it is postmodern (figure 18).

And let us not forget that Guibert's feat in writing *Cytomégalovirus* is all the more extraordinary for the Barthesian intertextuality encoded in it, as we saw in chapter 2. It seems eerily appropriate that both of Guibert's original mentors should be, in this manner, both present and absent in Guibert's last work, Barthes at the level of the writing and Foucault at the level of the (hi)story that the writing recounts.

Guibert often wrote in that dangerous frontier-like zone that unites rather than separates life and art. Reading him is therefore a special experience. So-called reality effects (*effets de réel*) are not as simple as they appear, and they are never simple "effects." Rather, they are like the foundation or the substratum of something else, whether we choose to call it false truth or true falsehood. As the critic Raymond Bellour has written, "[Hervé Guibert] always played with the vanishing point of truth-falsehood to preserve on the razor's edge the gap now tiny now massive (as manifest as it is imperceptible) that allows him to at once live and write and to attribute qualities of the one to the other" ("Vérités

16 Guibert may well have been thinking of two texts written in the late 1960s: Foucault, "What Is an Author?" (1969) in *Language, Counter-Memory, Practice* (113–38) and Barthes, "The Death of the Author" (1968) in *Image Music Text* (142–8). Whether or not Guibert knew about both these articles (he seems to have been familiar with Foucault's ideas on the subject; see chapter 1), the fact remains that both *À l'ami qui ne m'a pas sauvé la vie* and *Cytomégalovirus* present disturbing parallels with them. While his older friends had described the theoretical disappearance of the author – a popular critical notion in the France of the late 1960s, when writing was conceived of solely as textual production – it is typical of Guibert in the 1990s to describe the fatal illnesses of actual writers. Thereby he concretizes a theoretical notion, giving it a whole new meaning. On the death of the author, see Chambers, *Facing It*.

et mensonges," 69). What might have passed for an amusing puzzle in an earlier work – *L'Incognito* – in *L'Ami* becomes a real test or trial from which readers will not return untouched. *À l'ami qui ne m'a pas sauvé la vie* is true not simply because it imports elements from real life but because it tells stories that are shattering in a manner that is at once more ingenious and more disturbing than any nonfiction. Michel Foucault said his own works were true precisely because they were fictitious: "I realize everything I have ever written is fiction. I don't mean by that it is not the truth. It seems to me that it is possible to make fiction work in [the cause of] truth, to induce truth effects through the discourse of fiction, and to do so in order that the discourse of truth leads to, 'fabricates' something that didn't yet exist, and therefore 'fictionalizes'" (*Dits et Écrits*, 3:236). In light of the preceding quotation, we can understand why fiction is more powerful than a critical metatext. When the metatextual function of a work is incorporated into a literary text, it "fictions," to translate Foucault's term, thereby producing an "effect of truth" which outperforms all that is supposedly objective and verifiable. Today we know that in the field of signs, whether literary or cultural, the old dream of rigorous scientificity was an illusion; we know also that texts create rather than reproduce reality. It is no doubt for these reasons that Guibert proposed to write a kind of essay on Thomas Bernhard "by means of a fiction" (*Ami*, 217).

The use of quotations, allusions, commentary, pastiche, and intertextual rewriting in *L'Ami* guarantees and underscores the materiality of the work as text. This materiality is crucial to Guibert's first AIDS fiction since it allows him to proclaim, for himself and for others, a firm NO in the face of the virus and public indifference. People living with AIDS risk being caught up between silence,[17] which is equivalent to death, and an ever-expanding body of scientific and medical discourse, much of the latter supposedly about them even if they cannot recognize them-

---

17 At times Guibert thematizes this silence before he is able to begin the description of what, for the moment, leaves him almost without words: "Rien écrit ce soir. Trop choqué. J'essaierai demain" (*Cyto.*, 59) ("Wrote nothing this evening. Too shellshocked. I'll try tomorrow" [*CMV*, 49]); "Chez moi, j'ouvris mon journal, et j'y écrivis: 'Fibroscopie.' Rien d'autre, rien de plus, aucune explication, aucune description de l'examen et aucun commentaire sur ma souffrance, impossible d'aligner deux mots, le sifflet coupé, bouche bée. J'étais devenu incapable de raconter mon expérience" (*PC*, 60) ("When I got home, I opened my journal and wrote 'Fibroscopy.' Nothing else, nothing more, no explanation, no description of the examination and no commentary on my sufferings, it was impossible to put two words together, I was speechless, mouth agape. I had become incapable of recounting my experience" [*CP*, 48]).

selves in the masses of facts and figures.[18] Faced with this dilemma, Guibert opted for life and writing, not of just any kind, but a writing that textualizes and metatextualizes itself like the shimmering circles of a lake into which a stone has been thrown. This is the solution he found to combat the monological and univocal discourse in which he found himself snared as he learned to fight both illness and modern medicine. Guibert's first empowering tactic is to throw back in the face of, first, the general public and, second, all medical workers the same technical terms that he would like to use with as much facility as a doctor.[19] More important, *À l'ami qui ne m'a pas sauvé la vie* presents itself as a textual artifact that, instead of hiding its status, continually underscores its stance as an overt piece of writing. In other words, we are dealing with an AIDS novel that is also a *text*, a metastatic work where signifiers and signifieds are piled one on top of the other so that one can never forget textuality, where pain is articulated by an unbearable even cancerous accumulation of details, where "normal" taxonomies and binary oppositions (life/death, text/metatext, fiction/nonfiction) are swept out despite every narratological protocol, where insult and public outrage are attached not to the description of the sexual act but to the impotence of the medical establishment and the corruption of the pharmaceutical industry, where the real scandal is not the identities of the models of characters but the illness that has killed Foucault, Guibert, and so many others. If an AIDS work is equivalent to life, then this novel represents life to the nth power, proclaiming as it does the victory of words. For some it may seem a Pyrrhic victory, but it is nonetheless an assertion of life by a writer whom I as critic mourn by bearing witness to his accomplishments, not the least of which is a readerly protocol founded not on simple empathy but on empowering compassion.

---

18 The slogan of ACT-UP, Silence = Death, reminds us of Guibert's AIDS writing. As Lawrence Schehr has argued, "Guibert writes texts that are the literary equivalent of ACT-UP; no previous situation can explain the need, the behavior, and the struggle. After Guibert, the AIDS text cannot ever be the same ..." (*Alcibiades at the Door*, 182).

19 "[J]'aimerais manier parfaitement le jargon des médecins, c'est comme un truc codé" (*PC*, 105) ("I'd like to be able to use medical jargon perfectly, it's like a code" [*CP*, 89]); "[J]'adore le langage pro" (*Cyto.*, 15) ["I love using the lingo of the pros" [*CMV*, 8, trans. alt.]).

Chapter Eight

Partners in Writing

> Guibert ... ne peut que me sembler tombé d'une autre planète; mais c'est moi, bien sûr, qui suis parfaitement étranger sur celle-ci ...
> Renaud Camus, *La Guerre de Transylvanie*, 138

> To me Guibert ... can only seem to have come from another planet; but for sure it is I who am a perfect alien on this one ...

> si Dieu existe, Hervé Guibert est un ange ...
> Yvonne Baby, *La Vie retrouvée*, 318

> if God exists, Hervé Guibert is an angel ...

> Le coeur, avec Guibert, a toujours dominé le sexe.
> Christophe Donner, *L'Esprit de vengeance*, 47

> With Guibert, my heart has always dominated my genitals.

Like Marguerite Duras, who claimed that she would never stop writing, Hervé Guibert too has kept on writing even after his death, as witnessed by the numerous posthumous publications. In this chapter, however, I shall concentrate on the three writers quoted above and their intertextual dialogues with him and his works.

RENAUD CAMUS

Born in 1946, Renaud Camus, who is no relation to Albert Camus, and Hervé Guibert have much in common. Both are novelists and diarists, but they have also engaged in other forms of writing, short stories and journalism in Guibert's case, and travel writing and elegies in Camus's. Camus is a prolific writer: to date, he has authored some forty books, and shows no signs of slowing down. Other areas Camus and Guibert have in common are their interest in art (painting) and writing about daily life that involves roughly the same milieu – the Paris of artists and intellectuals. For example, both knew Roland Barthes, and they had at least one other friend in common. Their careers followed a similar path for several years, since Guibert held a fellowship at the Villa Médicis (1987–9) just after Camus received the same honor (1985–7). What is more, both wrote a book about their experiences in Rome: Camus's *Journal romain* (1987) was published two years before *L'Incognito*. Both have also written novels in which madness is textualized: Camus's *Roman furieux* and Guibert's *Paradis*. More anecdotal is the fact that in their adolescence, both men visited England, where they had rather bizarre experiences at a time when they were becoming aware of their sexual orientation (*Fendre l'air*, 399–400; *Mes*, 75–6 [*My*, 64–6]). As well, both writers know the work of Thomas Bernhard, although Guibert was strongly influenced by the Austrian writer, unlike Camus.[1] Both have written about the photographer Duane Michals, and both had problems dealing with Marguerite Duras.[2] Finally, Camus and Guibert share their gay sexuality, about which both have written frequently, although Camus more than Guibert. Indeed, his *Tricks* (1979) has become something of a classic work about gay sex; although not pornographic in intention or effect, it has often been taken for such, which is perhaps why it is the work of Camus that has sold the best. In his preface Roland Barthes, a more sensitive reader than most, compares *Tricks* to haikus, or even a series of mini-novels (16).

And yet, despite the similarities in the careers and interests of Guibert

---

1 Camus, *La Guerre de Transylvanie*, 286–7.
2 In the volume of his diary devoted to 1988 (*Aguets*, 334), Camus mentions a short text he wrote about Michals; Guibert collaborated on *Changements: Photographies et textes de Duane Michals* (1981). He also wrote an article about Michals for *Le Monde*. In his "roman cocasse," *Mon valet et moi*, Guibert describes the pleasure that the old man has when his valet drives him to a factory in the forest of Rambouillet where the books of Marguerite Duras are pulped (54–5). Guibert elaborated on his relations with Duras, an "author whom he respected but who on the other hand didn't respect other writers," in his interview with Jérôme Garcin (108). Camus describes Duras as impossible to associate with (*Incomparable*, 86).

and Camus, there are also differences. For example, Barthes did not write a preface for the continuation of *La Mort propagande.* Guibert wrote extensively about AIDS, whereas Camus has not.[3] Unlike Guibert's diary, which to date remains unpublished, eight hefty tomes of Camus's journal have been published covering the years 1985 to 1993. It is an ongoing enterprise of Herculian proportions that, despite the difference in form, recalls the efforts of Michel Butor in *L'Emploi du temps* and *Degrés* or Claude Mauriac in *La marquise sortit à cinq heures* and *L'Agrandissement* for quasi-exhaustivity. In Camus's case, however, we are dealing not with a so-called New Novel, but with diary writing that seeks to chronicle in minute detail the author's activities, although not always on a day-to-day basis, as well as the evolution of his ideas about art, music, and politics. Guibert's diary, much shorter – only eight hundred pages in all, apparently – was kept intermittently and served as a hothouse for the incubation of themes and characters that were later to find their way into his fiction. Camus's published diary, by contrast, remains more distinct from his fiction, although a novel such as *Voyageur en automne* (1992) and the diary volume for 1991, *La Guerre de Transylvanie,* share the common theme of a journey to Eastern Europe. But the most important difference between these two writers is the huge success Guibert attained with the publication of his first AIDS novel. No work by Camus has known a similar success, although a recent work, *Etc.: abécédaire,* inspired by Roland Barthes's autobiography, is reported to be selling well.

One telling example of the different approaches to life and writing of these two writers is illustrated by their visits to Sicily: Guibert in 1983, Camus in 1987. Camus, as is usual when he writes about his many travels in Europe and America, pays as much attention to the countryside, the people, and their manners as he does to the museums and other "official" points of interest. Forever seeking an ideal of civilized life and *savoir-vivre* equal to the natural beauty of the land, Camus finds himself again and again disturbed and disappointed by the encroachments of twentieth-century ugliness, whether in the form of bad architecture, unattractive design, or lack of civility (his outcries of protest against general bad manners reach their peak when he writes about the French, and Parisians in particular). The following passage is typical of many in

---

3 Camus's *Élégies pour quelques-uns* (1988) is about lives lost to AIDS, but the syndrome is never named, just as it is never named in *Voyageur en automne* (1992), although one might interpret this novel as a kind of crypto-AIDS fiction. To date, *L'Épuisant Désir des choses* (1995) is his only novel in which a character is HIV-positive.

his diary, although here the protest takes on a melancholic air rather than a bellicose stance as is sometimes the case:

> on trouve partout des choses belles, mais à quoi servent-elles si leur beauté ne rayonne pas, si elle est constamment humiliée, flétrie, si elle ne débouche pas, aujourd'hui, pour nous, sur une civilisation de la beauté, sur une douceur, une paix, un art de vivre? (*Vigiles*, 166)
>
> everywhere one finds beautiful things, but what use are they if their beauty does not make itself felt, if it is constantly humiliated, stigmatized, if it does not lead, for us today, to a civilization of beauty, gentleness, peace, an art of living?

The reason I choose to quote this passage is because on the same page Camus mentions *en passant* visiting the famous Palagonia museum (devoted to monstrosities) in Palermo that inspired Guibert to write a text entitled "Sur une manipulation courante: (mémoire d'un dysmorphophobe)," which was included in *Photographies* (n.p.) as well as *La Piqûre d'amour...* (102–7). Instead of lamenting the fact that beauty does not lead to an "art of living," Guibert concentrates on himself. He allows – indeed, invites – a photograph to be taken of him naked in this museum devoted to a princely collection of ugly, odd-sized objects and furniture. Displaying his body so openly seemed appropriate in a place devoted to ugliness (we must remember that Guibert considered his body to be monstrous on account of the cavity in his chest). Apparently, he thought that the brightness of the light in the museum would make the cavity in his chest seem almost invisible.[4] Later on, he destroyed most of the contact sheets; but one negative ended up in the hands of a young man who eagerly developed the photograph and, by using various techniques, made Guibert's deformity visible to all. The text ends with the following sentence: "La photo, malgré toutes mes stratégies de recul, de dénégation, était une statue supplémentaire élevée par le prince Palagonia dans le temple de la monstruosité" (*PA*, 107) (The photo, in spite of all my delaying and negating tactics, was an additional statue erected by Prince Palagonia in his temple of monstrosity). Camus,

---

4 The unpublished photograph taken in Sicily reminds one of the photo in which an X-ray of Guibert's chest figures prominently (figure 7). Clearly, although Guibert claimed to feel ashamed of his body, he also felt the need to exhibit it through various photographic or narrative "slips."

by contrast, does not even describe the museum or the collection: clearly, for him ugliness is not something to delight in, and he is inspired by it only to the extent that he deplores its existence. Guibert shows himself to be in the tradition of Rabelais and other writers of excess such as Genet and Bataille, whereas Camus belongs with Racine and Chateaubriand and the French tradition of restraint.

One can well imagine Camus's reaction to Guibert's novel *Vous m'avez fait former des fantômes*, a title inspired by one of Sade's letters to his wife. In the novel, "infanteros" fight with children in corridas that correspond to a traditional bullfight.[5] Camus is horrified by what he reads, and I would agree that at times it is difficult *not* to put down Guibert's novel, so vivid are some of the descriptions about the training and putting to death of the children. As is typical of the reaction of Camus to Guibert's subsequent works – although not for the same reasons – he finds himself unable to judge the novel's literary worth, "trop horrifié par ce que je lis, trop tendu dans l'effort de continuer, pour pouvoir objectivement apprécier, en l'occurrence, un style ou un talent" (*Aguets*, 66) (too horrified by what I am reading, too tensed up by the effort to continue on to appreciate objectively style or talent in such circumstances). Later, Camus is upset by a book review of Hugo Marsan in which the critic wrote that Camus doesn't like Guibert: as Camus claims, it was the subject matter of the novel that turned him off rather than its author. Nonetheless, Camus is forced to admit that he "ne trouve pas Guibert, à aimer, tout à fait si facile que cela; de sorte que, au fond ..." (*La Guerre de Transylvanie*, 39) (does not find it so easy as all that to like Guibert, so that deep down ...).

As though seeking deliberately to alienate Camus, the ever-mischievous Guibert includes a character modeled on his fellow writer in *L'Incognito*. Named Quickly, presumably because of the "quickies" described in *Tricks*, this character precedes Hector Lenoir, as Guibert

---

5 Letter 162 in *Oeuvres complètes du Marquis de Sade*, 12:397. *Vous m'avez fait former des fantômes* could be read as an allegorical critique of bull fighting. One could also read it in light of Michel Leiris's comparison of the dangers posed by life writing with those faced by a bullfighter, as he outlined in his famous 1935 essay "De la littérature considérée comme une tauromachie." Although so many of Guibert's autofictions and other works could be considered to illustrate Leiris's theory about a form of writing that is at once confessional, obsessive, and authentic, it is also typical of Guibert to take an abstract concept and to concretize it in the form of a novel in which children replace bulls in the ceremonial confines of the arena! See Owen Heathcote's studies "L'érotisme, la violence et le jeu dans *Vous m'avez fait former des fantômes*" and "Jobs for Boys? Or: What's New about the Male Hunter in Duvert, Guibert and Jourdan?"

calls himself in his novel, at the fictitious Spanish Academy based on the Villa Médicis. Where Camus's diary about his experiences in Rome is a careful and erudite recounting of visits to museums and churches interspersed by his attempts to cruise men, most of which turn out to be ill-fated in the Italian capital, Guibert's novel is a hilarious carnivalesque tale of administrative incompetence, jokes played on the other inhabitants of the so-called academy, and visits to a bar whose denizens engage in hustling and drug dealing, as well as crimes of a more violent nature. Towards the end, the novel takes on the aura of a detective story when a gay classics professor is discovered dead. Overall, the verve of Guibert's prose stands in sharp contrast to the sober and rather somber descriptions in Camus (he writes of sex with almost the same detachment he brings to the description of a baroque church).

Guibert describes how everyone in the Academy is reading Quickly's travel diary about Rome, and in a subsequent volume of the diary, Camus inevitably narrates his own reading experience of *L'Incognito*. Camus seems less shocked by Guibert's revelations of Quickly's sexual preferences (which are fallacious, as Camus points out) than envious of the possibilities afforded a writer of an autobiographical fiction, although he does not use the term: "Le genre dans sa bâtardise est toutefois un peu spécieux: tout est vrai, peut dire l'auteur, c'est un *journal*; mais si certains détails sont faux, rien que de très normal: il s'agit d'un roman ..." (*Fendre l'air*, 291) (Such a bastard genre is nevertheless somewhat specious: everything is true, the author can say, it's a diary; but if certain details are false, it is entirely normal, after all, we are dealing with a novel). Since Camus remains more faithful to the separation of literary genres, he cannot take such liberties with truth, which allow Guibert to be more hard-hitting than Camus was when denouncing the abuses of power at the Villa Médicis:

> les plaintes de Guibert, confronté à la même situation et aux mêmes protagonistes, sont bien autrement virulentes que les miennes. À l'abri qu'il est sous le commode pavillon "roman," ayant changé tous les noms et transporté la scène à l'"Académie espagnole" (!!! ... Mais cette académie espagnole dépend de Paris ...), il peut se montrer beaucoup plus cruel que je n'ai jamais songé à le faire, beaucoup plus féroce dans le tableau qu'il dresse de ce petit monde clos et de son fonctionnement, beaucoup plus précis dans les traits qu'il décoche et dans ceux qu'il dépeint; et d'autant plus qu'il ne paraît pas autrement sensible, lui, à la beauté ni à la richesse d'art de la Villa, ni de la Ville. (Ibid., 300-1)

the complaints of Guibert, who was confronted by the same situation and the same actors, are much more virulent than my own. Sheltered as he is by the handy label "novel," having changed all the names and transported the scene to the "Spanish Academy" (!!! ... But this Spanish Academy is answerable to Paris ...), he can allow himself to be much crueler than I would ever have thought of being, much more ferocious in the picture he paints of that closed little world and the way it runs, much more precise in the shots he lets fly and in the features he delineates, all the more so since he does not seem particularly sensitive either to the beauty or the artistic riches of the Villa, or of the city for that matter.

Not only does Guibert enjoy the protection afforded by the umbrella of fiction, his novel gets a long review in *Le Monde* that doesn't even mention Camus's *Journal romain* (ibid., 306)! In spite of all this, Camus does not hide how much he enjoyed reading *L'Incognito*, so much so in fact that he finds himself as incapable of making a literary judgment about it as was the case, although for different reasons, with the Sadean-inspired novel. Despite what he says, Camus in fact is quite sensitive to some of Guibert's qualities as a writer, as he demonstrates in the following passage:

> Guibert, à part cela, n'a guère de chance avec moi; je suis incapable de le lire d'un point de vue purement littéraire, et de me faire une objective idée de ses mérites artistiques. La dernière fois (*Vous m'avez fait former des fantômes*), c'était parce qu'il me mettait sous le nez des monstruosités et des tortures que je n'avais pas la force de regarder très attentivement, ni le moyen d'apprécier esthétiquement. Cette fois-ci, c'est parce que ce qu'il me raconte dispose sur moi, tout à l'inverse, d'un tel pouvoir de fascination, que je serais un lecteur captif quand bien même il serait, lui, un narrateur incompétent. Mais il me semble au contraire qu'*il est vif, efficace, plutôt gai, corrosif et bon observateur.* (Ibid., 301; my emphasis)

Apart from that [corroborating what Camus wrote about the Villa Médicis] Guibert has no luck with me; I am incapable of reading him from a purely literary point of view, and of forming an objective idea about his artistic merits. The last time (*Vous m'avez fait former des fantômes*) it was because he shoved under my nose monstrosities and tortures that I did not have either the strength to look at very attentively or the means to appreciate aesthetically. This time it is because what he is recounting inversely exerts such a power of fascination on me that I would be a captive reader even if he were an incompetent narrator. But he seems to me, on the contrary, to be *lively, effective, rather gay, caustic, and a good observer.*

Strangely, Camus remains silent about one of the most troubling themes in *L'Incognito*: AIDS. Although not what I have characterized as an AIDS autofiction like the three parts of the trilogy, this novel does mention the syndrome numerous times, often in a personal context, as in this sentence on the first page: "J'avais arrêté de travailler, j'étais persuadé d'avoir le sida" (*I,* 11) (I had stopped working, I was convinced I had AIDS).[6] AIDS is an almost constant concern of the narrator in *L'Incognito,* and it is all the more distressing because he is still uncertain about his HIV status. Guibert's seropositivity, which he had long suspected, was confirmed in January 1988 (*Ami,* chapter 49), while he was living at the Villa Médicis, but he does not say so in the novel about Rome. On the other hand, in *L'Incognito* the first-person narrator does write about impending insanity brought on by AIDS-related illness:

> Ce livre menace ma raison. Peut-être l'ai-je déjà perdue tout à fait, ou suis-je en train de la perdre, elle s'égrène et se brise entre chaque page qui l'engloutit. On dit que le virus se tapit dans le cerveau et épuise le système nerveux. Je me sens à la veille d'un coma. Avec le livre j'ai l'impression d'effacer le temps, au fur et à mesure, de plus en plus vite, pour laisser le moins de marge possible entre le temps conscient et le temps perdu de la mort. (*I,* 180-1)

> This book threatens my sanity. Perhaps I've already lost it entirely, or maybe I'm in the process of losing it, it's falling apart, breaking up between every page that engulfs it. They say the virus lurks within the brain and wears out the nervous system. I feel like I'm about to go into a coma. As I proceed in writing this book I have the impression I'm rubbing out time with increasing speed, leaving the least possible margin between the time of consciousness and the lost time of death.

L'Incognito contains a seemingly endless series of peripeteia in which the

---

6 There are more than a dozen other references to AIDS in *L'Incognito* (11, 12, 27, 54, 76, 79, 97-8, 114, 121, 129, 156, 180, 185, 195, 222-3). The first sentence of *L'Incognito* can be read as a kind of transitory step between the last sentence in the abandoned manuscript, *Adultes!*: "Gaspar pense qu'il a le sida" (f. 182, quoted with the permission of Christine Guibert) and the first sentence of *À l'ami qui ne m'a pas sauvé la vie*: "J'ai eu le sida pendant trois mois" (9) ("I had AIDS for three months").

reader risks getting lost, but the obsessive fear of AIDS that crops up throughout the novel takes on the aura of a haunting leitmotif. Indeed, the title itself can be read as a reference to AIDS, for in this quasi-detective story the unknown murderer of Guido Jallo is mirrored by the virus circulating "incognito" among the clients of bars such as L'Incognito in Rome, Le Knolle in Berlin, L'Ochsengarten in Munich, and Le Keller in Paris (*I*, 195), the last being the bar that Muzil was said to frequent in *L'Ami*.[7] As Guibert wrote on the publicity blurb for the back cover of *L'Incognito*, 4:00 a.m. is the time when murders take place by an exchange of fluids. But in the text of the novel itself, Guibert alias Hector Lenoir is aware of and practices safer sex, also a preoccupation of Camus in his *Journal romain*.

What we are dealing with is Guibert's forthrightness, which so many readers, especially journalists, have interpreted as indiscretion rather than frankness, versus Camus's sense of privacy and discretion. Even in the case of *À l'ami qui ne m'a pas sauvé la vie*, many readers wondered if Guibert had invented a new story, this time about his supposed – but in fact real – seropositivity; and he freely admitted that he would have been quite capable of basing the narrative on the experience of someone other than himself, as we have seen. Perhaps because Camus judges AIDS too difficult or, as is more likely, too personal a topic to write about, especially when it comes up in such slippery terrain as a novel with an autobiographical underpinning, he occults what is undoubtedly one of the most important themes in *L'Incognito*: AIDS. HIV manages to circulate, unnoticed, in the milieu frequented by the narrator, undoubtedly killing more victims than the murderer of the gay professor. The latter's death nonetheless remains remarkable, since it reminds us of the murder of one of Guibert's heroes: Pier Paolo Pasolini.

Renaud Camus also enjoyed reading *Fou de Vincent*, although he disapproved of Guibert's use of colloquial French, such as *bises* or *bisous* instead of *baisers* for kisses. Nevertheless, Camus is forced to admit that Guibert's informal style is no doubt an accurate reflection of the language as it is spoken today. He appreciates Guibert's sense of humor, as

---

7 No doubt Guibert was thinking of the model for the character who was to be named Muzil in the next novel when he describes these bars as *mouroirs* (*I*, 195). He uses the same unpleasant word in *À l'ami qui ne m'a pas sauvé la vie* to describe a project for a hospice in which Dr. Nacier, a friend of Hervé's, sought to interest Muzil. The philosopher's reaction was that a much better idea would be to establish a false hospice that would allow people merely to pretend to die, so that they might assume a new identity (*Ami*, chapter 9).

in the following sentence about a telephone conversation Hervé had with Vincent's mother: "'C'est à quel sujet?' me demande la mère de Vincent; envie de lui répondre: c'est au sujet de sa bite, Madame, j'aurais besoin de la sucer dans les meilleurs délais" (*FV,* 59) ("What is the purpose of your call?" Vincent's mother asks me; feel like answering her: it's about his cock, Madame, I need to suck it A.S.A.P.). The humor, for Camus, resides not in the use of *bite,* a colloquial term for penis, but the formal expression that follows that sounds like a business letter: "the comic *punctum* of the sentence, for me, is rather the expression 'dans les meilleurs délais'" (*Fendre l'air,* 314). Although Camus does not mention Barthes by name in this context, the use of the term *punctum,* borrowed from *Camera Lucida,* indicates that he was sensitive to the Barthesian intertextuality in Guibert's short book about his friendship with Vincent.

À *l'ami qui ne m'a pas sauvé la vie* was the book that had the greatest impact on Camus, as was the case for so many readers of Guibert. But unlike most of these readers, Camus knows the model who unwittingly posed for "Bill," since it was to him that *Tricks* was dedicated: Philippe St. In his diary entries about Guibert's novel, Camus attempts to hide the identity of their mutual friend, using ellipses to protect him. But there are clues that indicate we are dealing with the dedicatee of his most successful book. For example, Camus comments on the terrible irony of the two dedications to the same person, framing as they do the period of gay liberation followed by the advent of AIDS: "Si l'on songe au jeu des dédicaces, douze ans d'écart écrivent une histoire terrible" (*L'Esprit des terrasses,* 74) (If one thinks of the interplay between the two dedications, the twelve years separating them tell a terrible story). And, of course, Camus cannot erase what has already been published in earlier volumes of the ongoing diary, when he had no reason to suspect just how far Guibert was capable of going in his "games of truth," to use Foucault's expression. For example, Camus described having dinner with Philippe and Guibert on 14 December 1987 (*Vigiles,* 458–9), a dinner also evoked by Guibert (*I,* 82), although he calls "Bill" Phil at that point. Further comparison of the two writers' works leads to other discoveries. "Bill" and Philippe share the same birthday (or almost): 28 January (*Ami,* 225) or 29 January (*La Guerre de Transylvanie,* 64). Both men visit France at irregular intervals when on leave from their work in Florida; they both mention gay men in Québec (*Vigiles,* 349; *Ami,* chapter 96). Like so many other readers of Guibert's most famous novel, Camus remained blind to the different interpretations that can be made of the title, preferring to see it only as an ironic dedication to Philippe. For

Camus, Philippe Ier – or Philippe le Grand, as he is sometimes called in the journal – represents an ideal of culture, good breeding, and generosity: in a word, the perfect host (*Vigiles*, 81), whereas for Guibert he represents something quite different.

Guibert met Phil a.k.a. Bill in the fall of 1973 while dining alone on a shrimp salad at the so-called Drugstore at the corner of Boulevard Saint-Germain and Rue de Rennes, outside of which gay hustlers used to gather. (Guibert describes the hustlers in a preparatory note included with the scenario for *L'Homme blessé* [171].) At the time Guibert was down on his luck: he had recently moved to Paris, and had failed the entrance examination to a film school (Institut des Hautes Études Cinématographiques). Bill invited him to accompany him to Africa: "Ce n'est pas du tout compliqué, me dit-il, d'aller en Afrique, il suffit de prendre tous les jours votre Nivaquine, cinq jours avant le départ, j'en ai là, si vous voulez ..." (*Mes*, 103) ("'There's nothing complicated about going to Africa,' he tells me, 'you only have to take your Nivaquine every day for five days before you go; I've got some if you want it ...'" [*My*, 92]). For several weeks they remained in contact by telephone, and Guibert did indeed begin to take quinine in preparation for the trip to Africa. In the end, however, the trip was canceled. As the character inspired by "Bill" says, "Mauvais calcul. C'est la saison des pluies. La terre est trempée. Les grands animaux ne sortent plus. Nous n'aurions rien vu, mon pauvre ..." (*HB*, 109) (Bad timing. It's the rainy season. The earth is soaked. The big game animals will be hidden. We wouldn't have seen anything, dear fellow). Perhaps Philippe a.k.a. Bosmans was intimidated by Hervé's youth and beauty as only an older homosexual man can be, which may explain the oddly phrased invitation. In any case, the words remained imprinted in Guibert's memory, since he was to use them in *L'Homme blessé* (41–2), the film scenario on which he and Patrice Chéreau labored for six years, as well as in *Mes parents* and *À l'ami qui ne m'a pas sauvé la vie* (178–9 [*Friend*, 161–2]). Camus did not pick up on this when he saw the film of *L'Homme blessé*, since there is no physical resemblance between the actor playing the role of Bosmans (Roland Bertin) and Philippe (*L'Esprit des terrasses*, 79), and of course Camus would not have had any way of knowing that the invitation Bosmans extends to Henri in the film was based on the words of their mutual friend. Guibert claimed that he later observed "Bill" as a spy whenever they subsequently dined together, writing down phrases and sentences on table napkins, not all of which however ended up in the scenario (cf. *HB*, 186–7; *PA*, 134).

An example of how intrigued Guibert was by Bill's highflying if somewhat bizarre lifestyle can be seen in one of the fragments of *L'Image fantôme*, "La collection." In turn, it helps us elucidate the penultimate chapter of *L'Ami*, in which we see Bill as both victim and victimizer of the young men whom he attempts to "collect." In order to understand chapter 99 of the novel, the reader needs to compare Bill with a certain P. who entertains a series of young men on a *bateau-mouche* in order to obtain their photographs (taken by the house photographer of the restaurant), which he then stores in a plastic bag (*IF*, 106–8; *GI*, 97–9). Despite Guibert's dislike of collectors, he concludes that "[l]a collection de P. est bien un petit cimetière secret, mais la photo [est] une prise de possession moins violente que le crime (on pourrait dire qu'elle est la condition de la grâce de P.: qu'il soit gracié)" (*IF*, 108) ("P.'s collection is really a secret little cemetery, but a photograph is a less violent means of taking possession of someone than a crime. [We could say that it is the condition of P.'s pardon: let him be pardoned]" [*GI*, 98–9, trans. alt.]). Clearly, this "pardon" will be temporary.[8]

As Guibert writes in *L'Ami*, when he learned that his old friend Bill was involved in research on a new anti-AIDS vaccine, everything made sense. Suddenly, it seemed as if he had been destined to be approached by this rather strange man more than fifteen years earlier:

> Je confirmai cette nuit-là à moi-même que j'étais un phénomène du destin: pourquoi était-ce moi qui avais chopé le sida et pourquoi était-ce Bill, mon ami Bill qui allait être un des premiers au monde à détenir la clef capable d'effacer mon cauchemar, ou ma joie d'être enfin parvenu au but? ... Mais ce Bill n'était-il pas, davantage que moi, un de ces phénomènes stupéfiants du destin, un de ces monstres absolus du sort, qu'ils semblent tordre et sculpter à leur guise? (*Ami*, 178–9)

> That night I told myself that I was a phenomenon of destiny: why had I been the one to catch AIDS and why was Bill, my friend Bill, going to be one of the first people in the world to hold the key to dispelling my nightmare, or my joy at having finally achieved my end? ... But wasn't Bill, even more than I, one of those astounding phenomena of destiny, one of those absolute monsters of fate which they seem to twist and shape at will? (*Friend*, 161–2; trans. alt.)

---

8 "Bill," as he is called in *À l'ami qui ne m'a pas sauvé la vie*, appears in the following works by Guibert: *IF*, 106–8 (*GI*, 97–9); *HB*, 41–2, and passim; *Mes*, 103 (*My*, 92); *G*, 8, 65 (*Gang.*, 10, 64); *I*, 69, 82; *Ami*, passim; *PA*, 46–50, 134.

In *L'Ami* Bill plays the role of a *deus ex machina* who is going to accomplish the impossible by curing Hervé. When Bill reappears from time to time in Hervé's life, he seems to be some kind of god, literally dropping from the sky in the plane that he pilots himself! But as the novel progresses, Hervé and his friends become progressively more disillusioned with the United States–based researcher and his unkept promises about securing them the vaccine before it is marketed. In the end, Hervé holds Bill responsible for his diminished state if not his imminent death, as some of the last words of the novel attest ("Jusqu'où souhaites-tu me voir sombrer? Pends-toi Bill!" (*Ami*, 267) ("Just how deep do you want me to sink? Fuck you, Bill" [*To the Friend*, 246]). In an interview with Antoine de Gaudemar, however, Guibert expressed great ambivalence towards "Bill": "By treating me the way he treated me, he is killing me, and me, I'm killing him with this book. The book is my weapon for killing him. I'm flabbergasted by the existence of such a character, as fantastic [*romanesque*] as you could wish for. While I have every reason to hate him, I can't prevent myself from feeling a curious kind of detachment towards him, nor can I get rid of a certain affection." ("La vie sida," 20).

Camus's interpretation is completely different. He and his older friend and mentor Jean Puyaubert find it perfectly normal that Philippe did not give Guibert the vaccine, preferring to use it on a PLA with less-advanced symptoms (*L'Esprit des terrasses*, 79). Camus is shocked not by his friend's treatment of Guibert, but by Guibert's treatment of his friend. There is, however, one point on which the two writers are in agreement: Bill/Philippe is an eminently novelistic character: "un personnage éminemment *romanesque*, d'une ombreuse complexité, et tel que son pouvoir, sa fortune, son autorité naturelle et acquise, l'usage qu'il en fait, souvent très généreux, par foucades, le mettent nécessairement en évidence dans les imaginations et dans les vies" (ibid.; my emphasis) (a true literary character of shady complexity, and such that his power, his money, his natural and acquired authority, the use he makes of them, often very generously, whimsically, of necessity put him in the limelight of people's imaginations and lives). And in Guibert's own words: "Avant de voir le salaud dans Bill, j'y vois un personnage en or massif" (*Ami*, 257) ("Before seeing the bastard in Bill, I see him as a character made out of solid gold" [*Friend*, 237]). The difference, of course, is that Camus has not taken the step of turning his friend into a literary character, although he appears in the journal.[9]

---

9 Philippe appears briefly in the guise of Méphisto as the mentor of Othon – a character

Camus reveals that even after the publication of À l'ami qui ne m'a pas sauvé la vie, Guibert continued to keep in contact with their mutual friend: "[Guibert] a mis à sac, avec L'ami qui ne m'a pas sauvé la vie, une bonne part de l'existence de l'ami en question, qui se trouve être aussi le mien; mais ensuite il lui fait des cadeaux, il l'invite à dîner, il lui téléphone trois fois par jour et s'étonne, ou feint de s'étonner, de sa réserve" (La Guerre de Transylvanie, 139) (With L'Ami he ransacked a good part of the existence of the friend in question, who also happens to be a friend of mine; but then he gives him gifts, he invites him to dinner, he phones him three times a day and is surprised, or pretends to be surprised, by his reserve). Camus concludes that Guibert's ethics are based on the principle of *aime-moi quand même*, by which he means that the author of L'Ami is capable of the greatest betrayals, but that he wants to be loved *anyway*, as though nothing had happened to test if not put an end to the friendship.[10] Putting words in Guibert's mouth, Camus expresses his disapproval in the form of an imaginary temper tantrum on the part of the younger writer: "[J]e ne suis pas gentil, je ne suis pas aimable, je vous ai fait des coups pendables et il est vraisemblable que je vais bientôt vous en faire d'autres, mais vous allez m'aimer tout de même, il le faut, je le veux" (ibid.) (I'm not nice, I'm not lovable, I've played lousy tricks on you and it's likely I will do so again, but you shall like me anyway, you must, I require it). No doubt there is some truth in what Camus says: Guibert was known for his betrayals of secrets, and he was quite aware that his autofictional writing placed huge demands on his friends: "With each book, I place exorbitant demands on my friends, abusive demands for love. But I've been very lucky. My friends have never censored or put me down [*brimé*]; they have always accepted me as the writer I wanted to be" (Interview with Gaudemar, "La vie sida," 20). On the other hand, he was also capable of abandoning a project when

---

based on Renaud Camus himself – in a novel authored by a certain Rémi Santerre; in this incarnation of "Bill" he is "a man too polite to be honest" (L'Écart, 143–4). Philippe appears numerous times in Camus's journal, as well as a recent autobiographical work: *Journal romain*, 22, 78, 175, 219, 272, 347, 364, 367, 404, 558; *Vigiles*, 81, 349, 350–1, 379, 385, 451–3, 480, 558–9; *Aguets*, 28, 30–1, 51, 73, 75, 85, 93, 99, 145, 285, 293, 331; *Fendre l'air*, 21–2, 260, 318, 356, 360, 411; *L'Esprit des terrasses*, 71, 79, 202, 311, 361–2; *La Guerre de Transylvanie*, 14, 17, 64, 139, 180, 464; *P.A. (petite annonce)*, 235, 297, 301. (In the last reference in *La Guerre de Transylvanie*, Camus tells how he learned about the death of Hervé Guibert from Philippe on 28 December 1991.)

10 "'[Guibert] was exasperating. He did everything to make one reject him and at the same time he had an enormous need for affection'" (Régine Deforges, quoted by François Buot, *Hervé Guibert: le jeune homme et la mort*, 65).

he learned that it would be too painful for those whom he loved (Interview with Donner, 137–8). As for Guibert's treatment of Philippe in real life after the publication of *L'Ami*, there seems to be no reason to doubt the veracity of what Camus says. As we have just seen, even in the interview where Guibert describes that novel as his way of killing Bill off, he also admits to still having a great deal of affection for the man. After all, the very ambiguity of Bill's actions and words fits in perfectly with Guibert's AIDS writing and the principle of irreducible uncertainty that underpins it!

In the diary for 1991, Camus describes seeing Guibert on television, presumably on the program *Ex libris* broadcast on 7 March where he appeared after the publication of *Le Protocole compassionnel* a few weeks earlier. Camus uses this occasion to write his most detailed critique of Guibert, the man and the writer. Camus begins by stating that he harbors no feelings of rivalry with Guibert, even though his fellow writer has had great popular success and he little or none. Furthermore, Camus is fully aware of just how unpopular a stance he is taking: it must be remembered he wrote this volume of his diary in 1991, at the height of the media frenzy surrounding Guibert:

> je suis absolument persuadé, au plus profond de moi, qu'il n'entre pas le moindre sentiment de rivalité frustrée dans le retrait où je me tiens, par rapport à l'admiration générale à son égard; et que je préférerais nettement partager, même, car ma position, si position il y a, s'en trouverait infiniment simplifiée, et en tout cas plus sympathique. (*La Guerre de Transylvanie*, 138)

> I am absolutely convinced, in my deepest being, that not the slightest feeling of frustrated rivalry enters into my reticence concerning the general admiration for [Guibert]; clearly I would prefer to share it, especially since my position, if one can call it a position, would be infinitely simplified – in any case, more pleasant.

Camus criticizes Guibert's spoken French in much the same way as he did for the written transposition of colloquial expressions in *Fou de Vincent*. This time, however, it is a no-holds-barred denunciation of Guibert's way of speaking, "proof" in Camus's eyes that Guibert is *not* a great writer: "[J]'ai tendance à penser qu'on ne peut pas être un grand écrivain français si l'on ne peut pas ouvrir la bouche sans dire *quoi, bon*, ou *plein de* ..." (ibid., 139) (I tend to think that one cannot be a great French writer if one cannot open one's mouth without saying *what, okay,* or *loads of*). As is typical of Camus, he admits that his position is extreme; but he does not seem to take into account that Guibert was a very sick man when he gave the *Ex libris* interview, although it is possible, of course, that he might have spoken in the same manner had he been in perfect health. On the other hand, it seems unlikely that few other people who saw this interview of the unearthly-looking Guibert, wearing his famous red hat, speaking in a hoarse whisper, confiding some of his most personal thoughts about his writing and the evolution of AIDS as it affected his visibly frail body, would have thought of reproaching him for using less than classically correct French! After several twists, turns, and parenthetical comments, Camus comes to the crux of his argument: he shares neither Guibert's language nor his ethics. Camus reproaches Guibert with having revealed the cause of Foucault's death: "Il révèle, de Foucault, tout ce que sa famille et lui avaient mis beaucoup de soin à cacher, mais il proclame que c'est par respect à son égard" (ibid.) (He reveals everything that Foucault's family and Foucault himself had taken such care to hide, but he proclaims that it is out of respect for him). Here one could rebut Camus's argument by quoting what Guibert said about Foucault as a figure of history: "I believe that *after his death* Foucault's private life belongs to world history as well as literary history" (Interview with Eribon, 89; my emphasis). Clearly, Camus sets greater store by loyalty to family than does Guibert. It is equally clear that Guibert understood the *jeux de vérité* that link, rather than divide, history and fiction.

Camus concludes his comments on Guibert with an extraordinary comparison: he perceives Guibert's linguistic and ethical fluidity, as he terms it, to be on a par with French public opinion about the Gulf War, a position that Camus finds pusillanimous at best:

> Autant que sa langue avec le français tel qu'on le parle, cette éthique du fluide, qu'on lui voit, et qui aurait pour elle la justesse, la complexité, la résignation à l'inévitable, est sans doute parfaitement en accord avec la France aujourd'hui.
>
> C'est même à peu près, me semble-t-il, celle qu'on vient de voir à l'oeuvre dans nos positions nationales, à propos de la récente guerre du Golfe; non pas dans l'action gouvernementale officielle, qui n'en était qu'une nécessaire sous-section; mais dans l'ensemble des attitudes de l'opinion publique et du pays. Ne me jugez pas sur mes actes, et l'autre [Guibert] non plus: tout est toujours *beaucoup plus compliqué* ... (*La Guerre de Transylvanie*, 139; original ellipsis)

> Just as his French is no doubt in perfect harmony with the language as it is spoken today, so too this ethics of fluidity that is his and which has going for it correctness, complexity, resignation to the inevitable is perfectly in accord with today's France.
> This is even more or less, it seems to me, the ethics that we have just seen at work in our national positions concerning the recent Gulf War, not in official government actions, which were only an inevitable subsection of them, but by and large in the public opinion of this country. Don't judge me by my actions, like the other one [Guibert]: everything is always *much more complicated* ...

Guibert is, in the end, summarily rejected: "l'autre non plus."[11] After reading this passage that mixes topics as different as stylistic registers, ethics, and national politics, it is difficult to credit, as Camus would like us to believe, that he harbors no professional jealousy toward his fellow writer.

Addendum: in the last published volume of the diary Camus seems to have changed his position. If he does not agree with Guibert, then at the very least he has accepted the inevitable. By his "éthique du fluide" Guibert is now credited with having changed forever the form and content of what can or cannot be said. Describing the French translation of Pier Vittorio Tondelli's last novel, *Chambres séparées* (1992), Camus reproaches the Italian author for being too discreet! Despite its autobiographical content, Tondelli's novel is narrated in the third person; it's hero is named Leo; and AIDS is never mentioned:

> Tondelli a eu grand tort d'être si discret. Il faut bien dire que pour un roman si manifestement autobiographique le recours à un personnage central, écrivain venu d'un gros bourg d'Emilie, a quelque chose d'un

---

11 Renaud Camus reproaches the French nation for its cowardice in the face of Iraq's invasion and occupation of Kuwait. Camus's *bête noire* is the so-called ideology of the "sympa," which he perceives to be the dominant discourse in contemporary France. Such an ideology, according to Camus, takes the form of a kind of French "political correctness" based on sloppy thinking, as denounced in the following quotation: "Le comble, c'est que tous les pacifistes *sympas* ... de l'année dernière, qui trouvaient inadmissible qu'on aille se battre pour le Koweït, jugent maintenant imbécile qu'on ne se soit pas battu plus longtemps, ni plus loin, et qu'on n'en ait pas fini une bonne fois avec Saddam Hussein" (*La Guerre de Transylvanie*, 191) (The limit is all these "nice" pacifists ... from last year who found it inadmissible to fight for Koweit and who now judge that we did not fight long enough or far enough, and that we should have finished once and for all with Saddam Hussein).

> peu ridicule, dans le climat actuel. Guibert a balayé d'un coup toutes ces précautions parfaitement vaines. (*Le Château de Seix*, 86)

> Tondelli was wrong to be so discreet. One has to acknowledge that for a novel so openly autobiographical, using as a main character a writer from a large town in Emilia-Romagna is somewhat ridiculous in today's climate. With one blow Guibert swept away all these precautions which are perfectly useless.

It would seem that Guibert may have won over even his rival in the end. In any case, Camus is certainly correct in believing that Guibert has left his mark on the French literary scene, just as he has had a long-lasting influence on the way AIDS was constructed in France at the end of the twentieth century.

Renaud Camus is an important writer. With Guibert, I believe that he may have allowed feelings of rivalry to get in the way of the works themselves, at least from *Fou de Vincent* on. (Camus does not comment directly on any of Guibert's works published after *L'Ami*, although he does mention how impressed a friend of his was with *Le Protocole compassionnel*.) Despite – or because of – having so much in common, Guibert and Camus might have lived on different planets. There is a fundamental foreignness about Guibert that Camus neither accepts nor really understands. His judgment of Guibert – and Camus is not one to shrink from judging – is more ideological than political, more linguistic than literary, and more ethical than aesthetic.

It is possible that Camus's negative reaction to Guibert may have been exacerbated by what the younger writer said about Barthes at the dinner hosted by Philippe, not to mention the incident that led the former to write his "Fragments pour H." (We know that Camus identified completely with Barthes against the willfully hurtful intentions of the "other man," although it is not clear if he knew from the outset the identity of H.) Here is what Camus has to say about a certain G.:

> Je me moquais jadis de G., qui reprochait à Barthes d'être un hypocrite et un faux jeton, parce qu'il lui avait fait un compliment sur son livre, lorsqu'ils s'étaient rencontrés, mais n'en avait jamais rien dit en public, et moins encore écrit. Il me semblait, à moi, que le message était bien clair, et que G. devait se donner beaucoup de mal pour ne pas l'entendre: Barthes trouvait le livre de G. assez bon pour pouvoir lui en dire un mot aimable en situation mondaine, mais pas assez, de toute évidence,

> pour engager sur lui, dans la presse, son prestige, ou sa responsabilité vis-à-vis des lecteurs. (*L'Esprit des terrasses*, 76)
>
> In the past I used to make fun of G., who reproached Barthes for being a hypocrite and a devious character because he had complimented him about his book when they met but did not say anything in public, much less write anything. It seemed to me that the message was clear and that G. must have been hard put not to understand it: Barthes thought highly enough of G.'s book to be able to say a few nice words about it in a social situation, but clearly not highly enough to commit himself, in the press, in terms of his prestige and his responsibility to his readers.[12]

Although Camus never says directly that it was Guibert who criticized Barthes for refusing to write a preface for one of his books, the context in which Camus raises G.'s supposed insensitivity and tactlessness would seem to indicate that he was thinking of Guibert; for example, the passage quoted was written on 5 March 1990, the day after Camus mentions *L'Ami* for the first time. Perhaps Camus was unaware of the original agreement between Barthes and Guibert that stipulated a preface for a night of love. As we know, Barthes reneged on that "contract" after the scene in his apartment in December 1977. Camus wrote earlier about Barthes's ideas concerning preface-writing within the body of *Tricks* (437–8) – an ironic twist given that Barthes did preface Camus's most famous book. Later on, we learn that Barthes was more interested in Camus's person than his writing (*La Guerre de Transylvanie*, 400), although he points out that they were never lovers (*P.A. [petite annonce]*, 53; *Incomparable*, 12, 58).

It is likely that Camus has not had his last word on the subject of Guibert, but it is already clear that the author of *Tricks* remains fiercely loyal to Barthes,[13] placing him on a higher plane that Guibert's erstwhile mentor, Foucault. In a recent volume of the journal, for example, Camus expresses approval, albeit not ecstatic, of what his friend nicknamed Flatters – in reality, the painter Jean-Paul Marcheschi – says about the relative statures of Michel Foucault and Roland Barthes in the pantheon of French critical thought: "Fl. pense que Barthes est loin d'avoir encore sa juste place, qui est immense; et qu'on s'apercevra

---

12 See also *Fendre l'air*, 308. Although Barthes refused to commit himself in print regarding Guibert's juvenilia, Foucault did so in an interview a few months after the publication of *La Mort propagande* ("Non au sexe roi," *Dits et écrits*, 3:261–2).
13 See Camus's novels *Roman roi*, 498–9, and *Roman furieux*, 77, 492, for a sympathetic portrait of Barthes in the guise of Orlando or Roland.

bientôt de tout ce qui le met à cent coudées au-dessus d'un Foucault, par exemple, traité au passage de *lourdaud*. Bon, bon, bon, très bien" (*Le Château de Seix*, 37) (Fl. thinks that Barthes is far from having his rightful place, which is immense; and that we shall realize soon what makes him a hundred times more important than Foucault, for example, described in passing as "oafish." Well, well, well, very good).[14]

We are dealing not only with vastly different personalities but also with radically divergent views about writing and living. Camus is a social conservative and a classical writer in terms of the aesthetic choices he makes, choosing, for example, not to mix his diary and his fiction, at least not to the extent that Guibert claimed he did. Camus thinks Guibert was infinitely more in tune with the spirit of the times, whereas he often decries the language and ideology of his peers, though to no avail. In 1990 – the year that *À l'ami qui ne m'a pas sauvé la vie* was published – Camus wrote to Alain Buisine to express his astonishment on reading an article that the French critic had published about Camus's writing: "'Mais cela tendrait-il à signifier, Monsieur, que j'existe?'" (Does this tend to mean, Sir, that I exist?)[15] The point, of course, is that Camus remains alive but may not feel he exists, whereas Guibert is dead but continues to live on as a writer. But then the critical reception of a author's oeuvre is something that must be gauged over decades, not just a few years, and who can tell how readers of the twenty-first century will judge these two writers?

YVONNE BABY

A former journalist at *Le Monde*, where she worked from 1957 to 1985, Yvonne Baby (b. 1931) has written several novels. In 1977, while she was head of the cultural section of France's most prestigious newspaper, she hired Hervé Guibert to become the first photography critic of *Le Monde*, a position that he was to occupy until 1985, when he left the paper in a gesture of solidarity with Baby. It has been argued that *La Vie retrouvée*, published by Baby in 1992, would never have been written without the example of her protégé's autobiographical novels.[16] Whether or not this

14 In the volume of his diary for 1993, Camus returns yet again to Guibert, this time to remark how indifferent he was to Guibert's so-called beauty (*Graal-Plieux*, 151).
15 Letter quoted by Buisine, "Renaud Camus: pas vu, pas lu," 355.
16 Garcin, "Au nom de Guibert." Baby appears in *À l'ami qui ne m'a pas sauvé la vie* under the guise of Eugénie, 42–3, 122 (*Friend*, 34, 108); cf. *IF*, 63–4 (*GI*, 60–1); *Voy.*, 103; *AS*, 46; *SV*, 60; *HCR*, 83, 87 (*MRH*, 56, 61); *Let. é.*, 53; "L'autre journal d'Hervé Guibert," 76.

is true, the fact remains that Baby's book presents numerous similarities with Guibert's works, in terms of both content and style.

La Vie retrouvée, for example, is written in long run-on sentences reminiscent of the style of Thomas Bernhard, to whom Baby refers several times. Baby has other interests in common with Guibert; both of them collected postcards of Rembrandt's self-portraits (*La Vie retrouvée* [henceforth abbreviated *VR*], 85, 123). Indeed, it was Baby who sent Guibert the first postcard in his Rembrandt collection, as he explains in *L'Image fantôme*. And like Guibert, Baby is not shy about describing an early sexual experience in *La Vie retrouvée*, which is a kind of long self-portrait:

> Je vais te montrer la serre, m'a dit le jeune jardinier. Au bout du jardin, je respire les roses et prend [*sic*] un pétale rouge fuchsia, le déchire, le lèche et le colle sur ma bouche – habitude de Bénac –, et soudain, il se peut que des lèvres d'enfant se transmuent en bouche pourpre de femme, qu'une bouche ourlée, surprenante, invitante, se penche vers ce sexe de serre, comme bruni de terre, plante parmi les plantes qui ombragent les fleurs, un cri épouvanté interrompt ces délices, dont je crois avoir saisi la saveur particulièrement illicite, et peut-être délétère, un cri, Ma mère, ai-je dit, me levant aussitôt très droite, quelques gouttes blanches, bave de limaces, ai-je eu le temps de penser, sans dégoût ni embarras, me rappelant la chasse aux limaces avec ma grand-mère, après les averses d'été à Bénac, ou encore ce lait qui a jailli, il y a un instant, d'une tige coupée dans cette même serre. Quelques gouttes tombent, sont tombées sur le bord ajouré de ma socquette en coton perlé, j'ai également le temps de les enlever, m'essuyant aux feuilles plates que j'arrache, ultime délice, à un arbuste exotique ... (*VR*, 212–13)

> I'll show you the greenhouse, the young gardener said to me. At the end of the garden, I can smell the roses, I pick a red fuchsia petal, tear it, lick it, and stick it to my mouth – a habit from Bénac – and suddenly it comes about that a child's lips are tranformed into the crimson lips of a woman, a rimmed mouth, astonishing, inviting, bends down toward that greenhouse sex organ, like brown earth, a plant among the plants that shade the flowers, a cry of terror interrupts these delights, whose specially illicit savor I believe I have captured, a cry, Mother, I said, immediately standing up straight, several white drops, slug slime, I had the time to think, without disgust or embarrassment, remembering when I used to hunt for slugs with my grandmother after summer rain storms in Bénac, or even that milk which a moment ago had squirted out of a stem

> cut in two in this same greenhouse. A few drops fall, fell on the laced edge of my ankle socks of beaded cotton, I also have the time to take them off, wiping myself off on the flat leaves I tear from an exotic shrub, a final source of pleasure ...

In this case, Baby has outperformed Guibert in terms of precociousness in her description of oral sex engaged in by a child! At the same time, the reference to the trace left by the slugs, and the milky sap of a plant – metonymic analogues of the young gardener's semen – are reminiscent of Proust's description of the first time Marcel masturbates in the "petit cabinet sentant l'iris," a scene reprised by Guibert in *Mes parents*.[17] Proust is ever present in Baby's autobiographical novel, as witnessed not only by the title but also by the themes of childhood, love, time, and memory. All of these themes are also to be found in *Mes parents*, Guibert's most overtly autobiographical work, although strangely enough he did not attempt to give much textual depth in that early attempt at autobiographical writing.

To be sure, Baby, being older than Guibert, writes of an earlier period, including the German occupation of France during most of the Second World War, and some of her most important themes, such as marriage and maternity, are different from the younger writer's usual concerns. Nevertheless, one can also detect an influence of Guibert on Baby even in passages that initially might seem foreign to his universe. For example, Baby's love for and complicity with her two sons, Nicolas and Olivier, echo the pages in *Mes parents* where Guibert describes how intensively his parents cared for him. The dual shift in point of view – from a male to a female narrator and from an adult recalling his childhood to an adult remembering her own offspring's childhood – seems less like a fundamental ontological difference than a typically Guibertian transposition. And while Guibert never had children, the intense love he describes in *L'Ami* for Loulou and Titi – the children of his lover Jules and Berthe, whom Hervé eventually married – is mirrored in *La Vie retrouvée*. Whether it be Hervé and his parents, Hervé and "his" children, or Baby and hers, we are dealing with a form of total love of flesh and blood, one that is "carnal" (of the flesh but not sexual), as Louise describes the first relationship (*Mes*, 125; *My*, 113). While the idea of "writing the body" has lost favor in certain critical circles recently, nothing can better describe both Baby's and Guibert's inscription of their loved ones' bodies.

---

17 *Mes*, 89; *My*, 78–9. Cf. Proust, *À la recherche du temps perdu*, I:156; *Remembrance of Things Past*, I:172.

When Yvonne Baby gets to the point in her story where Guibert arrives on the scene, her narrative takes on a prelapsarian quality. She first met him in 1977, after he had published *La Mort propagande* with Régine Deforges, but he asked Baby not to read it, since he feared she would be shocked by it. Baby makes the point that she was looking less for stylistic perfection than for real writing ability in the journalists working for her: "la perfection, que m'importe, je cherche l'écriture, je cherche le style, et c'est ce journalisme-là que je défendrai, bonheur féroce, entraînée par l'élan fondateur du service culturel ..." (*VR*, 322–3) (what have I to do with perfection, I'm looking for writing, I'm looking for style, and that is the journalism I'll defend, a ferocious happiness, caught up as I am in the founding rush of the cultural service). As the previous sentence illustrates, Baby's syntax is often loose, approximate even, just like her protégé's, although his writing in *Le Monde* was usually more rigorously correct than in his books. Clearly, Guibert's humorous and self-denigrating article about his experiences at the festival, "An author in search of an audience," impressed Yvonne Baby, for she asked him to become her photography critic shortly after its publication in August 1977:

> soyez notre critique [de photographie], ai-je dit aussi, contente, à ce sourire qui articule très poliment, Parfait, puis qui s'agrandit, s'agrandit, familier déjà, un sourire docile et un sourire hooligan, un sourire qui lèche les petitesses et goûte la grandeur, vais-je découvrir, un sourire à qui l'on abandonne tout, sans réfléchir, même s'il ne vous cède jamais rien ... (*VR*, 318)

> be our photography critic, I said, heartened by a smile that articulates very politely, Perfect, and then gets bigger and bigger, already familiar, a meek smile and a hooligan's smile, a smile that laps up pettiness and savors greatness, as I will discover, a smile to which one is willing to forsake everything without thinking, even if it never gives up anything to you ...

The result was a success: Guibert wrote on photography, but also on film and other spectacles, such as the Folies Bergères in his article "Le luxe, jusqu'à l'épuisement." It is clear that Baby is still proud of the team she put together, for she describes the time spent working with Guibert, nicknamed Lapin, "rabbit," and his colleague Claire Devarrieux, called "Clarinette," as a paradise (*VR*, 323).

Baby appreciates the angelic side of Hervé, while acknowledging that there was another dimension to him. As the following quotation makes clear, Baby, like so many others, was not indifferent to Guibert's physical beauty:

> ce diable voluptueux et goulu, narquois, amusé, joufflu, je le vois souffler dans une trompette en verre de Murano ... regardez-le, n'est-il pas l'ange de Pier Paolo Pasolini, le voyou au front bouclé de *l'Accatone* et, s'écartant des faubourgs, le visiteur policé de *Théorème*, fuyez à son passage, si vous en avez l'énergie, il risque de dévaster ce qu'il embellit, les lys peuvent pâlir à la lumière crue, choc rimbaldien, il convient de resaluer la beauté ... (*VR*, 318–19)

> that voluptuous and greedy devil, sardonic, beguiling, chubby-cheeked, I can imagine him blowing on a trumpet made out of Murano glass ... look at him, isn't he Pier Paolo Pasolini's angel, the thug with his forehead covered in curls in *Accatone* and, far removed from the inner city, the civilized visitor in *Teorema*, flee his approach if you have the energy, he could devastate all that he embellishes, lilies can go pale in a hard light, a Rimbaud-like shock, beauty must be saluted anew ...

Such a paen of Surrealist-like free associations praising Guibert's good looks reminds us that Yvonne Baby met him when he was in the flower of his young manhood, when he was, as he says in *L'Ami*, "master of the world." Here was a beautiful young writer and photographer who took in films, exhibitions, galleries, and museums, whether in Paris, Berlin, or New York. He met and/or interviewed the great and the famous, such as Francis Bacon, Balthus, Cartier-Bresson, Gina Lollobrigida, and Orson Welles; he knew Isabelle Adjani, Agathe Gaillard, Roland Barthes, and Patrice Chéreau, but also – and on a more daily basis – Michel Foucault, Mathieu Lindon, and, of course, Yvonne Baby herself; his books were published by one of France's most innovative and prestigious publishing houses, Les Éditions de Minuit; and his journalism was published by the premier newspaper in the French-speaking world.[18] He was, like Miss Jean Brodie, in his prime although he was better look-

---

18 Guibert took photographs of Adjani, Balthus, Cartier-Bresson, Chéreau, Lollobrigida, Foucault (figure 4), and Welles, as well as Yvonne Baby, Hans-Georg Berger, Bernard Faucon, Agathe Gaillard, Mathieu Lindon, and Eugène Savitzkaya (see *Le Seul Visage* and *Photographies*).

ing and younger in mind and body than that fascistic high school teacher! Hervé's angelic appearance and unearthly powers to influence people were demonstrated when Baby's elder son Nicolas became gravely ill with peritonitis at age seventeen (cf. figure 19). Guibert visited the young man in hospital and took a photograph of him, which Baby describes as follows:

> Hervé Guibert les cerne, ces yeux, et les creuse en les photographiant pendant une visite, l'ange blond croise l'ange noir, dans l'oeil d'Hervé, voleur d'âmes, Nicolas devient ce mauvais garçon, ce compagnon d'*Accatone* ou de *Théorème*, à l'image, on le croirait revenu blessé d'une rixe sur les longues plages indolentes et perverses au pied du rocher Circé, où Pier Paolo Pasolini fut assassiné ... (*VR*, 363)

> Hervé Guibert puts shadows around those eyes, and makes them seem hollow as he photographs them during a visit, the blond angel meets the black-haired angel, in the vision of Hervé, that thief of souls, Nicolas becomes a bad boy, a companion of *Accatone* or *Teorema*, to judge by the picture you would think he'd come back wounded from a fight on the perverse and indolent long beaches at the base of the Circé rock where Pier Paolo Pasolini was murdered ...

Once again Hervé is associated with two of Pasolini's films, including *Teorema*, the restricted film that he ardently desired to see in his young adolescence (*Mes*, 67; *My*, 57). Both Hervé and Nicolas are described as angels, the one blond, the other dark-haired. Indeed, Hervé seems to have co-opted Baby's son into his own vicious circle of homoerotic desire and perverse indolence. Nicolas has been made to look like one of the young men whom Baby imagines frequenting the beach where Pasolini died. We recall how Guibert did much the same thing with his mother, as described in the eponymic text of *L'Image fantôme*. As in that case, the *Spectrum* is positioned and if necessary made up to look like a mirror image of Hervé's own desire, whether it be for the actor who played Tadzio (in whose image Guibert cast his mother) or Terrence Stamp in *Teorema*.[19] In looking at the photo of her son, Baby sees not merely his image but a reflection of the homoerotic desire projected on

---

19 According to Guibert, the first man he fell in love with was the actor Terrence Stamp, whom he only knew as a photograph (*IF*, 19–21 [*GI*, 17–19]). As an adult, he wrote a film review of *Teorema* ("L'allégorie absolue") that was published in *Le Monde*.

to him by the photographer. Baby is perfectly well aware of this mimetic performance: Hervé is destiny's inevitable agent who allows her to see Nicolas as a sexual object, hence the briefest expression of jealousy on her part when she describes Guibert as a "thief of souls." In fact, the photo will serve as a means to help cure the sick youth in a kind of laying on of hands that is at once real and symbolic, thereby emphasizing the angelic qualities of Hervé Guibert. After all, as Murray Pratt has reminded us, when an angel descends to earth, there are always shattering results ("L'autoprésentation, l'écriture autre et l'ange," 149–50):

> quand j'étends mes mains sur ces mains qu'Hervé Guibert, parachevant sa photo d'archangélique manière, a posées à plat, ailées, sur le torse encore halé, encore musclé, atteint par la gaze qui monte si haut et n'empêche pas, au-dessous, criminelle et impalpable, l'embolie pulmonaire, ce caillot de la taille d'une balle de ping-pong, dira le médecin, une balle, plutôt une boule de glace qui doit fondre, qui fondra ... (*VR*, 364)

> when I extend my hands on these hands that Hervé Guibert, like an archangel, putting the finishing touches on his photo, had placed flat out, winged, on [Nicolas's] still tanned, still muscular torso, touched by the gauze that comes up so far and does not prevent, beneath, the criminal and unpalpable pulmonary embolism, that clot the size of a ping-pong ball, as the doctor will say, a ball, or rather a scoop of icecream that must melt, that will melt ...

The contrast with Renaud Camus's description of Guibert could not be greater. Yvonne Baby's portrait of her young colleague takes the form of an encomium to a friend who seems still alive, although she does mention a photograph that foreshadows death.[20] She does not write about Guibert's books directly. Rather, she has followed his example by imitating certain elements of his style, thereby turning her own work into a mimotext; in fact one could discern in *La Vie retrouvée* a mimo-mimotext – like *À l'ami qui ne m'a pas sauvé la vie* – as different layers of textuality interpenetrate each other: Guibert, Bernhard, Proust ...

---

20 "cette photo qu'il m'a offerte, photo-miroir, photo-icône, masque clair-obscur, la mort est blanche, l'empreinte immortelle, des griffes pourtant menacent l'ange" (*VR*, 319) (that photo he gave me, a photo-mirror, a photo-icone, a chiaroscuro mask, death is white, the immortal imprint, nevertheless claws threaten the angel).

Instead of judging Guibert as Camus does, Baby seems to have an intuitive grasp of his seductive powers, to which she is clearly not immune, as well as his talent for camaraderie and friendship, not to mention a darker side that she finds less frightening than intriguing.

CHRISTOPHE DONNER

"*Vengeance is mine ...*, saith the Lord" (Rom. 12:19). At the basis of *L'Esprit de vengeance* (1992, henceforth abbreviated as *EV*) by Christophe Donner (b. 1956) is his desire to write about his grandfather, Jean Gosset: "Je veux venger mon grand-père. C'est un saint, résistant, philosophe, et je ne suis rien de tout ça" (*EV*, 64) (I want to avenge my grandfather. He was a saint, a member of the Resistance, a philosopher, and I am none of these). A protégé of Emmanuel Mounier, Gosset was a mild-mannered man who became sick to his stomach at the mere thought of giving oral examinations to high school students; but during the Second World War Donner's grandfather worked in the French Resistance, performing many dangerous assignments. He was captured and deported to Germany, where he died in the Neuengamme concentration camp in 1944. According to Donner, upon Gosset's death the position for which Mounier had been grooming him in the small community of Les Manteaux blancs founded by the famous father of personalism was taken up by a younger philosopher. As a result of a series of complicated circumstances Christophe Donner ended up living with this man's family for a number of years; but no one initially made the connection with his grandfather, whom the philosopher had known as a student. Donner first fictionalized this family in his novel *Les Sentiments* (1990), although he did not name them in that book, as he did in *L'Esprit de vengeance*. In the case of the second book, the family obtained a court injunction against the publisher, Les Éditions Bernard Grasset, requiring removal of all the direct references to their name, and payment of five thousand francs to the family for having violated their privacy. An emended edition was required, in which the family name is replaced by a blank, as indicated by the following sentence in italics on the verso side of the title page: "*À la suite d'une décision du Tribunal de Grande Instance de Paris, il a été fait interdiction à l'auteur de citer un certain patronyme dans son livre. Ce patronyme a donc été caviardé dans la présente édition*" (*EV*, [6]) (As a result of a decision by the Tribunal de Grande Instance of Paris, the author has been forbidden to quote a certain family name in his book. Thus the name has been removed from this edition).²¹ Although it is not difficult to determine the identity of the philosopher, since one of his titles is mentioned in *L'Esprit de vengeance*, I have decided to respect the privacy of the family about whom Donner wrote in such detail. Despite its title, the book is a hymn of praise not just to Donner's grandfather and, paradoxically, the philosopher, his wife, and their children, but also to Hervé Guibert, whom Donner met twice before his long interview with him in the winter of 1991 just after the publication of *Le Protocole compassionnel*.

The status of Christophe Donner's book is problematic: supposedly written over a period of twelve days, it is, as he describes it, an example of "écriture immédiate" (*EV*, 8), a reference not to the *écriture automatique* of the Surrealists, but to the production of an autobiographical work that contains, *en abîme* as it were, the story of its own genesis. One thinks, of course, not only of *À la recherche du temps perdu* but also of *À l'ami qui ne m'a pas sauvé la vie*. But even though Guibert was capable of working quickly – his first AIDS fiction was, he claimed, written in the space of a few months – there is no indication that he attempted to accomplish what Donner seeks to do, that is, to write without erasure or revision, simply to keep on going and, if necessary, to return to the same character or theme in a later part of the work. Donner's *parti-pris* of diary writing is in fact part and parcel of his reaction to Guibert, his writing, and the success it brought him.

Donner wanted to imitate the example of Guibert – and Renaud Camus, who is not mentioned – by spending two years in Rome at the Villa Médicis. His proposal to the committee, about which he talked with Guibert who encouraged him, involved writing a book about his grandfather:

> Je voulais partir à la Villa Médicis de Rome pendant deux ans afin d'écrire ce livre sur mon grand-père. Je voulais aussi faire comme Hervé Guibert: être reçu par le grand prix de Rome ... Au départ ... ça marchait comme sur des roulettes, j'avais été sélectionné parmi les quatre finalistes, j'avais rencontré Guibert qui m'avait encouragé à être brillant lors de mon passage devant le jury. Il était heureux pour moi que je passe deux ans dans ce mouroir. Il disait: C'est les deux plus belles années de ma vie. (*EV*, 158)

---

21 The facts of the case are described in a short unsigned article published in *Le Monde* (22 Feb. 1992): 24.

> I wanted to go to the Villa Médicis in Rome for two years to write this book about my grandfather. I also wanted to do as Hervé Guibert had done: receive the great Prize of Rome ... At first ... everything went like clockwork, I was selected among the four finalists, I met Guibert who encouraged me to be sparkling when I appeared before the fellowship committee. He was happy that I could spend two years in that asylum. He said: They were the two most beautiful years of my life.

According to his initial project, Donner intended to write a fictional version of his grandfather's life in order to distinguish his writing from the diary-inspired writing of Guibert's autofictions: "Ce que je criais à l'examen de passage de la villa Médicis: 'La fiction! je veux faire une fiction!' C'était ça, une volonté farouche de me différencier d'Hervé Guibert et de son Journal ..." (*EV*, 301) (Which is what I shouted at the interview for the Villa Médicis: "Fiction! I want to write fiction!" That was it, an unflinching desire to differentiate myself from Hervé Guibert and his diary). Apparently Donner panicked at the interview, and failed to answer satisfactorily the questions put to him about why he wanted to go to the Villa Médicis. Although not used to examination-like situations such as the interview with the board, Donner claims that what really put him off was having learned a few days earlier that Guibert had AIDS (*EV*, 159). He did not get the fellowship, with the result that he was obliged to find his own writing retreat in Sicily, which he did with much difficulty. It was while there and in the process of writing what appears initially to be a diary about the book he cannot write that Donner comes to the realization that the diary is in fact the book: "C'est à ce moment-là que j'ai décidé que le livre serait ça, le Journal et rien d'autre" (*EV*, 71) (It was then that I decided that the book would be this, the diary and nothing else).

Donner interviewed Guibert for *La Règle du jeu* on 16 February 1991; a month later he began writing *L'Esprit de vengeance*. The interview remains fresh in his mind, and he refers to it several times. For example, he asked Guibert about the fracture or split (*déchirement*) between his diary and his fiction: "Depuis quand vis-tu le déchirement entre le journal et la fiction?" (*EV*, 138) (Since when have you been living the split between your diary and your fiction?). Of course, Guibert answered that there was no split, since, as we know, it was in his diary that many of his books were "born":

> Ce n'est pas un déchirement, c'est plutôt les limites entre l'un et l'autre

> sont assez indécises, assez floues, elles s'interpénètrent toujours un peu. J'ai toujours mis à sac mon journal pour y voler certaines choses, pour mettre dans un livre ... (Interview with Donner, 138)

> There is no split, rather the boundaries between the two are quite imprecise, quite blurred, they always penetrate each other somewhat. I have always ransacked my diary to steal certain things in order to put them in a book.

In *L'Esprit de vengeance* Donner returns to his question and Guibert's response:

> Dans mon entretien avec Guibert, je lui posais la question du déchirement entre le récit et le Journal, il disait que ce n'était pas pour lui un déchirement. Pour moi ça l'est, et c'est beau, un déchirement, j'aime ce mot, j'aime le geste, le bruit, cette douleur particulière à le vivre ... L'écrivain qui se déchire entre la fiction et le présent méditatif. (*EV*, 150)

> In my interview with Guibert I asked him a question about the fracture between his narratives and his diary, he told me there was no split for him. For me there is one, a *fracture* is a beautiful thing, I like the word, I like the gesture, the noise, the particular pain of living it ... The writer splitting himself between fiction and the meditative present.

Wanting to avoid imitating Guibert, Donner lives and writes this fracture, first, by proposing to write a work more fictional than autobiographical, and, second, by in fact writing a diary-like work that he perceives to be nonfictional. In either case, however, it is the "anxiety of influence" that is the driving force behind the writing of his grandfather's story. But since he ends up opting for a writing style that is more personal, his own story – including his relations with the philosopher and his family as well as Guibert – takes on an ever greater importance. On the other hand, the story of the grandfather does not disappear, and indeed when Donner recounts his meeting with a man who as a boy knew Jean Gosset at Neuengamme, *L'Esprit de vengeance* takes on a dramatic quality second only to the narrator's description of the jealousy he felt for Guibert.

This writerly jealousy, which underpins the entire work, reaches its high point when Donner decides to throw away his copies of Guibert's books, letters received from Guibert, as well as the tape of the interview. Donner woke up early the morning after this acting out, and retrieved the plastic garbage bag containing the Guibert material, fortunately for us, since the interview is an important document in Guibert's career. At twenty-two pages, it is the longest interview published. At the same time, it is somewhat frustrating to read, since Donner seems to have based many of his questions on his own concerns and preoccupations ("Our desire for sainthood is spoiled by that which saves the narrator's life" [Interview with Donner, 154]). On the other hand, Donner did not ask Guibert some of the questions that would seem obvious, such as the relevance of homosexuality to his writing. Hence Guibert was obliged to improvise answers to the questions that Donner did not ask him, which he commented on: "[J]e réponds toujours à côté, chaque fois ..." (ibid., 147; original ellipsis) (My answers are always off the point, every time ...).

One of the questions that Guibert did not answer, according to Donner, was the first one put to him, concerning the effect of taking or not taking drugs on one's writing. In fact, Guibert did address the issue raised by discussing AZT, but it is true that in his answer he began speaking about his nonexistent sexual life: "Sexualité impossible, disait-il, douloureusement, atrocement impossible. Parce que malade et affaibli, sa sexualité a été impossible et reste impossible pour le bébé-Auschwitz" (*EV,* 46) (Sex is impossible, he said, painfully, atrociously impossible. Because he was sick and weakened, his sexuality had become impossible and remains impossible for Bébé-Auschwitz). We remember that Guibert used the expression "Auschwitz baby" in *Le Protocole compassionnel* (chapter 27) to describe his own ravaged body. Donner's use of it here is thus both intertextually and intratextually overdetermined. For example, he will draw a parallel between AIDS writing and the writing of deportees who returned from death camps in Germany after the Second World War:

> cet homme [Guibert] dont l'écriture m'a toujours ensorcelé, non seulement parce que je la considère comme une des plus belles qui soient, avec peut-être, pourquoi pas, ce pressentiment qu'elle ressemblerait un jour si étonnamment à une écriture de déportée, de héros, de saint, mais ensorcelante aussi parce qu'elle était écrite par un homme de mon âge qui, par certains traits (mais surtout par certains silences ou regards), me ressemblait. (*EV,* 300–1)

> Guibert whose writing has always bewitched me, not only because I consider it to be one of the most beautiful there is, with perhaps, why not, a

premonition that one day it would resemble the writing of a deportee, a hero, a saint, but also spellbinding because it was the work of a man of my age who, because of certain traits (but especially certain silences or looks), resembled me.

Even the ddI of the dead dancer is, in Donner's eyes, a story that recalls Holocaust narratives:

> Parce qu'à tout point de vue, l'histoire de la DDI du danseur mort ressemble au pain du copain mort, morceau de pain qui prolongera la vie du déporté peut-être assez pour en sortir un jour, peut-être assez de DDI pour voir arriver le remède. Voilà pourquoi j'aime Guibert. (*EV*, 123)

> Because from every point of view, the story of the ddI of the dead dancer resembles the bread of the dead friend, the piece of bread that will prolong the life of the deportee perhaps just long enough for him to get out one day, perhaps enough ddI to last until a cure is discovered. That's why I love Guibert.

Using the examples of his grandfather and Guibert, Donner continues to develop the parallel between a concentration camp inmate and a Person Living with AIDS. The metaphor first used in *L'Ami* and then in *Le Protocole compassionnel* is continued and developed in *L'Esprit de vengeance*, where its textual potential is fully realized.

Donner interprets Guibert first response about sex, or the lack of it, in two ways. First of all, he believes that it was Guibert's way of telling Donner that he could not have sex with him:

> En fait, face à moi qui l'aime d'amour, il devait m'alerter là-dessus, c'est pour ça qu'il a répondu ainsi à ma question. Il a fait semblant de parler littérature, et Thomas Bernhard sur le tapis bien sûr, mais en fait il devait m'alerter que nous ne coucherions pas ensemble. Quel garçon prévenant et délicat, à la réflexion. Baiser, coucher, faire l'amour avec Guibert, c'est une question qui m'est souvent venue à l'esprit mais qui n'est jamais descendue à l'endroit où il est tout de même nécessaire qu'elle descende: le sexe. Le coeur, avec Guibert, a toujours dominé le sexe. Mon amour pour lui n'a même, je crois, jamais produit le moindre fantasme charnel. (*EV*, 47)

> In fact, with me, with my genuine love for him, he had to alert me to the

fact, that's why he answered my question as he did. He pretended to be talking about literature, bringing up Thomas Bernhard, of course, but in fact he had to tell me that we wouldn't be going to bed. What a thoughtful, considerate man, on reflexion. To fuck, to go to bed, to make love with Guibert, it's a question I've often thought about but which never got down to the place where it has to go: the genitals. With Guibert, my heart has always dominated my genitals. My love for him has, I believe, never even produced the slightest sexual fantasy.

As Guibert explained, sex seemed to have been replaced in his life by the pursuit and acquisition of paintings:

> Le manque de la sexualité me ravage, me travaille, est douloureux au possible, et pratiquement intolérable, donc je crois que je cherche des substituts, je crois que le fait de chercher des tableaux, ces espèces de chasses, d'acquisitions, de négociations des tableaux, de possessions, pour moi c'est des présences, des présences au sens érotique ... (Interview with Donner, 139)

> This lack of sex torments me, tortures me, it is as painful as possible, practically intolerable, so I think I look for substitutes, I believe that looking for pictures, those sorts of hunting expeditions, acquisitions, negotiations about pictures, about possessions, for me they are presences, presences in the erotic sense ...

It is interesting here to note how Guibert's response anticipates *L'Homme au chapeau rouge*, his most painterly novel, most or all of which was already written at the time of the interview occasioned by the publication of the previous novel, *Le Protocole compassionnel*. Whether or not Guibert was trying to indicate to Donner in a diplomatic way that sex between the writer and his admiring reader was out of the question is, of course, impossible to know.

What Guibert did say was that he gave up on sex for the same reason that he gave up on writing for almost a year: lack of energy: "Je n'ai pas écrit pendant pratiquement un an parce que l'écriture c'est comme la sexualité: une dépense d'énergie, et je n'avais plus les moyens de me permettre cette dépense-là, plus la force physique et plus la force morale d'écrire" (ibid., 136) (I didn't write for practically a year because writing is like sex: an expenditure of energy, and I didn't have the means to allow myself that expenditure, neither the physical or moral strength).²² However, Donner has another interpretation – even more idiosyncratic than the first – about the reason why Guibert desired to speak about sex: "Hervé Guibert allait me donner une réponse sur la sexualité des gens des camps, sur celle de mon grand-père" (*EV*, 46) (Hervé Guibert was going to give me an answer about the sexuality of people in the camps, including my grandfather). For the author of *L'Esprit de vengeance*, Guibert has become the spokesman of Jean Gosset. Just as Donner adores his fellow writer, so too he adores the memory of the grandfather whom he never knew. Guibert a.k.a. Bébé-Auschwitz seems to have a direct link and personal contact with the Resistance hero who died in a German concentration camp. The writer's diminished physical state seems to have made him into a kind of spiritual medium in touch with those who, like Donner's grandfather, are already in paradise, to quote the title of Guibert's last novel:

> Lui que je venais de voir, squelettique, de profil, et près de la mort comme mon grand-père, il me répondait à côté de la question, directement pour m'informer sur la sexualité de ce grand-père qui fut soumis à un martyre physique et moral assez proche du sien avec sa maladie, et jusqu'à la sainteté où je place tous les deux. C'était un message de l'au-delà, un message de mon grand-père passant par la bouche de celui que j'admire le plus *sur* cette terre (et non dessous!). (*EV*, 47)

> He whom I'd just seen, with his skeletal profile, near death like my grandfather, he answered me beside the point, directly in order to inform me about the sexuality of my grandfather who was made to suffer a physical and moral martyrdom quite close to his with illness, even unto the sainthood that I attribute to them both. It was a message from the great beyond, a message from my grandfather coming from the mouth of the person I admire most *on* (and not under!) this earth.

---

22 This is not the only interview in which Guibert claimed to have been unable to write for a period as long as a year. Yet he accomplished a great deal in the last three years of his life. Not only did he write the three AIDS fictions (*À l'ami qui ne m'a pas sauvé la vie*, *Le Protocole compassionnel*, *L'Homme au chapeau rouge*), he also found time to write *Mon valet et moi*, *Le Paradis*, and *Cytomégalovirus*, as well as to work on the enlarged edition of *La Mort propagande et autres textes de jeunesse*. He also wrote the novella entitled *La Chaire fraîche* included in the posthumous volume of short stories (*La Piqûre d'amour*). Even without the editorial work involved in transcribing earlier works, this represents some nine hundred and sixty pages of print. (Cf. p. 212 of this book.)

Donner's hero – Guibert the martyr, Guibert the wounded man – has become Saint Guibert, equal in stature to the figure of the absent grandfather.

In the absence of Jean Gosset, Christophe Donner elected a new grandfatherly figure, the philosopher whose name cannot be written in this context. Indeed, one could read Donner's autobiographical narrative as a biblical tale in which first Mounier then the other philosopher play godlike roles, whereas Gosset is the Christ-figure. (Gosset used Christophe as his wartime pseudonym.) But just as there are two characters whose destinies put them on a par with the divinity, so too are there two Christ-like figures, the other being Hervé Guibert himself, whose martydom is equal to Gosset's. Finally, the author of *L'Esprit de vengeance* can be cast in the role of the Holy Spirit. Such an interpretation gains in credence what it lacks in realism when one recalls that Mounier was responsible for creating the intellectual community where the philosopher, his family, and Christophe lived together, a kind of miniature garden of Eden from which Donner was eventually expelled.

Ever conscious of the necessity to differentiate himself from Guibert, whose influence he wants to escape all the while he sings his mentor's praise, Donner saw himself on the side of life, as opposed to the other writer's "morbidité, son penchant pour le suicide, son corps sans cesse harcelé par la maladie" (*EV,* 301) (morbidity, his inclination to suicide, his body harassed by illness). Later, however, Donner realizes that such a distinction does not correspond to reality: "Aujourd'hui ces pseudo-différences tombent en poussière" (ibid.) (Today these pseudo-differences are reduced to dust); for Guibert no more represents death than Donner does life. But if the author of *L'Esprit de vengeance,* like the author of *Le Protocole compassionel,* uses the autofictional format, if Donner is no more on the side of life than Guibert symbolizes death, if their writing styles, like that of Yvonne Baby, are both heavily influenced by Thomas Bernhard (*EV,* 285), if both writers (who also made films) do their best work in Italy (Elba, Sicily), and if both of them lived in the company or circle of a famous French philosopher, what then distinguishes them? Donner, like Renaud Camus, finds himself wondering if he exists in his own right as a writer:

> Il est bon de se dire que personne ne se soucie de moi, ni Guibert, ni personne, et de rester petit, pas né, toujours dans l'imminence d'apparaître. Mais il arrive un moment où ça ne tient plus. Il arrive un moment où la putain, même de luxe, doit annoncer son prix, et affirmer, face à la concurrence, sa "différence" ... (*EV,* 301–2)

> It is good to say to oneself that no one is concerned about me, neither Guibert, nor anyone, and to remain small, unborn, always on the point of appearing. But there comes a time when it doesn't work any more. There comes a time when the prostitute, even the expensive call girl, must state her price and, faced by the competition, assert her "difference" ...

All that Donner can come up with in the way of a deciding difference between Guibert and himself is that the former was so exasperated by his friends that he wrote a hurtful text about them, although he later "condemned" it to oblivion. Donner, by contrast, claims to love his friends, to fear hurting them. Ironically, the real difference between the two writers is that Guibert successfully managed to bring off his autofictional writing, no matter how audacious it was,[23] whereas Donner's most blatant attempt to rival and perhaps even outdo Guibert led him to a trial, judgment, and condemnation at the instigation of his adopted grandfather, the philosopher whom he must have hurt deeply by writing about him and his family.[24] Donner wrote that the spirit of vengeance would be put into action, if Guibert were to die before him, which is what happened. But when the Lord said that vengeance was his, the meaning is clear: it is not for us mortals to try to usurp his role. Donner lived in the company of a godly man and he worshipped a writer whom he thought of as a saintly martyr, but in the end he was to lose the former because of what he wrote about him, just as he was to lose the latter to death.

Clearly, to follow in the steps of Hervé Guibert can be a journey fraught with pitfalls in the no-man's-land that both separates and connects life and writing. Whether one finds him difficult to like as does Renaud Camus, is attracted to him like Yvonne Baby, or worships him like Christophe Donner, and whether one seeks to write in his manner or not, Hervé Guibert is not an easy figure – nor an easy "act" – to follow. It is a tribute to Guibert that, hard as it may be, it was impossible for these writers not to attempt to follow him, one way or another. In all three cases we have seen that this fascination with Guibert is not only with his writ-

---

23 Guibert himself narrowly avoided prosecution. Whether or not the model for Bill contemplated legal action, I do not know, but apparently Isabelle Adjani thought of suing Guibert for his portrait of the actress Marine in *L'Ami* (Assouline, "Les vrais héros," 29–30).
24 In a recent work entitled *Contre l'imagination* Donner justifies using a friend's real name in a literary work since it forces the writer to remain closer to reality (54–6).

ing but also with his person, especially in the case of Baby and Donner, although even to some extent in the case of Camus. With Guibert we are dealing with a man, a body, as well as the inscription of that body in works that "autofictionalize" its suffering. No doubt this is why a "purely" literary response becomes impossible with Guibert. The effect of his writing on all of these writers is to incorporate their readerly responses, not in a book review, essay, or erudite study but in books of their own. In this, the example of Guibert is truly productive, his writing generating new writing, new books that inevitably intertexualize his own.

Camus's response to Guibert is the most traditional, in both form and content, but it is clear he has been touched by the example of this gay writer, however much they differ in outlook and style. The proof of this is the number of times that Camus returns to Guibert in his diary. Much of what Camus reproaches Guibert with is associated with larger issues. The indignation Camus expresses about Guibert's revelations about friends, for example, is part and parcel of his critique of autofiction, a genre for which he professes to have little patience, although in a recent text he describes his interest in a form of nonfictional novel that would be closer to *auto-graphie* than autofiction (*Etc.*, 162). Guibert's fluid style, so unlike Camus's traditionally molded and syntactically pure sentences, corresponds to the way French is spoken today more than the way it is supposed to be spoken, much less written. Camus belongs to the generation of Frenchmen who completed high school before the breath of fresh air brought in by the troubles and the subsequent education reforms of May 1968, whereas Guibert belongs to the first generation of post-68 students. This may explain some of the differences in the way each man approaches writing. Finally, Camus's critique of Guibert can also be explained by the former's dislike of eroticism on account of the association of sexuality with transgression and the theme of death, both of which play such a prominent part in some of Guibert's most important works, including *Vous m'avez fait former des fantômes* and *À l'ami qui ne m'a pas sauvé la vie*.

With Yvonne Baby there is a huge affective investment in the memory of her former protégé. She mentions none of his books, but it is clear that she has read her Guibert, in particular *À l'ami qui ne m'a pas sauvé la vie*. Its example, in terms of style – long run-on sentences – and content – the need to say everything (or almost) about oneself – has deeply influenced her. Baby allows us to realize just how charismatic Guibert was in the flesh. While Donner will perceive Guibert as a saint, Baby sees him as an angel (if God exists, as she wrote). The angelic image no doubt had a great deal to do with his looks, but there is a strong hint that she sees in him a celestial messenger, in an altogether different way to Camus's perception of his rival having come from another planet! For this woman who lived through a bitter struggle to hang on to her job at *Le Monde* and felt obliged to leave in the end, the example of Guibert is an empowering one, allowing her to sublimate her feelings in a book that covers her entire life going back to her Second World War experiences. Without Guibert it seems unlikely that Baby would have had the will, the courage, and the strength to complete such a massive undertaking.[25]

As for Christophe Donner, he has known the unhappy fate of what can happen to a writer who attempts to outperform Guibert. Despite the accusations of journalists there is a certain discretion in Guibert: usually, he does not use real names, and however autobiographical his works may be, they still remain fiction. In this, discretion in Guibert is truly disguised! Donner made the mistake of trying to both imitate and differentiate himself from Guibert. The result is a mixed success, even without taking into account the fate of his book in the French courts. To be certain, Guibert wrote quickly, but not as quickly or as uncritically as Donner claimed he did in the case of *L'Esprit de vengeance*. Still, one can only admire his sincerity, his almost childlike adoration for Guibert and the person he most closely identifies with him, Jean Gosset, his grandfather, the Resistance fighter who died in a concentration camp.

The terrible scourges of Nazism and AIDS are more than ample, though not complete, evidence of the sad state of humankind in the twentieth century. And Donner, like Guibert, is right to associate them, however different these evils may be. For, Susan Sontag to the contrary, metaphor can be an effective means in the attempt to inscribe – and therefore to remember – the unspeakable that, whether we be direct witnesses or not, is part and parcel of our story, our bequest to all those who will follow us.

---

25 See Yvonne Baby's preface to *La Photo, inéluctablement*, in which she recalls telling Guibert that he was an "indestructible angel" the day before he died ([vi]).

Chapter Nine

Ghost Writing

> l'amour de la littérature est aussi un voisinage avec des morts.
> *L'Incognito*, 183
>
> loving literature also means being on neighborly terms with the dead.

> Ils croisèrent des mythes, ce n'étaient peut-être que des hallucinations provoquées par leur faiblesse, des rappels de lectures d'enfance.
> *Les Lubies d'Arthur*, 47
>
> They encountered myths, perhaps they were only hallucinations brought on by their weakness, memories of things read about in childhood.

This chapter started out as an article I never completed on various portrayals of Michel Foucault in contemporary fiction. I was going to use John L'Heureux's biting satire of academic politics and life, *The Handmaid of Desire* (1996), as well as a postmodern play entitled *More Divine: A Performance for Roland Barthes* (1995) by Sky Gilbert, a Canadian dramatist and theater director, as well as a drag queen notorious for his female persona Jane.[1] Foucault "appears" in the former as the subject of a seminar taught by the formidable Olga Kominska, and in the latter – in the flesh – as a philosopher who is both more masculine and more open about being gay compared to his rather feeble and lifeless colleague, Roland Barthes. One could also include the fleeting references to a certain Scherner in *Les Samouraïs* (1990) by Julia Kristeva, although in that

---

1 Margaret Webb, "What's Eating Sky Gilbert?"

novel he plays a definite second fiddle to the beloved Armand Bréhal, the character based on Barthes.² Like Hervé Guibert, Kristeva "outs" Foucault for his sexuality and AIDS. In *The Farewell Symphony* (1997) by Edmund White, although Foucault only "occupies" a few pages – out of four hundred – he is a "fully drawn character" (Benfey, "The Dead," 11), since we do get an inkling of his cult of friendship among males, his modesty, as well as his illness and death.³ But apart from Guibert's "Les secrets d'un homme" (*MV*, 101–11) and *À l'ami qui ne m'a pas sauvé la vie*, to date the most extraordinary work of fiction to be devoted to Foucault's memory must surely be Patricia Duncker's *Hallucinating Foucault* (1996).

Writing in the *New York Times Book Review*, Allen Lincoln described Duncker's novel as "a fascinating drama of knowledge and power, reason and desire" ("Author! Author!" 15). In his book review of the French translation, Hugo Marsan wrote as follows in *Le Monde*: "[T]his intelligent and ardent text extirpates the roots of literary creation and exposes the latent madness of novelists" ("Histoire de l'amour fou"). Translated as *La Folie Foucault* by Céline Schwaller-Balay, the novel received more praise than usual for a translation, especially of a first novel. According to the dust jacket, Paul Rabinow, the well-known Foucault scholar, has written: "This lacerating novel invents a stunning fiction of Foucault and his doubles."

Patricia Duncker teaches at the University of Wales and lives for part of the year in France, according to the author's blurb. Although *Hallucinating Foucault* is her first novel, it is neither her first book nor her only work of fiction. She has edited a collection of lesbian fiction entitled *In and Out of Time* (1990), and is the author of a study of contemporary feminist fiction, *Sisters and Strangers* (1992). Since the publication of *Hallucinating Foucault*, a volume of her short stories – some previously published as early as 1991 – entitled *Monsieur Shoushana's Lemon Trees* (1997) has appeared. Hervé Guibert, by contrast, was anything but an academic, although because of his fascination with and love for women he could well be considered a proto-feminist. The most obvious point where Duncker (b. 1951) and Guibert meet is in their attempt to write

---

2 The first novel in which a character inspired by Foucault appears is Georges Lapassade's *Le Bordel andalou* (1971). Foucault also appears briefly in *Les Petits garçons* by Guy Hocquenghem (1983). I am indebted to *The Lives of Michel Foucault* by David Macey for these two titles.

3 *The Farewell Symphony*, 376–7, 383. In his review article, entitled "Love Stories," White described meeting Guibert at one of Foucault's dinner parties (3).

about Michel Foucault. I will argue, however, that the intertextuality between Duncker and Guibert goes beyond the fact that they have incorporated the famous philosopher into their fictions. Indeed, important as Foucault is in the Duncker novel, I believe *Hallucinating Foucault* is also about Guibert himself and his unique style. An early clue to Guibert's influence on Duncker can be found in her book *Sisters and Strangers* where, rehearsing the introduction to what was to be the penultimate volume of her *The History of Sexuality*, she writes: "Living and thinking differently from the heteropatriarchal world takes a great deal of emotional and intellectual effort; there are not many books written by men which offer any help whatsoever. The ones that do are fictional/poetical. But that is *another story*" (269; my emphasis). My hypothesis is that Guibert's works are part and parcel of that story, which Duncker has chosen to tell in her own words by writing a novel that is in large part a metatextual homage to another writer's work. In their reviews, Lincoln picks up on the allusions to Genet, and Marsan finds that the figure of the novelist in *Hallucinating Foucault* could be anyone of several real writers, including Althusser, Artaud, Duvert, or Hocquenghem. While it is clear that Duncker is familiar with the history of French literature – there are allusions to Balzac, Baudelaire, Rimbaud, and Claude Simon – I believe that her novel is nothing less than an attempt to write not so much in the shadow of Hervé Guibert as between the very lines of his works.

Duncker's novel tells the story of an unnamed graduate student at Cambridge who is doing his PhD dissertation on a gay French writer named Paul Michel (1947–93). (Paul-Michel was the full Christian name of Foucault, which means that any discussion of the main character of Duncker's novel immediately takes on a hallucinatory quality.) At the time the action of *Hallucinating Foucault* takes place, Michel no longer writes, and in fact he has disappeared from view since his hospitalization for schizophrenia in 1984. With the help of his girlfriend, a Germanist working on Schiller, the first-person narrator goes to France, discovers the asylum in Clermont-Ferrand where Paul Michel is interned, succeeds in getting him released, and goes on a vacation with him. Although the student perceived himself to be exclusively heterosexual up to that time, he falls in love with "his" writer, and they enjoy a passionate summer together before it all ends too quickly when Paul Michel dies in a car accident. The final pages recount the aftermath of the affair, including the funeral: "le petit," as his erstwhile lover called him, goes on to finish his dissertation on Michel's fiction, but he will never forget the man he loved and of whom he still has a recurring hallucinatory-like dream. The novel concludes with brief chronologies of the lives of Paul Michel and Michel Foucault set out in parallel columns.

Foucault never appears in person in Duncker's novel, which can be explained by the fact that the action of the novel takes place in the summer of 1993. And unlike Guibert and Foucault, the fictitious Paul Michel and the famous philosopher were not personal friends. They were close, however, for we learn that Paul Michel attended Foucault's courses at the Institut de France. More important, he wrote letters to Foucault about his writing and his life. (Four of these letters are "quoted" in the novel.) The student narrator unearths this correspondence in Paris, and discovers that the letters were never posted. This does not reduce the importance of Foucault for Paul Michel. Indeed, for him Foucault was his implied even ideal reader. They dialogued with each other not in person but through their writing, Foucault in his great tomes about knowledge, prisons, and sexuality, Paul Michel in his five novels: *La Fuite*; *Ne demande pas* (whose title is an ironical allusion to United States policy on gays and lesbians in the miliary – "Don't ask, don't tell"); *Maison d'été*, for which the author supposedly received the Prix Goncourt in 1976;[4] *Midi*; and *L'Évadé*. All of Paul Michel's books were published supposedly between 1968 and 1983, during the time when Foucault was working on *L'Archéologie du savoir*, *Surveiller et punir*, and *Histoire de la sexualité*.

Unlike Guibert, Paul Michel does not have AIDS. Their birth dates are different, Guibert having been born in 1955, and Michel in 1947. Michel's constant moves and living out of a suitcase bring Genet to mind more than Guibert, who certainly did not stop writing after the death of Michel Foucault. Guibert died at age thirty-six, Paul Michel at forty-six. But both died by suicide. And Guibert did have writer's block for a time in his mid-thirties, about the same age at which Michel stopped writing. Although never interned in a mental institution, Guibert was hospitalized, as he described in *Cytomégalovirus*. Two extratextual bits of evidence regarding Guibert are to be found in Patricia Duncker's novel: like Guibert, Paul Michel is gay, and like the real writer, the fictitious novelist is handsome.

So far, I have sketched out the basic details, the parallels as well as the differences, between these two writers, one of whom is real whereas the

---

[4] In fact Patrick Grainville received the Prix Goncourt in 1976 for his novel *Les Flamboyants*.

other is just a character in a novel. But since so much of Guibert's writing is autofictional, Hervé is also a character in many of his novels. As we will see, the writings of Duncker and Guibert intersect well beyond mere biographical details. After examining other striking similarities, I will concentrate on three common threads that interwine the books of Guibert with Duncker's novel: intergenerational friendships, Foucault, and madness.

OTHER SIMILARITIES

After securing Michel's release from the mental hospital, the graduate student drives south with his new friend at the height of the lemming-like summer exodus of the French from the north. The tale of their epic journey – the terrible heat, the nasty drivers, traveling through the night – might be considered a cultural cliché; but we should also remember that Guibert wrote about similar trips with his parents (*Mes*, 41–5; *My*, 32–6; *Hallucinating Foucault* [henceforth abbreviated as *HF*], 133–6). In both cases the adventures of the hapless *juilletistes*, or *aoûtiens* as the case may be, take on a Felliniesque quality.

Of somewhat more literary importance is the fact that Paul Michel (*HF*, 26), like Foucault and Guibert, was interviewed by Bernard Pivot for his "intellectual variety show" (*Friend*, 26), as Guibert describes the popular program *Apostrophes*. But it is when we get closer to their actual writing that certain similarities between the two writers become more blatant. For example, both Michel and Guibert tended to write in the south, the former in the Midi, where he "spent the days reading and writing, writing incessantly draft after draft" (*HF*, 54), the latter on the island of Elba. A friend of Guibert's compared his oeuvre to a house in which the rooms correspond to his reappearing characters: "'C'est comme une maison: il y a ta chambre, et puis il y a la chambre de l'ami, la chambre de tes grand-tantes, et puis les corridors qui relient toutes ces pièces'" (*PA*, 147) ("It's like a house: there is your room, and then there is the friend's room, the room of your great-aunts, and the hallways that connect all these rooms"). Paul Michel makes a similar – though not identical – point in one of his letters to Foucault: "My books are like a well-known and frequently visited château. All the corridors are completely straight and they lead from one room to another, the way out to the gardens or the courtyard clearly indicated" (*HF*, 72).

In *Hallucinating Foucault* there are two graduate students working on their PhDs: the Germanist who is working on Schiller, and "le petit" who is interested in the French writer who became insane. This recalls *Le Paradis*, in which there are also two graduate students researching their dissertations: Jayne, who works on insane writers, and Diane, who is writing about the fishing industry in Martinique! But the similarity does not end there, since in both novels it is a thesis-writing student who comes to the rescue of a more or less incapacitated writer with whom she or he has a sexual relationship. There is more, however. As the Germanist tells her boyfriend, "'If you're not in love with the subject of your thesis it'll all be very dry stuff, you know. Aren't you in love with Paul Michel?'" (*HF*, 13). The graduate student in French takes the message literally to heart, and ends up leaving the confines of a Cambridge library to share the bed of his "subject"! But the love between a writer and his readers is not limited to readers who are students of literature. Indeed, the principal theme of *Hallucinating Foucault* is this particular form of literary love. It was a type of love that Guibert himself cherished, not just the outpouring of affection of which he was the object after the publication of *L'Ami* and which he wrote about in *Le Protocole compassionnel*, but also the love he felt for those writers and other cultural workers such as Patrice Chéreau, whose productions he admired.[5] And in 1982 he wrote the following to and about the Belgian writer Eugène Savitzkaya in a public letter: "Je t'aime à travers ce que tu écris ... Je rêve d'une fraternité d'écriture ..." (*PA*, 64) (I love you through what you write ... I dream of a fraternity of writing). He was to echo this love for his fellow writer nine years later in his 1991 novel: "Eugène Savitzkaya is a very great poet, a very great writer whom I admire more than any other" (*CP*, 101). Towards the end of Duncker's novel, the Germanist writes a letter (redolent of Oscar Wilde's defense statement about a certain kind of love) to the now dead Paul Michel about a love that usually is not mentioned or studied: "'You [Paul Michel] said that the love between a writer and a reader is never celebrated, can never be proven to exist. That's not true.

---

5 Cf. the following about Patrice Chéreau: "Chaque fois qu'un de mes livres sortait, un de ces livres que peut-être je n'avais écrits et fait paraître que pour lui, non tant pour lui prouver que je pouvais marcher seul que par crainte qu'il ne m'abandonne un jour, dans ce travail que nous avions entrepris, et auquel je tenais par-dessus tout, parce qu'il était lié à lui, parce qu'il me liait à lui" (*PA*, 90) (Every time one of my books was published, one of those books that perhaps I had only written and published for his sake, not so much to prove to him that I could walk on my own as out of fear that one day he would abandon me and the project [*L'Homme blessé*] we had undertaken and which I valued above all else because it was linked to him and because it linked me to him).

I came back to find you. And when I had found you I never gave you up'" (*HF*, 166). The ever-practical Germanist sees to it that the letter she wrote but which just as easily could have been authored by "le petit" remains attached to Paul Michel's coffin, so he is buried with what is in fact a love letter from two of his admirers, a letter that speaks for all his readers. Needless to say, such a passage can be interpreted also as Duncker's own homage to Foucault or Guibert, or both.

When the French graduate student arrives at the Hôpital Sainte-Marie in Clermont-Ferrand, he discovers just how huge it is: "I was encircled by a small city, a city inhabited by the young, the middle-aged, the very old, a city of the mad" (*HF*, 91). This recalls Foucault's work on various "disciplinary spaces" (the hospital is described as "a great walled block, with a mass of interior buildings, like a convent or a prison, in the center of the city" (*HF*, 85)), as well as Guibert's novel *Des aveugles*, in which, as we have seen, the blind inhabit an institution that is a world of its own. Of course, there are real hospitals in Guibert's writings, such as the almost abandoned Claude-Bernard Hospital (*Ami*, chapter 18), the unnamed hospital to which the narrator of *Le Paradis* is taken when he falls into a coma (*P*, 114), or the hospital in *Cytomégalovirus*. Both Guibert and Duncker describe hospital personnel and their professional detachment that seems like brusqueness or worse, but which in fact can mask something much more positive. There are many doctors in Guibert's universe, but none is more favorably portrayed than the young Dr. Claudette Dumouchel in *Le Protocole compassionnel*. While entirely professional, Claudette is not adverse to joking with her difficult patient, who has (almost) complete trust in her. In Duncker's novel there is a similar character, also a woman (Dr. Pascale Vaury) who – apart from a nun who believes in the power of faith to heal – is Paul Michel's greatest ally in the mental hospital:

> "Écoute-moi. Sois sage," she said, turned on her heel and marched away. I stared after her. Paul Michel lay looking up into the trees, laughing slightly. I realized, for the first time, that all his rudeness to her face was a form of theater. There was an absolute trust and complicity between them. (*HF*, 125)

Guibert, we recall, describes his favorite doctors, especially Claudette Dumouchel, as more than professional health-care workers. They become his confidants, his advisers, and in a way his lovers. In fact, the love that unites a patient and his doctor can be interpreted as a variation on the theme of the love between reader and writer, since a doctor "reads" the patient's mind and body. Both Guibert and Duncker have chosen to celebrate this love in a context from which sex is excluded, although Guibert does think about it!

Like Guibert, Paul Michel commits suicide. While it is true that he actually dies in a car accident, he had swallowed enough drugs and alcohol to have killed him any way. This brings us to one of the most interesting motifs in Duncker's novel, owls:

> A gigantic white owl, drawn to the yellow lights and the swerving car, fixed its great eyes on [Paul Michel's] face and plummeted towards the Citroën. The creature smashed through the windscreen, sinking its claws into his face and throat. The car hurtled into the cliff. He was killed instantly. They laid him out on the stretcher with the great dead bird wrapped around his face. (*HF*, 158)

It seems a fitting end for someone for whom another – premonitory, as it turns out – owl appeared earlier in his life. In one of his unsent letters to Foucault, Paul Michel describes seeing a similar owl while he was out cruising for sex:

> "One night, walking alone in the Midi, in a town I hardly knew, I was searching, yes, I suppose I was, looking for the men leaning against their cars in the dark, watching for the glow of cigarettes in the doorways, I passed the church. And I heard the scream of an owl rising in the dark. I looked up. He suddenly took off from the lime trees above me, floodlit from beneath, a great white owl, his belly bleached white in the darkness, his huge white wings outstretched, crying in the night, flinging himself away into the darkness. And as I followed his flight into the dark, the night appeared to be a solid substance, matter to be written. I cannot believe that I have anything to fear." (*HF*, 62–3)

One can read the owl-motif in *Hallucinating Foucault* as revolving around the image of Foucault, for he was notorious for his owl-like gaze. Interpreted this way, the white owl that provokes the accident in which Paul Michel dies incarnates Foucault, his former mentor, rescuing Paul from this earth, so that he can join his elder brother in writing, the (arch-)reader of his works. Owls are connected with writing and reading in Duncker's novel, not simply because they look so wise, but also because of the owlish characteristics common to both the Germanist and Paul

Michel himself: "She had such thick lenses that they magnified her eyes. The result was an owl-like intensity, combined with an uncanny concentration. Somehow, you found yourself reflecting on the fact that owls ate live mammals" (*HF*, 17–18); "[Paul Michel] continued to gaze at me with terrible concentration. Suddenly, he reminded me of my Germanist. It was the same owlish, interrogating intensity. I was disconcerted" (*HF*, 96). The Germanist, whom Paul Michel had already met when she was a child, has always had an "owl-like glare" (*HF*, 152), so that it seems entirely fitting that it should be she who sets "le petit" on the path that will lead him to "his" writer, whose owlish gaze he initially finds disconcerting.

Owls figure prominently in Guibert's writing as well. For example, in *Des aveugles* Taillegueur makes a whistle that imitates the cry of an owl, using it to attract the attention of the boys playing in the courtyard during recess (*Av.*, 84, 99 [*Bl.*, 68, 81]). Guibert himself had a stuffed albino owl in his collection of rather bizarre objects that he often photographed (figure 20). According to Enda McCaffrey, they "reflect not only a sensitivity to the associative power of the object but a belief in the potential of that associative power" ("La superstition," 24). In the case of his owl, Guibert refers to it on several occasions in his books.[6] We might well wonder what is the meaning of these references to a stuffed owl, especially since Guibert appears to exploit their textual potential so little. I believe that owls had a particuliar significance for him. In mythology, the owl is associated with ugliness, with the night, and with the gift of clairvoyance, as well as with death (Chevalier and Gheerbrant, *Dictionnaire des symboles*, 246, 504–5), all of which are typically Guibertian concerns. Because owls avoid the light of day, they received a bad reputation in Christian times, but in the ancient world they were associated with knowledge on account of their connection with the *reflected* rays of moonlight. Here one thinks of the myopic Muzil, the untiring researcher who was still going to the library daily, peering over learned tomes in order to complete the footnotes to his *magnum opus*, right up to his final collapse in the kitchen of his apartment.[7]

The connection between sexual desire and owls is one that seemed to fascinate Guibert. For example, he used the following passage three

---

6 *Mes*, 154 (*My*, 141); *PC*, 117 (*CP*, 100); *I*, 16, 47, 63; *PA*, 80, 84.

7 Guibert refers to Muzil's myopia in *L'Ami* (chapter 11), and Foucault described himself as myopic in the letter written to Guibert on 28 July 1983 that is reproduced in "L'autre journal d'Hervé Guibert" (69).

times: first in "La semaine sainte," a short story published in the literary journal edited by his friend Mathieu Lindon, *Minuit*; second in *Les Lubies d'Arthur*; and third in *La Piqûre d'amour* (although published posthumously, the material in this collection of short texts was chosen by Guibert himself). Briefly, it is the story of a homosexual curate who wants to project erotic films out of doors; he fails, initially at least, since the images are lost in the screenless ether. But when an owl flies by, it becomes – for an instant – a living, flying backdrop against which can be seen images of "angelic vice":

> [Le curé] aurait voulu, carrément, projeter leur chute [of the erotic angels] sur le ciel, mais les images qui ne pouvaient buter contre aucune surface se dissipaient dans un rayon d'immatérialité. Dans la nuit, il recherchait une blancheur. Ce fut un oiseau, d'abord, qui la lui donna, mais trop fébrilement pour qu'il puisse y fixer une de ses fantasmagories. Une nuit, alors qu'il attendait depuis une heure, le pinceau rose des chairs humaines vint colorer le plumage triangulaire d'une effraie qui fut éblouie. (*PA*, 57–8; cf. *LA*, 101–2)

> What the curé would have really liked to do was project their downfall [of the erotic angels] against the sky, but the images, which could not fall on any surface, dissipated themselves in a ray of immateriality. In the dark of night he looked for something white. First a bird answered his gaze but too feverishly to serve as anchor for one of his phantasmagorias. One night, after he had been waiting for an hour, the pink light of human flesh abruptly colored the triangular plumage of a bedazzled barn owl.

I believe another passage in *La Piqûre d'amour* provides the missing clue about this association between owls and angels. Describing the genesis of *Les Lubies d'Arthur*, Guibert wrote in "L'ours," "Dans *La Légende dorée* une phrase m'avait mis la puce à l'oreille: 'Il releva la tête, et il vit une chouette, c'est-à-dire un ange' ..." (*PA*, 145) (In *The Golden Legend* a sentence had started me thinking: "He raised his head and saw an owl, which is to say an angel ...").[8] We recall that Yvonne Baby describes

---

8 Guibert read *The Golden Legend* as part of the preparatory work for writing the fantastic scenes in *Les Lubies d'Arthur*, a saint's life in its own right. The reference to an angel in the guise of an owl is to be found in the legend of Saint Peter in Chains in *The Golden Legend*: "The king [Herod] took pleasure in the thought that these eulogies were no more than his due, and made no effort to disown the divine honors offered to him.

Guibert as an angel, and that he himself wrote about his "charmante tête d'angelot bouclé" (*Ami*, 90) ("my charming curly-headed-cherub face" [*Friend*, 81]), that is before his locks were sacrificed to Jules's castrating scissors. In *La Piqûre d'amour* is to be found a text entitled "Nécrologie" written in 1984, in which Guibert describes inventing a fictitious obituary for someone real, which of course was in itself a fiction! According to this curious text, a famous ornithologist died as a result of too much intimate contact with his beloved birds:

> J'explicitai enfin les causes de sa mort, car après tout il n'était pas si vieux: accouplant sa bouche aux becs des oiseaux, mangeur de plumes, buveur de fientes, dormant sur un coussinet truffé d'os grêles de pigeons, il avait fini par attraper une ornithose, cette maladie infectieuse des oiseaux, transmissible à l'homme, chez qui elle peut prendre la forme d'une pneumonie. (*PA*, 117)

> Finally I clarified the cause of death, for after all he was not all that old: attaching his mouth to the beaks of birds, eating their feathers, drinking their droppings, sleeping on a small cushion stuffed with the frail bones of pigeons, he ended up catching ornithosis, that infectious bird disease which can be transmitted to humans as a kind of pneumonia.

As in Paul Michel's case, death is caused by direct contact between a human being and a bird or birds. Although Duncker's version is somewhat more realistic, "the great dead bird wrapped around [Michel's] face" (*HF*, 158) recalls the ornithologist "attaching his mouth to the beaks of birds." In both cases the sexual symbolism is clear. Indeed, in "Nécrologie" Guibert even goes so far as to say: "Au fond, pourquoi prétendais-je vouloir aimer P.? Il n'avait rien d'un oiseau" (*PA*, 118) (Deep down, why did I claim to want to love P.? There was nothing birdlike about him). After all, if Guibert is a self-perceived angel, to whom should he be attracted but other angels, or their earthly representatives, birds?

This fascination with birds is a topos that goes back even farther in

---

Then, looking up, he spied, perched on a rope over his head, an angel – that is, an owl. He realized that this was a harbinger of approaching death ..." (Jacobus de Voragine, *The Golden Legend*, 2:35). Guilbert seems to have remembered or to have chosen to place the words *angel* and *owl* in the opposite order; typically he places the more concrete entity, the owl, in first position. I am indebted to my colleague Richard Holdaway for finding the exact reference of this intertext.

Guibert's writing. For example, in a thinly disguised autobiographical text written in the 1970s, Guibert describes the love affair between Anton and a certain Aurélien. But "Aurélien is not a lover like others," as Guibert says, since he is a bird, albeit one that writes, with a thoracic cavity that is "too delicate" (*MP*, 110). And going back even farther, this time to the first text in the second edition of *La Mort propagande*, "Thérèse et son crocodile ailé," written when Guibert was only sixteen, we find a young girl who flies about on her pet crocodile. She also kills birds. In the end, Thérèse gives her boyfriend Alexandre a vampire-like kiss of death. Alexandre is described as a "blond archangel" (*MP*, 24).

At this point let us compare the two interpretations that I have been developing here. For the intratextual reader of *Hallucinating Foucault*, the great white owl that is the direct cause of Michel's death is related to the beloved addressee (Foucault) of the unsent letter in which the younger writer told the story of a magical moment with another owl, a moment that was associated, as we have seen, with homoerotic desire. For the intertextual reader, owls and owlish looks in Duncker's novel recall Guibert's writing, in particuliar the association of birds and sexual desire, whether on the part of Taillegueur or the frustrated curate who wanted to see "the angelic vice" (*LA*, 101) reflected in the sky, a fantasy that is realized for a moment when an owl flies by. Thus, the death of Paul Michel recalls and echoes Guibert as much as it does Foucault. Indeed, it would not be an exaggeration to say that Michel's meeting with the great white owl that ends up wrapped around his face is a symbolic rendering of his coming face to face with both Foucault *and* Guibert in a final, fatal act of love.[9]

INTERGENERATIONAL FRIENDSHIPS

> [Claudette Dumouchel] me dit: "Vous avez trente-cinq ans, c'est ça?" Le téléphone sonne. C'est le moment d'en profiter, le moment ou jamais, j'hésite, je me jette à l'eau, je demande: "Et vous? – Vingt-huit ans." ... Je calcule que j'ai sept ans de plus que Claudette, que j'en ai dix de plus que Vincent, dix de moins que Téo, soixante de moins que ma grand-tante Suzanne. (*PC*, 49)

---

9 In the manuscript of his unpublished novel *Adultes!* Guibert refers to a bird that "explose en plein vol contre le pare-brise" (f. 84) (explodes in full flight against the windshield) of a Jaguar driven by someone called Michel (quoted with the permission of Christine Guibert).

[Claudette Dumoucel] says: "You are thirty-five, aren't you?" The telephone rings, I have to seize this chance, it's now or never, I hesitate, I take the plunge, I ask her: "What about you?" "Twenty-eight." ... I calculate that I am seven years older than Claudette, ten years older than Vincent, ten younger than Téo, sixty years younger than my great-aunt Suzanne. (*CP,* 39)

In *Le Paradis* Jayne is some ten years younger than the narrator. He could also have added that there was a twenty-nine-year age difference between Foucault and himself. Although there was just a year's difference between Hervé and Jules, T., or Thierry as he is sometimes known, clearly, friendship for Guibert was not restricted to his contemporaries. In *Hallucinating Foucault* Duncker has portrayed characters "separated" by similar age gaps. For example, there is a twenty-one-year difference in age between Foucault and Paul Michel. As for the younger generation, the Germanist was born in 1967, "le petit" in 1971. This means that Michel was thirty-one when he first met the future Germanist, then aged eleven – his first true love, as he claims – and forty-six the summer of his short affair with the twenty-two-year-old graduate student from England. In one of Michel's letters to Foucault, he describes an episode clearly based on his experiences with the future Germanist. Michel's reader, as the student in French refers to himself, believes that none of the letters or any copies ever reached Foucault, which means that Paul Michel must have invented the reaction of *his* arch-reader to scenes that might be interpreted as having pedophilic overtones: "'I was also surprised and pleased that you noticed the episode with the boy on the beach. I knew I was taking a risk. The public becomes hysterical at the slightest hint of what could be called pedophilia'" (*HF,* 58). In fact, when we get to the description of the events of the summer of 1978, it becomes clear that, though deeply attracted to each other, the child, who was as sexually androgynous as she was intellectually precocious, and her adult friend did not engage in any sexual activities together. As we know, this is not the case with *Voyage avec deux enfants,* in which the twenty-six-year-old narrator plays erotic games with Vincent who, despite the fact that he is described as "l'enfant," must be sixteen at the time. The point here is hardly that Duncker is more "careful" than Guibert. Rather, what is at stake is the portrayal of intergenerational love, whether consummated or not. This is best summed up by Paul Michel when he states:

> "Yes, I suppose I did fall in love with that child. But there was something more important. We became friends. What equality is possible between a child of eleven and a man in his thirties? Friendship, complicity, trust make all things equal. You remind me of him." (*HF*, 155)

Friendship, complicity, trust – these are exactly what Guibert would like to receive from his friend, although it doesn't always work out that way. But in *Le Protocole compassionnel* all that is changed when the mere presence of Vincent has the ability to help Hervé forget his fatigue.

In reading the description of Paul Michel and the eleven-year-old child together on the Mediterranean beach, it is impossible not to think of Guibert's descriptions of time spent on a Moroccan beach a few years later: "Tomber amoureux. Tomber" (*Voy.*, 88) (Falling in love. Falling). Both children fulfill the role of muse for their respective writers. Referring to Vincent, Guibert said: "L'enfant m'avait remis dans ce sentiment d'enfance qui est propre à l'écriture ..." (*PA*, 142) (The child had made me feel like a child once again, which is so appropriate for writing ...). And in one of his letters to Foucault, Paul Michel will describe his version of the muse as "'a comrade, a friend, a traveling companion, shoulder to shoulder, someone to share the cost of this long, painful journey'" (*HF*, 58), which is exactly the role played by the child on the beach. According to Michel, the muse is usually portrayed as "'a piece of narcissistic nonsense in female form'" (ibid.), which doesn't correspond to Guibert's portrait of the "enfant perroquet" or, for that matter, to the eleven-year-old with whom Duncker's fictional novelist spends so many hours. Nevertheless, there is a feminine element in both cases. It takes some time for Michel to discover that his young friend is a girl and not a boy,[10] but he takes the news well (unlike Balzac's Sarrasine, who cannot accept the male gender of his beloved Zambinella, a castrato). For Guibert, there was no doubt, since from the outset he knew that Vincent was a boy; but he does insist on the androgynous quality of the adolescent, his "overwhelming femininity" (*Voy.*, 78): a boyish girl on the one hand and a feminine but not effeminate boy on the other. Gender bending plays havoc with the usual orthodoxy (neither Guibert nor

---

10 "'His [the child's] ambiguity suddenly broke over me with all the force of the sea against the great rocks. I had not mistaken the nature of this child. But I had certainly been deceived in her sex. She swung down from the solitary ledge and rushed into my arms'" (*HF*, 156).

Michel "should" be attracted to the feminine, since they are both homosexuals) in the same way that difference in age does, since such intense friendships are not "supposed" to exist between people of different generations. Certainly, one of the most refreshing aspects about both Duncker and Guibert is that neither is willing to play the game of political "correctness" as our society currently constructs it. In doing so, they risk alienating certain readers, a concern that Duncker addresses *en abîme* in her novel, as we have seen, whereas Guibert seems to take particular pleasure in describing the age difference and the sexual attraction between his two male subjects.

FOUCAULT

Like Paul Michel, who wrote four unposted letters to Foucault, Hervé Guibert also wrote his friend at least one letter that was never sent,[11] and in an interview he described the link between his books and letters (Interview with Cherer, 17). It seems unlikely that Guibert wrote the same type of letters as those written by Paul Michel in which the latter discusses his life and writing with the great philosopher, for the simple reason that Foucault and Guibert were in almost daily contact. There can be no doubt, however, that the love Guibert felt for Foucault was equal to if not greater than that attributed by Duncker to Paul Michel. In *Les Gangsters* Guibert describes Foucault's role in his life as that of a teacher who usually taught by example rather than precept: "son enseignement était diffus, léger" (*G*, 55) (his teaching was diffuse, not heavy-handed), the one exception being when Foucault told his younger friend always to lie about his sexual orientation if asked about it by the police. Perhaps no better indication of Foucault's place in Guibert's life can be found than when he finds himself faced by a panic-striken Vincent (*FV*, 70–1). As we saw earlier, in chapter 5, his young friend's pain obliges Hervé to assume the mantle of mentorship of "that irreplaceable friend" (*Ami*, 90).

We remember that the memory of the episode in which Hervé

11 Written on 26 March 1984, while Guibert was in Egypt with his friend and fellow photographer Hans Georg Berger, the letter begins thus: "Michel, T'écrire en ces jours est une chose délicate; ma conscience est troublée, et comme tu en es un peu le directeur ... J'ai repoussé ce moment comme une épreuve" (*Let. É.*, 53) (Michel, Writing to you at this time is delicate; my conscience is troubled, and since you are more or less its director ... I have been putting off this moment as though it were a trial [original ellipsis]).

washed out his mouth after kissing Muzil's hand paradoxically ends up being less shameful than empowering. I believe the real regret and no doubt the worst shame are the result of Hervé's having waited too long to tell his dying friend how much he loved him: "Ni David ni moi ne pûmes revoir Muzil, qui pourtant réclamait notre présence ... J'avais envoyé à la Pitié un mot au nom de Muzil dans lequel je lui disais que je l'aimais, c'était bien la peine d'avoir tant attendu cet instant ..." (*Ami*, 107) ("Neither David nor I was able to visit Muzil again, even though he wanted to see us ... I'd sent a note to La Pitié with Muzil's name on it telling him I loved him – I don't know why I waited until the last moment ..." [*Friend*, 94; trans. alt.]). Here the name of the hospital in which Foucault died, which has been omitted from the English-language translation, La Pitié[-Salpêtrière], rings out the cry of pity that Guibert asks from us his readers for the "crime" of needlessly having waited so long to express his true feelings to his friend. Surely Guibert wasn't afraid of another hysterical scene like the one he got himself into with Barthes! If Guibert is being honest here, it is horrible to think that during his last days Foucault was asking to see Mathieu Lindon (called David in *L'Ami*) and Hervé Guibert, while the French medical authorities limited visits to his blood relatives. As though Foucault's loved ones did not include his gay friends, the members of that circle of young men with whom he had shared so many dinners, so many thoughts and theories. In his review of the French translation of *Hallucinating Foucault* Hugo Marsan emphasizes that "Foucault saw in the networks of masculine friendships an even greater social transgression that the most frenetic of sexual practices" ("Histoire de l'amour fou").[12] Deprived of his friends' company, Foucault nonetheless still managed to talk and teach through the night with the doctor on duty (*Cyto.*, 40–1; *CMV*, 31).

12 Edmund White has also written about Foucault and friendship: "Inspired by the ancient Greeks, whom he was studying, he'd developed a cult of friendship. He thought that we had nothing else to value now; the death of God had resulted in the birth of friendship. If we could no longer enjoy an afterlife earned by our good deeds, we could at least leave behind a sense of our achievement, measured aesthetically, and the most beautiful art we could practice would be the art of self-realization through friendship" (*The Farewell Symphony*, 377). See also "Michel Foucault, une interview: Sexe, pouvoir et la politique de l'identité," in *Dits et écrits*, 4:744–5, first published in English as "Sex, Power and the Politics of Identity" in the American magazine *The Advocate*, although the 1982 interview by B. Gallagher and A. Wilson was originally intended for publication in *The Body Politic*, a now-defunct gay newspaper published in Toronto. Didier Eribon has written about Foucault and his cult of friendship among men in *Réflexions sur la question gay*, in particular chapter 12, "Les hommes entre eux" (468–80).

After reading about these events – as in the story of Christophe Donner's grandfather who up until his death still managed to discuss philosophical topics with a young friend in the Neuengamme concentration camp (*EV*, 263) – one is tempted to think that there is nothing that can be said in the face of the sublime, or the absurd, which so often turn out to be one and the same. But that would be a mistake. I believe that Duncker's example is one to be emulated. She, like Donner, has chosen to go beyond the passivity of reading, so decried by Proust, by writing in her own words another story, a story that renders as much homage to Guibert as it does to Foucault. Speaking of the author of *The History of Sexuality*, the Germanist says: "'He was the beloved, the unseen reader to be courted. I think that Paul Michel wrote every book for Foucault. For him and against him'" (*HF*, 35). In terms of intertextuality, such a passage can be read in the light of Guibert's friendship with Foucault, just as it allegorically refers to the link between Duncker's novel and the model upon which she (partially) has based it, Guibert's books, which can be interpreted as fictionalizations of some of Foucault's theories. Such a reading risks seeming more abstract than it is: perhaps what we need at this point is one of Paul Michel's huge laughs (*HF*, 128), a laugh that recalls those of Muzil/Foucault himself (*Ami*, 21, 24, 109; *HF*, 148)!

In Duncker's novel we learn that Foucault and Michel explored similar themes, although their styles were very different:

> But stylistically they were poles apart. Foucault's huge, dense, Baroque narratives, alive with detail, were like paintings by Hieronymous Bosch. There was an image, a conventional subject, a shape present in the picture, but the texture became vivid with extraordinary, surreal, disturbing effects ... Paul Michel wrote with the clarity and simplicity of a writer who lived in a world of precise weights and absolute colors, a world where each object deserved to be counted, desired and loved. He saw the world whole, but from an oblique angle. (*HF*, 6)

In this case there is both similarity and difference between the two pairs of writers. It is true that Guibert explored themes that were similar to those researched by Foucault; the ones mentioned in *Hallucinating Foucault* ("death, sexuality, crime, madness" [*HF*, 30]) pertain as much to Guibert as they are supposed to characterize the novels of Paul Michel. It is also true that the style of Guibert was not the same as Foucault's, but it would be difficult to describe the writing of the former as a model of "clarity and simplicity"! Indeed, it would be more appropriate to reverse Duncker's descriptions of the two types of prose. If we read the first part of the passage as pertaining to Guibert ("the texture became vivid with extraordinary, surreal, disturbing effects") and the second part as a description of Foucault's writing – especially in the last two volumes of *The History of Sexuality*, known for their clarity – then the metatextual commentary fits.

When dealing with a relationship between two writers – or rather two pairs of writers, albeit one of whom is supposedly fictitious – the question that is inevitably posed is whether they read each other's works and, if so, to what extent if any either one was influenced by the other. In *Hallucinating Foucault*, there is no doubt: "'We read each other with the passion of lovers. Then we began to write to one another, text for text'" (*HF*, 148) is how Paul explains his literary love affair with Foucault to his young friend. He continues:

> "They [critics] talk of influence, threads, preoccupations. They know nothing about the unspoken pact. That was absolutely clear between us. We knew each other's secrets, weaknesses and fears, petit. The things that were hidden from the world. He wanted to write fiction." (*HF*, 149)

This passage echoes "Les secrets d'un homme," that beautifully elegiac text written by a fellow writer on the death of one of his closest friends. The passage in *Hallucinating Foucault* also recalls one in which Guibert describes Muzil's self-deprecating evaluation of his own writing as less creative work than a novel: "charmant Muzil maniant le paradoxe et prétendant qu'une oeuvre philosophique n'était pas une oeuvre d'écriture comme le roman, courant toujours après la vérité ou le feignant alors qu'elle n'était évidemment chez lui qu'une pure fiction" (*P,* 122) (charming Muzil skillfully handling paradoxes and claiming that a philosophical work was not a literary work like a novel, always running after the truth or pretending to do so when clearly with him it was only a pure fiction).[13] At the same time, as we saw in chapter 7, Foucault himself compared all of his work to fiction, without diminishing the truth factor. As is becoming clearer, it is difficult if not impossible to distinguish between supposed nonfiction and fiction, whether the latter be the works of Guibert, Duncker, or White. What we are dealing with is a series of ever-expanding concentric circles as writing about writers and their writing gains ever-increasing intertextual magnitude.

---

13 Cf. "[Foucault had] said – with his modesty that was as pure and demanded as much concentration as a flame held between hands on a windy night – that I was 'a real writer,' unlike him" (White, *Farewell Symphony*, 377).

But let us return to Foucault, the man and his death, and the effect of the latter on a writer named Paul Michel. As described in an article supposedly published in *Gai Pied Hebdo*, "'On the night of 30 June 1984 Paul Michel was arrested in the graveyard of Père Lachaise. He was found screaming and crying, overturning tombstones with a crowbar'" (*HF*, 26–7). The death of Foucault deprived Paul Michel of his reader and his companion in writing, thereby provoking a schizophrenic crisis and his incarceration first in Paris at the Sainte-Anne psychiatric hospital and later in Clermont-Ferrand at the Sainte-Marie hospital,[14] not to mention the writer's block from which he will suffer supposedly for the rest of his life, although he is quite capable of covering the hospital walls with poetic graffiti. After all, why continue to write after one has lost one's reader? We know of course that none of this happened to Guibert, and that for the purposes of her novel Duncker has imagined a scenario that corresponds better to what happened to Antonin Artaud some forty years earlier. Nevertheless there is one fragment in *À l'ami qui ne m'a pas sauvé la vie* that recalls the terrible fate of Paul Michel:

> Muzil allait mourir, incessamment sous peu, et cette certitude me défigura dans le regard des passants qui me croisaient, ma face en bouillie s'écoulait dans mes pleurs et volait en morceaux dans mes cris, j'étais fou de douleur, j'étais le *Cri* de Munch. (*Ami*, 104)

> Muzil was going to die, and very soon, a certainty that disfigured me in the eyes of passersby, for my face disintegrated, washed away by my tears and shattered into fragments by my cries, I was crazed with grief, I was Munch's *Scream*. (*Friend*, 92; trans. alt.)

Simply put, Guibert's screams have been taken one step farther: a complete physical and mental breakdown from which only the love of Michel's student reader will save him for the duration of their brief friendship in the summer of 1993.

Both Guibert and Duncker describe the famous scene in the courtyard of the hospital after the removal of Foucault's body from the morgue, what is known in French as *la levée du corps*, a scene described

---

14 Foucault attended *présentations de malades* in the late 1940s and early 1950s at the Hôpital Sainte-Anne, where he later worked as a student in psychology; he lectured at the university in Clermont-Ferrand from 1960 until 1966 (Macey, *The Lives of Michel Foucault*, 36, 56, 109).

also by his biographer David Macey. (Yves Montand, Simone Signoret, Jacques Derrida, Michel Serres, Pierre Nora, Claude Gallimard, Jérôme Lindon, Paul Veyne, Pierre Boulez, Claude Mauriac, and Hélène Cixous, among many others, were present [*The Lives of Michel Foucault*, 471–2].) Guibert describes how a philosopher read a text (*Ami*, chapter 39), whereas in *Hallucinating Foucault* it is Paul Michel who is given the honor of rendering homage to his master. Guibert does not quote the text; indeed, he complains about not being able to hear the philosopher's whispers, so that it is possible that he did not understand what was being read. Duncker, by contrast, reproduces in English what was read in French. Here is the second paragraph:

> "People will say, perhaps, that these games with oneself need only go on behind the scenes; that they are, at best, part of those labors of preparation that efface themselves when they have had their effects. But what, then, is philosophy today – philosophical activity, I mean – if not the critical labor of thought upon itself? And if it does not consist, in place of legitimating what one already knows, in undertaking to know how, and up to what limit, it would be possible to think differently?" (*HF*, 30)[15]

According to the imaginary article about Paul Michel that quotes this passage by Foucault, it is taken from the preface to *La Volonté de savoir* (ibid.), which is not correct. It is important to note that his words are to be found in the introduction to *The Use of Pleasure*, the second volume of *The History of Sexuality*. It was there that Foucault explained the new turn his research had taken during the long period of gestation that separated the publication of the first and second volumes of his monumental work that Guibert so eloquently described in *À l'ami*. It is here that we see just how congruent are the writing projects of Foucault, Guibert, and Duncker, as well as the fictional Paul Michel. For all of them, "to think differently" is crucial.

Duncker does not describe Foucault's funeral, whereas Guibert did so three times: in *Des aveugles* (132–4; *Bl.*, 111–12), where the description refers ostensibly to Taillegueur's funeral; in *Mauve le vierge* (111); and in *À l'ami qui ne m'a pas sauvé la vie* (chapter 39). On the other hand, Duncker's description of the burial of Paul Michel bears certain similarities to Guibert's versions of what happened. There is a regal old lady in

---

15 See Foucault, *History of Sexuality*, vol. 2, 8–9; Macey, 471; Eribon, *Michel Foucault* (1991), 353.

both cases (either Muzil's mother or Michel's aunt). The coffin is buried with the roses that cover it. And finally a great writer – whether we simply call him "a man," as Guibert does in *Mauve le vierge*, or Muzil in *L'Ami*, or Paul Michel as does Duncker – is buried with a letter. Guibert wrote: "On ne chassa pas la lettre qu'un inconnu avait déposé à la levée du corps, sans se soucier qu'elle fût d'amour ou d'injures, les fleurs coupées l'ensevelirent" (*MV*, 111) (No one removed the letter that a stranger had placed [on the coffin] at the *levée du corps*, without worrying if it were a message of love or insults, the cut flowers shrouded it). Paradoxically but appropriately, it is the Germanist who writes this letter, so that in *Hallucinating Foucault*, we get to read what even Guibert dared not invent. In her letter she describes the love that is so seldom celebrated or even acknowledged, the love of a reader for a favorite writer, whether his name is Paul Michel or not:

> "I was your reader too. [Foucault] was not your only reader. You had no right to abandon me. Now you leave me in the same chasm which you faced when you lost the reader you loved best of all ... I followed you, across page after page after page. I wrote back in the margins of your books, on the flyleaf, on the title page. You were never alone, never forgotten, never abandoned. I was here, reading, waiting." (*HF*, 165)

MADNESS

Since the beginning, the most prevalent theme in Guibert's writing was not sex but the threat posed by impending madness. Sometimes writing is the cause, as in *Voyage avec deux enfants* and *L'Incognito*; whereas at others it is love, as in the appropriately entitled *Fou de Vincent*; sometimes it is physical pain, as in *Les Gangsters*; at other times it is the loss of a loved one, Muzil in *À l'ami qui ne m'a pas sauvé la vie*, and Suzanne in *Le Paradis*. For example, in his last novel Guibert continually refers to the fact that he believes himself to be insane: "Je suis fou, fou à lier" (*P*, 117) (I'm crazy, stark raving mad); "la nuit de ma folie" (*P*, 128) (the night of my madness).[16] Like Paul Michel in *Hallucinating Foucault*, Guibert is forced to seek the help of a psychiatrist and to take medication (*P*, 122). The major difference between the two writers is that Guibert continues to write even as his worst fears about what is happening to him seem

---

16 There are numerous references to mental illness in *Le Paradis*, approximately one per every three pages.

confirmed, whereas the fictitious novelist stops writing altogether after his night of folly and violence in the Père-Lachaise cemetery following the death of Foucault. Michel's fate seems particularly appropriate when we remember the title of one of Foucault's early articles: "La folie, l'absence d'oeuvre" (*Dits et Écrits*, 1:412–20). Whether it be the sad example of what happened to Artaud or Foucault's friend Jacques Martin, "the philosopher without an oeuvre," the ultimate effect of madness is silence, which no doubt explains why Guibert describes himself as an unpublished writer at one point in *Le Paradis* (58), although he later contradicts this by stating that he does remember his books.

Before describing the final step into total silence, both novelists have chosen to portray various writerly stances in relation to madness. For example, Jayne Heinz is supposed to be writing a doctoral dissertation about her "grands fous," and of course the example of Foucault's great work on folly in the age of reason looms in the background, although the narrator of *Le Paradis* claims that Muzil only understood what real madness was much later, after taking drugs in California (*P*, 121). In *Hallucinating Foucault* Paul Michel describes madness as an "excess of possibility (*HF*, 121), whereas writing for him is about "reducing possibility to one idea, one book, one sentence, one word" (ibid.). In general, Duncker makes more of a distinction between madness and writing than does Guibert. For example, to write about madness, as does Jayne, presupposes that one can distinguish the passage from sanity to insanity, or from feigned insanity to real insanity, or from a description of past insanity to present lucidity, none of which is self-evident or in the end even possible, unless perhaps one were to lose one's own sanity:

> C'est vraiment infernal, avec ce Strindberg, c'est comme une spirale qui vous noie très lentement, il est fou à lier bien entendu – paranoïa, délire de la persécution ..., mais on ne sait jamais au moment où il écrit s'il est hors folie, s'il relate un épisode de folie dont il s'est dépris et dont il se moquerait presque maintenant, ou s'il est en plein dans la folie, et si son livre, par son édification insensée, participe en premier lieu de cette folie. C'est à perdre soi-même les pédales. (*P*, 82)

> It's really devilishly tricky with this Strindberg guy, it's like a spiral that drowns you very slowly, he's raving mad, of course – paranoia, persecution complex ... but you never know if he is sane when he is writing, if he is relating an episode of madness he's gotten over and which he is almost making fun of now, or if he is in the middle of a crisis, and if his

book, by its senseless construction, is part and parcel of such madness. It's enough to drive you crazy.

How to distinguish the dancer from the dance, or the madness from the writing when surely the very lack of any dividing line furnishes proof of the artist's success? Needless to say, everything Jayne says about Strindberg could be applied to Guibert's writing in *Le Paradis*.

The next "logical" step is to write not of but *in* madness. Using the same expression as Guibert, Paul Michel makes the point that all writers are "somewhere or other, mad. Not les grands fous, like Rimbaud, but mad, yes, mad" (*HF*, 120). Rimbaud also comes up in *Le Paradis*, an example made all the more relevant, given the narrator's recent trip to Africa:

> Je suis allé en Afrique pour trouver l'oubli et m'oublier moi-même, Rimbaud pour effacer son passé en devenant chasseur d'éléphants qui rêve d'épouser une petite femme à Charleville avec tout l'ivoire qu'il aura raflé, loin de ses frasques de jeunesse et de son écriture d'antan. (*P,* 114–15)

> I went to Africa to find oblivion and to forget myself, Rimbaud went to efface his past by becoming an elephant hunter who dreams of marrying a little woman in Charleville with all the ivory he's swiped, far from the high jinks of his youth and his writings of yesteryear.

Guibert continues in a self-reflexive mode, as he finds himself confusing words, for example, almost writing *enfant* ("child") for its homonym *antan* ("yesteryear"), a revealing Freudian slip that seems all the more appropriate since he is in the process of writing about the "child" poet Arthur Rimbaud (1854–91), who stopped writing before his twentieth birthday and went to Africa after the end of his tumultuous love affair with Paul Verlaine. Guibert wonders if this is the beginning of the end, whether he has gotten to the point where he will no longer be able to write, on account of not just a lack of sufficient mental concentration but also the lack of the motor reflexes that writing requires, whatever material process is involved:

> Ne plus savoir écrire. L'écriture est aussi un réflexe moteur qui se transmet du cerveau à la main, j'ai disjoncté cette nuit. Mes souvenirs sont de la bouillasse et il n'est même pas sûr que je puisse continuer à tenir le stylo, le mien, convenablement, pour continuer, pour me raccrocher à ça, au moins. (*P,* 115)

> Not knowing how to write anymore. Writing is also a motor reflex that is transmitted from the brain to the hand, I blew a fuse last night. My memories are as clear as mud and it is by no means certain that I can go on holding my pen properly, to continue, to hang on to that at least.

The impending paranoia that Guibert feels coming on him means that the very fear of not being able to write may be itself a symptom of madness. Instead of living in the terror of not being able to write, he wonders if it would be better to accept the fact that he may have already crossed the borderline between the "ordinary" folly of writing and the lunacy of "les grands fous":

> Paranoïa. Quand vais-je aller me rouler un patin à un cheval stationné devant l'hôtel? Quand accepterai-je la folie des grands fous, de Nietzsche et d'Artaud avec ses pustules de syphilis sur le front, de Strindberg qui peignait des vagues et des champignons vénéneux? (*P*, 116)

> Paranoia. When am I going to French kiss a horse tied up in front of the hotel? When will I accept the madness of the truly insane, of Nietzsche and Artaud with his syphilitic pustules on his forehead, of Strindberg who painted waves and poisonous mushrooms?

Guibert wonders if he now has become like the truly insane, "les grands fous," as he describes them, such as Artaud, Strindberg, and Nietzsche. In the penultimate fragment of *Camera Lucida* Barthes also alludes to Nietzsche when the French critic describes how he felt himself going mad while obsessively scrutinizing certain photographs.[17] After the death of Jayne, has Hervé gone one step farther than she by entering into the space of madness itself? Some might see proof of impending madness in the fact that the narrator claims he no longer knows how to organize a novel, a passage that is in both the final version of the novel and the manuscript of *Congolo gâté (roman fou)*. In "Les secrets d'un homme" Guibert described a hospitalized philosopher who no longer clearly remembers the books he has written: "L'existence même de ses livres se dissipa: qu'avait-il écrit? avait-il même jamais écrit? Parfois il

---

17 "I entered crazily into the spectacle, into the image, taking into my arms what is dead, what is going to die, as Nietzsche did when, as Podach tells us, on January 3, 1889, he threw himself in tears on the neck of a beaten horse: gone mad for Pity's sake" (*Camera Lucida*, 117). Barthes is referring to E.-F. Podach's 1931 book *L'Effondrement de Nietzsche*, which was reissued in 1978 in Gallimard's pocketbook collection "Idées."

n'était plus sûr" (*MV*, 107; cf. *Ami*, 99–100) (Even the existence of his books melted away: what had he written? had he ever really written? Some times he wasn't sure). In Guibert's own case, things appear not to have gotten quite that far. And yet amnesia is present, at least as far as some of the basic narratological tools that a novelist needs. After all, in *Le Paradis* Guibert does sacrifice any coherent chronology. But even though we never get to learn in exactly what order he made the trips to Martinique, Bora Bora, and Africa, does it really matter? And so, like Jayne, wondering about Strindberg, we also ask ourselves if we are dealing with "real" or "feigned" madness. But what then is feigned madness in a fiction and, what is more, an autofiction in which the autodiegetic narrator both is and is not identical to the writer?

Perhaps much if not all writing is equivalent to madness. Even in his first novel, Guibert seems to espouse this hypothesis: "J'ai peur de continuer à m'enfoncer dans l'écriture comme dans la folie ..." (*Voy.*, 62) (I'm afraid to continue being swallowed up by writing like madness). In his last novel, he says: "Writing is madness ..." (*P*, 125). But for Paul Michel, "'Madness is ... the opposite of creativity'" (*HF*, 121). And he goes on to state, "'You cannot make anything that can be separated from yourself if you are mad'" (ibid.). Having lost his reader in the person of Foucault, Paul Michel lost his reason and the ability to express himself in any way other than his madness itself. For Guibert things are not so cut and dried. In the passage quoted from page 125 of *Le Paradis*, he goes on to say that writing "est à la fois la folie et la raison, le raisonnement de la folie" (is at once madness and reason, reasoning with madness). He feels he has no choice but to reason – perhaps one should use the word *quibble* in this context – with madness by and through the process of writing. For Guibert it was impossible to conceive of a life worth living without writing ("Quand je n'écris plus je me meurs" [*P*, 130] [When I can't write any more, I feel like I'm dying]), so that the only solution is to write through the madness in order, if not to tame it, then at least to ensure that what critics of the New Novel used to call *discohérence* does not become total incoherence. Writing interfaces with madness; but it is also the therapy that allows the writer to continue to go on. As Paul Michel says, "'My language was my protection against madness ...'" (*HF*, 121). But of what use is language if there is no one to listen, no one to read ("'my language vanished along with my reader'" [ibid.])? Going one step farther than Guibert, Duncker takes the problem of writerly madness and firmly places it on the shoulders of the reader. Guibert, by contrast, seems to assume that there will always be a reader out there; for him the problem is at the production end of things, perhaps because he had not lost his ideal reader, Mathieu Lindon.[18] In any case, it is clear that both Guibert and Duncker have used madness as more than a mere theme. For both of them, it is intimately linked to the processes whereby texts, including the novel we are reading, become performative acts – from the mechanics of writing to the fundamentals of narratological construction, from questions of coherence and readability to the death of the reader and the confinement of the writer in that noisy "silence" of the asylum to which, over the years of so many centuries, society has condemned some of its most creative thinkers. As such, Duncker's novel offers a biting indictment of society's need to incarcerate all those who do "not fit in," just as Guibert's paints a troubling portrait of what it means to write when meaning is challenged by the painful onset of what is perceived to be madness.

In *Hallucinating Foucault* hallucinations – whether of "le petit" or Paul Michel – are mentioned several times (*HF*, 84, 105, 106, 120), which is hardly surprising given the topic of madness as well as the many uncanny situations narrated. The novel ends with a hallucination, or rather a dream of "hallucinatory intensity" (*HF*, 171). The English graduate student, now an instructor at a London college, recounts a recurring dream in which he sees Paul Michel in a field. "Le petit" stumbles toward his beloved writer but to no avail, since he never gets any closer. It is winter, and the field is littered with stubble fires; through the smoke the narrator perceives a distant figure:

> The shape of a man, a long way off, *behind Paul Michel*, glimmers through the smoke ... I cannot make him out. I do not know who he is. The scene freezes before me like a painting I can never enter, a scene whose meaning remains unreachable, obscure. (*HF*, 172; my emphasis)

The dreamer awakes, "shivering, wretched and alone" (ibid.).

The end of the narrative is followed by two brief biographies set out in parallel columns, the fictitious writer on the left, the real philosopher on the right:

Paul MICHEL   Michel FOUCAULT

---

18 On the role of Mathieu Lindon as Guibert's ideal reader, see the interview with François Jonquet, "'Je disparaîtrai et je n'aurai rien caché ...'" (108).

It seems clear that the other man in the field is Foucault: after all, the novel is entitled *Hallucinating Foucault*.

I suppose many readers have interpreted the novel this way; nonetheless, such a reading raises some problems. For instance, why would the former student not be able to recognize Foucault, whose appearance was so distinctive? Could it be because he doesn't want to share Paul Michel with the latter's ideal reader? Could it be because the narrator never really elucidated the role played by Foucault in Paul Michel's life and writing, and is, at a subconscious level, fearful of confronting his own hermeneutic failure? Could it be because he hasn't come to terms with his sexuality and sees himself as forever remaining on the outside of a community made up of same-sex partners? All of these reasons seem plausible enough, but they beg the question by presuming that the dream man is Foucault. What if he were someone else, such as Hervé Guibert? Since the graduate student never mentions Guibert, perhaps we should exclude that possibility. On the other hand, it is just a dream, albeit of "hallucinatory intensity," or rather a fictitious dream as written and constructed by Patricia Duncker. I believe that she has added this extra level of intertextual indeterminacy as an acknowledgment of her legacy as one of Guibert's literary offspring. Such an interpretation might seem fanciful, and yet there are ample phantom effects within the novel. For example, when the student first meets his writer, there is someone else present: "I looked up and I saw Paul Michel, grinning wickedly, the immaculate white nurse standing *behind him*" (*HF*, 100; my emphasis). It is thanks to this nurse, a "large blond man in impeccably starched white" (*HF*, 92) that we – like the student – first get to "see" Paul Michel.[19] This no doubt explains why the name of the nurse is Hervé (*HF*, 90–1)! That he should be standing behind the dreamed-of image of the beloved novelist recalls other forms of writing in which words and names are hidden *behind* other words and names, as in the anagrams studied by Ferdinand de Saussure in *Les Mots sous les mots*. It also explains why I consider *Hallucinating Foucault*, which could just as easily have been entitled *Hallucinating Guibert*, not only a superb novel but also a wonderful commentary similar to that found in *À l'ami qui ne m'a pas sauvé la vie* where Guibert temporarily became Thomas Bernhard's "ghost writer." In her own way, Patricia Duncker has brought

---

19 In case anyone should miss the intertextual clues, the cover of the 1998 Vintage edition of *Hallucinating Foucault* is made up of two of Guibert's photographs, one of them a 1981 self-portrait.

Guibert back from the dead, using a type of hallucinatory and fragmented intertextuality that makes for a haunting reading experience (figure 21).

Afterword

> De nouveau je pourrais appeler ce livre, comme tous les autres livres que j'ai déjà faits, *L'Inachèvement.*
>
> *L'Homme au chapeau rouge,* 154

> Once more I could call this book, like all the other books I've already written, *Incompletion.*
>
> *The Man in the Red Hat,* 111 (trans. alt.)

Along with many other authors – ancient, pre-modern, modern, and contemporary – Hervé Guibert is a dead white male. But his works represent anything but what that expression usually conjures up in people's minds when they hear it: canonical figures whose works are surrounded if not buried by tomes of learned commentary and gloss. At the same time, Guibert was neither "politically correct" nor politically involved. No doubt he could best be described as someone who chose to think and write "differently," to use Foucault's expression. The very incompletion to which Guibert referred at the end of *L'Homme au chapeau rouge* is part and parcel of that difference, as is the combination of truth and fiction in his unique form of self-writing.

To understand Guibert is to understand the all-important figure of the monster, whether it be an animal, a hybrid, or Guibert himself. If one were to isolate a single key to his oeuvre, it would be the key in *Des aveugles* that Josette offers to the besotted monster who wastes no time in swallowing her whole. Monstrosity for Guibert elicits less sympathy than complicity, less fear than friendship, less pity than adoration. Traditionally, the monster is the one, the "thing," who is perceived to be different and hence worth being exhibited (*montré*) in public spaces, while at the same time the monster must be isolated, confined, and sheltered, supposedly for the good of everyone concerned. Such vicious treatment tires, humiliates, and enslaves the monster but does not change his or her fundamental alterity, a monstrosity that at once intrigues and repels ordinary folk, which, of course, is the whole point. Guibert's descriptions of zoos, museums of vice, and palaces where "desirable monsters" are imprisoned remind us of other disciplinary spaces, including various types of institutes for the disabled, psychiatric hospitals, and the sanatoriums for PLAs (*sidatoriums*) that have been proposed by right-wing politicians in France (Düttmann, *At Odds with AIDS*, 47).

As much as the incarceration of so-called monsters in cages or cells is fundamentally vicious, self-revelation (*dévoilement de soi*) is the exact opposite, since it means coming out of the cell or closet to which Guibert might have allowed others to confine him. If the theme of the monster is the key to this oeuvre, then the self-portrait – whether photographic or written – is its keystone. To reveal oneself to television viewers, journalists, Spectators (in the Barthesian sense of viewers and amateurs of photographs), and readers requires a form of self-regard and self-image that underpins what some have perceived to be narcissism and others to be exhibitionism. In fact, Guibert's project of self-revelation, while it does imply a strong sense of self-identity, is more related to the practice of self-reflexivity. Given that the body, his body, is the central focus for so much of his writing and photography, to reveal it is to reveal the physical essence, materiality, or corporality without which there would be no author, much less the death of the author. In other words, between the body and the work it produced, the corpus, lies a set of interrelated links, as emblematized by the act of writing by hand. To write oneself, to write about writing, to write about writing oneself are – if not one and the same – so entwined that it is difficult as well as pointless to attempt to separate out the factors or actors involved.

Self-revelation and life-writing presume and assume that secrets will be told, circulated as Guibert said at the end of *L'Image fantôme*. But this does not mean that everything can be told or is in fact told. Guibert's notorious indiscretion is more often than not a clever form of disguised or camouflaged discretion, hence the play with names, initials, and dates, as well as the vertiginous series of reversals and inversions, the recourse to the fantastic, and the use of nonlinear narrative. As much as the self is important in Guibert's project, it is inconceivable without the other. Underlying his works is the desire to bear witness to his love for his friends, including – as the dedication to *Le Protocole compassionnel* states – his readers. Testimonials of friendship in Guibert are neither saccharine nor maudlin; on the contrary, they are frank and hardhitting, and may be tempered by irony and, in some cases, a deep-rooted sense of ambivalence. His characters are often based on real-life models – sometimes, as with Proust, on more than one at the same time – and some can be traced, as we have seen, from one book to another and from one medium to another, as witnessed by his multiple "inscriptions" in writing, photographs, and video of his two great-aunts. As much as relationships based on family ties – whether conventional or in the new style of the "Club des cinq" – friendship, or sexual desire, those based on mentoring are crucial in Guibert. It is impossible to conceive of what his work would have been like without the influence of Roland Barthes and Michel Foucault. No doubt if Guibert had lived longer he too would have become a mentor to other writers, such as Christophe Donner. Friendship was as necessary as writing for Guibert. Indeed, the two go hand in hand.

Writing for Guibert is a dangerous activity. It represents a limit-experience or an experience of limits (*expérience limite*), that is, a transformative experience in which a person risks his or her well-being, safety, or life by going to the very limit of what he or she is physically and mentally capable (Cf. Philippe Sollers, *Writing and the Experience of Limits*, 199–205). Writing was neither a self-evident nor a banal activity for the writers who influenced Guibert, such as Bataille, Bernhard, Foucault, Genet, and Leiris. Other limit-experiences could be intense love, fear, or physical pain. It is, of course, not by chance that so much of Guibert's writing is precisely about such experiences. The uncanniness, the dangers, and the sense of living beyond the pale of what can be tolerated are part and parcel of the practice of writing for him. Indeed, whether it be living with unrequited love or with AIDS, to take the experience to the limit means that it must be written down. As such, writing allows Guibert to wrestle with many scary demons, and the publication and reception of the written work continue and prolong the sense of living not only dangerously but taking the experience or experiment (in French they are the same word) to the extreme frontier – and beyond – of what is knowable or doable in this world. As a limit-experience, life-writing means at once to play for high stakes, to live with a heightened and hallucinatory sense of reality, and to flirt with the irreality or nonreality of what lies ahead after death.

At the same time Guibert's writing style is, as we have seen, grounded in the concrete, the material, and the corporeal. He will take a theoretical concept such as the death of the author and "literalize" it, whether in a photograph (figure 7) or a text (*À l'ami qui ne m'a pas sauvé la vie*, *Cytomégalovirus*) or a video (*La Pudeur ou l'Impudeur*). He will take the notion of literary pastiche and turn it into a textually productive metaphor for HIV. He will take a dead metaphor and reanimate it, as with the expression *mise en abîme*, where the idea of the chasm and the abyss is resurrected, so to speak. Such reincarnation or reincorporation leads to the question of intertextuality, by means of which bits and pieces of other texts, allusions or quotations, find their way into Guibert's works. Just as it is often difficult to identify an intertext in a literary work, it is also difficult to know with which books an author was familiar. As well as the more traditional forms of influence based on remembering texts that one has read, I think that we should also consider the likelihood of a kind of oral intertextuality. By this I mean that Guibert no doubt became aware of many authors and works through conversations with Foucault, as was apparently the case with Marcus Aurelius's *Meditations*. One can well imagine Foucault describing a work or reading passages from a book taken from his bookshelves during the course of their dinners together. In this way, one can appreciate how friendship, mentoring, reading, and writing are related in Guibert's career. This does not exclude a genealogy of knowledge transmitted between different generations of mentors and friends going back, for example, to Foucault's own intellectual masters, such as Georges Canguilhem, Georges Dumézil, and Jean Hippolite.

Writing for Guibert means a mix of truth and fiction – or better – truth as fiction rather than the more conventional binary opposition of truth or fiction. As he said in *Le Protocole compassionnel*, "It is when what I am writing takes the form of a journal that I most strongly feel that I am writing fiction" (*CP*, 72). In this he is faithful to Foucault's notion of games of truth. Whether we call Guibert's life-writing autofictions or something else, the main point is that not only are truth and fiction mixed but that it is often impossible to determine with which one is dealing. In fact, to attempt to do so is like fighting with windmills or looking for the way out in a hall of mirrors. The fundamentally irreducible ambiguity that underpins Guibert's writing is for some as disturbing as the representation of same-sex desire. But if one can accept the idea of a fictitious truth or a truthful fiction, then Guibert's works can be appreciated for what they are: ludic constructs with which the reader is invited to work and play. Such ambiguity extends to other domains, in particular, Guibert's prognosis as a PLA living before combination therapy. There are many enigmas in Guibert and while some are solved, there are so many decoys and lures, like HIV itself, that indeterminacy is the ultimate result.

Writing, then, is an experience that allows Guibert to go up to – even beyond – the edge of human experience. Writing is anchored in the fragile, artisan-like inscription of traces of black ink on unlined sheets of white paper, a process powered by the brain-hand motor impulses over which he feared he would eventually lose all control, as described in *Le Paradis*. Writing is like entering a great chamber in which the echoes of other texts rebound and reverberate. For Hervé Guibert there can be no writing without reading, and the author elected to accompany the composition of a new work may end up being incorporated into its fictional fabric. I have already mentioned the confessional, the corporeal, the self-reflexive, and the testimonial aspects of Guibert's works; to which one must add the links between writing and illness, including madness, that lie at the heart of so much of his work.

Whether it be the effect of viewing his photographs, in which the absence inherent in all photography is illustrated again and again, or of reading books that challenge so many of our ethical and aesthetic preconceptions, Guibert's works are unlikely to leave his viewing and reading public indifferent. To be sure, there is more than one way to react to this impact. Patricia Duncker's notion of a reader's love for an author is a good antidote to the kind of methodological rigor that some of us used to try to achieve in studying literary works, a rigor that in fact had more in common with *rigor mortis* than with either literature or methodology. To attempt to remove one's subjective self completely from the writing of criticism is neither helpful nor in the final analysis possible, as Barthes – among others – demonstrated so eloquently. But even if he had not done so, then the example of the writing and the photography of Guibert would lead us to the same conclusion. As for the "compassion protocol," that highly charged version of the reader-writer contract, it cannot be refused, ignored, or denied in the name of some higher critical or metacritical principle. As Ross Chambers has demonstrated in his work on AIDS witnessing in texts and films, it is possible to mourn the death of an author, by celebrating his or her works, and to testify to their impact upon us without compromising intellectual honesty.

Not all of Guibert's admirers will go on to write a book as Yvonne Baby did; but that does not mean that the impact of his photography and books has been necessarily any less. As stated at the outset of this afterword, Guibert was able to think differently (*penser différemment*) or, if you prefer, to think *otherwise*. This manner of thinking affects form as much as content, with the result that we cannot avoid putting into question the *doxa* – detested by Roland Barthes and Renaud Camus alike – as seen in the heterosexist, stereotypical, and linear approaches to so much of what passes for thinking in today's mediatized and information-obsessed world. Reading Guibert, we become aware that we have indeed begun to think about many issues differently. Not that his works are pedagogical in either intent or style. But they do act upon his Spectators/readers, modifying us, transforming us. This is the result not of some kind of didactic discourse or message attached to the works but rather of their overall *performative* effect. I look upon the process as akin to taking a medication or receiving an inoculation. The works themselves act or work on us, without our knowing it, causing us to perceive the world, including ourselves, in a fresh manner. Our minds are opened up to new associations and connections. In this, Guibert's work can be likened to the *pharmakon* – the remedy made from dangerous components that can cure an illness, the illness here being our acculturation to perceiving reality in ways that, however reassuring, are far off the mark. But once Guibert's *pharmakon* of photographs and texts has been "absorbed" and goes to work on us, we are able to understand that notions such as completion and incompletion, truth and falsehood, sickness and health, morality and immorality, or weakness and strength are neither necessarily self-evident nor mutually exclusive. We have acquired an immunity against preconceived ideas that we heretofore presumed certain and well established, be it friendship, family values, desire, vice, blindness, love, reading, writing, or the body in dis/ease. This "vaccine" is Guibert's ultimate gift to us. I close by quoting the words of Michel Foucault taken from *The Use of Pleasure*.

> There are times in life when the question of knowing if one can think differently than one thinks, and perceive differently than one sees, is absolutely necessary if one is to go on looking and reflecting at all.

Bibliography

WORKS BY HERVÉ GUIBERT

À l'ami qui ne m'a pas sauvé la vie. Paris: Gallimard, 1990.
Adultes! Ms. Fonds Hervé Guibert. Institut Mémoires de l'Édition Contemporaine, Paris.
Les Aventures singulières. Paris: Minuit, 1982.
Des aveugles. Paris: Gallimard, 1985.
Blindsight. Trans. James Kirkup. New York: Braziller, 1996.
Les Chiens. Paris: Minuit, 1982.
The Compassion Protocol. Trans. James Kirkup. New York: Braziller, 1994.
Congolo gâté (roman fou). Ms. Fonds Hervé Guibert. Institut Mémoires de l'Édition Contemporaine, Paris.
Cytomégalovirus: journal d'hospitalisation. Paris: Seuil, 1992.
Cytomegalovirus. A Hospitalization Diary. Trans. Clara Orban with the assistance of Elliot Weisenberg. Lanham, MD: UP of America, 1996.
Enquête autour d'un portait (Sur Balthus). Preface by Éric de Chassey. Paris: Les Autodidactes, 1997.
Fou de Vincent. Paris: Minuit, 1989.
Fou de Vincent. Ms. Fonds Hervé Guibert. Institut Mémoires de l'Édition Contemporaine, Paris.
Les Gangsters. Paris: Minuit, 1988.
The Gangsters. Trans. Iain White. New York: Serpent's Tail, 1992.
Ghost Image. Trans. Robert Bononno. Los Angeles: Sun and Moon P, 1996.
L'Homme au chapeau rouge. Paris: Gallimard, 1992.
L'Homme blessé, with Patrice Chéreau. Paris: Minuit, 1983.
L'Homme blessé. Screenplay and dialogue by Hervé Guibert and Patrice Chéreau. Dir. Patrice Chéreau. Perf. Jean-Hughes Anglade, Vittorio Mezzogiorno, and Roland Bertin. 100 min. Cinevista, 1988. Videocassette.

L'Image fantôme. Paris: Minuit, 1981.
L'Incognito. Paris: Gallimard, 1989.
Lettres d'Égypte: du Caire à Assouan, 19.. [photographs by Hans Georg Berger]. Arles: Actes Sud, 1995.
Les Lubies d'Arthur. Paris: Minuit, 1983.
The Man in the Red Hat. Trans. James Kirkup. London: Quartet Books, 1993.
Mauve le vierge. Paris: Gallimard, 1988.
Mes parents. Paris: Gallimard, 1986.
"M'évanouir me guette." [words for a song]. http://www.pagina.tm.fr. 3 Nov. 1997.
"Mirage geisho." Recording by Carole Laure, 1991.
"Mon petit gant" [words for a song]. http://www.pagina.tm.fr. 3 Nov. 1997.
Mon valet et moi: Roman cocasse. Paris: Seuil, 1991.
La Mort propagande. Paris: Régine Deforges, 1977.
La Mort propagande et autres textes de jeunesse. Paris: Régine Deforges, 1991.
My Parents. Trans. Liz Heron. New York: Serpent's Tail, 1993.
Le Paradis. Paris: Gallimard, 1992.
Le Paradis. Ms. Fonds Hervé Guibert. Institut Mémoires de l'Édition Contemporaine, Paris.
La Photo, inéluctablement: Recueil d'articles sur la photographie, 1977–1985. Preface by Yvonne Baby. Paris: Gallimard, 1999.
Photographies. Paris: Gallimard, 1993.
La Piqûre d'amour et autres textes suivi de *La Chair fraîche.* Paris: Gallimard, 1994.
Le Protocole compassionnel. Paris: Gallimard, 1991.
La Pudeur ou l'Impudeur. TF1. 30 Jan. 1992.
Le Seul Visage. Paris: Minuit, 1984.
Suzanne et Louise. Paris: Éditions libres Hallier, 1980.
To the Friend Who Did Not Save My Life. Trans. Linda Coverdale. New York: Serpent's Tail, 1994.
Vice. Paris: Jacques Bertoin, 1991.
Vole mon dragon. Paris: Gallimard, 1994.
Vous m'avez fait former des fantômes. Paris: Gallimard, 1987.
Voyage avec deux enfants. Paris: Minuit, 1982.

PREFACES BY HERVÉ GUIBERT

Barceló, Miguel. *Le Peintre aux métamorphoses.* Nîmes: Musée d'Art Contemporain, 1991.
Berger, Hans Georg. *Dialogue d'images.* Bordeaux: William Blake, 1992.
– *L'Image de soi, ou l'injonction de son beau moment?* Bordeaux: William Blake, 1988.

Faucon, Bernard. *Tables d'amis: vingt-et-un menus légers, mais consistants, faciles à préparer pour nourrir ses amis.* Bordeaux: William Blake, 1991.
Laget, Denis. *Peintre.* 1991.
Michals, Duane. *Changements.* Paris: Herscher, 1981.

SELECTED ARTICLES BY HERVÉ GUIBERT

"L'allégorie absolue." *Le Monde,* 18–19 Nov. 1984: 13.
"Un auteur en quête de spectateurs." *Le Monde,* 11 Aug. 1977: 17.
"Autoportraits." *Le Monde,* 12 Aug. 1981: 9.
"L'autre journal d'Hervé Guibert." *L'Autre Journal,* December 1985: 65–76.
"Beau à tout prix." *Le Monde,* 8 Apr. 1980: 18.
"La Belle Époque en tableaux animés." *Le Monde,* 4 Sept. 1979: 11.
"'Le coeur fatigué': extraits inédits du journal d'Hervé Guibert – autour du *Paradis.*" *Libération,* 14 Jan. 1993: 23.
"L'Égypte au temps de Flaubert." *Le Monde,* 27 Aug. 1980: 10.
"Histoires photographiques de Duane Michals." *Le Monde,* 9 Feb. 1978: 15.
"Les jeunes aveugles et la culture." *Le Monde,* 14 July 1983: 10–11.
"Le jour où les animaux empaillés se révoltèrent." *Le Monde,* 28 June 1984: 16.
"Le luxe, jusqu'à l'épuisement." *Le Monde,* 28 Dec. 1978: 12+.
"Une matière de feuillage." *Le Monde,* 10 Nov. 1977: 20.
"Rendez-vous avec Vincent." *Le Monde,* 11 Feb. 1982: 10–11.
"Le rêve de la transparence." *Le Monde,* 17 Aug. 1978: 9.
"La sincérité du sujet." *Le Monde,* 28 Feb. 1980: 22.
"La tête coupée de Mao Tse-toung. *Le Monde,* 2 Nov. 1978: 8.

SELECTED INTERVIEWS WITH HERVÉ GUIBERT

Arsand, Daniel, and Jean-Michel Quiblier. "Entretien avec Hervé Guibert." *Masques,* Winter 1984–5: 72–5.
Cherer, Sophie. "Guibert gagne." *7 à Paris,* 24–30 Apr. 1991: 14–19.
Donner, Christophe. "Pour répondre aux quelques questions qui se posent ..." *La Règle du jeu,* 3.7 (1992): 135–57.
Dulaure, Antoine. "Hervé Guibert: les messagers des morts." *L'Autre Journal,* April 1985: 54–6.
Eribon, Didier. "Hervé Guibert et son double." *Le Nouvel Observateur,* 18–24 July 1991: 87–9.
Francblin, Catherine. "Les aveugles d'Hervé Guibert." *Art Press,* April 1985: 44–6.
Garcin, Jérôme. "Hervé Guibert – son dernier entretien." *L'Evénement du jeudi,* 2–8 Jan. 1992: 108–9.

Gaudemar, Antoine de. "Les aveux permanents d'Hervé Guibert." *Libération*, 20 Oct. 1988: XII.
– "La vie sida." *Libération*, 1 Mar. 1990: 19–21.
Jonquet, François. "'Je disparaîtrai et je n'aurai rien caché ...'" *Globe*, February 1992: 102–13.
Lançon, Philippe. "'Hervé Guibert: Foucault a été mon maître, je devais écrire sa mort ...'" *L'Evénement du jeudi*, 1–7 Mar. 1990: 82–5.
Mauraisin, Olivier. "Hervé Guibert: l'écrivain amoureux." *Gai pied*, 18 Dec. 1982: 33.
Pivot, Bernard. "Le sexe homicide." *Apostrophes*, Antenne 2, 16 Mar. 1990.
Poivre d'Arvor, Patrick. *Ex libris*. TF1. 7 Mar. 1991.
Tournier, Françoise. "Chronique d'une mort annoncée." *Elle*, 21 May 1990: 182–3.
– "Hervé Guibert: 'Je n'ai jamais autant aimé la vie.'" *Elle*, 11 Mar. 1991: 156–7.

SELECTED WORKS ABOUT HERVÉ GUIBERT

Apter, Emily. "Fantom Images: Hervé Guibert and the Writing of 'sida' in France." In Murphy and Poirier, eds, *Writing AIDS*, 83–97.
Arsand, Daniel. "Hervé Guibert: le seul texte." *Masques*, Winter 1984–5: 67–71.
Assouline, Pierre. "Les vrais héros des romans à clefs." *Lire*, March 1992: 23–32.
Bellour, Raymond. "Double jeu." *Magazine littéraire* 292 (Oct. 1991): 84–5.
– "Entre les images et les mots." *Magazine littéraire* 180 (Jan. 1982): 56.
– "Folie d'écrire." *Magazine littéraire* 270 (Oct. 1989): 124–5.
– "Guibert ou l'indécidable." *Magazine littéraire* 260 (Dec. 1988): 80–1.
– "Hervé Guibert, l'inéluctable." *Magazine littéraire* 331 (Apr. 1995): 68.
– "Des instants de 'l'espèce humaine.'" *Magazine littéraire* 286 (Mar. 1991): 68–9.
– "Lumières aveuglantes." *Magazine littéraire* 218 (Apr. 1985): 63.
– "La machine à fictions." *Magazine littéraire* 331 (Apr. 1995): 112.
– "Oser imaginer." *Magazine littéraire* 248 (Dec. 1987): 91–2.
– "'Quand je n'écris plus, je me meurs.'" *Magazine littéraire* 307 (Feb. 1993): 64–5.
– "Trompe-la-mort." *Magazine littéraire* 276 (Apr. 1990): 54–6.
– "Vérités et mensonges." *Magazine littéraire* 296 (Feb. 1992): 68–70.
Bernstein, Michèle. "Hervé Guibert: À l'ami." *Libération*, 1 Mar. 1990: 21.
Bianciotti, Hector. *Comme la trace de l'oiseau dans l'air*, 130–45. Paris: Bernard Grasset, 1999.
Boulé, Jean-Pierre. "Bibliographie." In Boulé, ed., *Hervé Guibert*, 133–58.
– "Guibert ou la radicalisation du projet sartrien d'écriture existentielle." In Sarkonak, ed., *Le Corps textuel d'Hervé Guibert*, 25–42.

- *Hervé Guibert: "À l'ami qui ne m'a pas sauvé la vie" and Other Writings.* Glasgow: U of Glasgow French and German Publications, 1995.
- "Hervé Guibert à la télévision: vérité et séduction." In Boulé, ed., *Hervé Guibert*, 112–20.
- *Hervé Guibert: Voices of the Self.* Trans. John Fletcher. Liverpool: Liverpool UP, 1999.
- "The Postponing of *La Pudeur ou l'Impudeur*: Modesty or Hypocrisy on the Part of French Television." *French Cultural Studies* 3 (1992): 299–304.
- "'Tout ange est terrible' (À propos des articles nécrologiques sur Hervé Guibert)." *L'Esprit créateur* 37.3 (1997): 61–71.
- Boulé, Jean-Pierre, *Hervé Guibert.* Spec. issue of *Nottingham French Studies* 34.1 (1995).

Braudeau, Michel. "Ecrire contre la montre." *Le Monde*, 2 Mar. 1990: 30.

Buisine, Alain. "À toute allure, Hervé Guibert." In Sarkonak, ed., *Le Corps textuel d'Hervé Guibert*, 97–112.
- "Le photographique plutôt que la photographie." In Boulé, ed., *Hervé Guibert*, 32–41.
- "Tel Orphée ..." *Revue des sciences humaines* 81.210 (1988): 125–49.

Buot, François. *Hervé Guibert: le jeune homme et la mort.* Paris: Grasset, 1999.

Chambers, Ross. "The Suicide Experiment: Hervé Guibert's AIDS Video, *La Pudeur ou l'Impudeur*." *L'Esprit créateur* 37.3 (1997): 72–82.

Charrière, Christian. "L'homme et son double." *Le Figaro*, 12 Nov. 1991: 4.

Cherer, Sophie. "Christophe Donner: 'Hervé Guibert, mon frère de sang d'encre.'" *L'Événement du jeudi*, 21–27 Feb. 1991: 65–6.

Czarny, Norbert. "La 'maladie' acceptée." *La Quinzaine littéraire*, 1–15 Apr. 1990: 9.

Darrieussecq, Marie. "De l'autobiographie à l'autofiction: *Mes parents*, un roman?" In Sarkonak, ed., *Le Corps textuel d'Hervé Guibert*, 115–32.
- "La notion de leurre chez Hervé Guibert: décryptage d'un roman-leurre, *L'Incognito*." In Boulé, ed., *Hervé Guibert*, 82–8.

Duncan, Derek. "Gestes autobiographiques: le sida et les formes d'expressions artistiques du moi." In Boulé, ed., *Hervé Guibert*, 100–11.

Epps, Brad. "Le corps 'techno-ascétique': Guibert, le sida et l'art de la maîtrise de soi." In Sarkonak, ed., *Le Corps textuel d'Hervé Guibert*, 43–62.

Favereau, Eric, and Annick Peigné-Giuly. "Le sida d'Hervé Guibert trouble l'écran." *Libération*, 20 Jan. 1992: 25–6.

Gaillard, Agathe. *Mai-Photographies* [exhibition catalogue]. Quimper, 1994.

Garcin, Jérôme. "Hervé Guibert raconte l'agonie de Michel Foucault." *L'Evénement du jeudi*, 1–7 Mar. 1990: 80–1.
- "Au nom de Guibert." *L'Événement du jeudi*, 27 Feb.–4 Mar. 1992: 100–1.

Gaudemar, Antoine de. "Livret d'infamille." *Libération*, 22 May 1986: 35.
Godard, Colette. "Dialogue sur l'île d'Elbe." *Le Monde*, 2 Jul. 1992: 32.
Grisi, Stéphane. *Dans l'intimité des malades: de Montaigne à Hervé Guibert*. Paris: Desclée de Brouwer, 1996.
Guilbard, Anne-Cécile. "De la pratique du narcissisme à la recherche de l'image vraie." In Boulé, ed., *Hervé Guibert*, 42–8.
Heathcote, Owen. "*Les Chiens* d'Hervé Guibert: analyse d'une 'plaquette pornographique.'" In Boulé, ed., *Hervé Guibert*, 61–9.
– "From Cold War to AIDS War." *Modern and Contemporary France* 3.4 (1995): 427–37.
– "L'érotisme, la violence et le jeu dans *Vous m'avez fait former des fantômes*." In Sarkonak, ed., *Le Corps textuel d'Hervé Guibert*, 189–211.
– "Jobs for the Boys? Or: What's New about the Male Hunter in Duvert, Guibert and Jourdan." In Heathcote et al., eds, *Gay Signatures*, 173–91.
Hill, Leslie. "Écrire – la maladie (à propos de quelques textes d'Hervé Guibert)." In Boulé, ed., *Hervé Guibert*, 89–99.
Jaccomard, Hélène. "La thanatologie chez Hervé Guibert." *Journal of European Studies* 25.99 (1995): 283–302.
Keegan, Paul. "The Lesson of the Master." *Times Literary Supplement*, 28 Sept.–4 Oct. 1990: 1038.
Leclère, Marie-Françoise. "Hervé Guibert: les années sida." *Le Point*, 12 Mar. 1990: 25.
Lloyd, Christopher. "Le laboratoire du corps: Hervé Guibert et le sida." In Christopher Lloyd, ed., *Epidemics and Sickness in French Literature and Culure*, 171–82. Durham: U of Durham P, 1995.
McCaffrey, Enda. "La superstition dans *Vous m'avez fait former des fantômes*." In Boulé, ed., *Hervé Guibert*, 24–31.
Mazureck, Maureen. "'Sa façon de regarder un lézard!'" [interview]. *Libération*, 18–19 Jan. 1992: 23.
Michelena, Jean-Michel. "Hervé Guibert: une vie *choisie*." *L'Infini* 39 (1992): 126–8.
Pratt, Murray. "L'autoprésentation, l'écriture autre et l'ange." In Sarkonak, ed., *Le Corps textuel d'Hervé Guibert*, 133–54.
– "De la désidentification à l'incognito: à la recherche d'une autobiographie homosexuelle." In Boulé, ed., *Hervé Guibert*, 70–81.
– "Hôtel Old Cataract: image, texte." In Boulé, ed., *Hervé Guibert*, 5–7.
– "'A Walk along the Side of the Motorway': AIDS and the Spectacular Body of Hervé Guibert." In Heathcote et al., eds, *Gay Signatures*, 151–72.
Saint-Amand, Pierre. "Mort à blanc: Guibert et la photographie." In Sarkonak, ed., *Le Corps textuel d'Hervé Guibert*, 81–95.

Sarkonak, Ralph. "Hervé Guibert: *Vice* de formes." In Boulé, ed., *Hervé Guibert*, 49–60.
- "Une histoire de corps." In Sarkonak, ed., *Le Corps textuel d'Hervé Guibert*, 5–22.
- "De la métastase au métatexte: Hervé Guibert." *TEXTE* 15–16 (1994): 229–59. Repr. as "Du para- au métatexte: À *l'ami qui ne m'a pas sauvé la vie.*" In Sarkonak, ed., *Le Corps textuel d'Hervé Guibert*, 155–85.
- "Traces and Shadows: Fragments of Hervé Guibert." In Mahuzier et al., eds, *Same Sex/Different Text?* 172–202.

Sarkonak, Ralph, ed. *Le Corps textuel d'Hervé Guibert*. Paris: Les Lettres Modernes, 1997.

Scheher, Lawrence R. "Cippus: Guibert." In *Alcibiades at the Door: Gay Discourses in French Literature*, 155–96. Stanford: Stanford UP, 1995.
- "Jus." In Sarkonak, ed., *Le Corps textuel d'Hervé Guibert*, 213–28.

Sion, Brigitte. "Deux écrivains face à la maladie: Thomas Bernhard – Hervé Guibert." *Équinoxe* 5 (1991): 127–39.

Smith, Richard. "Le pouvoir n'est pas une institution: humour et politique dans *Des aveugles*." In Boulé, ed., *Hervé Guibert*, 15–23.

Smyth, Edmund. "*Des aveugles*: modes d'articulation." In Boulé, ed., *Hervé Guibert*, 8–14.

White, Edmund. "Love Stories." *London Review of Books*, 4 Nov. 1993: 3+. [Repr. in David Bergman, ed., *The Burning Library. Essays*, 355–66. New York: Knopf, 1994].

Wilkerson, Donna. "Hervé Guibert: Writing the Spectral Image." *Studies in 20th Century Literature* 19.2 (1995): 269–88.

Worton, Michael. "En (d)écrivant le corps, en imaginant l'homme: le 'vrai corps' de Guibert." In Sarkonak, ed., *Le Corps textuel d'Hervé Guibert*, 63–77.

OTHER WORKS CONSULTED

Baby, Yvonne. *La Vie retrouvée*. Paris: Éditions de l'Olivier, 1992.

Baetens, Jan, ed. *Camus*. Spec. issue of *écritures* 10 (1998).

Barthes, Roland. *Camera Lucida: Reflections on Photography*. Trans. Richard Howard. New York: Hill and Wang, 1981.
- "Fragments pour H." *L'Autre Journal*, 19–25 Mar. 1986: 81–2.
- *Image Music Text*. Trans. Stephen Heath. New York: Hill and Wang, 1977.
- *Incidents*. Trans. Richard Howard. Berkeley: U of California P, 1992.
- *A Lover's Discourse: Fragments*. Trans. Richard Howard. New York: Hill and Wang, 1978.
- *Oeuvres complètes*. Ed. Éric Marty. 3 vol. Paris: Seuil, 1993–95.
- *The Pleasure of the Text*. Trans. Richard Miller. New York: Hill and Wang, 1975.

- *Roland Barthes by Roland Barthes.* Trans. Richard Howard. New York: Hill and Wang, 1977.
- *Sade Fourier Loyola.* Trans. Richard Miller. New York: Hill and Wang, 1976.
- *S/Z.* Trans. Richard Miller. New York: Hill and Wang, 1974.

Bataille, Georges. *Madame Edwarda, Le Mort, Histoire de l'oeil.* Paris: Pauvert, coll. "10:18," 1979.

Baudelaire, Charles. *Oeuvres complètes.* Ed. Marcel A. Ruff. Paris: Seuil, 1968.

Benfey, Christopher. "The Dead." *New York Times Book Review,* 14 Sept. 1997: 11–12.

Benveniste, Émile. *Problèmes de linguistique générale.* Paris: Gallimard, 1966.

Bernhard, Thomas. *Alte Meister.* Frankfurt am Main: Suhrkamp, 1985. [*Old Masters.* Trans. Ewald Osers. New York: Quartet, 1989.]
- *Der Atem: Eine Entscheidung.* Salzburg: Residenz, 1978. [*Breath. Gathering Evidence.* Trans. David McLintock. New York: Knopf, 1985.]
- *Beton.* Frankfurt am Main: Suhrkamp, 1983. [*Concrete.* Trans. David McLintock. London: Dent, 1984.]
- *Die Kälte: Eine Isolation.* Salzburg: Residenz, 1981. [*In the Cold. Gathering Evidence.* Trans. David McLintock. New York: Knopf, 1985.]
- *Der Untergeher.* Frankfurt am Main: Suhrkamp, 1983. [*The Loser.* Trans. Jack Dawson. Afterword by Mark M. Anderson. New York: Vintage, 1993.]

Boffin, Tessa, and Sunil Gupta, eds. *Ecstatic Antibodies: Resisting the AIDS Mythology.* London: Rivers Oram P, 1990.

Boswell, John. *Same-Sex Unions in Premodern Europe.* New York: Villard, 1994.

Boulé, Jean-Pierre, and Murray Pratt, eds. *AIDS in France.* Spec. issue of *French Cultural Studies* 9:27 (1998).

Buisine, Alain. "Renaud Camus: pas vu, pas lu." *French Forum* 18.3 (1993): 355–65.

Burner, Michel-Antoine, and Patrick Rambaud. *Le Roland-Barthes sans peine.* Paris: Balland, 1978.

Calvet, Louis-Jean. *Roland Barthes 1915–1980.* Paris: Flammarion, 1990.

Camus, Renaud. *Aguets: journal 1988.* Paris: P.O.L, 1990.
- *Le Château de Seix: journal 1992.* Paris: P.O.L, 1997.
- *Élégies pour quelques-uns.* Paris: P.O.L, 1988.
- *L'Épuisant Désir de ces choses.* Paris: P.O.L, 1995.
- *L'Esprit des terrasses: journal 1990.* Paris: P.O.L, 1994.
- *Etc.: abécédaire.* Paris: P.O.L, 1998.
- *Fendre l'air: journal 1989.* Paris: P.O.L, 1991.
- *Graal-Plieux: journal 1993.* Paris: P.O.L, 1998.
- *La Guerre de Transylvanie: journal 1991.* Paris: P.O.L, 1996.
- *Journal romain: 1985–1986.* Paris: P.O.L, 1987.
- *P.A. (petite annonce).* Paris: P.O.L, 1997.

- *Roman furieux.* Paris: P.O.L, 1987.
- *Roman roi.* Paris: P.O.L, 1983.
- *Tricks.* Preface by Roland Barthes. Paris: P.O.L, 1988 [1979].
- *Vigiles: journal 1987.* Paris: P.O.L, 1989.
- *Voyageur en automne.* Paris: P.O.L, 1992.

Camus, Renaud, and Farid Tali. *Incomparable.* Paris: P.O.L, 1999.

Chambers, Ross. *Facing It: AIDS Diaries and the Death of the Author.* Ann Arbor, U of Michigan P, 1998.

Chevalier, Jean, and Alain Gheerbrant. *Dictionnaire des symboles.* Paris: Robert Laffont/Jupiter, 1982.

Clark, Charles F. *AIDS and the Arrows of Pestilence.* Golden, CO: Fulcrum, 1994.

Couser, G. Thomas. *Recovering Bodies: Illness, Disability, and Life Writing.* Foreword by Nancy Mairs. Madison: U of Wisconsin P, 1997.

Crimp, Douglas. "AIDS: Cultural Analysis/Cultural Activism." *October* 43 (1987): 3–16.

- *On the Museum's Ruins.* Cambridge, MA: MIT P, 1993.

Cummings, Kate. "Reading AIDS." *College Literature* 21.1 (1994): 157–62.

Danthe, Michel. "Le sida et les lettres: un bilan francophone." *Equinoxe* 5 (Spring 1991): 51–85.

Darrieussecq, Marie. "L'autofiction, un genre pas sérieux." *Poétique* 107 (1996): 369–80.

Delbo, Charlotte. *Auschwitz and After.* Trans. Rosette C. Lamont. Intro. Lawrence L. Langer. New Haven: Yale UP, 1995 [1965–70].

Dellamora, Richard. "Apocalyptic Utterance in Edmund White's 'An Oracle.'" In Murphy and Poirier, eds, *Writing AIDS*, 98–116.

Denneny, Michael. "AIDS Writing and the Creation of a Gay Culture." In Pastore, ed., *Confronting AIDS through Literature*, 36–54.

Derrida, Jacques. *Memoirs of the Blind: The Self-Portrait and Other Ruins.* Trans. Pascale-Anne Brault and Michael Naas. Chicago: U of Chicago P, 1993.

Dewey, Joseph. "Music for a Closing: Responses to AIDS in Three American Novels." In Nelson, ed., *AIDS: The Literary Response*, 23–38.

Diderot, Denis. *Oeuvres.* Ed. André Billy. Paris: Gallimard, coll. "Bibliothèque de la Pléiade," 1951.

Donato, Eugenio. "The Museum's Furnace: Notes towards a Contextual Reading of *Bouvard et Pécuchet.*" In Josué V. Harari, ed., *Textual Strategies: Perspectives in Post-Structuralist Criticism*, 213–38. Ithaca: Cornell UP, 1979.

Donner, Christophe. *Contre l'imagination.* Paris: Fayard, 1998.

- *L'Esprit de vengeance.* Paris: Grasset, 1992.
- *Les Sentiments.* Paris: Seuil, 1990.

Duncker, Patricia. *Hallucinating Foucault.* New York: Vintage International, 1998

[1996]. [*La Folie Foucault*. Trans. Céline Schwaller-Balay. Paris: Calmann-Lévy, 1997.]
- *Monsieur Shoushana's Lemon Trees*. London: Picador, 1998 [1997].
- *Sisters and Strangers: An Introduction to Contemporary Feminist Fiction*. Oxford: Blackwell, 1992.

Duncker, Patricia, ed. *In and Out of Time: Lesbian Feminist Fiction*. London: Onlywomen Press, 1990.

Dupriez, Bernard. *A Dictionary of Literary Devices: "Gradus, A-Z."* Trans. Albert W. Halsall. Toronto: U of Toronto P, 1991.

Düttmann, Alexander García. *At Odds with AIDS: Thinking and Talking about a Virus*. Trans. Peter Gilgen and Conrad Scott-Curtis. Stanford: Stanford UP, 1996 [1993].

Edelman, Lee. *Homographesis: Essays in Gay Literary and Cultural Theory*. New York: Routledge, 1994.

Eribon, Didier. *Michel Foucault et ses contemporains*. Paris: Fayard, 1994.
- *Michel Foucault 1926–1984*. Paris: Flammarion, coll. "Champs," 1991.
- *Réflexions sur la question gay*. Paris: Fayard, 1999.

Estène, Casimir (pseud. Rémi Santerre). *L'Écart*. Paris: Gallimard, 1969.

Feldman, Douglas A., ed. *Culture and AIDS*. New York: Praeger, 1990.

Flaubert, Gustave. *Salammbô*. Ed. Pierre Moreau. Paris: Gallimard, coll. "Folio," 1970.
- *Trois contes*. Ed. Pierre-Marc de Biasi. Paris: GF-Flammarion, 1986.

Foucault, Michel. *Les Anormaux: cours au Collège de France (1974–1975)*. Ed. Valerio Marchetti and Antonella Salomoni under the direction of François Ewald and Alessandro Fontana. Paris: Gallimard/Seuil, coll. "Hautes Études," 1999.
- *Discipline and Punish: The Birth of the Prison*. Trans. Alan Sheridan. New York: Vintage, 1995.
- *Dits et Écrits 1954–1988*. Ed. Daniel Defert and François Ewald. 4 vol. Paris: Gallimard, 1994.
- *Histoire de la folie à l'âge classique*. Paris: Gallimard, coll. "Tel," 1972.
- *Histoire de la sexualité*. 3 vol. Paris: Gallimard, coll. "Bibliothèque des Histoires," 1976–84.
- *The History of Sexuality*. Trans. Robert Hurley. 3 vol. New York: Vintage, 1990.
- *Language, Counter-Memory, Practice: Selected Essays and Interviews*. Ed. Donald F. Bouchard. Trans. Donald F. Bouchard and Sherry Simon. Ithaca: Cornell UP, 1977.
- *Madness and Civilization: A History of Insanity in the Age of Reason*. Trans. Richard Howard. New York: Vintage, 1988.
- *Raymond Roussel*. Paris: Gallimard, 1963.

- "Sex, Power and the Politics of Identity" [Interview with B. Gallagher and A. Wilson]. *The Advocate* 400 (7 Aug. 1984): 26–30, 58.
- *Surveiller et punir: naissance de la prison.* Paris: Gallimard, coll. "Bibliothèque des Histoires," 1975.

Fuss, Diana, ed. *Inside/Out: Lesbian Theories, Gay Theories.* New York: Routledge, 1991.

Genette, Gérard. *Palimpsests: Literature in the Second Degree.* Trans. Channa Newman and Claude Doubinsky. Lincoln: U of Nebraska P, 1997 [1982].

- *Paratexts: Thresholds of Interpretation.* Trans. Jane E. Lewin. Cambridge: Cambridge UP, 1997 [1987].

Gervais, André, with Renald Bérubé. *Petit glossaire des termes en "texte."* Paris: Lettres Modernes Minard, coll. "Archives," 1998.

Gide, André. *La Séquestrée de Poitiers.* Paris: Gallimard, 1930.

Gilbert, Sky. "More Divine: A Performance for Roland Barthes." In *This Unknown Flesh: A Selection of Plays*, 183–233. Toronto: Coach House P, 1995.

Goethe, Johann Wolfgang. *The Sorrows of Young Werther and Selected Writings.* Trans. Catherine Hutter. New York: New American Library, 1982.

Gott, Ted, ed. *Don't Leave Me This Way: Art in the Age of AIDS.* Canberra: National Gallery of Australia, 1994.

Halperin, David M. *Saint Foucault: Towards a Gay Hagiography.* New York: Oxford UP, 1995.

Harvey, Robert. "Sidéens/Sidaïques: French Discourse on AIDS." In Lawrence Schehr, ed., *Discourses and Sex.* Spec. Issue of *Contemporary French Civilization* 16.2 (1992): 308–35.

Heathcote, Owen, Alex Hughes, and James S. Williams, eds. *Gay Signatures: Gay and Lesbian Theory, Fiction and Film in France, 1945–1995.* New York: Berg, 1998.

Hoffman, Amy. *Hospital Time.* Foreword by Urvashi Vaid. Durham: Duke UP, 1997.

Holborn, Mark, and Dimitri Levas, eds. *Mapplethorpe.* New York: Random House, 1992.

Howe, Lawrence. "Critical Anthologies of the Plague Years: Responding to AIDS Literature." *Contemporary Literature* 35.2 (1994): 395–416.

Jarman, Derek. *Queer Edward II.* London: British Film Institute, 1991.

Klusacek, Allan, and Ken Morrison, eds. *A Leap in the Dark: AIDS, Art and Contemporary Culture.* Montreal: Véhicule P, 1992.

Kristeva, Julia. *Les Samouraïs.* Paris, Fayard, 1990.

Leiris, Michel. *Manhood: A Journey from Childhood into the Fierce Order of Virility.* Trans. Richard Howard. Foreword by Susan Sontag. Chicago: U of Chicago P, 1984 [1939, 1946].

Lejeune, Philippe. *Moi aussi.* Paris: Seuil, coll. "Poétique," 1986.

Lévy, Joseph, and Alexis Nouss. *Sida-Fiction: essai d'anthropologie romanesque.* Pref. François Laplantine. Lyon: Presses universitaires de Lyon, 1994.
L'Heureux, John. *The Handmaid of Desire.* New York: Soho, 1996.
Lincoln, Allen. "Author! Author!" *New York Times Book Review,* 16 Feb. 1997: 15.
MacQueen, John. *Numerology: Theory and Outline History of a Literary Mode.* Edinburgh: Edinburgh UP, 1985.
Macey, David. *The Lives of Michel Foucault.* London: Hutchinson, 1993.
Magné, Bernard. "Métatextuel et lisibilité." *Protée,* Spring-Summer 1986: 77–88.
Maher, Winifred Barbara, and Brendan Maher. "The Ship of Fools: *Stultifera Navis* or *Ignis Fatuus?*" *American Psychologist* 37.7 (1982): 756–61.
Mahuzier, Brigitte, Karen McPherson, Charles A. Porter, and Ralph Sarkonak, eds. *Same Sex/Different Text? Gay and Lesbian Writing in French.* Spec. issue of *Yale French Studies* 90 (1996).
Marc-Aurèle. *Pensées pour moi-même suivies du Manuel d'Épictète.* Trans. Mario Meunier. Paris: GF-Flammarion, 1992.
Marsan, Hugo. "Histoire de l'amour fou." *Le Monde,* 21 Feb. 1997: ix.
− "Sida: l'amour fatal." *Magazine littéraire* 301 (July 1992): 56–9.
Ménil, Alain. *Sain(t)s et Saufs. Sida: une épidémie de l'interprétation.* Paris: Belles Lettres, 1997.
Michaels, Eric. *Unbecoming.* Ed. Paul Foss. Durham: Duke UP, 1997.
Miller, James E. *The Passion of Michel Foucault.* New York: Simon, 1993.
Miller, James L. "AIDS in the Novel: Getting It Straight." In Miller, ed., *Fluid Exchanges,* 257–71.
Miller, James L. ed. *Fluid Exchanges: Artists and Critics in the AIDS Crisis.* Toronto: U of Toronto P, 1992.
Miquel Barceló 1984–1994. London: Whitechapel, 1994.
Monette, Paul. *Afterlife.* New York: Avon, 1990.
− *Borrowed Time: An AIDS Memoir.* New York: Avon, 1988.
Montaigne, Michel de. *Essais.* Ed. Maurice Rat. 2 vol. Paris: Garnier, 1962.
Murphy, Timothy F. *Ethics in an Epidemic: AIDS, Morality, and Culture.* Berkeley: U of California P, 1994.
− "Testimony." In Murphy and Poirier, eds, *Writing AIDS,* 306–20.
Murphy, Timothy F., and Suzanne Poirier, eds. *Writing AIDS: Gay Literature, Language, and Analysis.* New York: Columbia UP, 1993.
Nelson, Emmanuel S., ed. *AIDS: The Literary Response.* New York: Twayne, 1992.
Olson, Michael P. "Thomas Bernhard, Glenn Gould, and the Art of the Fugue: Contrapuntal Variations in *Der Untergeher.*" *Modern Austrian Literature* 24.2/3 (1991): 73–83.
Pastore, Judith Lawrence. "Introduction." In Pastore, ed., *Confronting AIDS through Literature,* 1–12.

- "What Are the Responsibilities of Representing AIDS?" In Pastore, ed., *Confronting AIDS through Literature*, 15–35.
Pastore, Judith Laurence, ed. *Confronting AIDS through Literature: The Responsibilities of Representation*. Urbana: U of Illinois P, 1993.
Patton, Brian. "Cell Wars: Military Metaphors and the Crisis of Authority in the AIDS Epidemic." In J.L. Miller, ed., *Fluid Exhanges*, 272–86.
Poe, Edgar Allan. "Marginalia." In *Complete Works*, vol. 16. Ed. James A. Harrison. New York: AMS Press, 1965.
- *Oeuvres en prose*. Trans. Charles Baudelaire. Ed. Y.-G. Le Dantec. Paris: Gallimard, coll. "Bibliothèque de la Pléiade," 1951.
Proust, Marcel. *À la recherche du temps perdu*. Ed. Jean-Yves Tadié. 4 vol. Paris: Gallimard, coll. "Bibliothèque de la Pléiade," 1987–9.
- *Remembrance of Things Past*. Trans. C.K. Scott Moncrieff, Terence Kilmartin, and Andreas Mayor. 3 vol. London: Penguin, 1981.
Rabelais, François. *Oeuvres complètes*. Ed. P. Jourda. 2 vol. Paris: Garnier, 1962.
Robinson, Christopher. *Scandal in the Ink: Male and Female Homosexuality in Twentieth-Century French Literature*. London: Cassell, 1995.
Sade, Marquis de. *Oeuvres complètes*. Ed. Gilbert Lely. Vol. 12. Paris: Cercle du livre précieux, 1967.
Saint-Amand, Pierre. "The Secretive Body: Roland Barthes's Gay Erotics." In Mahuzier et al., eds, *Same Sex/Different Text?* 153–71.
Santerre, Rémi. *See* Estène, Casimir.
Sarkonak, Ralph. "Roland Barthes and the Spectre of Photography." *L'Esprit créateur* 22.1 (1982): 48–68.
Saussure, Ferdinand de. *See* Starobinski, Jean.
Schehr, Lawrence R. *Parts of an Andrology: On Representations of Men's Bodies*. Stanford: Stanford UP, 1997.
- *The Shock of Men: Homosexual Hermeneutics in French Writing*. Stanford: Stanford UP, 1995.
Il secondo '800 italiano: Le poetiche del vero. Milan: Mazzotta, 1988.
Simon, Claude. *Album d'un amateur*. Remagen-Rolandseck: Rommerskirschen, 1988.
- *Les Géorgiques*. Paris: Minuit, 1981.
- *The Georgics*. Trans. Beryl and John Fletcher. London: Calder, 1989.
Sollers, Philippe. *Femmes*. Paris: Gallimard, coll. "Folio," 1983.
- *Writing and the Experience of Limits*. Trans. Philip Barnard with David Hayman. New York: Columbia UP, 1983.
Sontag, Susan. *AIDS and Its Metaphors*. New York: Farrar, 1989.
- *Illness as Metaphor*. New York: Farrar, 1978.

Starobinski, Jean. *Les Mots sous les mots: Les anagrammes de Ferdinand de Saussure.* Paris: Gallimard, 1971.
Taylor, Christopher C. "AIDS and the Pathogenesis of Metaphor." In Feldman, ed., *Culture and AIDS*, 55–65.
Thomas, Chantal. *Thomas Bernhard.* Paris: Seuil, coll. "Les Contemporains," 1990.
Tournier, Michel. *Le Roi des Aulnes.* Paris: Gallimard, coll. "Folio," 1981 [1970].
– *Le Vent Paraclet.* Paris: Gallimard, coll. "Folio," 1977.
Tondelli, Pier Vittorio. *Chambres séparées.* Trans. Nicole Sels. Paris: Seuil, 1992.
Treichler, Paula A. *How to Have Theory in an Epidemic: Cultural Chronicles of AIDS.* Durham: Duke UP, 1999.
Voragine, Jacobus de. *The Golden Legend: Readings on the Saints.* Trans. William Granger Ryan. 2 vol. Princeton: Princeton UP, 1993.
Watney, Simon. *Policing Desire: Pornography, AIDS and the Media.* Minneapolis: U of Minnesota P, 1987.
– *Practices of Freedom: Selected Writings on HIV/AIDS.* Durham: Duke UP, 1994.
Webb, Margaret. "What's Eating Sky Gilbert?" *Toronto Life,* March 1997: 45+.
Wetsel, David. "The Best of Times, the Worst of Times: The Emerging Literature of AIDS in France." In Nelson, ed., *AIDS: The Literary Response,* 95–113.
White, Edmund. *The Farewell Symphony.* New York: Knopf, 1997.
– "On Gay Fiction." *London Review of Books,* 9 March 1995: 6–8.
Woods, Gregory. "AIDS to Remembrance: The Uses of Elegy." In Nelson, ed., *AIDS: The Literary Response,* 155–66.
– "Ce pays de malheur." *Times Literary Supplement,* 8 Oct. 1993: 7–8.
– *A History of Gay Literature: The Male Tradition.* New Haven: Yale UP, 1998.
Wright, Les. "Gay Genocide as Literary Trope." In Nelson, ed., *AIDS: The Literary Response,* 50–68.
Yingling, Thomas E. *AIDS and the National Body.* Ed. Robyn Wiegman. Durham: Duke UP, 1997.

Index

Adjani, Isabelle, 241, 253
Adrien, Philippe, 122
Adultes!, 7, 30, 60, 189–90, 199, 225, 267
Alembert, Jean le Rond d', 103
Althusser, Louis, 258
À l'ami qui ne m'a pas sauvé la vie, 4, 7, 10–11, 15–18, 20–6, 28, 53–4, 60–1, 72, 77–9, 96, 115, 125, 136–8, 142, 146, 149–54, 156–9, 161–3, 165–6, 168–72, 175, 178–82, 184–5, 187–91, 193–217, 225–31, 235–7, 239, 241, 243, 245, 249, 251, 254, 257, 260–2, 266, 270–2, 274–6, 280, 282–3, 287
Anderson, Mark, 202
Apostrophes, 4, 260
Apter, Emily, 150–1, 154, 157, 177, 191
Arsand, Daniel, 12
Artaud, Antonin, 258, 274, 277, 279
Assouline, Pierre, 253
Autre Journal, L', 12, 40, 43, 56
"Autre journal d'Hervé Guibert, L'," 20, 237, 264
Aventures singulières, Les, 74, 197, 237
Aveugles, Des, 4, 7, 13–14, 86–114, 122, 145, 186–7, 197, 213–14, 262, 264, 267, 275, 284

Baby, Yvonne, 32, 218, 237–44, 252–5, 265–6, 288
Bacchus, Saint, 11
Bach, Johann Sebastian, 202
Bacon, Francis, 29, 167, 241
Balthus. *See* Klossowski, Balthazar
Balzac, Honoré de, 6, 41, 160, 258, 269
Barbedette, Gilles, 197
Barceló, Miquel, 163, 173
Barthes, Henriette, 31–3, 37, 42–3, 45–6
Barthes, Roland, 4, 9, 20–1, 28–65, 70, 74, 80, 99, 122, 130–1, 133, 160, 183, 185, 215, 219–20, 235–6, 241, 256–7, 271, 286, 288–9
 – *Bruissement de la langue, Le*, 31
 – *Camera Lucida*, 10, 33–5, 37, 43–6, 49–51, 53, 55, 64, 74, 227, 279
 – "Fragments pour H.," 36–44, 56, 58, 60, 64, 183, 235
 – *Image Music Text*, 215
 – *Incidents*, 43, 59, 63–4

- *Lover's Discourse, A*, 31, 36–7, 39–40, 42, 44, 50, 64, 131, 133
- *Pleasure of the Text, The*, 52
- *Roland Barthes by Roland Barthes*, 29, 36, 50
- *Sade Fourier Loyola*, 62
- *S/Z*, 41, 160

Bataille, Georges, 5, 30, 99, 109, 114, 222, 286
Baudelaire, Charles, 21, 85, 101, 165, 167, 177, 189, 258
Bellour, Raymond, 7, 71, 195, 215
Benfey, Christopher, 257
Benjamin, Walter, 69
Bentham, Jeremy, 80
Benveniste, Émile, 183
Berger, Hans Georg, 5, 122, 147, 241, 270; *Dialogue d'images*, 5; *Image de soi, L', ou l'injonction de son beau moment?*, 5
Berlin, Peter, 16
Bernhard, Thomas, 5, 64, 179–80, 200–6, 209, 216, 219, 228, 243, 249–50, 252, 283, 286
Bernstein, Michèle, 195
Bertin, Roland, 228
Beyle, Henri, 104
Blair, Eric Arthur, 132
Blindsight. See *Aveugles*
Blyton, Enid, 23–4
Borges, Jorge Luis, 99
Bosch, Hieronymus, 94
Boswell, John, 11
Boudinet, Daniel, 34
Bouffin, Tessa, 191
Bouissac, Paul, 10
Boulé, Jean-Pierre, 5, 7, 12, 97, 118, 130, 143–4, 151, 157, 173, 191, 194–5, 205
Braudeau, Michel, 205

Brueghel, Pieter the Elder, 94
Buisine, Alain, 22, 237
Buot, François, 5, 173, 231
Burner, Michel-Antoine, 52
Butor, Michel, 190, 220

Cadinot, Jean-Daniel, 113
Calvet, Louis-Jean, 31, 43, 61
Camus, Albert, 190, 218
Camus, Renaud, 56–7, 60, 144, 218–37, 243–5, 252–4, 289
Canguilhem, Georges, 287
Cartier-Bresson, Henri, 241
Chambers, Ross, 54, 151, 153, 161, 164, 194, 215, 288
Charrière, Christian, 67
Chateaubriand, François René, 111, 222
Chéreau, Patrice, 71, 96, 228, 241, 261
Cherer, Sophie, 156, 270
Chiens, Les, 17, 31
Christie, Agatha, 23
Christopher, Saint, 73
Clark, Charles, 166
"Coeur fatigué, Le," 6, 144
Compassion Protocol, The. See *Protocole compassionnel*
Condillac, Étienne Bonnot de, 102
Congolo gâté (Roman fou). See *Paradis*
Courbet, Gustave, 71, 96
Couser, G. Thomas, 192
Crimp, Douglas, 83, 149, 151
Cummings, Kate, 151–2
Cytomégalovirus: journal d'hospitalisation, 4, 6, 14, 63–4, 146, 189, 191, 193, 212–17, 251, 259, 262, 271, 287
Czarny, Norbert, 205

Danthe, Michel, 184

Darrieussecq, Marie, 156
Deforges, Régine, 231, 240
Delbo, Charlotte, 191
Denneny, Michael, 149, 160
Derrida, Jacques, 71, 87, 96, 98–9, 275
Devarrieux, Claire, 240
Dewey, Joseph, 150
Diderot, Denis, 86, 90, 92, 100–3, 109, 114
Donato, Eugenio, 84
Donner, Christophe, 3, 8, 26, 28, 44, 218, 232, 244–55, 286
du Camp, Maxime, 122
Dulaure, Antoine, 102
Dumézil, Georges, 14, 287
Duncan, Derek, 13, 26
Duncker, Patricia, 257–83, 288
Duras, Marguerite, 218–19
Düttmann, Alexander Garcia, 285
Duvert, Tony, 258

Edelman, Lee, 172, 181, 184, 191
Epictetus, 153
Eribon, Didier, 14, 28–9, 31–2, 41, 63, 206, 233, 271, 275
Estène, Casimir, 231
Ex Libris, 4, 232–3

Faucon, Bernard, 241
Flaubert, Gustave, 110, 114, 118, 122, 133–4, 137
Foucault, Michel, 10–11, 13–16, 19–21, 27–31, 57, 60, 63, 70, 80, 82–3, 89, 95, 111–14, 152, 154, 159–60, 174, 185, 197–8, 204–10, 213–17, 227, 233, 236, 241, 256–60, 262–4, 267–9, 270–7, 280, 282, 284, 286–7, 289
– *Anormaux, Les*, 79, 83–4

– *Archéologie du savoir, L'*, 104, 259
– *Discipline and Punish*, 80–1, 89, 92, 96, 259
– *Dits et Écrits*, 113, 271, 277
– *History of Sexuality, The*, 83, 96, 159–60, 179, 207–8, 258–9, 273, 275, 289
– *Language, Counter-Memory, Practice*, 215
– *Madness and Civilization*, 84, 89, 93, 96, 112
– *Raymond Roussel*, 109
Fou de Vincent, 14, 20–1, 57, 123, 130–8, 140, 142–3, 147–8, 189, 191, 197, 226–7, 232, 235, 270, 276
Francblin, Catherine, 87, 96

Gaillard, Agathe, 9–10, 17, 241
Galileo, 92
Gallagher, B., 271
Gangsters, Les, 4, 11, 14, 25, 57–9, 125–7, 130, 136–8, 147, 229, 270, 276
Garcin, Jérôme, 67, 205, 219, 237
Gaudemar, Antoine de, 4, 7, 15, 73, 115, 156, 206, 230–1
Genet, Jean, 5, 30, 38, 222, 258–9, 286
Genette, Gérard, 87, 195, 198, 200, 203, 206
Ghost Image. See *Image fantôme*
Gide, André, 210
Gilbert, Sky, 256
Godard, Colette, 147
Goethe, Johann Wolfgang von, 39, 41, 64
Gordon, Charles George, 153
Gosset, Jean, 244–7, 249, 251–2, 255, 272
Gott, Ted, 191
Gould, Glenn, 201–2
Grainville, Patrick, 259

Guibert, Hervé. *See titles of individual works*
Gupta, Sunil, 191

Halperin, David, 11, 14, 25
Heathcote, Owen, 222
Hippolite, Jean, 287
Hocquenghem, Guy, 257–8
Homer, 99
Homme blessé, L', 96, 122, 228–9, 261
Homme au chapeau rouge, L', 4, 6, 17, 56, 134, 136, 141, 144, 149, 155–6, 158, 161, 163, 167–8, 174, 179–80, 186–7, 189, 191–2, 211, 237, 250–1, 284
Howard, Richard, 59

Image fantôme, L', 4, 12, 16–17, 20, 22, 26, 28, 32–4, 45–55, 64, 67, 76, 83, 113, 116, 125, 133, 152, 155, 171, 229, 237–8, 242, 285
Incognito, L', 21–2, 58–9, 64, 125, 134, 136, 189–90, 216, 219, 222–7, 229, 256, 264, 276
Institut des Hautes Études Cinématographiques (IHEC), 228
Institut des Jeunes Aveugles, 7, 87, 102–3, 145
Institut Mémoires de l'Édition Contemporaine (IMEC), 6, 9, 144

Jakobson, Roman, 150
Jarman, Derek, 191
Joan of Arc, 13, 24, 99, 179
Jonquet, François, 22, 73, 147, 155, 209, 215, 281
Jouy, Charles, 83
Joyce, James, 99
Julien l'Hospitalier, Saint. *See* Flaubert

Kafka, Franz, 64
Keller, Helen, 100
Kirkup, James, 93, 161, 179
Klossowski, Balthazar, 241
Kristeva, Julia, 256–7

Lançon, Philippe, 206
Langer, Lawrence L., 191
Lapassade, Georges, 257
Leclère, Marie-Françoise, 195
Lettres d'Égypte: du Caire à Assouan, 19.., 6, 14, 121, 237, 270
Leiris, Michel, 32, 167, 222, 286
Lejeune, Philippe, 156
Le Vau, Louis, 80
Lévy, Joseph, 191
L'Heureux, John, 256
Libération, 173, 205
Lincoln, Allan, 257–8
Lindon, Mathieu, 144, 241, 265, 271, 281
Locke, John, 103
Lollobrigida, Gina, 241
Louis XIV, 80
Louis XVII, 13, 24, 179
Lubies d'Arthur, Les, 20, 53, 121, 147, 256, 265, 267

Macey, David, 10, 14, 80, 113, 206, 274–5
MacQueen, John, 178
Maher, Winifred Barbara, and Brendan Maher, 94
Mallarmé, Stéphane, 42
Mancini, Antonio, 153, 187
Mann, Thomas, 48, 113
Man in the Red Hat, The. *See Homme au chapeau rouge*
Mapplethorpe, Robert, 16, 172–3, 188

Marchais, Georges, 41–2
Marcheschi, Jean-Paul, 236–7
Marcus Aurelius, 61, 152–3, 187, 287
Marie-Antoinette, 179
Marsan, Hugo, 222, 257–8, 271
Martin, Jacques, 277
Mauriac, Claude, 220, 275
Mauve le vierge, 13–14, 20–1, 57, 68, 70, 72, 104, 123, 128–30, 134–5, 189, 209–11, 257, 265, 273, 275–6, 279–80
Mazureck, Maureen, 164
McCaffrey, Enda, 264
Ménil, Alain, 181
Merleau-Ponty, Maurice, 104
Mes parents, 4, 11, 14, 20, 25, 30, 55–6, 70, 133, 184, 189, 210, 219, 228–9, 239, 242, 260, 264
Michaels, Eric, 153, 187
Michals, Duane, 16, 219
Miller, James E., 13–14, 16, 205–6, 210
Miller, James L., 149, 181, 191
Milton, John, 99, 178
Mitterand, François, 43
Molyneux, William, 103
Monde, Le, 4–6, 8, 19, 32, 34–5, 44–5, 56, 76, 87, 156, 219, 224, 237, 240, 242, 245, 255, 257
Monette, Paul, 160
Montaigne, Michel de, 8, 10, 44, 86, 165, 167
Mon valet et moi, 63, 67, 219, 251
Mort propagande, La (first edition), 4, 6, 11, 28–30, 67, 116, 167, 220, 240
Mort propagande et autres textes de jeunesse, La, 13, 20, 29, 31, 47, 68, 70, 74, 122, 183, 210, 251, 267

Mounier, Émmanuel, 244, 252
Musée Grévin, 12, 68, 179
Musil, Robert, 14
My parents. See *Mes parents*

Nietzsche, Friedrich, 141, 279
Nouss, Alexis, 191

Olson, Michael P., 202
Orwell, George. *See* Blair, Eric Arthur
"Ours, L'." See *Piqûre d'amour et autres textes ...*

Paradis, Le, 6, 63, 104, 125, 141–6, 158, 179, 191, 219, 251, 261–2, 268, 273, 276–81, 288
Pasolini, Pier Paolo, 226, 241–2
Pastore, Judith, 149–50, 159, 182
Patton, Brian, 181
Peter in Chains, Saint, 265
Photographies, 6, 12, 18, 67, 121, 221, 241
"Pièce d'Oedipe, La." See *Mort propagande et autres textes de jeunesse*
Pinget, Robert, 92
Piqûre d'amour et autres textes, La suivi de *La Chair fraîche*, 6, 20, 53, 96, 121, 125–6, 189, 221, 228–9, 251, 260–1, 264–6, 269
Pivot, Bernard, 260
Plato, 103–4, 178
Podach, E.F., 279
Poe, Edgar Allan, 166–7, 188–9
Ponge, Francis, 68
Pratt, Murray, 26, 212, 243
Protocole compassionnel, Le, 4–5, 9, 14, 17, 20, 26, 61–3, 112, 115–17, 125, 136, 138–43, 145–7, 149, 154–5, 158–9, 161, 163–4, 168, 172–3, 176–80, 182–91, 196, 211–12, 214,

216–17, 232, 235, 245, 248–52, 261–2, 264, 267–9, 286–7
Proust, Marcel, 7, 38–41, 53, 120, 127–8, 131–3, 143, 146, 156, 170, 176, 203, 239, 243, 245, 272, 286
Pudeur ou l'Impudeur, La, 5, 11, 13, 19, 25, 54, 161, 164–5, 189, 287
Puyaubert, Jean, 230

Rabelais, François, 92, 222
Rabinow, Paul, 257
Racine, Jean, 222
Rambaud, Patrick, 52
Règle du jeu, La, 246
Rembrandt, 171, 238
Resnais, Alain, 182
Rimbaud, Arthur, 258, 278
Robbe-Grillet, Alain, 68
Roussel, Raymond, 109–10, 114
Rubens, 29

Sade, Marquis de, 5, 62, 178, 222
Saint-Amand, Pierre, 16
Salignac, Mélanie de, 103
Samson, 99
Santerre, Rémi. *See* Estène, Casimir
Sartre, Jean-Paul, 11, 38
Saunderson, Nicolas, 103
Saussure, Ferdinand de, 282
Savitzkaya, Eugène, 155, 241, 261
Schehr, Lawrence, 64, 150, 157–9, 183, 193, 217
Schiller, Friedrich von, 258, 260
Schwaller-Balay, Céline, 257
Sebastian, Saint, 166
"Secrets d'un homme, Les." *See* Mauve le vierge
Serge, Saint, 11
Seul Visage, Le, 12, 15, 55–6, 152, 237, 241

Shakespeare, William, 23
Simon, Claude, 83, 104, 132, 190, 258
"Sincérité du sujet, La," 43–4
Sion, Brigitte, 200
Smith, Richard, 93, 110, 113, 122
Sollers, Philippe, 60, 286
Sontag, Susan, 181, 184, 191, 255
Stamp, Terrence, 242
Stendhal. *See* Beyle, Henri
Strindberg, August, 141, 277–80
Suzanne et Louise (photo-roman), 11–12, 34, 49, 67, 77
"Suzanne et Louise" (play), 32

Teiresias, 93
Teresa of Avila, Saint, 74
To the Friend Who Did Not Save My Life. *See* À l'ami qui ne m'a pas sauvé la vie
Tondelli, Pier Vittorio, 234–5
Tournier, Françoise, 27
Tournier, Michel, 73
Treichler, Paula, 166, 181, 191
Tutankhamen, 122

Verlaine, Paul, 278
Vice, 6, 12, 53, 66–85, 106
Vingt ans, 4
Visconti, Luchino, 48, 113
Vole mon dragon, 6, 57, 61, 121–3, 126, 129, 140
Volland, Sophie, 103
Voragine, Jacobus de, 121, 138, 167, 265–6
Vous m'avez fait former des fantômes, 17, 99, 124–5, 178–9, 222, 224, 254
Voyage avec deux enfants, 14, 20, 53, 115–22, 124, 126–30, 137, 142, 145–7, 189, 191, 237, 268–9, 276, 280

Index

Wagner, Richard, 32
Walser, Robert, 141
Watney, Simon, 149
Welles, Orson, 62, 161, 241
White, Edmund, 5–6, 8, 157, 180, 197, 257, 271, 273
Wiertz, Antoine, 29
Wilde, Oscar, 261

Wilkerson, Donna, 160
Wilson, A., 271
Woods, Gregory, 150, 152, 154, 176, 191
Wright, Les, 182

Yuon, Juno, 10